THE
GREAT
COMMISSION
RESURGENCE

THE

GREAT
COMMISSION
RESURGENCE

FULFILLING GOD'S MANDATE IN OUR TIME

CHUCK LAWLESS AND
ADAM W. GREENWAY, EDITORS

ACADEMIC

Nashville, Tennessee

The Great Commission Resurgence:
Fulfilling God's Mandate in Our Time

Copyright © 2010 by Chuck Lawless and Adam W. Greenway

ISBN: 978-1-4336-6970-5

Published by B&H Publishing Group
Nashville, Tennessee

Dewey Decimal Classification: 269.2
Subject Heading: EVANGELISTIC WORK \ MISSIONS \
DOCTRINAL THEOLOGY

Printed in the United States of America

1 2 3 4 5 6 7 8 9 10 11 12 • 17 16 15 14 13 12 11 10

BP

CONTENTS

Contents

SECTION 2: FROM THE WORD

SECTION 3: FOR THE WORLD

SECTION 4: VIA THE CHURCH

Contents

SECTION 5: THE WAY FORWARD

Daniel L. Akin
President and Professor of Preaching and Theology,
Southeastern Baptist Theological Seminary

Ed Stetzer and Philip Nation
Director of LifeWay Research and Missiologist-in-Residence, LifeWay
Christian Resources / Director of Ministry Development, LifeWay Research

Convictional Yet Cooperative:
David S. Dockery
President and Professor of Christian Studies, Union University

Adam W. Greenway
Associate Vice President for Extension Education and Applied
Ministries; Director of Research Doctoral Studies, Billy Graham School
of Missions and Evangelism; Assistant Professor of Evangelism and
Applied Apologetics, The Southern Baptist Theological Seminary

DEDICATION

LAWLESS:

To the members of Pisgah Heights Baptist Church
(now Liberty Heights Church),
West Chester, Ohio,
who first gave me a passion for evangelism
and, as always,
to my wife, Pam,
who models for me a Great Commission heart

GREENWAY:

To the local community of believers
called First Baptist Church,
Frostproof, Florida,
whose Great Commission obedience transformed my life
and to Carla, my wife,
a gifted partner in Great Commission ministry
Soli Deo Gloria!

FOREWORD

Johnny M. Hunt

How refreshing it is, from time to time, to pick up a book that deals so completely with a subject for which the Lord has captured your heart! When I think of the Great Commission, a fire ignites within my soul; indeed, it is none other than our precious Lord Jesus. I have often thought through the years that if the body of Christ—the local church in general and me in particular—would get serious about the last words that Jesus spoke to the local church, we could fulfill the Great Commission in our generation. What a challenge and encouragement that is to my own heart.

Chuck Lawless and Adam Greenway have done all of us a great favor in showing us where we are as a Southern Baptist Convention. They have brought together great historians, theologians, and pastors—men who represent different parts of Christ's body—to speak in a mighty, prophetic, and scholarly way into our hearts. It has often been said that if we really desire to be where God wants us, we must honestly appraise where we are now and then make sure we have a clear path based on his precious Word to lead us to where he would have us to be. In this book, *The Great Commission Resurgence: Fulfilling God's Mandate in Our Time*, we have an opportunity to look at where we are. "Facts are our friends"—and the bottom line fact is that we are a denomination in decline. It has been many years since we have shown a positive increase as it pertains to reaching the population of people with whom God has called us to share the Good News.

The Lord has been good to the Southern Baptist Convention. In this book, you will have an opportunity both to view our history and to get glimpses of what our future could look like. Vision has stirred the passion in my heart. This book will help sharpen our vision as we take a look at the big picture of the Great Commission and the difference we can make, beginning now. Is there tension and different views concerning how we can get there? Of course! But, as I have often had to remind myself, the reality is that our agreements are so much greater than our differences. For the greater cause of God's glory, may all Southern Baptists join hands for the expressed purpose of making Christ known to all peoples. Theology has always been at the forefront of the Southern Baptist Convention, and until this day it remains our passionate desire to have a missiology driven by biblical principles. As we think about the nations and their need of the gospel, we here in North America also realize that the United States is the third largest lost nation on the planet. May we never neglect taking the gospel to our neighbors and to the nations!

One of the great personal challenges in my life today is how much I have bought into the American dream. The Spirit of God now seems to be helping me to "back out," to be better able to embrace his vision for the nations as opposed to my dream for my own life and family. The Lord often convicts me that many times I desire for you and for others to embrace something that I am not fully embracing myself. If, indeed, I desire to see the nations come to know Christ, and particularly our own nation, and to have a church that would make much of the glory of God, may it first begin in my own personal life. May I, as a pastor, find myself not only preaching for a Great Commission Resurgence, but living to embrace this passion and vision for my own heart. Charles Haddon Spurgeon and D. L. Moody both said many years ago that if we are to reach this nation, we must get serious about planting churches in the major urban context. I pray that God will move us to become personal soul-winners and evangelists with mission hearts to touch this nation—the under-served and the vast pockets of lostness—as we take Christ to the nations of the world.

This book inspires me because I believe its content. I believe there is a new Southern Baptist Convention coming—one that has the potential of being stronger, more useful, and bringing greater glory to God than ever before. It is my prayer that you will not only read this book, but embrace its vision for the nations and for the glory of God.

INTRODUCTION

Chuck Lawless

In June 1985 as a 24-year-old pastor, I attended my first Southern Baptist Convention. Meeting that year in Dallas, Texas, more than 40,000 messengers gathered for what would become a tumultuous, often rancorous meeting. Thousands of messengers waited for the doors to open every morning in order to secure the best seats to make a motion. "Points of order" often echoed through the convention hall. Tempers flared. Meal breaks became opportunities for more heated discussions.

I left that meeting alarmed by the obvious division in my denomination, but also grateful for believers who were taking a clear stand on the Word of God. Somehow, I just knew that something significant was happening, even though I did not fully understand all of the issues.

Frankly, I had become a Southern Baptist almost by accident several years earlier. A seventh-grade classmate in Ohio had first told me the gospel. I had never heard the gospel before age 12, even though my family lived within a short driving distance of more than a hundred Southern Baptist churches. My classmate was both tactless and relentless in his evangelistic approach, and I decided to attend church only one time simply to "get that crazy Christian off my back."

At the time, our neighbors beside us and behind us were both Southern Baptist families. Each drove past our home at least twice a week on their way to church, and each family had at least invited me to attend. It only made sense to attend with them—but only one time. Little did I know that God was soon going to change my world.

I found in that Southern Baptist church a group of people who genuinely loved Jesus and who grew to love me. They transported me to church, challenged me to learn, taught me the Word, and modeled Christian living. In that church family I found people who became my family. "Brother" and "sister" became much more to me than simply titles to use for church folks whose names I had forgotten.

More than anything, this church gave me a strong belief in the authority of the Word of God. God inspired His Word, they told me, and God is perfect. What God inspired is inerrant and thus trustworthy. It was years later before I investigated those claims more fully, but my foundation was secure. Further learning only solidified that belief.

Thus, as a messenger to the 1985 Southern Baptist Convention, I believed that the stand we took there really did matter. And indeed it did. Southern Baptists have said repeatedly that we are a people of the Book, a people who are unwilling to compromise on the authority of the Word. The years of what became known as the "Conservative Resurgence" were not without pain, but I am honored to be part of a denomination willing to take such a stand.

That same Southern Baptist church in Ohio gave me not only a belief in the Word, but also a heart for evangelism. My pastor allowed me to make evangelistic visits with him. The associate pastor invited me to join his "bus ministry" team (I'm dating myself here, I know . . .). A deacon took me with him when he made hospital visits. Week after week, month after month, I had the unbelievable privilege of telling others about Jesus and His grace. In fact, I could not understand why everybody did not quickly follow Christ after hearing the story.

I assumed that every Southern Baptist church was like this one, but it did not take long to learn otherwise. I found it hard to believe, but some churches preached evangelism while not *doing* evangelism! The Great Commission (Matt 28:18–20) was more a heading for a biblical text than a lifestyle to be lived. Southern Baptists, I learned, sometimes do not follow the very Word for which we would take such a strong stand.

That very issue gives rise to this book. Throughout this book, you will find contributors who love Southern Baptists—but who are deeply concerned about our denomination. We are all members of the family, but troubled at some level that we as a family are not living up to our biblical obligations. We have churches, numbers, dollars, and opportunities, but we have seemingly lost (if we ever really had) a passion for the Great Commission. As I have written elsewhere, "Somehow, we have stood faithfully for a message that we have chosen to keep to ourselves."[1]

---

1 Chuck Lawless, "The Great Commission and the Local Church," in Thom Rainer et al., *Great Commission Resurgence* (Nashville: LifeWay, 2008), 26.

Now, many of us are longing for a Great Commission Resurgence. Within this text are challenges from denominational leaders, seminary and university presidents, professors, local church pastors and church planters, and church staff members—all of whom intensely desire for God to do something among us for which only He would get the credit. We want God to break our hearts over the lostness of the world.

So much is at stake here. Millions in North America do not know Jesus. More than 1.6 billion people around the globe have likely never heard of Jesus. Generation after generation of children and young people are following false religions, deceived by an enemy who wants to keep them in bondage (2 Cor 4:3–4). Families—even Christian families—are falling apart around us. Meanwhile, thousands of churches go through the motions Sunday after Sunday, making little eternal difference. We have increased our numbers significantly since 1950, but we are reaching no more today than we did then. We can only wonder if Satan would say to us what the demon said to the sons of Sceva in Acts 19:15, "Jesus I know, and Paul I recognize—but who are you?"

If, however, you have come to this book to find quick-fix, simple steps to a Great Commission Resurgence, you will likely be disappointed. In fact, you will find that we do not all agree on causes behind our denominational malaise, nor do we always agree on solutions. Some see the Great Commission primarily through an international lens, while others focus on North America. Some contributors hint at denominational restructuring; others affirm current structures even when suggesting change. Certain ideas in the book may be too radical for you, while others may not be radical enough.

At the same time, the contributors do not necessarily agree on every fine point of theology. We do agree, though, that God's Word is authoritative (2 Tim 3:16), that we are mandated to proclaim that Word (Luke 24:47; Rom 10:14), and that we must make disciples of all the people groups of the world (Matt 28:18–20). We affirm that Jesus Christ is the only Redeemer and that a personal relationship with Him is necessary for salvation (John 14:6; Acts 4:12; Rom 10:9–15). The church, we believe, is God's plan for doing the work of the Great Commission—and it is the privilege of all believers to play a role in that task.

Here is the reality: the Southern Baptist Convention will *never* be the center of a Great Commission Resurgence. Any genuine Great Commission Resurgence will occur only when God's people—his church, gathered in local congregations—admit our apathy, confess our sin, turn to him in brokenness, preach the Word in gratitude and obedience, invest personally in the lives of new believers, and give glory to God alone. It is impossible for our denomination to refocus on the Great Commission unless the individuals who make up our denomination first do so. That simple truth means that a Great Commission Resurgence will be intensely personal—and challenging. Great movements of God almost always begin with a few believers who are willing to pay the price of repentance and obedience.

As you read this book, may I challenge you to make these commitments? First, read *prayerfully*. You will find that the contributors to this work are passionate in our thinking and writing about the Great Commission. That is not to say, though, that we are natural evangelists. We do not claim to have overcome all of our own personal obstacles to doing the Great Commission. We continue to be reminded daily that making disciples in our Jerusalem, Judea, Samaria, and ends of the earth (Acts 1:8) happens only because God empowers us.

One danger in reading this book is that you will approach it only as an academic text. It is written with an academic audience in mind, but the goal is not simply imparting knowledge. Knowledge without passion breeds arrogance, and arrogance will always hinder a Resurgence. Prayerfully ask God now to make you desperate for Him and dependent upon Him.

Second, read *positively*. I feared as we put together this book that some readers would hear so much about the failure of the Southern Baptist church that they would give up on the church after reading this work. Please hear me: our goal is just the opposite. The church is still God's church, and Jesus is both the cornerstone and the head of His church (Eph 2:20, 5:23). In spite of our failures and shortcomings, God still loves us and seeks to use us. He will draw to Himself a people from every tribe, people, language, and nation (Rev 5:9–10), even through the efforts of an imperfect church.

The contributors to this work have hardly given up on the Southern Baptist church. We are acutely concerned, but not defeated. We still believe that the God whose church we are is bigger than any issue that we face. We choose, by faith, to be positive. Our prayer is that God will help you to do the same.

Third, read *practically*. That is, read with intentional change in mind. Status quo simply will not produce a Great Commission Resurgence among Southern Baptists; thus, each of us must be open to change as God leads. Maybe David Platt's sermon on taking risks for the Great Commission will challenge you to give up your "stuff" that the world thinks is so important. Perhaps Bill Henard will push you to take strategic steps to lead your church in personal evangelism. Reading chapters on theology (e.g., those by Russell Moore and Bruce Ashford) might guide you to increase your church's teaching on the theology of the Great Commission.

Now is not the time merely to read a book about the Great Commission, highlight the good points within, and then put the book back on the shelf. The truth of the gospel, the reality of hell, and the potential of Christ's return urgently demand action. We pray that this book will lead to discussions about the Great Commission, but discussions that do not lead to Great Commission actions will leave our denomination right where we are.[2]

Finally, read *personally*. Within the past few years, Southern Baptists have rightly challenged our congregations to be accurate and honest in reporting church membership. So many of our reported church members are inactive that our membership statistics are largely irrelevant. We are not nearly as strong or as numerous as we claim to be.

On the other hand, whether we have as many as sixteen million members or as few as sixteen members does not matter. A Great Commission Resurgence is not about what *everybody else* should be doing. Rather, it is about what *I* should be doing. It is about what *you* should be doing. It is ultimately about what *we* should be doing together as the body of Christ.

Read on now . . . prayerfully, positively, practically, and personally. May a Great Commission Resurgence begin with me and with you.

---

2   To facilitate the discussion of this book's concepts among church laity, LifeWay has also produced an accompanying trade book entitled *Retreat or Risk: A Call for a Great Commission Resurgence*, ed. Jedidiah Coppenger (Nashville: B&H, 2010).

SECTION 1
WHERE WE ARE

SBC DECLINE AND DEMOGRAPHIC CHANGE

Ed Stetzer

PREAMBLE

The state of the Southern Baptist Convention is a common topic of discussion lately. People ask me over and over again, "Are we in decline?" Based on current trends, my answer is, yes. The Southern Baptist Convention, on the aggregate, is in a state of decline. Th e follow-up questions include "why?" or "what caused this?" These secondary questions are far more challenging. In reality, a preponderance of factors is at work, both spiritual and demographic.

These questions drive the data analysis in this research report. Much has been said and many have speculated on decline scenarios. Many have put pieces together in a hodge-podge manner to say that the denomination is not in trouble. Others have just ignored the debate altogether. In attempting to provide additional evidence for decline and explanatory factors that may be at work, I presented a series of tables and graphs at a gathering of state convention newspaper editors at the 2009 Southern Baptist Convention annual meeting in Louisville, Kentucky. A number of media outlets, both inside and outside Southern Baptist life, reported on this presentation. In an effort to better document this recent research, I have put together this chapter, explaining my methodology and providing additional interpretation of results.

The trajectory of our current membership rolls and annual baptisms cannot be derived from any other source than the Annual Church Profile (ACP). In this sense, we rely on the excellent work of hundreds of church and denominational employees that bring this data together every year in understanding the current state of the Southern Baptist Convention. The

ACP is the primary data source for measuring the change in membership and baptisms over the past fifty years. This data also provides the source of our projections through 2050.

In explaining the decline we demonstrate in this chapter, it is imperative that we pinpoint the demographic changes of Southern Baptists *and* non-Southern Baptists in the United States. My basic thesis is the following: *America has changed, but Southern Baptists have not kept up with this change.* I am not speaking here of spiritual, moral, or even religious change in America. These sorts of debates can be taken up at another time. I am referring to the great demographic changes that have occurred in the United States over the past quarter century that are not reflected in our Southern Baptist churches. As America has changed demographically, Southern Baptists have not. This incongruity, I believe, is one major source for the current decline we are experiencing in our convention.

So how do we measure change? Well, we cannot do it by comparing entirely different datasets with completely different sampling strategies. Doing so would mean stringing together data sources and commentary of supposed experts to provide evidence for a particular viewpoint. As I have already stated, I believe we are currently a denomination in decline. That is my leading viewpoint, and I believe the evidence in this report is convincing. The reasons for the decline, however, are far more arbitrary and are open to a wide range of debate.

At LifeWay Research, our aim is to present fair and balanced evidence from the least biased data sources possible. Therefore, in order to answer this question of demographic change, we require a random sample of people that include both Southern Baptists and non-Southern Baptists with an adequate number within each subgroup. We also require data that have been consistently collected for several decades. And the data must be reliable: in other words, it must be a data source that has been used extensively within scholarly and popular publications. There is really only one adequate data source available in the United States that permits such an analysis, and it is the General Social Survey (GSS).

The General Social Survey has been conducted at least bi-annually since 1972 with the data for 2008 having just been released at the time of this writing.[1] The survey is heavily funded by the National Science Foundation and is the primary data source for social scientists looking at social trends over time.

---

1   A question regarding denominational affiliation was not added until 1984. For this reason, all results in this chapter using the GSS begin in that year.

In each survey year, a random sample of American adults (ages 18 and over) is asked a variety of questions including issues of economics, health, religion, social attitudes, and social interaction. I have used the GSS in the past and have come to appreciate its great qualities in answering questions that deal with trends over time as well as its wealth of data for analysis.

The GSS, however, as is the case for all data sources, is not without its limitations. At first sight, it may appear that there is not an adequate sample of SBC respondents for each survey year. The table below lists the number of SBC and non-SBC respondents. Although the number fluctuates from year to year, there are still in the vicinity of 150 to 200 SBC respondents each year in which to gauge demographic change relative to the non-SBC population. The GSS is the most recognized social survey of Americans in existence. If it is respected enough to be used as a primary source in researching for social trends by the world's leading researchers and scholars, it will suffice for our purposes.

Table 1. General Social Survey Number of Respondents for SBC and Non-SBC Populations by Year

Year	SBC	non-SBC	Total
1984	107 (7.26%)	1366	1473
1985	147 (9.58%)	1387	1534
1986	119 (8.10%)	1350	1469
1987	204 (11.22%)	1614	1818
1988	153 (10.34%)	1327	1480
1989	128 (8.33%)	1409	1537
1990	123 (8.97%)	1249	1372
1991	133 (8.77%)	1383	1516
1993	155 (9.66%)	1450	1605
1994	290 (9.70%)	2701	2991
1996	271 (9.34%)	2632	2903
1998	249 (8.80%)	2582	2831
2000	240 (8.52%)	2576	2816
2002	202 (7.31%)	2562	2764
2004	215 (7.65%)	2596	2811
2006	318 (7.05%)	4191	4509
2008	138 (6.82%)	1885	2023

If concern still exists for the lower than ideal number of SBC respondents in the GSS, however, each demographic difference between these two subgroups presented in this report has been tested for statistical significance using t-tests of means. A t-test takes into account the sample size for each group tested. Therefore, even when means may look radically different or remarkably similar, it is still possible that they are not statistically significant due to sample size for either or both of the subgroups. In verifying the validity of my argument, I will consistently refer to the statistical significance differences (probability of difference as accurate 95% of the time) between SBC and non-SBC groups for each graph presented in this report.

A secondary limitation to the GSS, and again for any other similar data source, is the expectation that Southern Baptists would be unequally selected compared to the non-Southern Baptist population. As it is a random sample, this should not be a concern. However, in looking at the particular variables under analysis in this report (i.e., age, percent other race, percent immigrant, and community size), it could be argued that certain portions of each of these demographic groups may be less likely to identify themselves as Southern Baptists than other demographic groups. For instance, the most likely candidates for bias are those individuals who are not white or black (i.e., other race), many of whom are immigrants. They may not identify themselves as Southern Baptist, even though they attend a Southern Baptist church. This is a selection issue that is worth noting, but the results are so dramatically different between the two subgroups that I expect this concern will be alleviated. Even if these few "missing" cases were reinserted, they would be few in number, and would not considerably alter the general trends presented in this report. Every sample or census that exists possesses this same problem, and due to the uniformity of sample error we can assume any differences in the GSS to be the same as the unique sample error in any other survey or census. The ACP possesses its own intricate liabilities, and due to this fact we will utilize both the GSS and ACP in order to gain the best perspective possible of trends within the SBC and the United States.

Lastly, let me add a few words about trends. This report relies on consistent trends for three or more years. A change from time period one to time period two could be due to a number of explanations other than actual socio-demographic change (i.e., measurement error, sampling error, etc.). Consistent change that continues into a third time period is notable. Such a trend, one lasting for more than three time periods, indicates a notable trend.

This report begins with an overview of SBC church membership and baptisms with projections through 2050 based on current trends. As I have already commented on this decline in my other writings, I will not linger on this point at length. The crux of the report is based on the GSS data in comparing Southern Baptist and non-Southern Baptist populations in explaining SBC decline. It is my hope that you will consider how we as Southern Baptists have remained rather static in our demographic composition while the communities around our churches have been dramatically changing. As further evidence of SBC decline, we replicated the results in this report for just the Southern regions of the United States. These results are found in the appendix and provide comparable results.

Before the data analysis, let me be clear in my intentions for this report. The report is not meant to be a doomsday prediction or a means for manipulating convention leadership to follow a particular constituency or group. In fact, my goal with this report is quite the opposite. Its purpose is to present a realistic picture of what the data shows. Most people to whom I have spoken have their own theory for explaining the current decline of our convention. In attempting to explain our current circumstance, I am presenting just one piece of the puzzle here. The findings speak for themselves.

Finally, the following results should not discourage us. Our God is bigger than our current state of affairs and as our Convention continues in the direction of fulfilling the Great Commission, our growing reliance upon Christ and His mission for the church gives me great hope. Reality should not frighten us. Reality should push us to be more effective for the sake of the gospel.

A DENOMINATION IN DECLINE

Membership

When we discuss the state of the Southern Baptist Convention, our point of reference often starts with the curve presented in Figure 1. Since 2000, the total membership of the Convention has remained more or less stagnant, hovering at just over 16 million. The past three years have seen a descending trend, however. We may be able to placate ourselves by believing that Southern Baptists are maintaining their population size, or we can quibble over whether the recent decrease in membership is of any real concern.

Predicting the future is a dangerous undertaking. If the last fifty years are predictive of our future, we will grow. If the last two years are predictive of our future, we will experience decline. There is no way to tell since the trends have changed over the last few years. Many observers look at the chart below and, from their observations rooted in basic math, see a pattern. The growth has slowed, and now we have declined for two years. Some, looking at the chart, believe we have peaked and the coming years will see more decline.

It is not the numbers in Figure 1 that provide the longest trends, but rather the results in Figure 2 and Figure 3.

Figure 2 takes the percent year-to-year change in SBC membership and extrapolates the trend (straight line) from 1950 through to 2050. Although we experienced membership growth for the majority of the years since 1950, that membership growth has become smaller and smaller, and passed into decline a few years ago.

There is a definitive trend downwards that if continued will accumulate into a reduction of about 3 percent a year in membership by 2050. In absolute numbers, if the trend continues, we can see in Figure 3 that the current total of 16 million members would be the peak. We do not know if that is the case. (And, we won't know for a few years—the 2009, 2010, and 2011 numbers will not suddenly alter the trend.) It will take

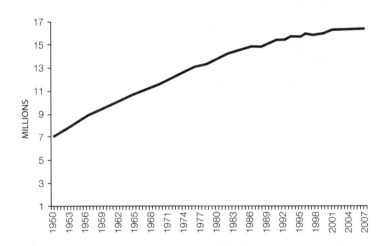

Figure 1. SBC Total Membership 1950–2008.
Source: Annual Church Profile 1950–2008.

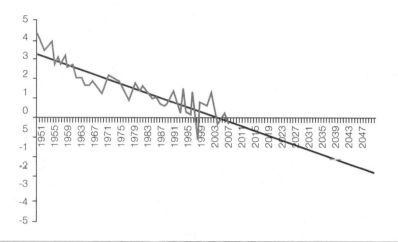

Figure 2. Year-to-Year Percent Change in SBC Membership, Projected to 2050. Source: Annual Church Profile 1950–2008.

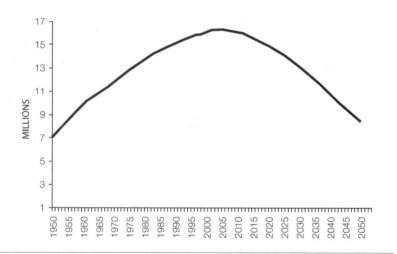

Figure 3. SBC Projected Total Membership to 2050. Source: Annual Church Profile 1950–2008.

several years of change. If that trend continues, however, by 2020, the current trend would put SBC membership around 15 million. If this trend were to continue *as it has for fifty years*, 8.6 million members would be the reality by 2050.

In the meantime, the population of the United States is not expected to remain static through 2050. Figure 4 demonstrates that the SBC share of the US population has been in a general state of decline since the latter part of the 1980s. Since the peak value of 11% in 1987, the percentage of Americans that claim to be Southern Baptist has declined to just fewer than 7% in 2008.

Baptisms

If we look at the other critical measurement, baptisms, the evidence for decline only accumulates. Figure 5 displays the baptism numbers since 1950. The trend is not nearly as consistent as the membership figures, but in the long term does not indicate substantial growth either. If we were to extrapolate the year-to-year percent change in baptisms to 2050, it would essentially be a flat line, indicating little growth or decline. In other words, although the decline in baptisms projected into the future does not look as challenging as the decline in membership, the study does not suggest a future trend of baptisms indicating sustained growth.

Many have rightfully asked if the decline in baptisms over the last ten years is part of the normal up and down that we have seen for fifty years and, if so, will they go up again. That is certainly what all Southern Baptists would want. But, there is no way to know for certain.

In order to ask if the SBC baptism decline of the last ten years was unusual, the North American Mission Board staff contacted the Assemblies

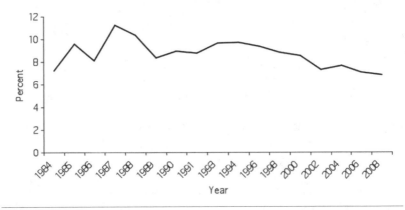

Figure 4. Percent of Americans that are Southern Baptist 1984–2008. Source: GSS 1984–2008.

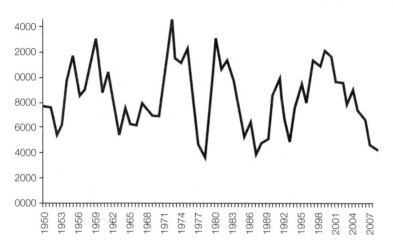

Figure 5. SBC Baptisms 1950–2008.
Source: Annual Church Profile.

of God and Nazarene denominations, two organizations that track their baptisms in similar ways. In order to compare the baptisms, they set a base-line year (1980) and then compared the percentage change from year to year. It turns out that making 1980 the baseline made the SBC baptisms appear much worse than would other years (note that 1980 was a good year). NAMB's research team leader (Richie Stanley) worked with Bill Gordon, from the evangelization team, to create a better baseline—averaging baptisms over three years.

The NAMB report concluded that a side-by-side comparison of these three denominations reveals a disquieting decline in SBC baptisms since 1997 when compared to the other two evangelical denominations.

Figure 6 shows the percentage change in baptisms of the three denominations. The average number of baptisms for the years 1980–1982 was used as a baseline for comparison purposes.

It is interesting to note that the baptisms actually track together in the 1980s (declining) and all go up in the 1990s. In the late 1990s and into the new millennium, however, the lines diverge. SBC baptisms decline much more clearly than the others. Again, there is no way to tell the future trends, but for many with a passion for evangelism, any decline in baptisms (even one that can be explained) is a cause for concern.

Figure 6. Percentage Change in Baptisms of Three Denominations 1980–2008.
Soure: NAMB.

Demographic Changes—SBC and US Population

As already mentioned, the explanation for current decline in the SBC is due to a host of factors. This report takes a demographic perspective, yet acknowledges that many other factors are at play.

Age. One category of growing difference between the SBC population and the US population is age. In Figure 7, we can see no obvious trend in the differences of age between SBC and non-SBC populations from 1984 through 1998. Although all groups are getting older, the lines do begin to diverge around 2000. The trends continue to widen from 2000 to 2008. In fact, since 2000, there is a statistically significant difference in age between the two groups in mean age, with the exception of 2008. Substantively, the mean difference in ages is only about three years, but as an average within the adult population, this can mean a great deal of difference to the age distribution within our congregations.

A caveat should be mentioned at this point. It is true that the GSS is an adult sample; therefore, a mean could be adjusted lower with an extra abundance of young children in Southern Baptist families compared to the US population. We investigated this possibility and came across the most recent research conducted by Conrad Hackett of the University of

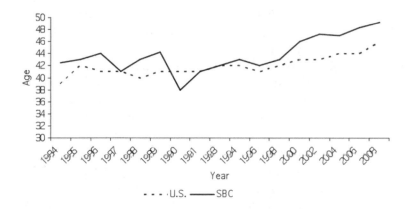

Figure 7. Median Age of the US Population and SBC Members by Year. Source: GSS 1984–2008.

Texas at Austin, who finds that Southern Baptists do not have a substantially greater fertility rate than the US population.[2] Therefore, we should not expect a mean age difference between Southern Baptists and the general US population to be altered substantially by including children in the sample. Figure 7 presents median rates of age within the SBC and the US rather than mean ages, due to the fact that this is the standard approach of presenting age demographics in American populations.

In summary, both Southern Baptists and the US population are aging, but Southern Baptists are aging more quickly. This reality can mean one of the following things:

- With each additional year, fewer young adults are part of Southern Baptist churches.
- With each additional year, there is an increase in seniors in our churches.
- With each additional year, the life expectancy of Southern Baptist seniors vis-à-vis the US population is higher and subsequently raises the average age of Southern Baptists compared to the US population.

---

2   Conrad P. Hackett, "Religion and Fertility in the United States: The Influence of Affiliation, Region, and Congregation" (Ph.D. diss., Princeton University, 2008).

I have written a great deal in support of the first hypothesis. If we look at the age group of 18 to 29 year olds and their frequency of church attendance, we see that non-Evangelicals are becoming less church-going while Evangelicals are mostly staying constant with a slight edge toward growth. The composition of Southern Baptist churches, on the aggregate, is becoming older than the US population. This will present further demographic difficulties in the future when this young adult population has children who may also not be in Southern Baptist churches, creating an even deeper decline in replacing older generations.

As Figure 8 indicates, the fact that rates of religious service attendance for 18 to 29 year olds is steady to slightly growing for Evangelicals as a whole leaves a quandary as to why the median age in the SBC is growing. Two explanations are possible for this dynamic. First, it is possible for the median age to grow while the number of 18 to 29 year olds in the SBC is also growing. The mass of Baby Boomers simply outnumbering a growing trend of young SBC attendees is possible. A second possibility is that the number of young Evangelicals is rising due to gains made by non-SBC congregations that make up for losses of young Evangelicals in SBC congregations. A good comparative category to examine this possibility is with nondenominational congregations. Figure 9 shows the proportion

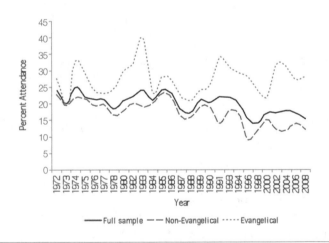

Figure 8. Percent of 18 to 29 Year Olds Attending Religious Services at Least Once a Week.
Source: GSS 1972–2008.

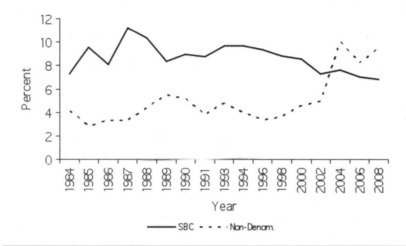

Figure 9. Proportion of Americans who are Southern Baptist as Compared to Nondenominational 1984–2008.
Source: GSS 1984–2008.

of Americans who claim to attend a nondenominational congregation as compared to a SBC congregation.

Southern Baptist attendees have historically outnumbered nondenominational attendees. This trend ended by 2004. Since 2004, more people claim to attend a nondenominational congregation than a Southern Baptist congregation. Though this finding is revealing, it alone does not substantiate evidence to support a theory that young adults are leaving the SBC for nondenominational congregations. It may be impossible to prove that this is happening, but it is possible to compare median and mean ages longitudinally. When the median age of nondenominational attendees is compared to the US population and the SBC, it is lower than both. Figure 10 shows that the median age for nondenominational attendees is more than 5 years less than the median age for SBC attendees. T-tests show that the SBC was significantly older than nondenominational attendees from 2000 to 2006. Some claim that the SBC is comparatively reaching younger demographics effectively. Figure 10 shows that this comparison obviously does not include nondenominational congregations.

Ethnicity/Immigration. Southern Baptists are known for their emphasis on language church work. Even before the era of the Home Mission Board director of language churches, Oscar Romo, Southern Baptists had

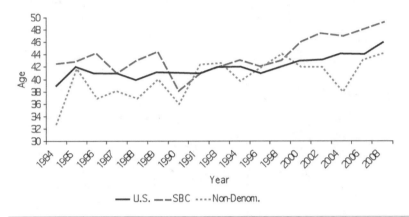

Figure 10. Median Age of the US Population, the SBC, and Nondenominational Attendees 1984–2008.
Source: GSS 1984–2008.

a long history of church planting and evangelism among people groups that do not speak English. But the question has to be asked: despite this amazing work among immigrants, has attendance in our denomination kept up with the demographic changes that immigrant groups are creating in US society?

I refer you first to Figure 11, which displays the percent other race (non-white, nonblack population) for SBC and non-SBC populations. Through the eighties and early nineties, there was little difference in the percentage of other race group for SBC and non-SBC populations; however, we see a dramatic diversion beginning in the mid-nineties that continues through 2008. In essence, the percentage of the other race group in the Southern Baptist Convention has remained fairly static for the past quarter century, whereas the US population has become increasingly more ethnically diverse. In fact, the difference in percentage of the other race group between the SBC and the general US population is statistically significant since 1993.

It is true that when dealing with very small percentages in the SBC population for the category "other race," one could posit that only a handful of respondents in the SBC subgroup does not tell us very much. That speculation could be justified if it were not for Figure 12, where we see a similar story as displayed in the preceding graph. Here we see the same divide in percent foreign-born between SBC and the general US population. At

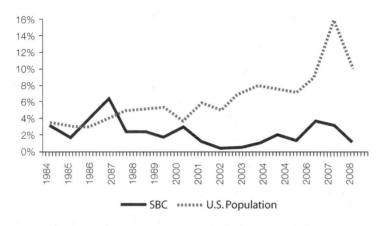

Figure 11. Percent Other Race (nonwhite, nonblack) of SBC and US Population by Year.
Source: General Social Survey 1984–2008.

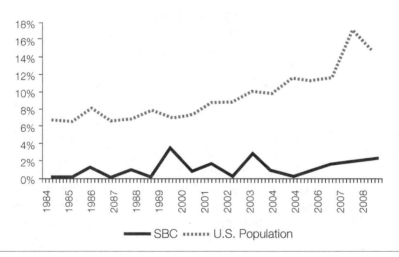

Figure 12. Percent Foreign-Born of SBC and US Populations by Year.
Source: General Social Survey 1984–2008.

the same point in the mid-1990s, the percentage of foreign-born people among Southern Baptists remained rather static, but the US population has continued to increase in its immigrant population.

Again, these findings are not to discredit the amazing work done among our language and people group missionaries. However, we are simply not keeping pace with this demographic change. As the contours of the US population changes, the Southern Baptist Convention will continue to decline if we are not better equipped and engaged in reaching immigrant populations. This is unfortunate since, as Phillip Connor has pointed out with ACP data, non-English speaking people groups in North America are indeed underrepresented in our convention compared to the US population, but the are also the groups with the highest baptism rates within our Convention.[3] In other words, the harvest is plentiful, but the laborers are still so few.

Interaction of Age and Ethnicity. Neither age nor ethnicity by itself can account for the dynamics at play in denominational change. The two properties intermingle in their effects on any social organization. Figure 13 displays the vast differences in median age by race and ethnicity since 2000.[4] The increased variation in median age since 2000 is due to the increasing age of the Baby Boomers, with lower than replacement rates of fertility among white, non-Hispanic women.[5]

The SBC has always possessed a high proportion of Whites. As discussed above, Southern Baptists have worked hard to add greater racial and ethnic diversity to the denomination. A longitudinal glimpse of the SBC's proportionality of Whites can be seen in Figure 14. This chart shows that the denomination has declined in proportionality of Whites since 1984, but very slightly. It is encouraging, though, to see that the proportion is not far off the US population as a whole. As a matter of fact, the SBC has been historically close to the national average and has only eclipsed the average in the last wave of the GSS, which was done in 2008.

In 2008, the SBC reported a population that is 81.9% white, whereas the nation at large reported being 77.6% white. This 4.3% difference is alarming, but represents only one year, thus failing to define any trend. Note that the reported 2008 proportion of 81.9% white is the highest

---

3   Phillip Connor, *A Biblical Missiology for North American People Groups* (Alpharetta, GA: Center for Missional Research, North American Mission Board, 2006).

4   The GSS did not ask an independent question regarding one's Hispanic ethnicity until 2000. Prior to this, Hispanics could have chosen either, "White" or "Other" on the racial variable. This accounts for a slight, and indeterminate, amount of the variation in the "White" and "Other" categories between the periods before 1998 and afterward.

5   Brady Hamilton and Stephanie Ventura, "Fertility and Abortion Rates in the United States, 1960–2002," *International Journal of Andrology* 29 (2006): 34–45.

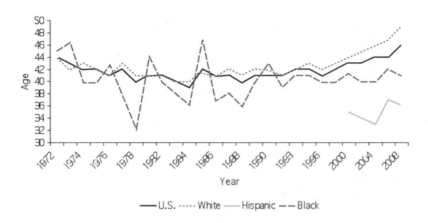

Figure 13. Median Age of Whites, Blacks, Hispanics, and US Population by Year.
Source: GSS 1972–2008.

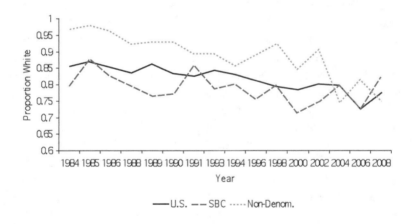

Figure 14. Proportion of Whites found in the SBC, Nondenominational Congregations, and the US Population.
Source: GSS 1984–2008.

proportion of whites that the SBC has had since 1991. This places a high level of importance on the direction of ethnicity rates over the next two reported years. If the value stays even or continues to increase in the near future it will indicate a reverse bell-shaped relationship with the proportionality of whites, showing an up-trend in white proportionality and the loss of past gains in diversity. One result would be a negative effect on denominational membership. Also note the proportion of whites among nondenominational attendees, included for comparative purposes. Nondenominational congregations historically have had heavy overrepresentation by whites. This trend has steadily declined since 1984. In 1985 Americans reporting to have attended nondenominational congregations were 97.7% white, while the SBC and American population were a full 10% lower at 87% white. In 2004, nondenominational attendees dropped below the rate of white in the SBC and the American population for the first time. In 2008, Nondenominational congregations were 75% white, which is 7% lower than the SBC for that year. Nondenominational congregations were significantly more proportionally white than SBC congregations in every wave with the exception of 1991, 1993, 1994, 2004, and 2008.

Figure 14[6] is a replication of Figure 10 with the addition of the median age for Whites. In accordance with the proportion of whites being so dominant in the SBC, the median age value is virtually the same as that of whites in the US from 1984 to the present. One glimpse into the dynamics of young adults in the SBC can be seen by the fact that the median age of nondenominational attendees began to separate from the pack in 2000, which is generally the same point when they began to look less like the SBC and more like the US population racially/ethnically. The entering of this new market or demographic may partly explain how their median age stayed virtually the same, with a slight decrease since 1998. Thereafter, the SBC began to increase drastically in median age, in accordance with the median age for white Americans.

It is impossible to tell whether the comparative youth of nondenominational congregations is due to increasing diversity, increasing attraction to Evangelical young adults, or a mixture of the two. In all likelihood it is due to a mixture of the two. If it were due merely to the racial/ethnic diversification of the congregations, the difference in median age in Figure 15 would not be so great. A sign of this mixture of factors is that in 2006 nondenominational congregations were reported to have a higher proportion of whites than SBC congregations, yet their median age was 5.35 years less in that year. Given the fact that the survey subjects are all 18 years or older, it follows that young people have more heavily populated

---

6   The proportion of whites is significantly different between the SBC and nondenominational congregations in 1984, 1985, 1986, 1987, 1988, 1989, 1990, 1996, 1998, 2000, 2002, and 2006.

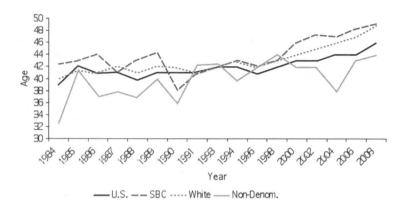

Figure 15. Median Age of the US Population, the SBC, Nondenominational Attendees and Whites 1984–2008.
Source: GSS 1984–2008.

nondenominational congregations since 2000. Unfortunately, the same is not the case for the SBC. There is an obvious connection between this influx of young adults to nondenominational congregational attendees and the decline in the number of young adults attending SBC churches for the first time in 2002.

Urbanization. The United States is moving to its cities. As a result, cities have become important centers of commerce throughout the country. These cities include all ranges of urban residences including inner city districts and suburban areas. Unfortunately, Southern Baptists have not kept up with the pace of urbanization within America. Figure 16 displays the average community size (in thousands) as self-reported by respondents in the GSS. As in the preceding demographics, the difference between the SBC and non-SBC populations during the eighties and early nineties was not that great; however, by the mid-nineties, a significant difference emerged as the US population continued to be highly urban, but Southern Baptists became less urban.

Church Age Effects. Recently, attention has been turned toward the effects of congregational age on decline and closure. Specifically, Kevin Dougherty, Jared Maier, and Brian Vander Lugt found a significant correlation between a congregation's age and its closure.[7] Assessing the

---

7   Kevin Dougherty, Jared Maier, and Brian Vander Lugt, "When the Final Bell Tolls: Patterns of Church Closings in Two Protestant Denominations," *Review of Religious Research* 50 (2008): 49–73.

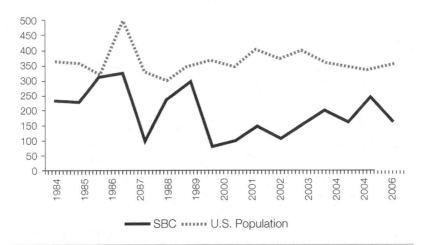

Figure 16. Average Self-reported Community Size in Thousands for SBC and US Populations by Year.
Source: General Social Survey 1984–2008. Note: The question of community size was not asked in the 2008 GSS.

Presbyterian Church (US) and the Church of the Nazarene, congregations were found to have a significantly higher risk of death in the first 15 years of existence and between the ages of 35 and 50. In a presentation at the 2009 annual meeting of the Southern Baptist Research Fellowship in 2009, Maier showed the results of a replication study, sponsored by NAMB, of the Southern Baptist Convention. He found that the exact same relationships existed for the SBC, as shown in Figure 17.

Dougherty and his co-authors state that there are three types of age liabilities for any social organization: "Newness Liabilities," "Adolescence Liabilities," and "Oldness Liabilities." Newness liabilities that affect social organizations are four-fold: (1) new roles have to be learned, which takes time and effort, (2) new roles can clash until standardized in an efficient way, (3) new organizations are based on relations between strangers, and (4) new organizations must find a way to establish external relationships. Due to the "Free Church" nature of the SBC congregations, the fourth point is especially difficult for our congregations to manage.[8] These four

---

8   Ibid.; Arthur L. Stinchcombe, "Social Structures and Organizations," in *Handbook of Organizations*, ed. James G. March (Chicago: Rand McNally, 1965).

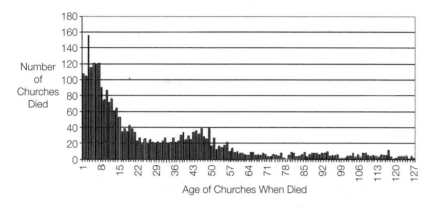

Figure 17: Age Distribution of Congregations at Time of Closure in the SBC, 1995-2007.
Source: Kevin Dougherty

points also illustrate why multi-site church plants have become desirable for many, for they already have some system of standardization, and many internal and external relationships are already established.

The second type of liability is that of Adolescence.[9] A spiked rate of organizational death tends to be found when an organization's "seed" money runs out. A church may be alive for quite some time solely dependent on resources that it possessed as "start-up" money. When this money runs out, the true instability of the congregation is realized and it begins a progression to closure.

The last type of liability is that of Oldness.[10] There are three main social dynamics that lead to oldness liabilities for organizations. The first

9   Michael T. Hannan, "Rethinking Age Dependence in Organizational Mortality: Logical Formalizations," *American Journal of Sociology* 104 (1998): 126–65; Mark Fichman and Daniel Levinthal, "Honeymoons and the Liability of Adolescence: A New Perspective on Duration Dependence in Social Organizational Relationships," *Academy of Management Review* 16 (1991): 442–68; Dougherty, Maier, and Vander Lugt, "When the Final Bell Tolls"; Josef Bruderl and Rudolf Schussler, "Organizational Mortality: The Liabilities of Newness and Adolescence," *Administrative Science Quarterly* 35 (1990): 530–47.

10   David N. Barron, Elizabeth West, and Michael T. Hannan, "A Time to Grow and a Time to Die: Growth and Mortality of Credit Unions in New York City, 1914–1990," *American Journal of Sociology* 100 (1994): 381–421; Heather A. Haveman, "Ghosts of Managers Past: Managerial Succession and Organizational Mortality," *Academy of Management Journal* 36 (1993): 864–81; Dougherty, Maier, and Vander Lugt, "When the Final Bell Tolls."

is *senescence*. Senescence indicates that the organization has succumbed to the "iron cage" of bureaucratization.[11] In other words, the organization has become so rationalized and structured that no effective decisions or actions can be made. In the case of churches, the congregation has "committee'd" itself to death. The second liability of oldness is *obsolescence*. Organizations can become obsolete in their given market and environment. Methodologies that once worked no longer hold the social power of appeal that they once possessed. The only organizations that are immune to this liability of age are those that have a fixed need, a fixed environment of consumers, and an immunity to technological advancements. Congregations are susceptible to this liability due to their lacking the latter two attributes. The last liability of oldness is *leadership transition*. The loss of a founding leader is catastrophic to any type of organization. Leadership transitions dramatically increase the risk of decline and closure.

Maier's research on closure in the SBC showed that the upward curve of oldness liabilities was also present in the 35–50 age range. This tells us that SBC congregations suffer from one, or all, of the three oldness liabilities. It would be prudent to take notice of this dynamic and to do all that is possible to assist congregations in being as vital as possible to their communities. Assistance could be made available to congregations that would help them navigate the untangling of committee gridlock, becoming culturally relevant, and transitioning pastorates (especially those that are experiencing pastoral change for the first time). Dougherty, Maier, and Vander Lugt admit that any guess to why the rate of death increases at the unique area of 35–50 years of age is purely conjecture.[12] Yet, they do suggest that it is most likely related to generational transition within the church, along with the exit of some founding pastors. Charter members of a church must pass the church on to a younger cohort during this unique point in time. Many churches seem to struggle with this hand off, which leads back to the culprits of senescence and obsolescence.

One approach to dealing with these issues would be for SBC congregations to incorporate as many younger adults as possible in the leadership and decision-making processes of the church. Without their inclusion, they are not likely to stay. It is less likely than ever before for a person in adulthood to be a member of the same church they attended as a child.

---

11   Max Weber, *The Protestant Ethic and the Spirit of Capitalism*, trans. Talcott Parsons (New York: Routledge, 2001), 123.

12   Dougherty, Maier, and Vander Lugt, "When the Final Bell Tolls."

Mobility, urbanization, suburbanization, and exurbanization are dictating this trend. Social dynamics such as these are changing the way that Americans become affiliated with a congregation. Many rural areas have become exurban, and many suburban areas have become urban. These trends change the dynamic and demography of the surrounding areas. To provide the best opportunity for vitality, congregations must take these demographic shifts into consideration in order to be culturally relevant and avoid falling prey to obsolescence.

CONCLUSION

As I stated at the beginning of this chapter, reality should not frighten us. Facts are our friends. Reality should inspire us to greater things. Much of the research in this report describes the challenges that Southern Baptists face for the mission of God over the next forty years. For God to move us to new places with Him the first step is for us to become uncomfortable with the current realities. The discomfort should begin with the lost, whereas our comfort is in knowing that God invites us to join His mission. Facts are our friends because they show us where we see God at work and where the church is failing to advance with Him.

Where do we go from here? Although one might expect a methodological formula or a prophetic sermon at this point, I think we have tired of words pontificated from papers and platforms. No one is surprised when preachers and researchers scream from the rooftops "the sky is falling." Few believe or really care. Like a flu vaccine, Southern Baptists have been injected with just enough doomsday sermons and statistics to become immune to them.

The change that must come *to* our churches must begin *in* our churches. American churches, specifically Southern Baptists, must seek a movement of God. Our decisions today must move beyond human strategies and explanation. Statistics that describe the realities of our churches and the people on our mission field are as much about spiritual realities as they are about demographic trends. Southern Baptists must awaken a passion for the nations that live in our country's borders like the passion that the early church had for those living in the Roman Empire. That is something only God can do. Maybe it would look something like this:

Current Realities > New Conversations > Discomfort and Conviction > Prayer > Obedience > Revival > Mission

You may be thinking, "That is not very realistic." You are right. But we have lived according to human realities for too long. God calls us to make disciples of all nations. As long as we are satisfied or apathetic in reaching every generation and every people group, we are showing disobedience to the Great Commission, especially when those generations and people groups live within our own cities.

The uncovering of one factor regarding the decline of our Convention is not the answer to the decline, but it is a place of insight for the decline. It is a place to begin our conversations with one another, and with Christ, because it is still His church that we lead. I believe one place for us to start reaching North America is through the avenue of the rich diversity He has placed within our culture. I find hope in picturing a racially rich and culturally diverse SBC penetrating every people group in America with the good news of the gospel of Jesus Christ. Imagine new and revitalized churches alive and on mission with people who are experiencing personal transformation. Imagine personal transformation bleeding over to change cities and communities beyond human explanation through the undeniable power of God. May the Spirit of God move Southern Baptists to reconnect with the heart of God for the unreached generations and ethnicities of our land, bringing the hope of the gospel of Jesus Christ to our nation and our world.

APPENDIX

Note: The following figures are based on GSS data for the US Southern population, including the following states: Texas, Oklahoma, Arkansas, Louisiana, Mississippi, Alabama, Georgia, Florida, Tennessee, Kentucky, West Virginia, District of Columbia, Maryland, Delaware, Virginia, North Carolina, and South Carolina. These states represent the South Census region. Unfortunately, the GSS does not permit further subdivision by state. For this reason, other influential SBC states like Missouri could not be added to this analysis.

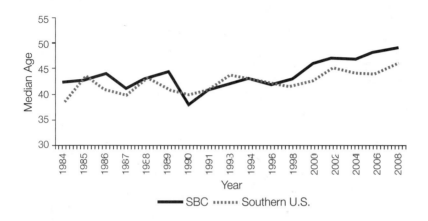

Figure A1. Median Age of SBC and US Southern Populations by Year.
Source: General Social Survey 1984–2008. Note: Mean Age differences between SBC and non-SBC Southern populations are statistically significant in 2004.

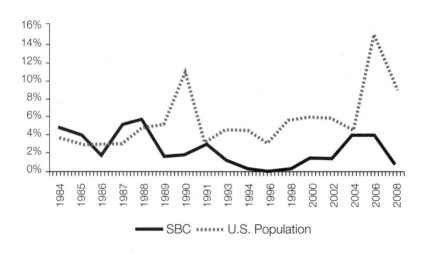

Figure A2. Percent Other Race (nonwhite, nonblack) of SBC and US Southern Populations by Year.
Source: General Social Survey 1984–2008. Note: Percent other race differences between SBC and US populations are statistically significant in all years since 1993, except for 2004.

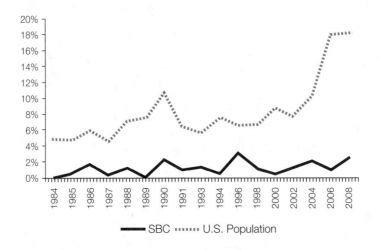

Figure A3. Percent Foreign-Born of SBC and US Southern Populations by Year.
Source: General Social Survey 1984–2008. Note: Percent immigrant differences between SBC and US populations are statistically significant for every year.

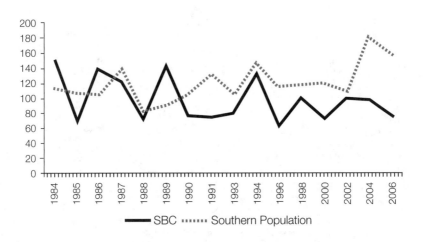

Figure A4. Average Self-reported Community Size in Thousands for SBC and US Southern Populations by Year.
Source: General Social Survey 1984–2008. Note: Community size differences between SBC and US populations are statistically significant in years 1996, 2000, 2004, and 2006. The question of community size was not asked in the 2008 GSS.

A RESURGENCE NOT YET FULFILLED

EVANGELISTIC EFFECTIVENESS IN THE SOUTHERN BAPTIST CONVENTION SINCE 1979[1]

Thom S. Rainer

When the Southern Baptist Convention elected Adrian Rogers its president in 1979, hopes were high among many conservatives that significant changes or improvements would take place in at least four areas. Both written and anecdotal sources make clear that the foremost issue was doctrinal and that the six Southern Baptist seminaries were the focus of the doctrinal reformation.

The strategy was cogent and clear. The president's appointment powers would eventually reach the boards of trustees of the seminaries, who would hire new conservative professors and administrators for those seminaries. Those professors would then teach new generations of students, who would in turn lead churches toward greater biblical conservatism. No informed observer can deny the efficacy of this strategy. Today all six seminaries are led by undeniably conservative presidents, and the faculties are dominated by conservative professors.

A second but related focus of reformation was the engagement of culture. Conservatives were anxious to make clear statements of biblical values on issues such as marriage, sexuality, and the sanctity of life. A primary venue for this expression was the annual Southern Baptist Convention, particularly through resolutions voted on by the messengers. Issues of

---

1   This chapter is a revised and expanded version of the author's original article, "A Resurgence Not Yet Realized: Evangelistic Effectiveness in the Southern Baptist Convention Since 1979," *The Southern Baptist Journal of Theology* 9, no. 1 (Spring 2005): 54–69.

cultural engagement from a conservative and biblical perspective continue to dominate the approved resolutions since 1979.

Southern Baptist leaders are at the forefront of cultural engagement. R. Albert Mohler Jr., the president of The Southern Baptist Theological Seminary, hosts a daily, nationally syndicated radio show that focuses primarily on cultural engagement.[2] Mohler also maintains a Web site where he regularly discusses cultural issues via his blog and e-commentaries.[3]

When George W. Bush was re-elected as president of the United States in 2004, pundits across the political spectrum expressed surprise at the significant role that "values" played in the president's victory.[4] Bush was a regular speaker, usually by live video, at the annual Southern Baptist Convention. He recognized the important role Southern Baptists played in moving forward his social and political agendas.

Many Southern Baptist leaders made regular visits to the White House under the conservative Bush administration. A national news magazine noted the close relationship between President Bush and Richard Land, president of the Ethics and Religious Liberty Commission of the Southern Baptist Convention. "As director of the political arm of the Southern Baptist Convention," the magazine noted, "Richard Land has enjoyed a long and close relationship with the born-again Bush."[5] The Conservative Resurgence can be credited with significant victories on both fronts of theological reformation and cultural engagement.

A third area of measurable success is in the arena of international missions. Many conservatives were concerned that the direction of the Foreign Mission Board was less conversionary, following the dialogical path of the mainline denominations. The newly named International Mission Board, however, took a clearly defined conservative and conversionary direction.

The numerical results are noteworthy. At the end of 2009, the IMB had 5,512 appointed field personnel. The church membership of affiliated IMB churches exceeded 10.3 million in 2008. In that same year the board

---

2 The radio show is called "The Albert Mohler Program," and is nationally syndicated by Salem Communications. The show airs five days a week, Monday through Friday. See http://www.albertmohler .com/radio/.

3 See http://www.albertmohler.com.

4 See, for example, "The Morals and Values Crowd," *US News and World Report*, 15 Nov. 2004, 42.

5 "Winner: Richard Land, A Spiritual Influence," *Time*, 15 Nov. 2004, 84.

reported over 565,000 overseas baptisms. Also in 2008, missionaries and nationals started 26,970 churches.[6]

Though pundits may disagree on the extent of the success of the Conservative Resurgence in these three major areas, few will argue that doctrinal fidelity, cultural engagement, and international missions are decidedly more conservative today than in 1979. But there was yet a fourth area of focus of the Conservative Resurgence, and it is the evaluation of that issue that is the subject of this chapter.

THE CONSERVATIVE RESURGENCE AND EVANGELISTIC EFFECTIVENESS

Prior to the impetus of the Conservative Resurgence, Dean Kelley wrote a landmark book demonstrating that conservative churches are much more likely to grow than moderate or liberal churches. The 1972 introduction of *Why Conservative Churches Are Growing* ignited a debate in the American church landscape on the relationship between theological beliefs and growth of churches.[7]

Kelley was no fundamentalist. He served as an executive with the liberal National Council of Churches. Southern Baptist conservatives pointed to that book and other studies to rally members and messengers to turn the convention to a more conservative direction. And one of the primary benefits of the resurgence, we were told, would be an unprecedented evangelistic harvest in the denomination. Did the resurgence succeed in this arena?

The Thesis: A Resurgence Not Yet Fulfilled

The thesis of this chapter is that the Conservative Resurgence that began in 1979 in the Southern Baptist Convention has *not* resulted in a greater evangelistic effectiveness in the denomination. A corollary to the thesis is that, without the resurgence, the evangelistic effectiveness of the denomination would be much worse.

---

6   "Fast Facts," International Mission Board of the Southern Baptist Convention [on-line]; accessed 10 Nov. 2009; available from http://www.imb.org/main/page.asp?StoryID=4452&LanguageID=1709; Internet.

7   Dean M. Kelley, *Why Conservative Churches Are Growing*, rev. ed. (Macon, GA: Mercer University Press, 1986).

To use a medical metaphor, the resurgence slowed the bleeding of lost effectiveness, but the patient is still not well. Despite great expectations of an evangelistic harvest, the Southern Baptist Convention is in no better condition evangelistically than it was in 1979.

This chapter will demonstrate the numerical realities of evangelistic stagnation in the denomination. But the research presented will be more than descriptive. Note the title of the chapter: "A Resurgence Not *Yet* Fulfilled." The research will provide several hypotheses for the stagnation and offer prescriptive suggestions for greater evangelistic health. The present picture is painted with some level of gloom, to be sure. The future picture, however, offers hope if definitive changes are made.

Methodology of the Research

The primary approach of this research is statistical and numerical analysis. Such an approach has admitted weaknesses.

First, numbers are not an ideal measurement in most Christian research. Indeed, some of my previous works have been criticized for an overemphasis on numerical realities. For example, baptismal numbers are among the key statistics we use. But numerical measurements of conversions are an approximation at best. We cannot know with certainty if a baptism measured is a true conversion. Matters of the heart between a person and God are not always best expressed by numerical measurement.

Second, numerical analyses do not take into account external and contextual factors. For example, a church that records twenty-five baptisms in a nongrowing community of 300 persons may be much more effective than a church with the same number of baptisms in a fast-growing metropolitan area of two million persons.

Third, corporate spiritual realities cannot be measured. The spiritual health of a church simply has no corresponding numerical reality.

Essentially, my research was aimed at three data-based components. The first component of the data was total baptisms. Although baptisms are often perceived to measure the total conversions in a Southern Baptist church, we should be cautious when equating baptisms with conversions.

First, on some occasions total baptisms may understate conversion growth. Some churches have evangelistic efforts that do not result in baptisms in their specific congregations. They may refer recent converts to another church for a variety of reasons. For example, children who receive Christ in one church's Vacation Bible School might be baptized in their "home" church.

Second, baptisms may also overstate conversion growth. In a recent survey of Southern Baptist members, we found that 17 percent of those surveyed had been baptized two or more times. While the reasons behind these multiple baptisms vary (and some are really strange), the net effect is that a conversion is counted more than once.

Perhaps the primary reason baptisms can overstate conversions relates to our polity of baptism by immersion. Most Southern Baptists believe that a Presbyterian can be a Christian without being immersed, even if we disagree with pedobaptism doctrinally. But typically, that Presbyterian is immersed when he or she becomes a Southern Baptist. That particular baptism then represents a person who has been a Christian for some time, not the recent conversion of an unregenerate person.

A second data component is church membership. That particular number can be more problematic than baptisms. A majority of Southern Baptist churches overstate their membership significantly by failing to keep accurate membership records. Those churches that have attempted to discover the number of "real" members often find a number of those on the rolls have died or cannot be located.

Despite the inherent problems with this data, we had to use the data that was available to us for this research. Thus, we must approach our work recognizing the limitations of the data used, but also recognizing that the data can give us valuable insights into the evangelistic health of our denominations.

Lastly, a third measurement is called the "baptismal ratio." It is actually a combination of the numerical measurements of baptisms and membership. We will explain this ratio more fully in a subsequent section of this chapter.

Total Baptisms as an Initial Indicator of Evangelistic Effectiveness

The Southern Baptist Convention has retained membership and baptismal data since 1845, with the exception of the period between 1861 and 1871. For the purpose of this study, I think that fifty years of data would be sufficient to demonstrate clear trends. So, I'll first look at total baptisms in the denomination from 1950 to 2008, the most current year for which we have data.[8]

My purpose in reviewing this data is straightforward. If baptisms are at least somewhat a reflection of conversion growth in the Southern Baptist Convention, a lengthy trend can give us insights into the overall evangelistic effectiveness of the denomination.

Another helpful feature of this data is the trend of baptismal growth since 1979, the beginning of the Conservative Resurgence in the denomination. The results are fascinating but discouraging.

Simply stated, the Southern Baptist Convention is reaching no more people today than it did in 1950. The pattern in the graph below is a classic plateau. In fact, the picture is bleak, indeed. In 1950 Southern Baptist churches baptized 376,085 persons. In 2008 the total baptisms were 342,198—a difference and decline of ten percent!

For over fifty years, the number of baptisms has been in a tight range. The highest recorded baptisms took place in 1972, a total of 445,725. The lowest in this period was 336,050 in 1978, the year before the onset of the Conservative Resurgence. Sadly, 2008 was only six thousands baptisms above the lowest total over the last fifty years.

What are the numerical results for baptisms from 1979 forward? Are there any discernible improvements in overall baptismal trends for the past quarter-century represented by the Conservative Resurgence? Sadly, the answer is "no."

Those of us who follow these trends found hope in the years 1994 to 1999. This period was the longest uptrend in baptisms since 1950, and is represented on the graph as "breakout years." Unfortunately, the growth trend did not continue. With the advent of the new millennium, baptisms in the Southern Baptist Convention have declined consistently. With the exception of an uptick in 2004, there has been a steady decline in total baptisms across the past decade.

Again, we should be cautious in looking at these results as precise measurements of evangelistic health. But with the limitations of the data noted, the conclusion must be that the evangelistic growth of the denomination

---

8 All of the data for the Southern Baptist Convention came from the Annual Church Profiles (previously called the Uniform Church Letter). This information is maintained by LifeWay Christian Resources, the denominational agency of the Southern Baptist Convention responsible for gathering and publishing the data. I specifically looked at total baptisms, total membership, and the resulting baptismal ratios.

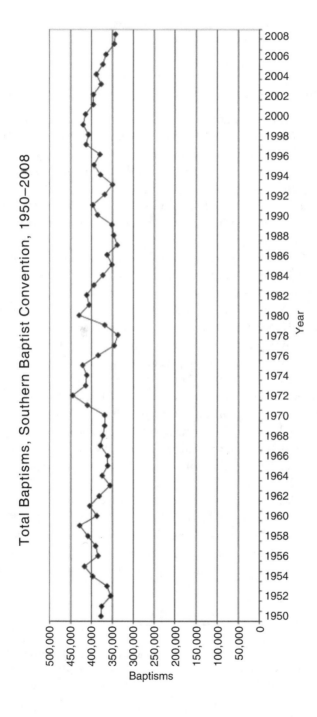

Total Baptisms, Southern Baptist Convention, 1950–2008

is stagnant, and that the onset of the Conservative Resurgence has done nothing to improve this trend.

Baptismal Ratio as a Measure of Evangelistic Effectiveness

In addition to utilizing total baptisms as a measure of evangelistic health, another measurement has been used for several years. The baptismal ratio utilizes both the membership of the church and the total baptisms.[9] We prefer this measurement of evangelistic health since it takes into consideration church size.

For example, a church with a membership of 800 should have more baptisms than a church of 30 in membership, all other factors being equal. The baptismal ratio thus measures numbers of members per baptism. In very rough terms, the ratio attempts to answer the question: "How many members does it take to reach one person for Christ in a year?"

The calculation of the ratio is simple. Total membership is divided by total baptisms. A church of 200 with 20 baptisms would thus have a baptismal ratio of 10, usually stated as 10 to 1. In other words, that particular church reaches one person for Christ each year for every ten members.

The ratio is informing on an aggregate basis as well. In 1845 the Southern Baptist Convention had 351,951 members; in 1950 the number was 7,079,889; and in 2008 the membership was 16,228,438. One would expect baptismal growth just due to the overall membership growth. The baptismal ratio, however, shows the number of members needed to reach one person, and thus allows a more accurate assessment of evangelistic effectiveness year by year. The following chart shows the baptismal ratio from 1950 to 2008.

Note that lower ratios depict greater evangelistic effectiveness. The upward trend noted in the chart is thus a negative trend. In 1950 one person was baptized for every 19 members. In 1978, the year prior to the beginning of the Conservative Resurgence, the denomination was baptizing one person for every 36 members. By 2008 the ratio had worsened to 47 to 1.

---

9 The use of the baptismal ratio as a measurement of evangelistic effectiveness dates back to at least the 1970s. The first book-length treatment of this measurement was Thom S. Rainer, *Effective Evangelistic Churches* (Nashville: B&H, 1996).

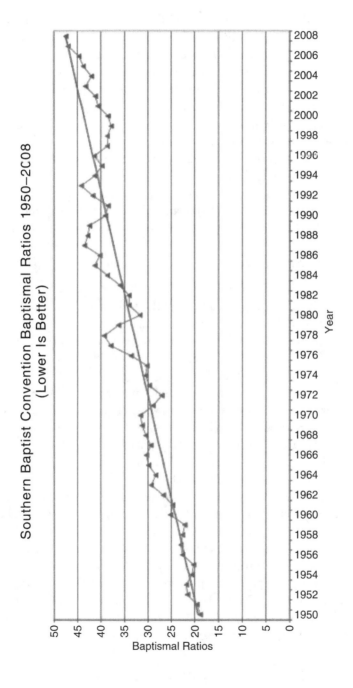

Southern Baptist Convention Baptismal Ratios 1950–2008
(Lower Is Better)

The trend in total baptisms in the Southern Baptist Convention thus depicts a clear pattern of plateau. But the more revealing measurement of baptismal ratios reveals consistent evangelistic deterioration.

The reality is that the baptismal ratio since the onset of the Conservative Resurgence has worsened. The trend is negative and disturbing. Though numbers are not ultimate measures of spiritual realities, the data we do have indicate a denomination in evangelistic crisis.

An honest evaluation of the data leads us to but one conclusion: *the Conservative Resurgence has not resulted in a greater zeal for evangelism in our churches*. According to the research, the Southern Baptist Convention is less evangelistic today than it was in the years preceding the Conservative Resurgence. A Great Commission Resurgence is needed desperately, indeed.

Possible Reasons for the Evangelistic Struggles of the SBC

The primary purpose of this chapter has been to gauge the realities of the evangelistic effectiveness of the Southern Baptist Convention utilizing widely available data. I have concluded that, evangelistically speaking, the denomination is on a path of slow but discernible deterioration. In this section, let me suggest several hypotheses that might help us discern possible reasons for the decline.

Hypothesis #1: The evangelistic fields in the United States are much less receptive than they were in past years. Jesus' teachings on the parable of the sower and soils (Mark 4:1–20) clearly depict different levels of receptivity to the gospel. Can the evangelistic struggles of the Southern Baptist Convention be explained by an American harvest field that is becoming less receptive to the gospel?

On the surface this hypothesis seems plausible. After all, few would deny a cultural trend exists in America that is clearly moving away from Christian values, and some consider America as "post-Christian." But does this trend mean that non-Christians are therefore less receptive to the gospel?

Unfortunately, I am not aware of any research that has attempted to measure gospel receptivity over the past fifty years. I did, however, lead a research team on a similar project for a single year. The concept of the research was to interview lost and unchurched Americans, attempting to discern their receptivity to the gospel.[10]

---

10   This complete research project is published in Thom S. Rainer, *The Unchurched Next Door* (Grand Rapids: Zondervan, 2003).

The researchers asked a series of thirty-three questions to over three hundred persons representing Americans of a variety of ages, both genders, and from varied geographical, racial, and ethnic backgrounds. Each person identified himself as an unchurched non-Christian. Though such surveys have obvious weaknesses when dealing with spiritual matters, we did uncover some revealing insights.

The researchers categorized the unchurched persons into five groups according to their responses. The group called U1 (unchurched one) represented the most receptive group to the gospel. The U5 group included those who were most antagonistic. Three other groups fell between these two extremes. Note the results.

U1	Highly Receptive	11%
U2	Receptive	27%
U3	Neutral	36%
U4	Resistant	27%
U5	Antagonistic	5%

We estimate that there are 160 million unchurched people in America. Nearly 61 million of these non-Christians are receptive or highly receptive to the gospel. Only 8 million have an antagonistic attitude toward Christians and the gospel. This research thus demonstrates that receptivity is not likely the reason that Southern Baptists are less evangelistic.

In another portion of this study, eight of ten unchurched indicated that they would come to church if they were invited. Unfortunately, few had ever been invited to church. It appears that receptivity to the gospel is strong, actually. And it appears that relatively few Southern Baptists are either inviting people to church or sharing the gospel with them.

Hypothesis #2: Socioeconomic gains tend to reduce evangelistic health in Christian groups. I think this hypothesis has merit, but I know of no study that has tracked the socioeconomic status of Southern Baptists since 1950. Material comfort may very well diminish evangelistic enthusiasm, but there is no definitive data to prove or disprove this hypothesis in the Southern Baptist Convention.

Hypothesis #3: Southern Baptist leaders are not personally evangelistic. The evangelistic health of a denomination is ultimately a local church issue. Denominations are neither evangelistic nor nonevangelistic; the churches and their members are the true indicators of evangelistic health.

Church members tend to follow the priorities of the leaders who serve in their churches, and the senior pastor is the person of primary influence.

In 2005, I conducted a study of senior pastors related to their habits of personal evangelism. Those surveyed were not exclusively Southern Baptists, but they included a good representation of SBC pastors.[11]

The surveys promised anonymity and were coded only by the level of evangelistic growth of the church of the pastor surveyed. We asked only one question: "How many times in the past six months have you shared the gospel with someone or developed a relationship with an unchurched person with the intention of sharing your faith with him or her?" The chart below provides a clear pattern.

2005 Survey	None	1–5 Times	6+ Times
Pastors of Growing Churches	6%	18%	76%
Pastors of Declining Churches	54%	38%	8%

LifeWay Research conducted a similar survey in 2008, specifically addressing SBC pastors' views and practices of personal evangelism. The data was not much better than the study I conducted four years ago. LifeWay Research found that 96 percent of the pastors surveyed witnessed to at least one person in the last six months. Sixty-six percent shared the gospel 1 to 15 times, 19 percent witnessed 16 to 40 times, and ten percent told 40 or more people about Jesus in the past six months. In addition, four percent did not share the gospel one time.[12]

The data, I believe, still indicate that this hypothesis has validity. Southern Baptist pastors today may not be as personally evangelistic as their predecessors, even though 81 percent feel responsible to lead their churches evangelistically by example. And the members of their churches may very well be following their poor example.

Hypothesis #4: The Southern Baptist Convention fails to recognize adequately churches with significant conversion growth. My assessment of this issue is largely anecdotal, based upon my work and interaction with other denominations. The Southern Baptist Convention does as well as any entity of which I am aware in recognizing conversion growth. Many state conventions publish annual baptismal counts of churches. The SBC as a national denomination has been sporadic in promoting evangelistic efforts.

---

11   This research is published in Thom S. Rainer, "The X Factor in Growing Churches," *Outreach* (January–February 2005): 16.

12   This research is found in "Southern Baptist Evangelism Today," by LifeWay Research. The data is available for purchase at http://www.lifeway.com/e5/shop/?id=005284845.

There is still a sense among many church leaders, however, that the denomination gives undue focus to larger churches at the expense of the midsize and smaller churches. Bigger is not necessarily better, unless the growth is the result of large numbers of conversions.

Hypothesis #5: The churches of the SBC are not evangelistic because they have many unregenerate members. An unregenerate person cannot share his or her experience of the redemptive power of Christ. Is it possible that we have significant numbers of non-Christians who have membership in our nearly 45,000 churches?

Another survey I conducted focused on persons who had been members of churches prior to becoming Christians, and asked them why they were in a church as a nonbeliever. The overwhelming number responded that they thought they *were* Christians. Yet later they would discover that they wrong.[13]

When I then asked them to share *why* they thought they had not become Christians as members, they gave four common responses. First, over one-half of those surveyed said they never heard a clear presentation of the gospel. One recent convert told me that sixty years of listening to sermons had not provided that clarity. Second, about four out of ten surveyed indicated that they had confused other issues with salvation. For some, church membership held the same meaning as being a Christian. Others indicated that "walking an aisle" or making a public statement of belief in Christ was a means of salvation. Third, some viewed doing ministry in the church as sufficient to get them into heaven. In other words, they had a works concept of salvation. Finally, about ten percent of those surveyed said that they joined the church originally understanding that they were *not* Christians. They were willing to be deceptive in order to gain the political or social capital that comes with being a member of a church.

How many members of churches are not Christians? Although the answer is elusive, let me make a modest attempt to answer the question, with the following caveat: when I provide statistical evidence of Christian church members, I do so with much caution. I recognize that my research is fallible and I realize that my discernment is far from perfect.

The methodology was simple. I asked 315 church members two "diagnostic" questions. The first question asked, "If you were to die today, do you know for certain that you would go to heaven?" The second question

---

13 This research is published in Thom S. Rainer, "Sharing the Gospel with Church Members," *Outreach* (May–June 2005): 17.

was: "If God were to ask you why He should let you into heaven, what would you say?"[14]

As a result of the research I categorized the responses of the church members into three groups. In the first group were those who clearly seemed not to have a grasp of the gospel. In the third group were those who seemed to grasp the gospel well, and who had assurance that they had placed their faith in Christ. In between these two groups was a small number difficult to place in either of the other two groups. The results are shown in the following table:

Church Members Who *Are Not* Christians	31%
Church Members Who *May Not Be* Christians	14%
Church Members Who *Are* Christians	55%

If the research approximates eternal realities, nearly one-half of all church members may not be Christians. This issue may very well be a major factor in the evangelistic apathy evident in many churches today.

Hypothesis #6: Only a small number of churches in the SBC have any significant evangelistic efforts. Less than ten percent of Southern Baptist churches accounted for over one-half of the total baptisms in 2008. The evidence is strong that most SBC churches are showing little evangelistic fruit. Note the significant number of churches with few or no baptisms in the table below.[15]

SBC Churches with 0 Baptisms in 2008	10,649 (23.7% of churches)
SBC Churches with 1 or Fewer Baptisms	13,982 (31.2%)
SBC Churches with 6 or Fewer Baptisms	26,101 (58.2%)
SBC Churches with 12 or Fewer Baptisms	32,245 (71.9%)

Nearly 25 percent of the SBC churches are baptizing no persons in a year, and almost 60 percent of the churches are baptizing six or fewer. Frankly, most Southern Baptist churches today are evangelistically anemic. The bulk of baptisms in the denomination are taking place in relatively few churches.

The lack of evangelistic growth in the Southern Baptist Convention since the Conservative Resurgence is disheartening. Is there hope? Certainly our hope always resides in a sovereign God. The concluding pages of this chapter

---

14   These two questions were first introduced by Dr. D. James Kennedy in *Evangelism Explosion*.

15   Annual Church Profiles, Southern Baptist Convention, 2008; LifeWay Christian Resources.

provide a modest path for the denomination to recapture an evangelistic zeal that has been waning for over fifty years. To that issue we now turn.

RECAPTURING OUR EVANGELISTIC HERITAGE: A MODEST PROPOSAL

Evangelistic effectiveness is ultimately an issue of each local congregation. The polity of our denomination is such that no denominational initiative can be effective unless the leadership of each church decides to implement it. And at least on an anecdotal basis, there seems to be widespread doubt about the efficacy of denominations in twenty-first century America.

Is there any point, therefore, in proposing any initiative from a denominational perspective? Is anyone really listening? Does anyone really care? Is it an exercise in both futility and presumption for me even to begin mapping possible alternatives?

Though I have no grand illusion that this chapter will be nailed to Southern Baptist church doors across America, I pray that God can use some portion of these suggestions for His glory and for an evangelistic denomination. The order of the following proposals is random and does not reflect any particular priority or significance.

Proposal #1: Seminaries Should Strive to Become Thoroughly Evangelistic

I can almost anticipate the response of some to this proposal. As the founding (and now former) dean of the Billy Graham School of Missions, Evangelism, and Church Growth at Southern Seminary, my heart beats for the evangelistic health and practice of pastors, churches, and denominations. This desire has not changed with my assuming the presidency of LifeWay Christian Resources. And yes, I still believe that denominational evangelistic effectiveness must begin in our seminaries.

First, I cannot argue against the presence of bias. I do hope that my bias does not cloud the stark picture of reality that I have already painted. The denomination is evangelistically sick, and some remedy is in order. Second, we must acknowledge that the majority of Southern Baptist pastors are not seminary-trained. An evangelistic revolution in the seminaries may not directly impact all pastors and church staff.

Still, the influence of seminaries is vast. The graduates of these institutions still go to many of the influential churches in our denomination, and those churches, for good or bad, become a model for others.

What does it mean for a seminary to be "thoroughly evangelistic"? I applaud seminaries that require all students in masters-level degree programs to take a course in personal evangelism. Such a requirement is important and necessary. But the thoroughly evangelistic vision of which I dream is more than the completion of a single course to satisfy graduation requirements.

The vision I have is that professors will be passionate about their respective fields of study *and* the Great Commission. Right theology should lead to evangelistic passion.[16] Proper comprehension of the Old Testament should lead to a burning desire to see all people saved. A right grasp of church history should drive persons to desire church growth that is biblical evangelistic growth. The best scholar without an evangelistic fire could lead future pastors and church staff to have an orthodoxy that is cold and lifeless.

Evangelistically passionate professors inspire students to evangelistic passion. Those students become pastors and other church leaders who inspire their congregations to evangelistic passion. And the evangelistic revolution of the Southern Baptist Convention ignites one church at a time to reach millions with the gospel of Christ.

Proposal #2: Recognize Effective Evangelistic Churches in the Southern Baptist Convention

Our denomination has done a credible job of recognizing high-baptismal churches. Many state conventions publish a list of the churches with the highest number of baptisms.

This proposal would extend the recognition to include those churches that have the best (lowest) baptismal ratios as well. A few state conventions already publish this list, which allow even the smallest of churches to be recognized for their evangelistic efforts.

---

16   I discussed the relationship between theology and evangelism on my blog in an entry entitled "When Theology Meets Evangelism," posted July 20, 2009, at http://www.thomrainer.com/2009/07/when-theology-meets-evangelism.php.

In 1996, with the publication of my book *Effective Evangelistic Churches*, the Billy Graham School began recognizing churches that met both criteria of number of baptisms and lower baptismal ratios. Named "The Spurgeon Awards" after the renowned nineteenth-century British Baptist pastor, this recognition includes both megachurches and smaller churches. A church must have at least twenty-six baptisms and a baptismal ratio of less than 20:1. In a typical year, less than five percent of Southern Baptist churches meet both criteria.

Proposal #3: Conduct More Research on Less Evangelistic Churches

Consider again the following revealing data from the 2008 Southern Baptist Convention statistical report:

- Of the 44,848 churches in the convention, 10,649 had zero baptisms. Stated differently, nearly 25 percent of all churches baptized no people.
- The total number of churches with six or fewer baptisms was 26,101, representing almost 60 percent of all SBC churches.
- The number of churches with twelve or fewer baptisms was 32,245, or 72 percent of the all SBC churches.[17]

The evidence is staggering, if not discouraging. One-fourth of the churches are baptizing no one. More than half of the churches are baptizing less than one person every two months. And more than seven of ten churches are baptizing less than one person per month.

To my knowledge, little research is being done to determine why more than 70 percent of our churches are clearly nonevangelistic.[18] How many of the "zero baptism" churches are churches that simply failed to report data? How many of the nonevangelistic churches were without a pastor during the reporting year? How many of the nonevangelistic churches have any type of evangelistic programs? The questions are endless, but the research could prove invaluable.

---

17   Percentages calculated from data from the Annual Church Profiles, Southern Baptist Convention, 2008; LifeWay Christian Resources.

18   I use the term nonevangelistic to refer to those churches that baptize twelve or fewer in a year. In other words, the nonevangelistic churches are baptizing one or less per month.

Statistically, if the nonevangelistic churches in the SBC (defined as those with twelve or fewer baptisms) increased their number of baptisms to a modest thirteen per year, the total baptisms in the Southern Baptist Convention would nearly double. If research on these less evangelistic churches could lead to new insights for more effective evangelism, the results could prove highly beneficial.

Proposal #4: Focus Evangelistic Training Resources on Pastors

The largest professional doctoral program at Southern Seminary is the D.Min. in evangelism and church growth. The students are typically full-time pastors and staff in local SBC churches with three or more years of post-Master of Divinity experience. I had the privilege of teaching in this program when I was dean of the Billy Graham School.

We required the students to take doctoral seminars as a cohort group. This approach engenders greater collegiality and accountability. The cohort approach also allows those of us who lead the program to see a "before and after" snapshot of the progress of the students in a group setting.[19]

One of the key emphases in the first doctoral seminar is that the pastor must take personal responsibility for the evangelistic growth of the church God has called him to lead. We are aware that numerous nonleadership factors are at work in evangelistic growth, but we also are keenly aware of the issue of pastoral leadership.

In 2003 I looked at the number of baptisms in the churches of fourteen men who were finishing their seminar work in the Doctor of Ministry program. I compared that to the number of baptisms in their churches two years earlier. Note the results:

Number of baptisms in 14 churches, 2001: 241	(17.2 baptisms per church)
Number of baptisms in 14 churches, 2003: 520	(37.1 baptisms per church)

---

19 This Doctor of Ministry program at The Southern Baptist Theological Seminary includes two years of on-campus seminars followed by the writing of a major ministry project. Students in this program must have a Master of Divinity degree (or its equivalent) and full-time ministry experience.

In just two years, the number of baptisms had more than doubled in these fourteen churches. How did the pastors explain the incredible increases? They all began to assume personal responsibility for evangelism in their local churches. Many of them developed accountability relationships with other persons in the area of personal evangelism. Some set goals for the number of persons with whom they would share the gospel each week. Still others brought evangelism training programs into the church where none had existed previously.

Once these pastors accepted the responsibility for leading their churches in evangelism, and once they began to model personal evangelism, the churches began to prosper evangelistically. On a larger scale, many of our denominational entities could focus significant resources on leading pastors to become more evangelistically accountable. If just one of five pastors would accept such training and accountability, the evangelistic results in our convention could prove significant.

Proposal #5: Encourage Pastors and Other Local Church Leaders to Lead Their Churches to a Time of Corporate Confession and Repentance for Their Lack of Evangelistic Zeal

Ultimately, evangelistic apathy is not a methodological failure—it is spiritual disobedience. The Bible is replete with commands and admonitions to communicate passionately the gospel with others. Our failure to do so is nothing less than sinful disobedience to the God who gave us unmerited favor through his Son Jesus Christ.

In 1986 I served in my first pastorate, a church with only seven in attendance the first Sunday I preached. I was a student at Southern Seminary, and I made the journey across the Ohio River into Indiana at least three or four times a week to the church. The church was evangelistically dead. There had been no baptisms in the recent memories of the few who remained in the church. I felt like a hospice worker, ministering to the people while waiting for a certain death.

My early actions were to confront the few members with their stark disobedience to God. My hard-hitting sermons, however, were not accompanied with the love of a shepherd for his flock. The members endured my preaching and anticipated the next seminary pastor who would do more of the same.

It was my custom to go to the 150-year-old sanctuary on Saturday evenings to pray for the service of the next day. And the subject of my prayers was usually a plea to God to change the hearts of the stubborn and spiritually anemic members of the church. But my prayers took a different turn one Saturday evening.

Somehow God got through my spiritual pride and attitude of superiority and confronted me with my own selfishness and disobedience. The church had not baptized anyone since I came as pastor six months earlier, but what had I done in obedience? I was good at sermonizing to others about their shortcomings, but I had become blind to my own. I left that small sanctuary a broken man.

I can only imagine the confusion of the church members the next Sunday morning as I preached. Gone was the self-sufficient and condescending pastor. The man they saw in the pulpit that Sunday was broken and totally dependent on God for everything.

I began to visit neighbors in the community and share the love of Christ. Some members soon accompanied me on these visits. People who had not been in a church in decades started visiting. Several accepted Christ. The church of seven grew to an attendance of seventy. And I learned an important lesson.

Evangelism and church growth does benefit from innovative programs. Research is helpful to grasp possible future paths of evangelistic strategy. But ultimately evangelism is a matter of the heart between the believer and a sovereign God. It is truly a spiritual matter. And if we are not personally and corporately evangelistic, the first response must be confession and repentance toward the God whose grace is sufficient to give us yet another opportunity.

CLOSING THOUGHTS:
A RESURGENCE NOT YET FULFILLED

The purpose of this chapter has been to examine the evangelistic effectiveness of the Southern Baptist Convention since 1979, the beginning of the Conservative Resurgence in the denomination. The conclusion is not encouraging. Evangelistic effectiveness is no better today than it was prior to 1979. Indeed the denomination is baptizing less than the totals of 1950, when the convention was less than half its size today.

In this chapter, I offered possible reasons for the anemic evangelistic growth in our denomination and suggested five modest proposals for reigniting evangelistic fires in our leaders and churches. But, as I articulated above, evangelistic apathy is first and foremost a spiritual problem. The first resolution must come from the disobedient Christian and his failure to obey the God who gave him eternal life.

The wording of the title of this chapter is not insignificant. It could have read "A Resurgence Not Fulfilled." Certainly the quantitative evidence is sufficient, if not overwhelming, to support the thesis that evangelistic health in the denomination has not improved since the Conservative Resurgence began in 1979. But the subtitle includes the little but hopeful word "yet." If we as a denomination had not pursued a path of biblical fidelity, we would have no hope for an evangelistic reformation. In the history of the church, God has not blessed those groups who have strayed from biblical truth.

The Conservative Resurgence brought back to our seminaries and agencies the demand that all leaders hold to the inerrancy of Scripture. God's Word is now held high in its total truthfulness. But total biblical fidelity requires more than a cognitive agreement on the parts and the sum of the Bible. True theological fidelity requires practical obedience as well. When we are passionately obedient about Christ's commission to share the gospel in all that we do, then the resurgence will have taken its full course.

When Peter and John were facing certain imprisonment and possible death for sharing Christ, the Sanhedrin gave them a simple mandate "against speaking to anyone in this name again" (Acts 4:17). The response of the two disciples was equally straightforward: "Whether it's right in the sight of God for us to listen to you rather than to listen to God, you decide; for we are unable to stop speaking about what we have seen and heard" (Acts 4:19–20).

The Conservative Resurgence means that we affirm the historical and spiritual truthfulness of the words above. But a true resurgence—a Great Commission Resurgence—means much more. We must embody those same words for our own personal evangelistic obedience. Then, and only then, will the resurgence be complete.

SOUTHERN BAPTIST HISTORY
A GREAT COMMISSION READING

Nathan A. Finn

Southern Baptists have always been a people concerned about the Great Commission. The Southern Baptist Convention is comprised of almost 45,000 local churches that voluntarily cooperate in numerous Great Commission endeavors. Two mission boards appoint, equip, and fund Southern Baptist missionaries who preach the gospel and plant churches in unevangelized regions of North America and every corner of the globe. Our six seminaries train present and future pastors, missionaries, and other Christian leaders to model a missional lifestyle in whatever ministry context they find themselves. LifeWay Christian Resources publishes materials that aid Southern Baptists and other Christians in missional living. Our Ethics and Religious Liberty Commission defends the freedom of all to preach the gospel and advocates gospel-centered values in our pluralistic culture. Even our annuity ministry, Guidestone Financial Resources, cares for the financial needs of pastors, missionaries, and denominational servants who seek to lead Southern Baptists in being a Great Commission people. The Great Commission has been Southern Baptists' *raison d'être* from the very beginning.

From time to time controversies have threatened our Great Commission priorities. This remains true today. This chapter offers a "Great Commission reading" of Southern Baptist history by articulating some historical and present threats to our Great Commission cooperation. It also contends that the time has come for our churches and denomination to move beyond hindrances to our cooperation and renew our commitment to the Great Commission.

PRECURSORS TO A GREAT
COMMISSION DENOMINATION

Baptists were concerned for the Great Commission for generations before there was a Southern Baptist Convention. The earliest Baptist "foreign missionaries" were black Baptists who were forced to relocate to other nations because of prejudice and persecution in America.[1] As early as 1783, an African American freeman and Baptist preacher named George Liele fled to Jamaica so that he could evade capture by hostile whites. His escape ultimately served missionary purposes as Liele established a gospel work on that island. One of Liele's converts, David George, helped establish an autonomous black Baptist church in America at Silver Bluff, South Carolina in the mid-1770s. George's congregation was probably the first permanent black Baptist church in America.[2]

Better known than these black Baptist missionary pioneers is William Carey, the cobbler-turned-pastor-turned-missionary. Carey wrote a book titled *An Enquiry into the Obligation of Christians to Use Means in the Conversion of the Heathens* (1792) in which he argued that the Great Commission did not expire with the apostles but is a binding command on every generation of Christians. He helped lead the English Particular Baptists to form a foreign mission society in 1792, volunteered to serve as one of the society's first missionaries, and spent the final forty years of his life in India where he preached the gospel, translated the Scriptures and other important works into Bengali and other languages, and established a Baptist college. He is widely considered to be the father of the modern missions movement in the English-speaking world.[3]

One future missionary whom Carey influenced was Adoniram Judson, the son of a Congregationalist pastor in Massachusetts. Judson and some of his classmates at Andover Seminary asked the Congregationalists to

---

1 Leroy Fitts, *A History of Black Baptists* (Nashville: Broadman, 1985), 109.

2 William H. Brackney, *Baptists in North America,* Religious Life in America (Oxford: Blackwell, 2006), 176–77. After a decade sojourn in Nova Scotia because of racial tensions in the South, George and almost 1200 other blacks left Canada and established a free black colony in Sierra Leone in West Africa in 1792.

3 The best recent biography of Carey is Timothy George, *Faithful Witness: The Life and Mission of William Carey* (Birmingham, AL: New Hope, 1991). A facsimile reproduction of Carey's *Enquiry* is available online at http://www.wmcarey.edu/carey/enquiry/enquiry.html. Many Baptists (and other Christians) became interested in foreign mission work through reading about Carey's exploits in popular religious periodicals.

support them as missionaries to India in 1810. Two years later, Judson, his wife Ann, and three others set out for India. They were the first formal foreign missionaries in American history. Shortly after their arrival in Calcutta, the Judsons received believer's baptism by immersion from an English Baptist missionary. The Judsons resigned their commission with the Congregationalists, became Baptists, and sent their colleague and fellow Baptist convert Luther Rice back to America to rally Baptists behind the cause of the Great Commission.[4]

Upon returning to America, Luther Rice traveled the Eastern Seaboard raising money for the Judsons. Some prominent pastors began to argue that American Baptists needed a foreign mission society like their English brethren. William B. Johnson, pastor of the Savannah Baptist Church in southeast Georgia, issued a call for a national meeting of Baptists who were committed to foreign missions.[5]

In 1814, Baptists formed the General Missionary Convention of the Baptist Denomination in the United States of America for Foreign Missions, more popularly known as the Triennial Convention because the body met every three years. Over the next dozen years the Triennial Convention undertook other ministry assignments, particularly home missions and theological education. This pleased the Baptists in the South, who wanted to see a strong centralized denomination that could unite Baptists in every endeavor that facilitated the Great Commission.[6]

---

4 Helpful studies of the Judsons include Courtney Anderson, *To the Golden Shore: The Life of Adoniram Judson*, reprint ed. (Valley Forge: Judson, 1987), and Joan Jacob Brumberg, *Mission for Life: The Story of the Family of Adoniram Judson, the Dramatic Events of the First American Foreign Mission, and the Course of Evangelical Religion in the Nineteenth Century* (New York: Free Press, 1980). For Luther Rice, see Evelyn Wingo Thompson, *Luther Rice: Believer in Tomorrow* (Nashville: Broadman, 1967).

5 Hortense C. Woodson, *Giant in the Land: The Life of William B. Johnson, First President of the Southern Baptist Convention, 1845–1851* (Nashville: Broadman, 1950; reprint, Springfield, MO: Particular Baptist Press, 2005), 32–35.

6 For the differing views of Baptists North and South concerning denominationalism, see H. Leon McBeth, *The Baptist Heritage: Four Centuries of Baptist Witness* (Nashville: Broadman, 1987), 347–50. Northern Baptists were less inclined to agree with a centralized denomination, preferring a number of autonomous societies, each of which would raise its own funds and establish its own priorities. Under the leadership of Boston pastor, editor, and future educator Francis Wayland, the 1826 Triennial Convention voted to revert back to a simple foreign mission society and ceased funding its other ministries. A Home Mission Society, Bible and Tract Society, and several schools developed over the next couple of decades, but Baptists in the South gave most of their financial support to the Triennial Convention because it was foreign missions that most captured their imagination.

During the 1820s and 1830s, several southern states formed Baptist conventions. These state conventions united all of the missionary Baptists in a given region. Among the principal concerns of each state body was helping to fund the foreign missions efforts of the Triennial Convention and facilitating church planting in unreached regions of the respective state. Several state conventions also sponsored their own foreign mission boards. These state conventions pioneered the cooperative strategy that came to characterize the Southern Baptist Convention.

There were some Baptists who opposed churches cooperating together in foreign missions work. There were several reasons that "anti-mission" Baptists rejected the validity of cooperative missions. Some, like Kentucky pastor John Taylor, were not opposed to missions *per se* but disliked fundraising and were concerned that mission societies were not good stewards of donated monies. Others, like New York pastor Alexander Campbell, argued that mission societies were unbiblical because the New Testament says nothing about them. Still others became convinced that missions work presumed upon God's sovereignty in salvation. These "Primitive Baptists" were similar in some ways to the English hyper-Calvinists who opposed the missionary efforts of Carey and his colleagues. Primitive Baptists believed God would accomplish the Great Commission in his own time and in his own way without human evangelistic efforts.[7]

Missionary Baptists in the South, with their strong commitment to centralized conventions, felt especially threatened by the Primitive Baptists in their midst. Georgia Baptists are perhaps the most notable example of this trend. Georgia Baptist pastor, editor, and denominational leader Jesse Mercer argued that it was possible to be firmly committed to God's sovereignty in salvation and believe that mission boards are a means God uses to save sinners. Mercer contended with the Primitive Baptists throughout the 1830s until the Primitives finally withdrew from the missionary Baptists, leaving the Georgia Baptist Convention, and often their local associations, and forming alternative, antimission associations. The Great Commission was enough of a priority to most

---

7 See Byron Cecil Lambert, *The Rise of the Antimission Baptists: Sources and Leaders, 1800–1840* (New York: Arno, 1980); John G. Crowley, *Primitive Baptists of the Wiregrass South, 1815–Present* (Gainesville: University of Florida Press, 1998); James R. Mathis, *The Making of the Primitive Baptists: A Cultural and Intellectual History of the Antimission Movement, 1800–1840* (New York: Routledge, 2004).

Baptists in the South that they would not tolerate those who had no use for missionary work and other related ministries.[8]

Tragically, missionary Baptists divided in 1845 along sectional lines. Similar divisions occurred among Methodists and Presbyterians around the same time, and many historians argue that these divisions contributed to the Civil War by exacerbating sectional tensions among religious people.[9] Much has been written about the role that slavery played in the 1845 division.[10] Yet even this controversy touches upon the Baptist commitment to the Great Commission. Without downplaying the role of slavery or whitewashing the racial prejudices of the antebellum South, it is important to remember that the slavery controversy occurred in the context of an internal debate among missionary Baptists concerning who was qualified for missionary appointment.

In 1841 and 1844, both the Triennial Convention and the Home Mission Society went on record affirming their respective neutrality on the slavery issue.[11] In 1844, the Georgia Baptist Convention tested the neutrality of the Home Mission Society by nominating James Reeves, a slaveholder, to serve as a home missionary. The society declined to act on the request because it determined the Reeves nomination was a test case. That same year the Alabama Baptist State Convention queried the Triennial Convention's board regarding whether or not that society would appoint a slaveholder as a missionary. The board responded, ". . . one thing is certain; we can never be a party to any arrangement which would imply approbation

---

8   Anthony L. Chute, *A Piety above the Common Standard: Jesse Mercer and the Defense of Evangelistic Calvinism* (Macon, GA: Mercer University Press, 2004), 127–59.

9   For example, see C. C. Goen, *Broken Churches, Broken Nation: Denominational Schisms and the Coming of the Civil War* (Macon, GA: Mercer University Press, 1985), and Mitchell Snay, *Gospel of Disunion: Religion and Separatism in the Antebellum South* (New York: Cambridge University Press, 1993).

10   For a survey of the various views proposed by Baptist historians, see Walter B. Shurden and Lori Redwine, "The Origins of the Southern Baptist Convention: A Historiographical Study," *Baptist History and Heritage* 37, no. 1 (Winter 2002): 71–96. As a general rule, earlier generations of historians downplayed the role slavery played in the division while contemporary historians act as though slavery were the only factor in the schism.

11   The events summarized in the next two paragraphs are recounted in detail in McBeth, *Baptist Heritage*, 385–88. The neutrality position reflected the tensions slavery was causing among Missionary Baptists, which was reflected in such actions as abolition movements among northern Baptists, banned books among Baptists in the South, and heated editorials by state Baptist paper editors on both sides of the debate.

of slavery."[12] Because of the slavery issue, both of the mission societies took actions that Baptists in the South believed undermined their ability to engage in missions work. Though slavery was undoubtedly the catalyst, it was differing opinions about missionary qualifications that led to the formation of the Southern Baptist Convention in 1845.

BUILDING A GREAT COMMISSION DENOMINATION

The Southern Baptist Convention (SBC) was formed May 10, 1845, in Augusta, Georgia. The almost three hundred delegates chose William B. Johnson to serve as president of the convention and to chair a committee charged with drafting a constitution. That constitution echoed the language of the Triennial Convention, arguing that the SBC was formed for "organizing a plan for eliciting, combining and directing the energies of the whole denomination in one sacred effort, for the propagation of the Gospel."[13] Southern Baptists wanted to be clear that the purpose of the new convention was missionary activity at home and abroad.

Because Southern Baptists were open to a more centralized denominational structure than their northern brethren, the new denomination immediately formed Foreign and Domestic Mission Boards as subsidiary ministries of the convention. The first Southern Baptist missionaries were southerners who were previously aligned with the northern boards but switched their allegiance to the SBC.[14] Throughout the nineteenth century, the Foreign Mission Board continued to appoint missionaries and expand into new fields of service. Money was always tight, and there were occasional controversies, the most notable being the Gospel Mission Controversy of the 1880s.[15] The Civil War also exacted a heavy price on the

---

12   See "The Alabama Resolutions and a Reply," in H. Leon McBeth, *A Sourcebook for Baptist Heritage* (Nashville: Broadman, 1990), 259.

13   "Original Constitution of the Southern Baptist Convention (1845)," available online at http://baptiststudiesonline.com/wp-content/uploads/2007/02/constitution-of-the-sbc.pdf.

14   William R. Estep, *Whole Gospel, Whole World: The Foreign Mission Board of the Southern Baptist Convention, 1845–1995* (Nashville: B&H, 1994), 65.

15   For more on the Gospel Mission Controversy, see Adrian Lamkin Jr., "The Gospel Mission Movement within the Southern Baptist Convention" (Ph.D. diss., The Southern Baptist Theological Seminary, 1980), and Keith E. Eitel, *Paradigm Wars: The Southern Baptist International Mission Board Faces the Third Millennium*, Regnum Studies in Mission (Waynesboro, GA: Paternoster, 2000), 31–72.

board and the wider denomination, but none of these obstacles permanently deterred Southern Baptist missions work in foreign countries.

The Domestic Mission Board was never as strong as the Foreign Board, and its earliest decades were marred by financial woes, inept leadership, unclear partnerships, and contested boundaries for missions work. That began to change in 1882 when Alabama pastor and educator I. T. Tichenor became corresponding secretary of the board. Under Tichenor's leadership, the Domestic Board embraced a number of new initiatives. The Board erected church buildings for frontier congregations, pursued church planting among Native Americans, began missions efforts in Cuba, established orphanages and grammar schools in Appalachia, and undertook theological education among freed African Americans, in partnership with Baptists in the North.[16]

Women played an important role in financing Southern Baptist missions causes, especially abroad. In 1888, the Woman's Missionary Union (WMU) was formed as an auxiliary to the SBC. Lottie Moon, a single missionary to China, was instrumental in calling for Southern Baptist women to rally together to help fund foreign missions work. Under the leadership of WMU corresponding secretary Annie Armstrong, the Foreign Board's annual total receipts increased from $86,000 in 1888 to over $315,000 in 1906. The WMU also initiated an annual Christmas offering named in honor of Lottie Moon in 1918. In 1907, the WMU Training School opened in Louisville, Kentucky, to train women for foreign missions work. WMU also developed missions education programs for elementary-aged children in SBC churches.[17]

Southern Baptists also embraced seminary education as a way to further their Great Commission ends. Under the leadership of South Carolina

---

16 The best biography of Tichenor is Michael E. Williams, *Isaac Taylor Tichenor: The Creation of the Baptist New South*, Religion and American Culture (Tuscaloosa: University of Alabama Press, 2005). Tichenor was also a leader in the wider convention, playing a crucial role in the formation of the Baptist Sunday School Board in 1891.

17 Many volumes have been devoted to both Moon and Armstrong. Helpful introductions include Catherine B. Allen, *The New Lottie Moon Story* (Nashville: Broadman, 1980), 1980), and Bobbie Sorrill, *Annie Armstrong: Dreamer in Action* (Nashville: Broadman, 1984). Keith Harper has edited the correspondence and shorter writings of both women. See Keith Harper, ed., *Send the Light: Lottie Moon's Letters and Other Writings* (Macon, GA: Mercer University Press, 2002), and idem, ed., *Rescue the Perishing: Selected Correspondence of Annie W. Armstrong* (Macon, GA: Mercer University Press, 2004). For a recent study of the WMU Training School, see T. Laine Scales, *All That Fits a Woman: Training Southern Baptist Women for Charity and Mission, 1907–1926* (Macon, GA: Mercer University Press, 2000).

pastor and educator James P. Boyce, The Southern Baptist Theological Seminary was founded in Greenville in 1859. The founding faculty members were committed to evangelism and missions; all of them were pastors before coming to Southern, and most served as Confederate chaplains during the Civil War. Several faculty members were also active in supporting foreign missions efforts.[18] The same priorities characterized the Southwestern Baptist Theological Seminary, formed in Waco, Texas in 1908. The founding president, B. H. Carroll, was widely known for his commitment to Great Commission priorities, which he instilled in the institution. Carroll protégé and second president Lee R. Scarborough was a respected evangelist and professor of evangelism. Since Scarborough's time, the evangelism chair at Southwestern has been nicknamed the "chair of fire."[19]

Southern Baptists continued to form new institutions into the early twentieth century. All of these agencies and boards were devoted in some way to furthering the cause of missions and evangelism among Southern Baptist churches. Unfortunately, this very institution-building unwittingly played a role in undermining the denomination's Great Commission cooperation. Between the 1920s and the 1960s, Southern Baptists became increasingly pragmatic, divorcing missions and evangelism from theology. This opened the door for the spread of a progressive theology that challenged orthodoxy, all the while trumpeting the cause of cooperative missions endeavors.

UNDERMINING GREAT COMMISSION PRIORITIES

Since World War II, there have been at least two internal dangers that undermined the Southern Baptist Convention's historic Great Commission priorities. These threats built upon each other until they became so great that Southern Baptists became embroiled in an internal controversy during the final decades of the twentieth century. The Southern Baptist Convention of the early twenty-first century is the product of both these dangers themselves and our collective response to them in the final years of the previous century.

---

18   See Gregory A. Wills, *Southern Baptist Theological Seminary, 1859–2009* (New York: Oxford University Press, 2009), and Tom J. Nettles, *James Petigru Boyce: A Southern Baptist Statesman*, American Reformed Biographies (Philipsburg, NJ: P&R, 2009).

19   See Robert A. Baker, *Tell the Generations Following: A History of Southwestern Baptist Theological Seminary, 1908–1983* (Nashville: Broadman, 1983); Alan J. Lefever, *Fighting the Good Fight: The Life and Work of Benajah Harvey Carroll* (Austin, TX: Eakin Press, 1994); Glenn Thomas, *Calling Out the Called: The Life and Work of Lee Rutland Scarborough* (Austin, TX: Eakin Press, 1996).

Programmatic Identity[20]

The first threat to the SBC's Great Commission heritage was the triumph of a programmatic identity during the mid-twentieth century. For the first seventy-five years or so of convention history, a basic theological consensus existed among the churches of the SBC. Southern Baptists as a denomination were characterized by a commitment to basic Christian orthodoxy, a broadly (though never uniformly) Calvinistic soteriology, a well-defined baptistic ecclesiology, a discomfort with ecumenical entanglements, and a zeal for missions work, especially in foreign countries. This consensus prevailed despite the absence of a convention-wide confession of faith. By the mid-twentieth century, the commitment to missions was the only aspect of the earlier consensus that continued to characterize Southern Baptists unambiguously, though even that commitment was transformed due to changes regarding the other convictions.

By the 1910s, the Southern Baptist Convention was evolving from a theological identity based upon doctrinal affinity to a programmatic identity based upon denominational loyalty. The transition occurred in several stages. Like most American denominations, the SBC was becoming increasingly centralized as it expanded its bureaucracy. In 1917, the denomination formed an Executive Committee to represent the churches between annual sessions, which expanded its influence over the next three decades. By the post-World War II era, the Executive Committee was presiding over the shift to a programmatic identity and stood at the center of a burgeoning Southern Baptist bureaucracy.[21]

From 1919 to 1924, the SBC launched a financial campaign to raise $75 million to fund the denomination's ministries. Though economic recession led to a final collection far below the amount pledged, the Seventy-five Million Campaign united Southern Baptists across geographical boundaries in a common endeavor. This led directly to the

---

20 This section draws heavily upon Nancy Tatom Ammerman, *Baptist Battles: Social Change and Religious Conflict in the Southern Baptist Convention* (New Brunswick, NJ: Rutgers University Press, 1990), 44–63; Bill J. Leonard, *God's Last and Only Hope: The Fragmentation of the Southern Baptist Convention* (Grand Rapids: Eerdmans, 1990), 25–64; Jerry Sutton, *The Baptist Reformation: The Conservative Resurgence in the Southern Baptist Convention* (Nashville: B&H, 2000), 31–59; David S. Dockery, *Southern Baptist Consensus and Renewal: A Biblical, Historical, and Theological Proposal* (Nashville: B&H Academic, 2008), 2–9.

21 See Albert McClellan, *The Executive Committee of the Southern Baptist Convention, 1917–1984* (Nashville: Broadman, 1985).

creation of the Cooperative Program (CP) in 1925. The CP was a centralized budget to fund all of the denomination's ministries, including domestic and foreign missions, which received the highest percentages of budgeted monies. The CP also created a closer bond between the SBC and the various state conventions, each of which was formally autonomous from the national denomination.[22] Though it furthered Great Commission causes, the Cooperative Program also funded the shift to a programmatic identity as finances gradually emerged as the central point of affinity among Southern Baptists.

Beginning with the pioneering work of Arthur Flake, Sunday school became the primary means through which local churches conducted evangelism and enlisted new members.[23] A number of denominational evangelism programs were designed to make Sunday school a more efficient tool in reaching prospective members. The most important program was "A Million More in '54," a convention-wide effort to enroll one million new Sunday school members during the 1953–1954 academic year.[24] Denominational programs, particularly those touting evangelism through the Sunday school, populated the shift to a programmatic identity and helped Southern Baptists grow from 5.3 million members in 1942 to over 12 million members by 1972.[25]

The mid-twentieth century was also a period of institutional expansion and bureaucratic efficiency. The convention formed three new commissions and expanded several others between 1945 and 1960. In 1950, the SBC adopted Golden Gate Baptist Theological Seminary and chartered Southeastern Baptist Theological Seminary. In 1957, the convention established Midwestern Baptist Theological Seminary. The Executive Committee, Sunday School Board, and Southern Seminary each contracted with business consulting firms and underwent corporate restructuring in the 1950s. Bureaucratic expansion and the quest for efficiency facilitated the

---

22 For a helpful introduction to the history and purpose of the Cooperative Program, see Chad Owen Brand and David E. Hankins, *One Sacred Effort: The Cooperative Program of the Southern Baptist Convention* (Nashville: B&H, 2005).

23 Arthur Flake, *Building a Standard Sunday School* (Nashville: Baptist Sunday School Board, 1919); idem, *The Department Sunday School* (Nashville: Baptist Sunday School Board, 1924).

24 *Encyclopedia of Southern Baptists*, vol. 2 (Nashville: Broadman, 1958), s.v. "Sunday School Board." The campaign resulted in a net of almost 600,000 in Sunday school enrollment.

25 Robert A. Baker, *The Southern Baptist Convention and Its People, 1607–1972* (Nashville: Broadman, 1974), 413.

shift to a programmatic identity and created a culture of denominational professionals in the convention's various agencies and boards.

The convention's programmatic emphasis downplayed (though never formally rejected) the importance of theological clarity, thus resulting in a pragmatic approach to intradenominational cooperation. By the middle of the twentieth century, Southern Baptists were held together less by doctrine than by a common commitment to cooperative missions and other activities that aided mission efforts. The Great Commission remained at the heart of the SBC but severed, at least informally, from sound doctrine and historic Baptist identity and practice. Progressive leader Cecil Sherman concedes this when he notes that the pre-1979 convention was primarily concerned with being a "missions delivery system," leaving theological issues to the discretion of the local churches. He flatly states, "The focus of the convention was missions, not theology."[26] For many mid-century Southern Baptists, theology was a distraction from missions work rather than the foundation of that work.

By the 1970s, many individual Southern Baptists had embraced what historian Greg Wills calls a "tribal" identity or "Southern Baptist ethnicity."[27] A generation's Baptist identity had been forged through the denomination's programs. Millions were converted through denominational evangelism initiatives, instructed through Sunday School Board curricula, nurtured through Royal Ambassadors, Girls in Action, and Acteens, encouraged through Baptist Student Union, educated through Baptist state colleges and convention-funded seminaries, and indoctrinated through Baptist Training Union. Being a missions-minded Southern Baptist meant loyalty to these programs and financial support of the Cooperative Program that funded them.

Progressive Theology

The second threat to the convention's Great Commission heritage was the rise of progressive theology. For the purposes of this chapter, progressive theology includes a variety of movements (modernism, neo-orthodoxy,

---

26 Cecil Sherman, *By My Own Reckoning* (Macon, GA: Smyth & Helwys, 2008), 132–33.

27 Gregory A. Wills, "Who are the True Baptists? The Conservative Resurgence and the Influence of Moderate Views of Baptist Identity," *The Southern Baptist Journal of Theology* 9, no. 1 (Spring 2005): 26; idem., "Southern Baptist Identity: A Historical Perspective," in *Southern Baptist Identity: An Evangelical Denomination Faces the Future*, ed. David S. Dockery (Wheaton: Crossway, 2009), 77–83.

liberation theology) that redefined or rejected the historic orthodox understanding of such doctrines as the inerrancy of Scripture, the deity of Christ, the Trinity, biblical miracles, human sinfulness, the atonement, and human salvation. Progressive theology slowly undermined the Great Commission by altering the content of the gospel message itself, substituting interfaith dialogue in the place of evangelism, and over-emphasizing social justice ministries and theological education on the mission field to the detriment of church planting.

Although progressive theology first entered the SBC in the late nineteenth century, it was in the first quarter of the twentieth century when institutions like Baylor University, Wake Forest University, Mercer University, and Southern Seminary began employing faculty members who allegedly embraced progressive views, particularly an affirmation of biological evolution.[28] Mirroring a wider trend in American denominations, in the 1920s some Southern Baptist conservatives began to speak out actively against the teaching of evolution and other progressive positions in denominational schools. These "fundamentalists," the most famous of whom was Texas pastor J. Frank Norris, were initially intradenominational dissenters who tried to work through the convention's polity to undermine leftward theological trends.[29]

By the mid-1920s, the Northern Baptist Convention was on the verge of splitting over a divide between fundamentalists and progressives. Southern Baptists did not want to face a similar scenario, so in 1925 the convention took the crucial step of adopting a denominational confession of faith. The *Baptist Faith and Message* was a revision of *The New Hampshire Confession* of 1833, probably the most popular Baptist confession in America

---

28 See James J. Thompson, *Tried As By Fire: Southern Baptists and the Religious Controversies of the 1920s* (Macon, GA: Mercer University Press, 1982), and Randall L. Hall, *William Louis Poteat: A Leader of the Progressive-Era South*, Religion in the South (Lexington: University Press of Kentucky, 2000).

29 Norris was an incessant critic of both progressive theology and programmatic emphases within the SBC. A pugnacious figure, his tactics wore thin on Southern Baptists, including many who were sympathetic to his concerns. By the 1930s he was no longer involved in convention life, though he remained a vocal critic of the denomination. Many fundamentalists followed Norris's lead and repudiated ties with the SBC, resulting in the birth of the Southern wing of the Independent Baptist movement. Other conservative dissenters remained within the convention, though very few of them showed any enthusiasm for the Cooperative Program or were active in the denomination's leadership. See Barry Hankins, *God's Rascal: J. Frank Norris & the Beginnings of Southern Fundamentalism*, Religion in the South (Lexington: University Press of Kentucky, 1996); Kenneth C. Hubbard, "Anti-Conventionism in the Southern Baptist Convention, 1940–1962" (Th.D. diss., Southwestern Baptist Theological Seminary, 1968); Nathan A. Finn, "The Development of Baptist Fundamentalism in the South, 1940–1980" (Ph.D. diss., Southeastern Baptist Theological Seminary, 2007), 76–127.

in the early twentieth century. Notably, the confession was adopted at the same annual session that established the Cooperative Program, arguably making the 1925 Memphis Convention one of the two most significant SBC annual meetings of the twentieth century.[30] The chief author of the *Baptist Faith and Message* was E. Y. Mullins, the president of Southern Seminary, immediate past president of the convention, perhaps the best known American Baptist in the world during the first quarter of the twentieth century, and considered by some scholars to be the most influential Baptist theologian North America has ever produced.[31]

Despite its articulation of historic Baptist theology, the *Baptist Faith and Message* was not widely used by Southern Baptists, including the denomination's bureaucracy.[32] By the mid-twentieth century, progressive theology was becoming increasingly visible in the convention's agencies and boards, particularly the seminaries. As Southern Baptists emphasized loyalty to programs and a financially driven cooperation, a broadly atheological atmosphere prevailed among the denomination's leadership.[33] This theological vacuum became a breeding ground for a number of progressive theological trends that were out of touch with the conservative convictions of grassroots Southern Baptists and posed a threat to Great Commission faithfulness.

The seminaries were the center of gravity for convention progressives. Southern Seminary countenanced progressive theology in a number of

---

30   James Edward Carter, "The Southern Baptist Convention and Confessions of Faith, 1845–1945" (Th.D. diss, Southwestern Baptist Theological Seminary, 1964), 103–35. The other most significant SBC annual meeting would be the 1979 Houston Convention, widely credited as the public launch of the Conservative Resurgence.

31   Mullins was a transitional theological figure in SBC life. Although he was conservative enough to be considered an ally in the wider fundamentalist movement, he was influenced by Friedrich Schleiermacher's emphasis on the primacy of religious experience. Mullins strongly advocated the doctrine of "soul competency," which for him was a highly individualistic understanding of the historic Baptist distinctive of liberty of conscience. Mullins's view of soul competency, which he popularized in his writings, public addresses, and seminary lectures, greatly influenced the pragmatic approach to cooperation that was emerging as the new consensus in the SBC. The standard biography of Mullins is William E. Ellis, *A Man of the Books and a Man of the People: E. Y. Mullins and the Crisis of Moderate Southern Baptist Leadership* (Macon, GA: Mercer University Press, 1985). For an introduction to Mullins's theology, see Fisher Humphries, "E. Y. Mullins," in *Baptist Theologians*, ed. Timothy George and David S. Dockery (Nashville: Broadman, 1990), 330–50.

32   Carter, "The Southern Baptist Convention and Confessions of Faith," 158–71.

33   See Leonard, *God's Last and Only Hope*, 56, 63, and Samuel Hill Jr., "Epilogue," in John Lee Eighmy, *Churches in Cultural Captivity: A History of the Social Attitudes of Southern Baptists* (Knoxville: University of Tennessee Press, 1972), 206.

ways, including inviting theological liberals to deliver academic lectures, employing openly progressive faculty members, and tolerating at least one professor's Arminian convictions.[34] New Orleans Seminary conducted a heresy trial for one professor who denied substitutionary atonement and terminated another professor for espousing progressive ideas about salvation.[35] Southeastern Seminary employed at least three New Testament professors who espoused Rudolf Bultmann's "demythologization" approach to Scripture, resulting in a series of investigations by the administration and trustees. Although Southeastern did not terminate any of the progressives, all three took new positions at other institutions.[36]

The 1960s and 1970s witnessed two different convention-wide controversies over the historical-critical method of biblical interpretation.[37] In both cases what ignited the fracases were denominationally published commentaries authored by Baptist professors and intended primarily for a Southern Baptist audience. In 1961, Broadman Press published *The Message of Genesis*, a popularly written commentary by Midwestern Seminary professor Ralph Elliott, that questioned the historicity of Genesis 1–11 and raised questions about Mosaic authorship of the Pentateuch.[38] In 1969, Broadman Press began publishing *The Broadman Bible Commentary*,

---

34 For progressive tendencies at Southern, see Clayton Sullivan, *Called to Preach, Condemned to Survive: The Education of Clayton Sullivan* (reprint paperback ed.; Macon, GA: Mercer University Press, 2003), 75; David O. Beale, *S.B.C.: House on the Sand?* (Greenville, SC: Unusual Press, 1985), 32–49; Dale Moody, *Apostasy: A Study in the Epistle to the Hebrews and Baptist History* (Greenville, SC: Smyth & Helwys, 1991), 1–6; Wills, *Southern Baptist Theological Seminary*, 308–436.

35 For progressive tendencies at New Orleans, see Mark R. Wilson, "Southern Theologian in Crisis: Frank Stagg, Atonement, and the Postwar South," *Perspectives in Religious Studies* 30, no. 1 (Spring 2003): 5–19, and Robert B. Sloan Jr., "Frank Stagg," in *Theologians of the Baptist Tradition*, ed. Timothy George and David S. Dockery (Nashville: B&H, 2001), 262–75.

36 For progressive tendencies at Southeastern, see Thomas A. Bland, ed., "In the Beginning," in *Servant Songs: Reflections on the History and Mission of Southeastern Baptist Theological Seminary, 1950–1988* (Macon, GA: Smyth & Helwys, 1994), 25–27; Donald E. Cook, "Our Message Be the Gospel Plain," in ibid., 115–16; James Leo Garrett, *Baptist Theology: A Four Century Study* (Macon, GA: Mercer University Press, 2009), 481.

37 For an extended discussion of these controversies and their effect on the SBC, see Jerry L. Faught II, "The Genesis Controversies: Denominational Compromise and the Resurgence and Expansion of Fundamentalism in the Southern Baptist Convention" (Ph.D. diss., Baylor University, 1995).

38 According to Elliott, he wrote the book at the invitation of Broadman for the purpose of introducing critical scholarship to Southern Baptist ministers and laypeople. He also argued that his views were normative among Southern Baptist academics at the time. See Ralph H. Elliott, *The "Genesis Controversy" and Continuity in Southern Baptist Chaos: A Eulogy for a Great Tradition* (Macon, GA: Mercer University Press, 1992), 7–12.

a series covering the entire Bible. The Genesis volume, authored by British Baptist scholar G. Henton Davies, articulated progressive views similar to those advocated by Elliott. Both commentaries sparked controversies at annual meetings of the SBC and resulted in revoked or revised books. The Elliott Controversy also led to a revision to the *Baptist Faith and Message* in 1963.[39] Most importantly, these controversies convinced many Southern Baptists that progressives were out of touch with the historic Baptist commitment to orthodox theology and Great Commission priorities.

RECOVERING A GREAT COMMISSION FOUNDATION

The Conservative Resurgence was a conservative theo-political movement that successfully gained control of the convention's denominational ministries through democratic processes during the final two decades of the twentieth century. Movement conservatives were a diverse group, but they shared a common opposition to leftward theological trends in the SBC and the wider American culture. Specifically, conservatives were convinced that the convention would thrive only if her leaders were both personally committed to and publicly advocates of the inerrancy of Scripture.[40] They also shared a common conviction that an orthodox theological consensus is necessary in order to pursue Great Commission priorities in a way consonant with Scriptural teachings.[41]

Prior to the Conservative Resurgence, SBC conservatives had normally mobilized regionally in response to controversies in particular states or institutions. They had also focused more on starting autonomous conservative

---

39   See David William Downs, "The Use of 'The Baptist Faith and Message,' 1963–1983: A Response to Pluralism in the Southern Baptist Convention" (Ph.D. diss., The Southern Baptist Theological Seminary, 1984), 103–48; Almer Jesse Smith, "The Making of the 1963 Baptist Faith and Message" (Ph.D. diss., The Southern Baptist Theological Seminary, 2004).

40   Paul Pressler, *A Hill on Which to Die: One Southern Baptist's Journey* (Nashville: B&H, 1998), 149–60.

41   Ibid., xi; Paige Patterson, *Anatomy of a Reformation: The Conservative Resurgence in the Southern Baptist Convention, 1978–2004*, 2nd ed. (Fort Worth: Southwestern Baptist Theological Seminary, 2006), 9. See also Sutton, *Baptist Reformation*, 258–86. For a negative assessment of the Conservative Resurgence's evangelistic fruit, see Thom S. Rainer's chapter, "A Resurgence Not Yet Fulfilled," in this volume. According to its key architects, the Conservative Resurgence was never an end unto itself, but was a movement to restore a firm theological foundation to the SBC so that the Convention's local churches could cooperate with theological integrity in their corporate pursuit of Great Commission ends.

ministries rather than reforming existing denominational ministries.[42] In the mid-1970s, a convention-wide conservative coalition began to come together under the leadership of Houston judge Paul Pressler and Criswell Institute president Paige Patterson. Pressler had been active in The Baptist Faith and Message Fellowship, a network formed in 1973 that included a number of conservative pastors who led large, evangelistic churches. Patterson earned two degrees from New Orleans Seminary, had pastoral experience, and was the son of a former pastor and executive secretary of the Baptist General Convention of Texas. Both men had deep Southern Baptist roots and desired to see the SBC return to a cooperation based on an orthodox theological consensus rather than a pragmatic commitment to missions, broadly defined.[43]

Pressler and Patterson began to build a network of like-minded conservative pastors and others who were willing to attempt to capture the convention's bureaucracy. They advocated a strategy that would take advantage of the appointive powers of the SBC president to reshape the denomination's institutions over the course of a decade or so. Convention messengers would elect a movement conservative as president, who would then appoint committed conservatives to key committees, who would in turn nominate sympathetic conservatives to vacant trustee positions at each SBC agency. The plan was contingent on electing a string of presidents who were not just conservative—there had been numerous conservative presidents in the past—but who were on board with the strategy.[44]

Key to the strategy's success was preventing conservatives from dividing over their own theological differences. To avoid internal fracturing,

---

42 For more information about conservative activism before the Conservative Resurgence, see Finn, "Development of Baptist Fundamentalism in the South," 155–57; Michael M. Soud, "A Critical Analysis of the Criswell College's Effect on the Southern Baptist Convention, 1980–2000" (Ph.D. diss., Southeastern Baptist Theological Seminary, 2003); James A. Patterson, "Alternative Theological Education in the Southern Baptist Convention: A Case Study of Mid-America Baptist Theological Seminary," *Journal of Baptist Studies* 1 (2007): 2–19, available online at http://baptiststudiesonline. com/wp-content/uploads/2007/03/james-patterson-article-2007.pdf (accessed July 2, 2009).

43 Patterson's and Pressler's respective roles in organizing the Conservative Resurgence have received considerable treatment by historians. For example, see Sutton, *The Baptist Reformation*, 62–90, and David T. Morgan, *The New Crusades, The New Holy Land: Conflict in the Southern Baptist Convention, 1969–1991* (Tuscaloosa: University of Alabama Press, 1996), 13–36. For their own reflections, see Pressler, *A Hill on Which To Die*, and Patterson, *Anatomy of a Reformation*.

44 Morgan, *The New Crusades, The New Holy Land*, 16, 36; Pressler, *A Hill on Which To Die*, 78–81. The strategy was actually developed by Bill Powell, the head of The Baptist Faith and Message Fellowship.

Pressler and Patterson encouraged conservatives to unite under the banner of inerrancy and avoid significant debates about other doctrinal matters. This approach would allow conservatives to win the rhetorical debate by framing the controversy as primarily a battle for the Bible, keep conservatives focused on a single issue on which they all agreed, and provide the epistemological basis for eventually adjudicating all of the contested theological issues.[45]

After spending more than a year drumming up grassroots support for the conservative cause, messengers to the 1979 annual session in Houston narrowly elected Memphis pastor Adrian Rogers on the first ballot, thus beginning the Conservative Resurgence. Rogers's term was followed by an unbroken chain of conservative presidents, all of whom took discernible steps in advancing the conservative cause. By the late 1980s conservatives were being selected for leadership vacancies at SBC agencies. By the early 1990s most progressives were disengaging from the convention and aligning with groups like the Alliance of Baptists and the Cooperative Baptist Fellowship.[46]

In an effort to streamline its ministries, the denomination underwent a bureaucratic restructuring in the mid-1990s under the name Covenant for a New Century. In 1997, the six seminary presidents publicly committed to govern their schools in a manner consistent with the beliefs and priorities of most Southern Baptists.[47] In 1998, the convention amended the *Baptist Faith and Message* to reflect conservative interpretations of gender roles within the family.

Perhaps the most significant conservative advance was the adoption of a new edition of the *Baptist Faith and Message* in 2000. Under the leadership of convention president Paige Patterson and a committee chaired by Adrian

---

45 See Patterson, *Anatomy of a Reformation*, 5, 7; Sutton, *The Baptist Reformation*, 1; Morgan, *The New Crusades, The New Holy Land*, 16; Pressler, *A Hill on Which to Die*, 191–92. See also Dennis Wiles' oral interview with Paige Patterson on June 22, 1990, available as Appendix 3 in Dennis Ray Wiles, "Factors Contributing to the Resurgence of Fundamentalism in the Southern Baptist Convention, 1979–1990" (Ph.D. diss., Southwestern Baptist Theological Seminary, 1992), 250.

46 For more information on the genesis of these movements, see Alan Neely, "The History of the Alliance of Baptists," in *The Struggle for the Soul of the SBC: Moderate Responses to the Fundamentalist Movement*, ed. Walter B. Shurden (Macon, GA: Mercer University Press, 1993), 101–28, and Daniel Vestal, "The History of the Cooperative Baptist Fellowship," in ibid., 253–74.

47 *One Faith, One Task, One Sacred Trust: A Covenant between Our Seminaries and Our Churches*, available online at http://www.baptistcenter.com/onefaithonetaskonesacredtrust.html (accessed July 2, 2009).

Rogers, the denomination revised its confession of faith at several points to reflect better a conservative theological consensus.[48] Although there are still periodic battles over biblical inerrancy, particularly in the state conventions, the Conservative Resurgence as a convention-wide movement ended with the adoption of the 2000 *Baptist Faith and Message*.

CURRENT THREATS TO GREAT COMMISSION COOPERATION

The contemporary SBC is the product of the Conservative Resurgence. Every Southern Baptist agency head, missionary, professor, and other denominational employee who has been hired in recent years is a theological conservative. Our mission boards are appointing sound missionaries, our seminaries are educating sound students, and our publishing house is producing sound curricula, books, and other resources. Our Ethics and Religious Liberty Commission is contending for traditional family values and moral conservatism.

While conservatives may have won our denominational civil war, the convention has yet to experience a lasting peace. Though the Conservative Resurgence successfully purged the SBC of progressive leadership, the internal differences among movement conservatives gradually began to cause tension in the denomination. Southern Baptists continue to debate the finer points of gender roles, miraculous gifts, Baptist distinctives, and Calvinism. Differences of opinions regarding musical worship styles and eschatology also cause occasional conflict, though typically at the local rather than convention-wide level. Each of these issues represents ongoing threats to Southern Baptist cooperation for the sake of the Great Commission.

Tensions over gender roles had been brewing since at least 1984, when the SBC passed a resolution opposing women in pastoral ministry.[49] Southern Seminary experienced controversy over gender roles in the mid-1990s when conservative president R. Albert Mohler Jr. enacted a new policy

---

48   See Adrian Rogers, "From the Chairman of the Committee on the Baptist Faith and Message," available online at http://www.sbc.net/bfm/bfmchairman.asp (accessed July 2, 2009); Douglas K. Blount and Joseph D. Wooddell, eds., *The Baptist Faith and Message 2000: Critical Issues in America's Largest Protestant Denomination* (Lanham, MD: Rowman & Littlefield, 2007); Charles S. Kelley Jr., Richard Land, and R. Albert Mohler Jr., *The Baptist Faith and Message* (Nashville: LifeWay, 2007).

49   "Resolution on Ordination and the Role of Women in Ministry," available online at http://www.sbc.net/resolutions/amResolution.asp?ID=1088 (accessed July 2, 2009).

that prospective faculty members must affirm not only inerrancy but also complementarianism, the theological name for the traditional view of gender roles.[50] The 1998 amendment to the *Baptist Faith and Message* and the 2000 revision of the confession codified traditional gender roles, making a commitment to complementarianism a litmus test for missionaries, seminary professors, and other convention employees.[51]

The second controversial issue is the alleged continuation of certain miraculous gifts. Local associations periodically spoke out against charismatic practices, sometimes ousting charismatic churches, and in 1987 the Home Mission Board passed a policy forbidding the appointment of charismatic Southern Baptists as domestic missionaries.[52] Since the late 1990s this has become an increasingly divisive issue. In 1999, Chattanooga Southern Baptist pastor Ron Phillips published *Awakened by the Spirit*, an

---

50 See Wills, *Southern Baptist Theological Seminary*, 519–35, and Barry Hankins, *Uneasy in Babylon: Southern Baptist Conservatives and American Culture*, Religion and American Culture (Tuscaloosa: University of Alabama Press, 2002), 82–88, 200–201.

51 Although virtually all Southern Baptists appear committed to the *principle* of complementarianism, there has been periodic tension over its *application*. Some have voiced concerns about churches that have female deacons, nonordained female ministerial staff, or even women teaching groups of mixed gender. The *Baptist Faith and Message* takes no position in these matters, but stricter complementarians argue that women serving in at least some of these roles potentially violate the Scriptures. Perhaps the most well-known controversy over the application of complementarianism was the 2006 dismissal of Old Testament professor Sheri Klouda from the faculty of Southwestern Seminary. Although Klouda was a complementarian, the seminary's administration determined that it violated biblical principles for a woman to serve as a professor in a theological discipline because those disciplines closely parallel pastoral ministry. A subsequent lawsuit Klouda brought against Southwestern was dismissed because the court refused to exert state influence in an ecclesiastical matter. See "Newspaper Reports Tenure Refusal for Southwestern Woman Prof," *Baptist Press* (January 22, 2007), available online at http://bpnews.net/bpnews.asp?id=24815; Hannah Elliott, "Bloggers Decry Southwestern's Dismissal for Teaching Men," *Associated Baptist Press* (January 24, 2007), available online at http://www.abpnews.com/index.php?option=com_content&task=view&id=1755&Itemid=12 0; Hannah Elliott, "Accrediting Agencies Asked to Probe Seminary's Dismissal of Female Prof," *Associated Baptist Press* (January 25, 2007), available online at http://www.abpnews.com/index.php?option=com _content&task=view&id=1757&Itemid=120; "Former Prof. Files Suit against SWBTS," *Baptist Press* (March 12, 2007), available online at http://bpnews.net/bpnews.asp?id=25152; Art Toalston, "Seminary Responds to Former Prof's Lawsuit," *Baptist Press* (April 11, 2007), available online at http:// bpnews.net/bpnews.asp?id=25367; Jerry Pierce, "Judge Dismisses Suit against Southwestern," *Baptist Press* (March 20, 2008), available online at http://bpnews.net/bpnews.asp?id=27676 (all accessed July 2, 2009).

52 C. Douglas Weaver, *In Search of the New Testament Church: The Baptist Story* (Macon, GA: Mercer University Press, 2008), 195.

apology for charismatic theology and practice.[53] Though it is difficult to prove, there is anecdotal evidence that the ministries of "Third Wave" Calvinistic theologians and pastors like Wayne Grudem, C. J. Mahaney, and Sam Storms have also influenced some within the SBC to be at least open to the possibility that miraculous gifts continue to the present.[54]

In 2005 and 2006, two widely reported incidents brought this issue to the forefront. In November 2005, the trustees of the International Mission Board passed new guidelines that forbade the appointment of missionaries who practice a "private prayer language," a form of speaking in tongues.[55] The new policy prompted protests from a number of Southern Baptist bloggers, most notably Oklahoma pastor Wade Burleson, then a trustee of the IMB.[56] In fall 2006, Texas pastor and Southwestern Seminary trustee Dwight McKissic preached a chapel sermon at Southwestern announcing that he practiced a private prayer language. Southwestern subsequently removed the sermon from its Web site, arguing that McKissic's sermon was tantamount to a critique of the IMB policies, though McKissic claimed he was unaware of the policies until after he preached the sermon.[57] In April 2007, McKissic's church hosted a Baptist Conference on the Holy Spirit that highlighted the differences of opinion about miraculous gifts; both McKissic and Burleson spoke at the conference.[58]

---

53   Ron M. Phillips, *Awakened by the Spirit: Reclaiming the Forgotten Gift of God* (Nashville: Thomas Nelson, 1999).

54   Internet searches for "Southern Baptists" and terms like "open but cautious," "Third Wave," and "continualist" result in thousands of hits, including blog posts, position papers, conferences, and articles in state Baptist periodicals.

55   Michael Chute, "Trustees Appoint 89 Missionaries, Adopt New Guidelines," *Baptist Press* (November 22, 2005), available online at http://bpnews.net/bpnews.asp?id=22133 (accessed July 2, 2009).

56   Burleson's blog, Grace and Truth to You, is available online at http://kerussocharis.blogspot .com (accessed July 2, 2009). Burleson recounts his response to the guidelines and the ensuing controversy in Wade Burleson, *Hardball Religion: Feeling the Fury of Fundamentalism* (Macon, GA: Smyth & Helwys, 2009). See also "Mission Board Trustees Seek Removal of Trustee Burleson," *Baptist Press* (January 11, 2006), available online at http://bpnews.net/bpnews.asp?id=22424 (accessed July 2, 2009).

57   Michael Foust, "Southwestern Trustee's Sermon on Tongues Prompts Response," *Baptist Press* (August 30, 2006), available online at http://bpnews.net/bpnews.asp?id=23882 (accessed July 2, 2009); "SWBTS Chapel Speaker Amplifies Stance; SBC's Page Sees 'Positive Outcomes,'" *Baptist Press* (August 31, 2006), available online at http://bpnews.net/bpnews.asp?id=23889 (accessed July 2, 2009).

58   Samuel Smith, "McKissic Leads Holy Spirit Conference," *Baptist Press* (April 30, 2007), available online at http://bpnews.net/bpnews.asp?id=25540 (accessed July 2, 2009); Hannah Elliott, "Holy Spirit Conference Urges Unity, Decries Its Absence in Baptist Life," *Associated Baptist Press* (April 30, 2007), available online at http://www.abpnews.com/index.php?option=com_content&task =view&id=2227&Itemid=120 (accessed July 2, 2009).

In part as a response to these controversies, in June 2007 LifeWay Research released a study that indicated half of Southern Baptist pastors believe private prayer languages are biblical, though critics disputed the findings.[59] Both Burleson and McKissic eventually resigned from their respective trustee appointments, the former after significant, prolonged controversy with the leadership of the IMB trustee board.[60]

The third controversial issue is actually a cluster of matters related to Baptist ecclesiological distinctives. Some have argued that a plurality of elders is more Presbyterian than Baptist and at least potentially undermines congregationalism. Others have advocated plural elders as a biblical option that has sometimes been popular among Baptists, though not in recent Southern Baptist practice.[61] Another issue is the terms of communion, specifically the question of whether or not immersion is prerequisite to participation in the Lord's Supper. While the *Baptist Faith and Message* clearly answers the question in the affirmative, it seems clear that many SBC churches practice open communion, inviting all believers to participate in the ordinance.[62]

---

59   Libby Lovelace, "LifeWay Research Studies the Use of Private Prayer Language," available online at http://www.lifeway.com/lwc/article_main_page/0%2C1703%2CA%25253D165593%252526M%25253D200906%2C00.html (accessed July 2, 2009); Malcolm B. Yarnell III, "Commentary on the LifeWay Research Division Study of Private Prayer Language," White Paper 17, Center for Theological Research, Southwestern Baptist Theological Seminary, 2007, available online at http://www.baptisttheology.org/documents/CommentaryontheLifewayStudyofPPL.pdf (accessed July 2, 2009).

60   "Burleson Resigns as IMB Trustee," *Baptist Press* (January 31, 2008), available online at http://bpnews.net/bpnews.asp?id=27291 (accessed July 2, 2009); Jerry Pierce, "McKissic Resigns as Seminary Trustee," *Baptist Press* (June 22, 2007), available online at http://bpnews.net/bpnews .asp?id=25958 (accessed July 2, 2009).

61   Most of the published material in this debate has been fair and irenic. For advocates of a plurality of elders, see Phil A. Newton, *Elders in Congregational Life: Rediscovering the Biblical Model for Church Leadership* (Grand Rapids: Kregel, 2005); John S. Hammett, *Biblical Foundations for Baptist Churches: A Contemporary Ecclesiology* (Grand Rapids: Kregel, 2005), 177–89; Mark Dever, *By Whose Authority?: Elders in Baptist Life* (Washington, DC: 9 Marks, 2006). For criticisms of the plurality view, see Gerald Cowen, *Who Rules the Church? Examining Congregational Leadership and Church Government* (Nashville: B&H, 2003); Daniel L. Akin, "The Single-Elder-Led Church: The Bible's Witness to a Congregational/Single-Elder-Led Polity," in Perspectives on *Church Government: Five Views, ed. Chad Owe*n Brand and R. Stanton Norman (Nashville: B&H, 2004), 25–86; Paige Patterson, "Single-Elder Congregationalism," in *Who Runs the Church? Four Views on Church Government*, Counterpoints, ed. Steve B. Cowan (Grand Rapids: Zondervan, 2004), 131–52.

62   For arguments that baptism is a prerequisite to the Lord's Supper, see Nathan A. Finn, "Baptism as a Prerequisite to the Lord's Supper,"; Emir F. Caner, "Fencing the Table: The Lord's Supper, Its Participants, and Its Relationship to Church Discipline," in *Restoring Integrity in Baptist Churches*,

Perhaps the most contentious ecclesiological matter is the nature of baptism. Although most Southern Baptists would probably agree in principle that some immersions do not pass biblical muster, this is an area where there are widely divergent views in application. In November 2005, the IMB trustees passed a baptism guideline in addition to their aforementioned private prayer language guideline. According to the trustees, any prospective missionary immersed in a church that does not embrace belief in the perseverance of the saints must be immersed in a Southern Baptist church. The IMB would consider this latter immersion a valid baptism, unlike the previous immersion.[63] This decision also generated considerable controversy among many Southern Baptists.

Proponents of the new guideline argue that the assumed invalid immersions are "alien immersions," similar to immersions performed by pedobaptist churches.[64] Opponents argue that any sincere believer who has been immersed by a church that preaches the gospel should not be required to be re-immersed, even if the church that administered the baptism was Arminian, pedobaptist, or both. This particular debate is exacerbated (plagued?) by inaccurate rhetoric, especially among those who frequent weblogs and online message boards. The pro-guideline camp accuses the anti-guideline camp of being ecumenists, a charge denied by those who criticize the guidelines. The anti-guideline party accuses the pro-guideline party of being Landmarkers or "neo-Landmarkers," labels that are often both inaccurate and intemperate.[65]

The final debate is over Calvinism, specifically the doctrines of unconditional election and limited atonement. The present debate stretches

---

ed. Thomas White, Jason G. Duesing, and Malcom B. Yarnell III (Grand Rapids: Kregel, 2008), 163–78. Many Southern Baptist bloggers have argued for an open communion position. For example, see David Rogers, "Response to Nathan Finn's 'Baptism as a Prerequisite to the Lord's Supper," *Love Each Stone*, September 18, 2006, available online at http://loveeachstone.blogspot.com/2006/09/reply -to-nathan-finns-baptism-as.html (accessed July 2, 2009); Alan Cross, "Which View of Communion Best Reflects Our Spiritual Unity with Christ?," Downshore Drift, February 27, 2009, available online at http://www.downshoredrift.com/downshoredrift/2009/02/why-open-communion-modified-best -reflects-our-spiritual-unity-in-christ.html (accessed July 2, 2009).

63 See Chute, "Trustees Appoint 89 Missionaries, Adopt New Guidelines."

64 The status of alien immersions is one of the perennial debates among Baptists, particularly in the American South. See *Encyclopedia of Southern Baptists*, vol. 1 (Nashville: Broadman, 1958), s.v. "Alien Immersion."

65 It is of course possible that some proponents are Landmarkers and some critics are ecumenists, but many times those who employ such descriptors are using them as epithets and painting with too broad a brush.

back into the 1980s, though since the 1990s it has periodically reignited with increasing intensity. Numerous studies have documented the recent growth of Calvinism among Southern Baptists and attempted to describe its influence.[66] Calvinists argue that their views are biblical and have deep roots in Baptist history in general and Southern Baptist history in particular. Non-Calvinists argue that at least some aspects of Calvinist theology are unbiblical and that Calvinists overestimate the role the doctrines of grace have played in Southern Baptist history. Non-Calvinists seem to be especially concerned with the influence of Founders Ministries, an informal Calvinist network within the SBC. Calvinists seem to be particularly concerned with the influence of revivalism and Keswick theology, both of which are popular in many SBC churches.[67]

The Calvinism debate, perhaps more than any other issue, is a threat to the ongoing cooperation of SBC conservatives, in part because of the intense feelings this debate provokes on all sides. Almost every effort to address this issue has furthered the tensions within the convention. Even conferences sponsored by recognized Southern Baptist leaders do little to calm the tensions over Calvinism and sometimes even contribute to those tensions. In November 2007, Southeastern Seminary, Founders Ministries, and LifeWay Christian Resources co-hosted the Building Bridges Conference at Ridgecrest Conference Center. The organizers invited representative Calvinist and non-Calvinist speakers to weigh in on some of the debated issues.[68] B&H Academic (a division of LifeWay) published the proceedings in a book titled *Calvinism: A Southern Baptist Dialogue*. Some non-Calvinists complained the conference and book were too friendly to Calvinism and criticized Southeastern and LifeWay for allowing Founders to co-host the confab.[69]

---

66 For example, see C. Douglas Weaver and Nathan A. Finn, "Youth for Calvin: Reformed Theology and Southern Baptist Collegians," *Baptist History and Heritage* 39 (Spring 2004): 19–41; Tom J. Nettles, *By His Grace and For His Glory: A Historical, Theological, and Practical Study of the Doctrines of Grace in Baptist Life*, 20th anniversary ed. (Cape Coral, FL: Founders Press, 2007), 250–302; Collin Hansen, *Young, Restless, and Reformed: A Journalist's Journey with the New Calvinists* (Wheaton: Crossway, 2008), 69–93.

67 These issues and others were covered in essays written by both Calvinists and non-Calvinists in E. Ray Clendenen and Brad J. Waggoner, eds., *Calvinism: A Southern Baptist Dialogue* (Nashville: B&H Academic, 2008).

68 For examples of accusations and caricatures from all parties involved, see Chuck Lawless, "Southern Baptist Non-Calvinists? Who Are We Really?" in ibid., 155–70, and Nathan A. Finn, "Southern Baptist Calvinism: Setting the Record Straight," in ibid., 171–94.

69 For example, see David L. Allen, "*Calvinism*: A Review," White Paper 25, Center for Theological Research, Southwestern Baptist Theological Seminary, 2008, available online at http://www.baptisttheology.org/documents/CalvinismaReview.pdf (accessed July 7, 2009).

In October 2008, Jerry Vines Ministries and several SBC seminaries co-hosted the John 3:16 Conference at First Baptist Church, Woodstock, Georgia. One participant claimed the conference was intended to be "a majoritarian Southern Baptist response to the 'Building Bridges' and 'Together for the Gospel' conferences."[70] The speakers, all non-Calvinists, critiqued the five points of Calvinism from a biblical and theological perspective and raised concerns about Calvinist influence in the convention. The proceedings were also published by B&H Academic in a book titled *Whosoever Will: A Biblical-Theological Critique of Five-Point Calvinism.*[71] These present tensions illustrate at least one potential downside to the Conservative Resurgence, albeit an unintentional one. A generation and a half of Southern Baptists was involved in a pitched battle for the future of the SBC. Many are still involved in such battles in their state conventions and associations. Most Southern Baptists would likely agree that these battles are important because truth matters. Nevertheless, Southern Baptists must recognize it is possible to become so accustomed to fighting during times of war that one does not know how to live peaceably with basically like-minded brothers and sisters once the battles are over.

This is not a mythical scenario. Many separatist fundamentalists, including many Independent Baptists, forgot how to be cooperative during the mid-twentieth century. After they lost the battles for their denominations and withdrew from those groups, they turned on each other. Within a generation, fundamentalists were shooting each other and often fracturing over matters such as cultural engagement, degrees of cooperation with and separation from other believers (even other conservatives), Calvinism, Landmarkism, the timing of the rapture, charismatic gifts, the age of the earth, and Bible translations.[72] To this day, there are Independent Baptists

---

70 See Steve W. Lemke's comment to Ed Stetzer, available online at http://blogs.lifeway.com/blog/edstetzer/2008/03/people_and_places_in_the_sbc_2.html (accessed July 7, 2009).

71 David L. Allen and Steve W. Lemke, eds., *Whosoever Will: A Biblical-Theological Critique of Five-Point Calvinism* (Nashville: B&H Academic, 2010).

72 See Nancy Tatom Ammerman, *Bible Believers: Fundamentalism in the Modern World* (New Brunswick, NJ: Rutgers University Press, 1987); David O. Beale, *In Pursuit of Purity: American Fundamentalism Since 1850* (Greenville, SC: Unusual Publications, 1986); Mark Taylor Dalhouse, *An Island in the Lake of Fire: Bob Jones University, Fundamentalism, and the Separatist Movement* (Athens: University of Georgia Press, 1996); George W. Dollar, *A History of Fundamentalism in America* (Greenville, SC: Bob Jones University Press, 1973); David Keith Bates Jr., "Moving Fundamentalism toward the Mainstream: John R. Rice and the Reengagement of America's Religious and Political Cultures" (Ph.D. diss., Kansas State University, 2006); Farley P. Butler Jr., "Billy Graham and the End of Evangelical Unity" (Ph.D. diss., University of Florida, 1976); Nathan A. Finn, "The Development of

who have as difficult a time getting along with some of their fellow funda-mentalists as they do the liberal Episcopal priest down the street.

Many sense a tendency toward this very type of infighting among some contemporary Southern Baptists. It has been demonstrated that we are fighting about some of the same issues over which our fundamentalist friends divided. Southern Baptists must be careful that we do not become too preoccupied with secondary and tertiary matters, lest these issues dis-tract us from the task at hand. We must remember that not all of our present battles are necessary. Some of our battles cause needless division among fellow conservatives. And when they do so, they distract us from our convention's main task: the proclamation of the gospel to all people.

Conservatives rightly criticize the pre-1979 SBC for emphasizing missions—and the financing thereof—to the exclusion of sound doctrine. This type of pragmatism created an atmosphere that tolerated and even encouraged aberrant theology so long as missionary enlistment increased and the Cooperative Program kept growing. Conservatives were wise to reject this paradigm and argue that one cannot do authentic missions with-out being committed to biblical theology and practice. This is a conviction that we must never surrender. But neither can conservative Southern Bap-tists so narrow the parameters of cooperation that much of our diversity is stifled for sake of doctrinal uniformity in nonessential matters.

TOWARD A GREAT COMMISSION FUTURE

This chapter has argued that the Great Commission has always been central to our convention of local churches. Despite our shared missional priorities, there have often been threats to our corporate pursuit of the Great Commission. This was true with the anti-mission movement of the mid-nineteenth century and the programmatic and progressive status quo of the mid-twentieth century. It remains true for the contemporary convention as the varieties of South-ern Baptist conservatism attempt to live together peacefully and cooperate together faithfully.

As this chapter comes to a conclusion, it bears repeating once again that Southern Baptists must not confuse the ends with the means. If we

---

Baptist Fundamentalism in the South"; Philip Dale Mitchell, "Come Out From Among Them and Be Ye Separate: A History of the Fundamental Baptist Fellowship" (Ph.D. diss., University of Colorado at Boulder, 1991).

are content with simply having theological conservatives leading our various ministries, then the Conservative Resurgence was only a half-victory. As Timothy George has quipped on a number of occasions, the mere replacement of one set of bureaucrats with another doth not a reformation make.[73] The Conservative Resurgence must result in a renewed zeal for the Great Commission. This is one reason why so many Southern Baptists have called for a "Great Commission Resurgence" in recent years.[74]

The use of the word *resurgence* is deliberate. Just as our commitment to conservative theology was interrupted during the generation prior to the Conservative Resurgence, our commitment to the primacy of missions and evangelism was interrupted during and after the Conservative Resurgence, at least in practice.[75] Important battles were fought within our denomination—battles that conservatives rightly believed would ultimately lead to theological renewal. With the success of the Conservative Resurgence, that theological renewal is underway.

The time has come for a missional renewal that flows from our doctrinal convictions. Zeal for the Great Commission needs to be restored to its place of prominence in Southern Baptist life, not just in theory and rhetoric, but also in practice. Although there is still work to be done to bring about further theological renewal in the convention, we cannot lose sight of the "one sacred effort" that has united us since our earliest days. The interruption is over. The distractions must be set aside. God is at work reconciling the world to Himself, and Southern Baptists need to get serious again about making ourselves available to the Lord to use in His great work of bringing salvation to people all over North America and in every corner of the earth. Theology and missions go hand in hand. One without the other is an incomplete agenda. One without the other is destined to fall short of what our Lord intends.

---

73   For example, see Timothy George, "Toward an Evangelical Future," in *Southern Baptists Observed: Multiple Perspectives on a Changing Denomination*, ed. Nancy Tatom Ammerman (Knoxville: University of Tennessee Press, 1993), 277.

74   In addition to this volume, see Daniel L. Akin, "Answering the Call to a Great Commission Resurgence," in Clendenen and Waggoner, *Calvinism*, 247–60; idem, "Marks of a Great Commission People" (sermon available from http://apps.sebts.edu/multimedia/?p=414); "SBC President's Declaration Calls for a Great Commission Resurgence," in *Baptist Press* (April 28, 2009), available online at http://www.bpnews.net/bpnews.asp?id=30387 (accessed July 6, 2009); Thom Rainer, "A Personal Great Commission Resurgence," in *Florida Baptist Witness* (June 30, 2009), available online at http://www.floridabaptistwitness.com/10439.article (accessed July 6, 2009).

75   See Rainer, "A Resurgence Not Yet Fulfilled," in this volume.

THE FUTURE OF THE SOUTHERN
BAPTIST CONVENTION[1]

R. Albert Mohler Jr.

The Southern Baptist Convention is asking important questions at a strategic moment in its history. There are countless opportunities not yet seized, and there is much work left undone. We live in a day when many denominations are concerned with merely staying alive or stemming massive losses; and in tragic cases of theological confusion, some even struggle to find a reason for being. The key issue is faithfulness. By the grace and mercy of God, we should pray and seek together to find ourselves faithful as we stand before the One who called us, saved us, and sends us out with His gospel.

Jesus said, "We must do the works of Him who sent Me while it is day. Night is coming when no one can work" (John 9:4). This warning should be our theme as we consider the urgency of our calling as ministers of the gospel. Night is coming when no one can work. Questions about the future of the Southern Baptist Convention are not mere abstract, bureaucratic, or structural concerns. These are questions about the Great Commission, the grace and glory of God, and the gospel of the Lord Jesus Christ. There must be urgency because we should be doing more to take the name of Jesus to the nations and to see every tongue and tribe exalt in the one, true, and living God.

Even as we think about what it means—and what it *can* mean—to be a Southern Baptist in the twenty-first century, the context of our discussion should begin with gratitude. We can think, pray, and plan for the *future* of the Southern Baptist Convention only because a multitude of

---

1 This chapter was first presented at a forum on the future of the Southern Baptist Convention at The Southern Baptist Theological Seminary on August 19, 2009.

people in the *past* gave so much to make this denomination what it is. Their sacrifice affords us the opportunity to have these important conversations about the future. Likewise, we should be thankful for present-day Southern Baptists throughout the world who demonstrate faithfulness in giving, praying, going, and sending. Without them, this discussion would not even be possible.

THE SOUTHERN BAPTIST CONVENTION IN HISTORICAL PERSPECTIVE

Putting the discussion of the Southern Baptist Convention into historical perspective requires looking back to its establishment, now well over 150 years ago. In 1845, when Baptists gathered together in Augusta, Georgia, they determined to establish a convention to unite the energy, conviction, and passion of the churches from which they came. They established what we would now call a mission statement, explaining that the formation of the Southern Baptist Convention was "for the eliciting, combining, and directing of the energies of the denomination for the propagation of the gospel."[2] Take note of those three very important participles: eliciting, combining, and directing. We still "elicit" today. "Combining" was the secret of the Southern Baptist Convention's organizational genius from the beginning, and it remains so today. "Directing," at least in 1845, had a singularly clear focus on missions.

Christian missionary endeavor was the motivating factor for the formation of the Southern Baptist Convention. The eliciting and combining eventuated in the directing of every dollar of missionary funds to expand the work of missions in North America and around the world. To this end, the Southern Baptist Convention formed two missionary boards. The Foreign Mission Board focused on missionary work outside the United States, while the Home Mission Board focused on evangelizing and planting churches in the frontier. As a reminder of how much has changed in terms of the geography of the United States, in 1845 the "frontier" began at Tuscaloosa, Alabama, and went westward from there. Even as so much has changed since 1845, the opportunities for reaching North America and the world have only multiplied.

---

2 Southern Baptist Convention, "Constitution," available at http://www.sbc.net/aboutus/legal/constitution.asp.

After the initial period of formation in the early nineteenth century, the Southern Baptist Convention progressed from holding triennial meetings into the present practice of annual meetings. Then, even as the United States experienced incredible growth in terms of population and geography, the Southern Baptist Convention also experienced abundant energy, dynamism, and expansion that exceeded even the originating dreams of the founders. By the end of the nineteenth century, Southern Baptists had expanded their mission through the addition of other organizations and purposes. Southern Baptists established The Southern Baptist Theological Seminary in 1859, making theological education a purpose of Southern Baptists—though it was not yet a purpose of the Southern Baptist Convention itself. Southern Baptists also established a publishing house in 1891, then known as the Baptist Sunday School Board. These are just two examples of the many endeavors and institutions into which Southern Baptists put their energies during this period of rapid expansion.[3]

A FOCUS ON EFFICIENCY

The Southern Baptist Convention now faces a critical crossroads and must either move into the future with denominational structures and methods open to change or face serious decline. The Southern Baptist Convention in 2009 continues to operate largely out of a model that the denomination adopted from corporate America in the early twentieth century, a model that prioritizes efficiency over theological conviction in carrying out the task of missions.

The great shift in the logic of the Southern Baptist Convention came early in the twentieth century, especially in the years from 1914 to 1919. During that period, a word came into Southern Baptist vocabulary, and it did not come from an undetectable source. The word was "efficiency," the code word of business in the early twentieth century. For the first time in the new business age, organizations began to think in terms of how they could be more efficient in their purposes. Efficiency experts arose as a new vocation in America. Time management, systems management, and

---

3 For a history of SBTS, see Gregory A. Wills, *Southern Baptist Theological Seminary, 1859–2009* (New York: Oxford University Press, 2009). For a history of LifeWay Christian Resources, see James T. Draper Jr. and John Perry, *LifeWay Legacy: A Personal History of LifeWay Christian Resources and the Sunday School Board of the Southern Baptist Convention* (Nashville: B&H, 2006).

organizational management—all these became a part of the early twentieth-century bureaucratic revolution.

Certainly in business, efficiency can be a make-or-break word between profit and loss. However, when it comes to missions, the work of our churches, and the work of the gospel around the world, efficiency has a limited application. What the efficiency model marked more than anything else was an infusion of a business culture into the life of the denomination. Churches became concerned with efficiency, and Christian leaders made decisions on the basis of efficiency.

In 1925, bowing to what was understood to be the necessity of having an ongoing entity for organizational coordination, the Southern Baptist Convention established the Executive Committee. There had never been anything like it before because the convention existed only during the days of the year in which the convention met, wherever it met. That is, when the annual meeting ended, the Southern Baptist Convention ceased to exist until the Convention met once again. Prior to 1925, there was no central organization, and there was an incredible resistance to the idea of establishing a headquarters.[4]

Not by coincidence, Southern Baptists also adopted the Cooperative Program in 1925. Again, the central concern was for efficiency in collecting contributions from the churches. Thinking back to those three words from 1845—"eliciting, combining, and directing"—the Cooperative Program was understood to be the answer to the question of how to fulfill this purpose efficiently. The Cooperative Program was not without controversy, even in its naming. "The Combined Program" and "Our Program" were two failed suggestions. Upon the establishment of the Executive Committee and the Cooperative Program, energy began to be directed toward the central coordination of the denomination. This redirection of energy was in evidence immediately in 1926 and 1927, as the Southern Baptist Convention gave an enormous expansion of powers to the Executive Committee.[5]

THE TOTAL CHURCH PROGRAM

During the 1950s, the managerial infusion into the life of the Southern Baptist Convention took a quantum leap forward. The Convention

---

4 Chad Owen Brand and David E. Hankins, *One Sacred Effort: The Cooperative Program of Southern Baptists* (Nashville: B&H, 2005), 145–59.

5 Ibid., 96–99.

formed a committee to study the "Total Church Program," resulting in the hiring of the management-consulting firm of Booz, Allen, and Hamilton. They made a thorough examination of the Southern Baptist Convention and brought recommendations concerning how the denomination could become more efficient. The report from the Convention committee, built on the analysis of the Booz, Allen, and Hamilton report, became known among Southern Baptists as the "Branch Report," named after committee chairman Douglas Branch. One of the proposals called for an office building in Nashville to house the Executive Committee and other entities. That building was approved in the late 1950s and occupied in 1963. Another proposal called for an Inter-Agency Council, while yet another called for program assignments to be given to every single Southern Baptist entity.[6]

With all the emphasis on restructuring and refocusing, what would be the logic and purpose of the Convention? In 1845, the answer to that question was clear and specific: "eliciting, combining, and directing the energies of the denomination for the propagation of the Gospel." When the Southern Baptist Convention received the report from Booz, Allen, and Hamilton, it came with the suggestion that the mission of the Convention should be: "To bring men closer to God through Jesus Christ."[7] As one would expect a management consulting firm to do, Booz, Allen, and Hamilton crafted the statement after interviewing multitudes of Southern Baptists to discover which three words they most commonly used in response to the question of what the Convention was to be.

This was not exactly "going back to the Scripture" for direction. Then again, this was not exactly a church or theological organization looking at the question. It was a management consulting firm that provided the direction and one that in many ways defined the whole science of business management in the mid-twentieth century—and still does so today. Booz, Allen, and Hamilton was the management consulting firm to many of America's largest corporations, and its managerial philosophy was reflected in the corporate ethos of America in the mid-twentieth century. In hiring Booz, Allen, and Hamilton, Southern Baptists were attempting explicitly and consciously to bring the denomination into the cultural mainstream in terms of this managerial revolution.

---

6 *SBC Annual*, Southern Baptist Convention Executive Committee, Nashville, 1958, 430–61.
7 Ibid.

PROGRAMMATIC IDENTITY: FIRST-HAND EXPERIENCE

Since the 1950s, another defining characteristic of the Southern Baptist Convention has been its programmatic identity. The basic ethos, driving energy, and organizational logic of the Convention has centered on creating identity through denominational programs. A church was Southern Baptist if it did certain things, had certain features, used certain offering envelopes and literature, and (one assumed) held to certain doctrines. Part of the history of the Convention is its reaffirmations of the doctrinal foundations of the gospel, as in the controversies which sprang up in the 1920s, necessitating the adoption of the *Baptist Faith and Message* in 1925. This statement was revised in 1963, and again in the year 2000. In analyzing the Southern Baptist Convention from 1945 to the present and in seeing the corporate management theory worked out in the churches, however, it becomes clear that though a concern to take the gospel to the nations was the driving energy, that concern became translated into a corporate structure with a programmatic identity.

There was a social context to this, especially in the southern states where the SBC and its churches functioned as something like the Roman Catholic Church. The Convention became "at ease in Zion," having both created and been created by the region. It achieved enormous dominance, and as a result, it was not controversial in the South to be a Southern Baptist. Rather, it was a matter of the social context in which churches knew who they were and with whom they worked in accomplishing what they believed to be Christ's commission to his church.

The Southern Baptist Convention took on a "cradle-to-grave" approach to denominational identity. In reality, the identity began *before* the cradle. In my office, I have a certificate whereby I was enrolled in "pre-cradle roll," as "Baby Mohler: Expected October 1959." There was literally a conception-to-grave understanding of denominational identity.

Once a baby was born, he or she would move up to the "cradle roll," becoming a Southern Baptist in the crib. The cradle-to-grave approach involved education, activities, and all the experiences of Southern Baptist babyhood and toddlerhood. Toddlers discovered that Jesus wanted them to be a "Sunbeam"—"To shine for him each day in every way to please him at home and work and play." I became a Sunbeam, and the songs, smells, and scents of what it meant to belong will be with me forever. Sunday was a full-body, total immersion experience for Southern Baptists, a four-fold activity consisting of Sunday school, morning worship, training union, and evening worship.

As a young person I was in every choir imaginable, because if one's parents were true Southern Baptists, then it was a genetic necessity that their children be there. When I was fifteen, I announced to my parents that I was dropping out of the youth choir. With a completely straight face, my father looked at me and said, "You didn't join." Upon further reflection, I realized that he was right. Being in the youth choir was a fact of birth, of identity, and of faithfulness.

There were also mission-oriented programs for children and adolescents: Girls in Action for girls and Royal Ambassadors for boys.[8] Every program came with its own literature. There were Sunday school quarterlies, Training Union quarterlies, books, and pamphlets. To be a Southern Baptist was to have printed material.

To be a Southern Baptist also meant that you arrived at your Sunday school class carrying an offering envelope with your name printed on it. There was a series of boxes on the envelope, and you checked those boxes to record your faithfulness. The boxes recorded things like your attendance, being on time, whether you brought your Bible.

The offering envelope was vital for Southern Baptist Convention identity because that was the method for compiling denominational statistics. My father, as the Director of Training Union, would promptly assemble those statistical reports. Back in those pre-computer days, I reasoned that they called these numbers into headquarters from the church, so that by Monday morning somebody in an SBC office somewhere knew that Al Mohler was "on time" and that he had "brought Bible" to his Training Union class.

Cradle-to-grave identity continued into the college years with youth camps, family assemblies (Ridgecrest, Glorieta, and state camps), and Baptist Student Union. Men progressed from RAs into the Brotherhood, and women moved from GAs into the Woman's Missionary Union. By the 1970s and 1980s, several state conventions even had retirement centers, so the SBC was literally a cradle-to-grave denomination.

What a lot of people do not know is that the planning concept of the Southern Baptist Convention was called "The Key Church" or "The Model Church Planning Concept." All SBC entities were accountable to a planning model that described a church as a "model church," a key church

---

8 See http://www.gapassport.com/ and http://www.royalambassadors.org/.

that was basically structured like a county-seat First Baptist church. If a church was truly Southern Baptist and with the program, then it would be organized in a certain way in terms of budget, deacon structure, and committees, etc. Furthermore, all of the Convention entities were accountable to that planning project. Every piece of Southern Baptist literature coming out of what was then called the Baptist Sunday School Board was accountable to that planning project.

When I was a student at Southern Seminary, we had a required course in which, as a class, we would go to the library to handle with our own hands and see with our own eyes every single type of literature published by the SBC. We could not graduate without this experience. In fact, this planning project was still in place when I was elected president of Southern Seminary in 1993.

All of this planning and work produced a great deal of solidarity of denominational identity. Churches were, and still are, sent a long survey known as the Annual Church Profile (ACP) in order to report their statistics: worship attendance, Sunday school enrollment and attendance, Brotherhood and WMU involvement, offering and mission giving, etc. As each church compiled and sent in their ACP, a statistical picture of Southern Baptist identity emerged from the data. This produced an incredible intactness and tightness to Southern Baptist identity. Our churches were recognizable because of this.

This solidarity was absolutely incredible, and it was policed by an informal but very real way of enforcing "orthodoxy." Some pastors would be dismissed from conversation because they led churches that used non-SBC Sunday school literature. A youth group was suspect if they chose to attend a parachurch summer activity instead of going to Ridgecrest or Glorieta. The mindset was that they would be getting outside the denominational program, and doing so could lead to a breakdown of SBC identity.

I will forever be thankful that I attended a church where nearly everyone there knew me and loved me. My family went to one of the "tall steeple" churches that had every one of these programs. My parents, family, and church were completely with the program. I was at church nearly every time the church doors opened, and we were often the people who opened the church. There was an enormous spiritual security in that identity. I grew up with warm-hearted Christians who knew me and loved me. When I was young enough to still wear those clunky white shoes, I would walk into church and shake hands with the old men, the "big people" who formed the Shaking Hands Committee. They were men who knew how to welcome you into the church, whether you were two or eighty. They treated you with respect, loved you, and scooted you up to your Sunday school class.

There was an incredible intactness to all this. I knew that surrounding me were Christians, organized together in a Southern Baptist church that had an identity. I did not wake up every morning wondering where my family belonged in the great scheme of things. This is who we were. Of course, it was also by conviction, but that was not the first thing that I came to know and experience—it was more the tribal cultural identity.

There has always been an enormous dynamic and brand loyalty within the life of the Southern Baptist Convention. Where there is brand loyalty, however, there is also the risk of brand disloyalty—a fact that leads directly to the present analysis and discussion of the Convention. The world that produced the Southern Baptist Convention of the 1950s has changed in so many different ways. That world is actually now long gone, even in geographical locations where Southern Baptists have historically been concentrated.

A CONTINUING PROCESS

Moving forward several decades, during the years 1993–1995, the Southern Baptist Convention established a "Program and Structure Committee," which brought a report called the "Covenant for a New Century." The report proposed that Southern Baptist entities be reduced in number from nineteen to twelve. The report also proposed the following mission statement: "The Southern Baptist Convention exists to facilitate, extend, and enlarge the Great Commission ministries of Southern Baptist churches, under the Lordship of Jesus Christ, upon the authority of Holy Scripture, and by the empowerment of the Holy Spirit."[9]

This statement is more theological, more scriptural, and certainly more evangelistic than the bureaucratic-sounding statement suggested by Booz, Allan, and Hamilton. Even so, the 1995 statement still reflects the cumbersome nature of the process it takes to combine the energies of thousands of churches. After much discussion and debate, the 1995 convention adopted the committee's report.

During the 2009 annual meeting in Louisville, Kentucky, the Convention established a Great Commission Task Force. Its assigned task

---

9 Brand and Hankins, *One Sacred Effort*, 124.

was to bring recommendations to the 2010 Southern Baptist Convention meeting in Orlando, Florida, concerning how the Southern Baptist Convention and its churches might be more faithful together in the cause of the Great Commission.

The history of the Southern Baptist Convention is the story of how Southern Baptists arrived where we are today. It is necessary to understand our history and to recognize how we took on such an immense corporate mentality. In their own day and time, Southern Baptists understood the corporate management shift to be the best way to accomplish the purposes of the denomination. Looking back, we now have the opportunity to evaluate whether inaugurating the corporate mentality was the best step for accomplishing the Great Commission. An even more urgent question for us to consider in this generation and at this time, though, is whether the corporate mentality *is* the best structure and ethos for a denomination—for today and for the future.

THE SOUTHERN BAPTIST CONVENTION AS GENERAL MOTORS

I want to suggest two analogies for thinking about the Southern Baptist Convention as it is today. The first analogy is the Southern Baptist Convention as General Motors.

William Durant incorporated General Motors in 1908 as a holding company, originally bringing in Buick and Oldsmobile. In 1909, Durant added Reliance Motor Truck Company (later becoming GMC), Cadillac, and other small manufacturers. At the time, Ford Motor Company was the dominant automobile corporation, and though it did not appear that anyone could *catch* Ford, Durant wanted to create a company that would grow and be able to *compete* with Ford. Durant held to the principle that achieving dominance in the pioneering automotive business would require combining as many facets of the business as possible into one giant corporation.

Another of Durant's principles was to avoid buying from suppliers because it made more sense simply to buy the suppliers themselves.[10] By 1910, Durant had brought into the GM corporation about twenty-five companies including manufacturers of automobiles, auto parts, and auto

---

10 Alfred P. Sloan, Jr. *My Years with General Motors* (New York: Doubleday, 1990), 6–7.

accessories.[11] At that point, General Motors became a cradle-to-grave employer—the company, the factories, the sales force, the massive dynamic and energy. Once individuals were "inside," they were *really* inside.

William Durant lost control of GM in 1910, regained it in 1916, and then lost it for good in 1920.[12] Alfred P. Sloan, considered by many to be the most brilliant CEO of the twentieth century, became President of GM in 1923 and Chairman in 1937. Sloan established the idea of a centralized headquarters with decentralized offerings. The manufacturing plants, suppliers, and dealers were distributed throughout the country, but there was a centralized logic in terms of the headquarters and the cradle-to-grave coverage.

At the time, Ford's philosophy could be summed up by Henry Ford's famous line: "Any customer can have a car painted any color that he wants, so long as it is black."[13] In contrast, GM discerned the desires of consumers and supplied the kinds of cars that Americans wanted to buy. In addition, customers also remained "inside the company" as they gauged their automobile purchasing power and selected the equivalent price-level of General Motors product.

Sloan described this product strategy as "a car for every purse and purpose."[14] At the entry level of cost and quality, a customer might purchase a Pontiac. Then, as his purchasing power increased, he would move on up the line to an Oldsmobile and then a Buick. And, if the apex of American automobile culture was reached, the customer would drive off the car lot in a Cadillac. The logic of General Motors was that customers never had to leave the corporation. Their identity was in the corporation, with its various brands of automobile culture and shared lines of automobile products.

Quicker than one might imagine, GM overtook Ford and led in global auto sales for seventy-seven consecutive years. GM had everything: manufacturers, supplies, a dynamic sales force, and a global reach for their products. In 1962, GM held 50.7 percent of the market share within the United States.[15] That is a truly amazing achievement as one considers that this one corporation accounted for more than half of all the automobiles

---

11 Ibid., 5.

12 William Pelfrey, *Billy, Alfred, and General Motors* (New York: Amacom, 2006), 281–83.

13 Henry Ford, *My Life and Work* (New York: Doubleday, 1923), 72.

14 Pelfrey, *Billy, Alfred, and General Motors*, 282.

15 William J. Holstein, *Why GM Matters: Inside the Race to Transform an American Icon* (New York: Walker), 5.

sold in the nation. As a result, General Motors emerged as the prototypical model of managerial dynamics. Other corporations looked at GM with envy, even as they also looked to gain the wisdom and managerial acumen practiced at GM.

From the 1980s to the present day, however, it became increasingly evident that GM was having serious economic and management troubles. GM declared bankruptcy in 2009, and ceased to be a publicly traded corporation. Through different legal means, GM was transformed into a new corporation owned by the taxpayers of the United States and the pension funds that hold its stock. The bankruptcy of General Motors was the second largest corporate bankruptcy in world history.[16]

Looking back at the corporate logic of GM, it is easy to see how it fit into the 1950s, 1960s, and 1970s. However, from the 1970s to the 1990s, GM lost much of its market share. While the car-buying culture changed in the late twentieth century, GM continued to operate out of a business model that worked well in the 1950s. Today, GM aspires to maintain its 20 percent share of the American automobile market, and its future is anything but certain. If the Southern Baptist Convention is indeed in some way analogous to General Motors, then the warning is that we can find ourselves in a similar crisis if we too are trapped in the organizational logic of the 1950s.

THE SOUTHERN BAPTIST CONVENTION AS A SHOPPING MALL

The second analogy for consideration is the Southern Baptist Convention as a shopping mall. Before the rise of the automobile, most retail activity was "in town," at department stores—beautiful buildings that served as competing temples of commerce. This was a pedestrian-driven commercial dynamic that combined big department stores with little storefront establishments. Going downtown meant that you were going to a *place*, and once there, you walked from store to store. As the automobile age developed, however, the idea of downtown shopping centers gave way to the idea of the shopping mall, the first of which was built in 1950: Northgate Mall in the suburbs of Seattle, Washington.[17]

---

16 Neil King Jr. and Sharon Terlep, "GM Collapses Into Government's Arms," *Wall Street Journal*, 2 June 2009, http://online.wsj.com/article/SB124385428627671889.html (accessed February 9, 2010).

17 See, "Northgate Shopping Mall (Seattle) Opens on April 21, 1950," accessed at http://www.historylink.org/index.cfm?DisplayPage=output.cfm&File_Id=3186.

The basic idea of a shopping mall was enclosed space, and in many ways this was a complete reversal of the downtown logic. When you shop in an enclosed space, you do not have to worry about rain, snow, or sleet because you are indoors and are separated from the weather. You are inside, and everybody is happy. The temperature and the humidity are controlled.

The logic of the mall is that its retail space is dominated with anchor tenants that are big department stores at the ends of the mall. The logic of mall shopping is that when you say you are going somewhere, you are going "to the mall"—this mall or another. The mall has a name. The names of the small stores are not even on the outside of the mall, which is a giant block sitting on pavement surrounded by thousands of parking spaces. Given their size and market dominance, the names of the anchor stores are on the outside, bringing people to the mall. However, most of what goes on *at* the mall is invisible until you get *inside* the mall.

Paco Underhill, a specialist in the history of retail, argues that one problem of the shopping mall is that it is a big wall with a little mouse hole (the door). Customers drive up to this massive thing, go in these little doors, and only then, on the inside, do they see the stores. Once they are in, they are in. The action and the identity are inside, not outside. On the outside, there is only a parking lot and cars, but the inside is where the action is.[18]

By 2008, there were 1,175 enclosed malls in the United States. From 1950 to 2000, the shopping mall displaced nearly all other retail contexts, rivaled only by the arrival in the 1990s of the "big-box" stores that tended to be clustered around malls. In the 1970s, *U.S. News and World Report* revealed that adult Americans spent more time at the mall than anywhere else other than home and work.[19] Incidentally, Underhill reports on one fact that should not come as a surprise: more than anything else, malls sell women's clothing.[20] A mall also has to sell additional items in order to get other customers in the door, however. Malls now offer food, entertainment, professional offices, dentists, insurance kiosks, banks, and coffee shops. Malls became full-service, but customers do not know this until they get inside the mall. Only on the inside can they find out about all the offerings.

In looking at trends in shopping and retail center development, a 2007 report showed that only one enclosed shopping mall was built in 2006, none were planned for 2007, and future trends continue in the same

---

18   Paco Underhill, *The Call of the Mall* (New York: Simon and Schuster, 2005), 17–22.
19   Ibid., 14.
20   Ibid., 126.

declining trajectory.[21] In fact, a big issue right now is the decision of what to do with malls that are being abandoned because the retail logic of the mall has collapsed. The retail energy in America is going into "lifestyle centers" or "affinity centers," which are outdoors—*not* enclosed. We are witnessing the creation of a new post-automobile era downtown. The customer will find popular stores within these affinity centers, but the retailers want their name out front. In these centers you actually drive your car within the proximity of the store. They have many of the services of the mall, but it is not enclosed space and the identity is primarily the store rather than the center.

The logic of the shopping mall is something of an analogy for the Southern Baptist Convention—who we are and how we arrived here. Just as I would argue that we are the General Motors of American denominations, it is also true that we are analogous to a great big shopping mall. We have two anchor stores—the International Mission Board and the North American Mission Board. Inside the mall we have all kinds of other offerings—seminaries, the Ethics and Religious Liberty Commission, LifeWay Christian Resources, Guidestone Financial Resources. On the state and associational levels, we offer a wide-range of programs and activities. We have all kinds of individual offerings, but they are sublimated within the mall and the enormity of the denomination—the logic of which becomes evident from the inside, not from the outside.

TEN QUESTIONS FOR THE SOUTHERN BAPTIST CONVENTION

I use these two metaphors to suggest that Southern Baptist Convention history *is* understandable, and it is not with a bitter sense of critique that we look back and say, "That was a sellout." Building a quest for efficiency on a corporate model was the best that Southern Baptists knew at the time, and there were many gains from this. There was efficiency in the Southern Baptist Convention that other denominations did not have, and there was solidarity to the Southern Baptist Convention that other denominations could only envy. As a result, many people and many millions of dollars were sent to the mission field.

---

21   Lisa Selin Davis, "When Downtown is in the Suburbs," *New York Times*, 30 September 2007, http://www.nytimes.com/2007/09/30/realestate/30nati.html (accessed 9 February, 2010).

However, now the question we Southern Baptists have to ask is the same question that General Motors should have been asking for the last twenty years: "What has changed, and why have we not?" Or, for those whose business is the shopping mall, the question is: "Has the logic of this particular organizational model and pattern now been eclipsed by something else?" Likewise, the Southern Baptist Convention must ask hard questions about our own denomination. As we think of the people in our churches and the people we seek to reach for Christ, are they attracted to our current model, pattern, mission, and logic, or does it seem like it comes from an age gone by?

In looking to the future, I want to suggest that the Southern Baptist Convention faces several questions about our identity. I am going to put these in terms of ten dichotomies. That is, I believe that Southern Baptists are going to choose one direction or the other. Now, when dichotomies like this are set up, the author clearly has a preferred option. As such, it will be very clear in which direction I hope to see the convention go.

Missiological or Bureaucratic

First, Southern Baptists must decide whether we are going to be *missiological* or *bureaucratic*. I would suggest that the missiological approach is the only logic that fits the church of the Lord Jesus Christ. Unless the Southern Baptist Convention clearly asserts an unashamed, undiluted, and ruthless missiological logic, we will find ourselves out of touch with our churches, with the generation now coming into leadership in ministry and missions, and with the world we are trying to reach. The logic of bureaucracy will never take us where we need to go. If the identity of the Southern Baptist Convention is bureaucratic rather than missiological, our logic will resemble mainline denominations. We will simply find ourselves dying and declining more slowly than they are, but we will be declining nonetheless.

Tribal or Theological

Second, Southern Baptists must decide whether our identity is *tribal* or *theological*. The reality is that we have had many shared convictions. However, in 1845, Southern Baptists did not even adopt a confession of faith. From reading Southern Baptist history, we know that one of the reasons why that happened is because every church was in close relationship with an association, and the associations were robustly confessional. However, by the time you get to the late nineteenth century, there is an aversion to being too specific about the convictional parameters and the theological foundations of our work together.

In the twentieth century, theological controversy showed the necessity of becoming clear in doctrinal conviction. Examples include the fundamentalist–modernist controversy in the twenties, the controversy over the historical-critical study of the Scripture in the sixties, and the struggle over the inerrancy of Scripture from the sixties through at least the eighties. Further issues made necessary the *2000 Baptist Faith and Message*, and if Southern Baptists think that adopting the 2000 *BFM* wrapped up all future theological responsibilities, we fool ourselves.

If we are going to assume a tribal-like identity, then we must first figure out a way to be a tribe when all the denominational structures are no longer as they once were. You may still be able to find churches that have the cradle-to-grave coverage, enrolling unborn children in the pre-cradle Sunday school department. However, that is not the norm. The entire world has changed, and the opportunity for a tribal identity is gone. Although in some quarters there is nostalgia for the tribal identity, we should see its loss as a gain. With the loss of tribal identity, the denomination will have to find a *theological* identity. And if the Convention finds the *right* theological identity, it will produce the right missiological logic.

Convictional or Confused

Third, Southern Baptists must decide whether the basis of our work together is *convictional* or *confused*. We can avoid talking about theological issues and minimize the theological logic of the Southern Baptist Convention, or we can make *every* issue a first-order issue. However, if we choose either one of those directions, then we are going to have a very confused people.

In this new era, Southern Baptists have no choice but to grow up theologically because we are no longer going to be insulated from theological and ideological currents swirling around us. Southern Baptist school children and teenagers are influenced by a clash of worldviews, now coming very early in life. Many Southern Baptist young people attend colleges and universities where they hear very strong challenges to their Christian faith. We no longer live in a region protected from those kinds of currents, and if we are not seriously convictional we will become more and more disastrously confused. Without embarrassment, Southern Baptists must be very clear that cooperation in missions necessitates that we share some very clear convictions. We must also be vigilant to defend the church against the many compromises, subversions, and rejections of biblical truth that arise in each generation. Southern Baptists must refuse to go down paths of theological compromise.

Secular or Sectarian

Fourth, Southern Baptists must decide whether our logic is going to be more *secular* or more *sectarian*. This will be difficult because we have never actually admitted that we *are* sectarian. However, now we will have to show up at the "Sectarians Anonymous" meeting and say, "Hello, I am a Southern Baptist. We are sectarian."

The classic sociological definition of a sect is that it stands out from the culture around it because of its mores, worldview, ideology, and convictions. If you grew up in the intact South and in the intact Southern Baptist Convention, you did not have to be sectarian because you were just here. This was more or less home. However, the South is no longer what it once was, and our responsibility is not just to the South anyway. The South became the Sun Belt, and the dominant religion of the Sun Belt is materialism. As a result, we now experience what sociologists call "cognitive contamination."[22] We are surrounded by various worldviews, and our own worldview has been shaped in ways that we may not even recognize.

We must recover the sense that the church of the Lord Jesus Christ is always, in a New Testament sense, sectarian. The church consists of resident aliens who are never fully at home in their culture. We cannot be fully at home in the culture because the culture is itself a "Genesis 3" culture, and the church is called to a different worldview, under allegiance to the Lord Jesus Christ. However, if we become more secular—and this is a real danger because it can come with such subtlety—the churches of the Southern Baptist Convention will be secularized before our eyes, even as we fail to recognize it. We will just begin to feel at home.

---

22 Peter L. Berger, *A Far Glory: The Quest for Faith in an Age of Credulity* (New York: Free Press, 1992), 38–40.

Younger or Dead

Fifth, the Southern Baptist Convention will become either *younger* or *dead*. Somewhere along the line between adolescence and adulthood, we are losing at least two-thirds of our young people, and we lose them in ways that are often more subtle than will first appear.[23] In some denominations and organizations, when you lose people, there is a statistical recognition that you have lost them. However, no one has to send in a resignation letter to the Southern Baptist Convention. People just stop showing up. Some become inactive, and some of them just openly leave and are never seen again.

One of the problems with the Southern Baptist Convention is that our own young people are very much a part of the generation that has reduced religion and Christianity to "moralistic therapeutic deism," believing that God basically wants them to do well and to do right and to be happy.[24] However, that is a false gospel, and to fight it requires a level of conviction and biblical clarity of evangelism and discipleship that goes beyond where Southern Baptists normally go.

The need to get younger also relates to how the Southern Baptist Convention is changing demographically. The birthrate of families in the Southern Baptist Convention has been cut roughly in half over the last thirty years. Now, let us just state the obvious. If your birthrate is cut by half, then your growth rate is also significantly cut because your first pool for evangelization should be the children of your own families. If you go from having 4.2 to 2.1 children per couple, then the nursery and the children's Sunday school will be smaller than they used to be. These declining demographics are also a part of where we are as Southern Baptists.

Diverse or Diminished

Sixth, the Southern Baptist Convention will be either more *diverse* or more *diminished*. We will either look more and more like America ethnically, or we are going to stand out for our standing out from the culture. Achieving ethnic diversity is going to be hard for the Southern Baptist Convention, but not primarily because of attitudes. Almost anyone you talk to is going to say that we need to be more diverse, but the process requires more than an

---

23   "LifeWay Research Uncovers Reasons 18 to 22 Year Olds Drop Out of Church," accessed at http://www.lifeway.com/article/?id=165949.

24   Christian Smith, *Souls in Transition: The Religious and Spiritual Lives of Emerging Adults* (Oxford: Oxford University Press, 2009), 154–65.

inclination toward diversity. It requires incredible strategy to become more diverse. It will require a lot of denominational energy and a lot of discomfort. If we are really going to reach America in all her diversity, then we are not all going to be singing out of the same hymnbook. For example, demographers predict that in the year 2050, one out of four Americans will have a Hispanic grandparent.[25] That is a different America, a different Sun Belt, and a different South—truly, a different world.

Missional or Methodological

Seventh, Southern Baptists will become either more *missional* or more *methodological*. Earlier, I used the term "missiological" as the theological logic for the denomination and its ethos. I take "missional" here as a strategic sense of application.

For a long time, if you asked, "Who is a Southern Baptist?" you would get a methodological answer. Now, certainly there is both a historical answer to the question and also a basic, minimally theological answer. However, in the past the predominant answer was methodological. That is not going to be a workable option for the future because you are not going to need Southern Baptists to do those methodological things. The church is not primarily an institution with a methodological mission. The church is faithful only when it is found to be missional, and the mission must be the strategic deployment for the cause of the gospel.

Strategic or Anemic

Eighth, Southern Baptists will become either more *strategic* or more *anemic*. When we say "more strategic," this means that churches will actually have to become missiological units. They must become a missiological think-tank to reach their community. They are not going to be able to just sit there and open the door, use the quarterlies, and still have faithfulness in reaching their community. It is going to take a lot of strategy. The global context will require Southern Baptists to update their strategies continually at every level because the fast-changing world requires us to be more than well-intentioned. Missional deployment requires energetic and strategic thinking.

---

25 "US Population Projections: 2005–2050," accessible at http://pewhispanic.org/reports/report.php?ReportID=85.

Bold or Boring

Ninth, the Southern Baptist Convention will become either increasingly *bold* or increasingly *boring*. This is a generation that will not be satisfied with boring. They can be bored anywhere. There is a kind of boring logic that operates by saying the same thing in roughly the same way, every time with no surprises. This simply will not work, and it is not the method of the New Testament.

The mission of the Lord Jesus Christ is so bold that it can never be boring. To become deeply involved in the logic of the Great Commission and in the mission of God in the world to the nations is to refute the possibility of boring. However, this means that we are going to have to take risks, and that is tough for any organization. It is especially tough for an organization that is feeling the pain of transition, and feeling the need for some quick reconsideration of strategy, purpose, and mission—but it is going to have to be.

We must become bolder, and we must have leadership that is bolder. We are going to have to take greater risks in finding out if faithfulness takes us here or there, if this model or that model helps us to be more faithful to the gospel. We must be willing to travel far outside our comfort zone, or our comfort zone will lead to death.

Happy or Bitter

Tenth, Southern Baptists must decide if we are going to be *happy* or *bitter*. We have a reputation for denominational crankiness, appearing angry and frustrated even as we insist that we are happy. Crankiness often erupts on the floor of the Southern Baptist Convention, as people who are not even present—or even Southern Baptist—are thoroughly criticized. Side issues are raised on the floor of the convention, as if those issues are where the Southern Baptist Convention *should* direct its energies. Often, a year will go by without a question being asked in an appropriate context, only to have it brought up on the floor of the convention in order to make some kind of cranky point.

The risk is that we will be cranky in all the wrong ways, because the reality is that if we stand by the scriptures, we *will* say hard things and the culture around us *will* consider us backward, unloving, and intolerant for standing by the truth. We will have to pay the cost for standing by the truth of God's Word on any number of issues, so we cannot afford to waste the opportunity to reach our neighbors by being cranky about things that are irrelevant, unhelpful, and extraneous to the life of the Southern Baptist Convention.

Our joy should be evident to all as we gather together. There should be a unity of purpose and a commonality of heart. If not, people will stop coming because they can be unhappy at home, unhappy at work, and unhappy in their local community. An unhappy marriage or an unhappy family is evidence of a problem because God's people should be joyful in whatever condition they find themselves. No matter what problems we have to deal with and no matter how difficult the decisions are that we have to make, there should still remain evident joy. If we are a denomination of unhappy cranks, we will decline and disappear—and we deserve to do so.

THE SOUTHERN BAPTIST CONVENTION AND THE FUTURE

The Southern Baptist Convention has both perception problems and reality problems. Though we say that we are sold out to missions, our financial infrastructure betrays that claim. Only a small portion of the offering plate dollars will ever make it to the international mission field. The Cooperative Program has been a great gift to the Southern Baptist Convention, allowing Southern Baptists to fund their commitment to missions, theological education, and the purposes of this denomination. However, the Cooperative Program is not enough, for two reasons.

First, it often sounds as though the greatest goal of the Cooperative Program is to cooperate. In that sense, the United States Army can have a "cooperative program." Instead, Southern Baptists need to perceive very clearly that the Cooperative Program, in both its ethos and its reality, is a way of reaching the nations with the gospel of Christ. Yes, we do cooperate. However, the pressing question in our day is whether Southern Baptists will be relevant in the mission of God and the world.

Second, we are not going to be able just to tell Southern Baptist churches of this generation how much they must do and how much they must give. Rather, we must make certain that we are worthy of the support of Southern Baptists who seek to reach the world with the gospel. They must see us as partners with the churches, not simply as recipients of their funds. Churches must be liberated to give as they will give, or they will not give as they otherwise would.

Despite efforts to the contrary, Southern Baptists continue to look like white-bread Protestantism, middle-class America still concentrated in the South and focused on North America. In reality, we *are* committed to world missions, but it does not yet look like we are as committed as we meant to be even in 1845. Nor are we as committed to missions as the New Testament calls us to be.

We must recover the primacy of the local church, and not just through speaking words we know we are supposed to say. We must discover where local churches urgently and passionately understand the mission of God and wish to be deployed. We must not make giving money the first and only logic of the passion of missions. Instead, Southern Baptist identity must be rooted in believing, being, going, sending, praying, suffering, and sacrificing. The giving should come at the end of the list, not at the beginning.

Every denominational board and agency must rethink these priorities. As a Convention, we must admit that it may have made sense to be General Motors at one point, and it may have made a great deal of sense to create a shopping mall at one point, but that world has passed. General Motors is bankrupt, and the malls are being boarded up. In the process of discovering how to be relevant to the purposes of God in this age, we must first go to the Scriptures and find a theological rationale. The logic of the Southern Baptist Convention cannot be bureaucratic, corporate, or drawn from business.

To use an analogy drawn from the very popular television commercial that promotes Apple computers, the Southern Baptist Convention consists primarily of PC guys. That is who we are. We grew up that way, and learned how to dress and talk that way—and all that really worked for a long time. Then, as you watch the commercial, you realize that the Apple guy is actually more focused on the future than the PC guy. The logic of these ads is that the PC guy and the Apple guy simply do not think alike. It is not just that one product is superior to another product. Rather, the message is that the logic is not the same. Apple obviously thinks that it is worth millions of their advertising dollars to tell you that their logic is different than the logic of the PC. Indeed, everyone that sees the advertisement immediately recognizes the truth of the message—they do operate from a different logic.

The Southern Baptist Convention is at a strategic moment in our history. We must not be seen as backward, cranky, and committed to the wrong kind of cultural identification. Instead, we must be missional, outwardly directed, future-oriented, and joyful in claiming and assuming the responsibility Christ invested in us. Our vision must be to gather and encourage Southern Baptists to work with other Christians to see the nations exalt the name of Jesus.

We must plant and nurture churches that bear all the biblical marks of the church. These marks are not reducible to statistics that can be sent in through the Annual Church Profile. Rather, they are only discernable by evaluating whether or not a church has the New Testament characteristics of a church. We will know these churches because they will show up on the mission field. They will show up in and among the nations. They will not just give money—they will pray, they will send, and they will go. As they go, these churches will either be alongside the Convention in the going, or they will be looking back, wondering why the Convention is not going with them.

CONCLUSION

The Southern Baptist Convention now stands at a great crossroads. There is so much more to consider. We could talk about the need to restructure, but structure is not the first issue. The ethos, mission, and purpose of the denomination—these are first issues for the present discussion. Southern Baptists must decide whether or not we will move into these questions of structure and method with theological conviction, knowing where we stand.

I am thankful that I am not in a denomination where the big theological and biblical questions are discussed as if they open for debate. But now, we must be a denomination that risks the structural and institutional questions being opened permanently—for the rest of our lives—seeking to be faithful at every turn as we look to the future.

Jesus said, "We must do the works of Him who sent Me while it is day. Night is coming when no one can work." Let us not be caught in the dark, wondering why we missed the opportunity while it was day.

SECTION 2
FROM THE WORD

THEOLOGY BLEEDS
WHY THEOLOGICAL VISION MATTERS FOR THE GREAT COMMISSION, AND VICE VERSA

Russell D. Moore

I am sitting up in bed in the middle of the night, computer in front of me, contemplating whether to type the next few words. I've been back and forth about it all night long, so far. I know if I say it, some of you will think it sounds kind of sacrilegious. But I really think it's true, and, in fact, I think we all know it's true, but too few of us want to say anything about it. The real problem for most Christians with the Great Commission is not, first of all, that it's so hard. The problem is that it's boring.

I can imagine some of you starting to object right now, so let me clarify. When I say the Great Commission is boring to many Christians, I don't mean the words spoken out with the Galilean accent of our King Jesus thousands of years ago in the Middle East. And I don't mean the words reiterating that event written down by the apostle Matthew as the Spirit of Jesus carried him along. And I don't mean the hidden revolution taking place even as you read this as persons around the world fall to their knees and cry out for mercy in Christ, or come dripping wet out of streams where they were baptized in the name of the Holy Trinity. I don't think many Christians ever hear the weight of that when they hear the words "Great Commission."

Too many of our churches—and too many of us—think of the Great Commission as little more than Jesus' way of promoting a Christmas offering or of marketing an evangelistic video series or propping up a denominational bureaucracy or giving a proof-text to get more people in the pews next to us at church. Someone tells us how the need is great, and we really should give more, for some abstract concept of "unreached people groups" with some abstract concept of "being on mission with Christ."

Come to think of it, Christian people often find missions boring for the exact same reasons that Christians find theology boring. The professor with his whiteboard behind him, dispassionately talking about the *ordo salutis* or the hypostatic union, is as lifeless to most Christians as a denominational program—or more so—and for the same reason. They are abstract. They seem disconnected from "real" life. We know the missions map on the wall and the confession of faith in our church constitutions are important—really, we know we ought to find them interesting—but for many of us they seem a bit, well, bloodless, compared to the bloody cross we picked up to follow when we first heard the word of the gospel.

Here's why. When theology loses mission, it becomes abstract—and boring. When mission loses theology, it becomes abstract—and boring. Both become boring when they become something other than what Jesus gave us. His sheep hear His voice, after all, and they run toward it (John 10:1–5). Our people don't resonate with the Great Commission largely because they've never seen the cosmic, panoramic view of what Jesus has actually called us to do.

The Scriptures, however, reveal an entirely different vision of the Great Commission. When Jesus announced the Commission to His disciples (Matt 28:16–20), He was not launching a global public relations campaign. *He was declaring war.* When Jesus grants the Great Commission, He is signaling the onset of the last days. The expansion of the gospel to the ends of the earth means that God has indeed granted Him the nations as His inheritance.

Thus, the Great Commission is a decisive stage in the warfare of God against the serpent of Eden. There is nothing programmatic about leading sinners to faith in Christ. Instead, the expansion of global missions represents the plundering of the kingdom of Satan (Mark 3:27; John 12:31–32; 2 Tim 2:25–26). The embrace of the gospel by sinners is more than just persuasion; it is the kingly activity of Jesus as the Son of David calling together a "flock" over which He rules as Shepherd (John 10:15–16; cf. Ezek 37:24).

The Great Commission points to faith in Christ and the forgiveness of sins as the vehicle for cosmic restoration and the salvation of the world. Those reconciled to God through Christ are receiving more than personal freedom from guilt—they are becoming "sons of God" who share with Jesus in an inheritance that includes the entire created order (Ps 89; Rom 4:13; 8:15–17; Gal 3:27–4:7).

The Great Commission is a theology of cosmic warfare—a theology centered on the unveiling of the long-hidden mystery of Christ and His church. It means the overthrow of the ancient powers that have long held the creation captive through sin and death. It means the triumph of a resurrected Messiah over every principality and power hostile to the reign of the Creator. It means that God is keeping His promises to His anointed King. If this bores us—or the nations and tribes around us—it's only because we don't see what's going on with the Great Commission.

It isn't boring. It's war.

THE GREAT COMMISSION AND THE REIGN OF DEATH

There was no Israelite Mission Board. Instead, the old covenant looked forward to the day when the nations would see the vindication of Israel, when Israel would be raised from the dead and cleansed from all sin (Ezek 36:33–36). "My dwelling place shall be with them, and I will be their God, and they shall be my people," Yahweh spoke through the prophet Ezekiel. "Then the nations will know that I am the LORD who sanctifies Israel, when my sanctuary is in their midst forevermore" (Ezek 37:27–28 ESV).

Israel therefore longed for the day when the ancient promises would be fulfilled, when the nations would come to Israel (Isa 60:1–14), when the ends of the earth would be given as an inheritance to the Son of David (Pss 2:8–9; 110:1–7). This would mean the reign of the Spirit-anointed King, the dawning of the messianic age (Isa 11:1–12), the kingdom of God. This is why the apostles inquired of the resurrected Jesus as to whether this was when He would "restore the kingdom to Israel" (Acts 1:6 ESV). Jesus answered their question by speaking of the power of the Spirit and the global task of the Great Commission (Acts 1:7–8). He was not changing the subject.

To understand the radical theology of the Great Commission, one must grasp the root problem—the tyranny of the demonic "principalities and powers" over the created order, created by Yahweh for His glory. As C. S. Lewis explained it:

> One of the things that surprised me when I first read the New Testament seriously was that it talked so much about a Dark Power in the universe—a mighty evil spirit who was held to be the Power behind death and disease, and sin. The difference is that Christianity thinks this Dark Power was created by God,

and was good when he was created, and went wrong. Christianity agrees with Dualism that this universe is at war. But it does not think this is a war between independent powers. It thinks it is a civil war, a rebellion, and that we are living in a part of the universe occupied by the rebel. Enemy-occupied territory—that is what this world is.[1]

This "enemy occupation" of the cosmos came through the deception of God's appointed king, the man Adam, who was given dominion over the creation (Gen 1:26–30; Ps 8:3–9). Because the human king surrendered his dominion to the Serpent-Conqueror, the creation is now in rebellion against its rightful rulers—the sons of man (Gen 3:16–19; Rom 8:19–23).

Therefore, the creation is under bondage to Satan because the creation's anointed rulers share a nature with the Evil One, the despotic "father" they have chosen for themselves (John 8:43–47; Eph 2:2–3). In order to restore human rule over the cosmos, the Serpent must be defeated by a man (Gen 3:15; Rev 12:5)—a human being who can destroy the satanic power over humanity, which is the guilt of sin and the curse of death (Heb 2:14–15). This is why Jesus confronts the demonic powers in His earthly ministry, why He demonstrates his authority over nature, and why He speaks of His crucifixion as the casting out of the ruler of this age (John 12:31; 14:30; 16:11).

As the church father Irenaeus noted, the humanity of Jesus is the fulfillment of our race's "war against the enemy." As such, Irenaeus contended, from the moment of Jesus' conception, He was "watching the head" of the Serpent—waiting to crush it beneath His feet.[2]

This is why the Great Commission requires cultural contextualization. Before we can announce Christ, we must know what the powers are encouraging our hearers to hide behind to shield them from the light of the glory of Christ. The apostolic mandate requires us to speak in such a way that our hearers know what it is that we're saying, a task modeled in the apostolic ministry of the apostle Paul (1 Cor 9:15–23). A theologically informed missiology understands that there are some aspects of human nature that transcend culture, rooted as they are in the creation and fall of humanity. The idolatries of racial supremacy fall before the New Testament's

---

1   C. S. Lewis, *Mere Christianity* (New York: Macmillan, 1943), 36.

2   Irenaeus of Lyons, *Against Heresies*, 5.21.1, in *The Ante-Nicene Fathers*, ed. Alexander Roberts and James Donaldson (Grand Rapids: Eerdmans, 1987), 1:548.

insistence on the unity of the human race in Adam (Acts 17:26). The missionary-evangelist further knows that all persons in all cultures have a real knowledge of God—a knowledge they universally suppress in unrighteousness (Rom 1:18–32).[3] "Evil must rationalize, and that is its weakness," notes philosopher J. Budziszewski. "But it can, and that is its strength."[4]

The missionary-evangelist knows that all persons in every culture know the objective standards of morality, and that all of them experience the indictments of the conscience for sin (Rom 2:14–16). The missionary-evangelist knows that all persons in every culture, whatever they do to deny it, fear death and the judgment to follow (Heb 2:14–15). This means that the message of the gospel across all cultures will address the common human plight of sin, righteousness, and judgment—the proclamation through which the Holy Spirit pierces consciences (John 16:8–11).

This means that a theology of the Great Commission recognizes that human hostility to the gospel is not primarily intellectual but moral. "And this is the judgment," the Gospel of John proclaims. "The light has come into the world, and people loved the darkness rather than the light because their deeds were evil" (John 3:19 ESV). The gospel, by its very nature, is threatening to the cherished autonomy of the sinner. But this understanding also means that missionaries and evangelists will not abandon a people group simply because they are initially unresponsive to the gospel—as though the gospel can be tested on a "focus group" of disinterested consumers.

Instead, a theology of the Great Commission understands that the problem for all persons—whether in Albania or Alabama—is captivity to the deception of the Evil One (2 Tim 2:25), a captivity that is overcome by the unabashed proclamation of the gospel (2 Cor 4:4–6). A biblical theology of the Great Commission sees gospel preaching as what it is: spiritual warfare.

And unregenerate humanity knows this—at some level. This is why warfare myths—from *Beowulf* to *Buffy the Vampire Slayer*—resonate with unbelievers. They don't know what is going on, but they sense that

---

3 For a discussion of the nature of this knowledge of God found in general revelation and in the *imago Dei*, see Carl F. H. Henry, *God, Revelation and Authority* (Waco, TX: Word, 1976; reprint, Wheaton: Crossway, 1999), 2:91–150.

4 J. Budziszewski, *The Revenge of Conscience: Politics and the Fall of Man* (Dallas: Spence, 1999), 35.

something more than meets the eye is in the air, that behind it all there is some ancient conspiracy. They try to quell it with bodily pleasure, mental diversions, and selfish ambitions. But somewhere behind it all, they seem to know there is a mystery stirring.

This is also why a biblical theology of the Great Commission will affect not just how we think, but how we *feel*. We preach, after all, the cross—a continual proclamation of the lostness of the world around us, and our own lostness apart from Christ. As poet Czeslaw Milosz puts it, "a religion of a crucified God is a religion of cosmic pain."[5] The Great Commission keeps our theology from being abstract thought. We, through the Spirit, "groan inwardly" as we see the curse of death in the cosmos around us, and in our own ongoing sin and despair (Rom 8:18–23, 26). Our pleadings then with our fellow dying sinners ought to project this sense of gravity, in order that consciences might hear in them the pleadings of Christ Jesus Himself.

Our theology saves our Great Commission activity from despair. After all, a realistic appraisal of the millions going out into the night of death every year, without mercy, is almost emotionally crushing. Right now, a four-year-old girl is being taught to bow before Allah; a nine-year-old boy in India is preparing an altar to an elephant-headed deity; an 81-year-old man in Alabama is dying, faithlessly, clinging to a repeated "sinner's prayer" that never expressed genuine trust in Christ. The reality of these things could lead us to wonder whether the gospel even "works" in a world like this. But we have a long view. We know that God raises up skeletons and makes them sons and daughters, and that He does it through the open speaking of His Word (Ezek 37:1–28).

THE GREAT COMMISSION AND THE ATONEMENT OF CHRIST

God's purpose is not just the rescue of some human beings, but also the restoration of human rule by conforming believers "to the image of his Son, so that he would be the firstborn among many brethren" (Rom 8:29 NASB). The Bible presents Jesus' death, resurrection, and His subsequent calling of sinners to repentance in strikingly cosmic terms, interpreting human redemption in the context of "an administration suitable to the fullness of the times, that is, the summing up of all things in Christ, things

---

5 Czeslaw Milosz, *Road-Side Dog* (New York: Farrar, Straus and Giroux, 1998), 135.

in the heavens and things on the earth" (Eph 1:10 NASB). Nowhere is the Christ-centered nature of redemption seen more clearly than in the content of Great Commission proclamation itself—the message of the crucified and resurrected Messiah (1 Cor 15:3–4), who bears the curse of God in the place of sinners. The Great Commission is anchored, of course, in what happened at the cross of Golgotha and the tomb of the Garden.

Because the kingdom comes through the gospel, there is no conflict between the understandings of the atonement as *Christus Victor*—Jesus' triumph over the demonic powers—and as a penal substitutionary sacrifice.[6] Yes, Jesus by His death and resurrection routs the demonic powers, but He does so by freeing humanity from what enslaves us to the demons in the first place: our condemnation before God for our sin and guilt (Rev 12:10–11). Christ is victorious precisely because He is our substitute, scapegoat, and sacrifice.[7]

The cross, then, changes the way we carry the Great Commission to the world. At the crucifixion stake, Jesus identified Himself with a sinful world (including the scandal of my sin). He was cursed by God in our place (Deut 21:23; Gal 3:13). This is why it seemed so reasonable to the shouting crowds to curse Him as a false Messiah—because only one rejected by God would ever be hanged on a tree. And that's why the apostle Paul had to insist repeatedly that he was not "ashamed" of the cross. At Golgotha, Jesus became sin (although He never sinned Himself) by bearing the sins of the world (2 Cor 5:21).

We are not, then, those who are "shocked" by sin. We are those who, with Jesus, identify ourselves with sinners, and are willing to go—with Him—where the misery of rebellion is the strongest, right into the dominion of the devilish rulers of this age. We do so as crucified people, those who can no longer be accused or condemned, but we do so with the chastened pride and the tender consciences of those who were accused and condemned—but are now liberated by God's mercy in the blood of Jesus. As twentieth-century evangelist-theologian Francis Schaeffer put it, "We

---

6   For a summary and defense of the *Christus Victor* view, see Gustaf Aulén's classic work *Christus Victor: A Historical Study of the Three Main Types of the Idea of Atonement*, trans. A. G. Hebert (New York: Macmillan, 1969). For a defense of the atonement as penal and substitutionary, see Michael S. Horton, *Lord and Servant: A Covenantal Christology* (Louisville: Westminster/John Knox, 2005), 178–241.

7   For a conversation between the *Christus Victor*, penal substitutionary, and other models of the atonement, see James Beilby and Paul R. Eddy, eds., *The Nature of the Atonement: Four Views* (Downers Grove, IL: InterVarsity Press, 2006).

cannot shout at people or scream down upon them. They must feel that we are with them, that we are saying that both of us are sinners, and they must know these are not just words, but that we mean what we say."[8] This isn't strategy or piety; it's how Jesus found us in the first place.

This is also part of the reason why so-called "social ministry" isn't a side issue to the Great Commission. The Great Commission teaches the nations, after all, "whatsoever I have commanded you" (Matt 28:20 KJV). Part of the way we teach the gospel of Christ is to teach what is *normal*— that is, what God created good and will redeem in the coming kingdom of Jesus. When we purify water or care for AIDS patients or combat poverty or alleviate hunger, we are announcing the kingdom by identifying the curse. This is not the way it's supposed to be, we demonstrate. And we show, by loving whole persons holistically, the kind of redemption Jesus has accomplished at the cross and empty tomb—deliverance from every aspect of the reign of death in the eternal kingdom of Christ.

The cross of Christ establishes both the universal scope of the mission of Christ and the freeness of the gospel offer. Jesus is, after all, the Savior of "the world" (literally, the word here is *cosmos*, John 3:16–17; 4:42). The sacrifice of Christ for the sins of the world further grounds the global and cosmic nature of the Great Commission.

Unlike some aberrant theologies of the recent past, the global scope of the cross doesn't mean simply that Christ's death makes humans objectively right with God apart from conversion to Christ. God propitiated our sins at the cross, yes, and we announce reconciliation everywhere through the cross. But this reconciliation comes through the sinner's union with Christ as his substitute and representative. Thus, the apostle John writes: "And *He Himself* is the propitiation for our sins, and not for ours only but also for the whole world" (1 John 2:2 NKJV, emphasis added).

The blessings of the atonement come only through union with Christ the covenant king, as we are "hidden in Christ" so that His life is our life and His death is our death (Col 3:3–4). Before our union with Christ, Scripture writes, we too were "children of wrath, like the rest of mankind" (Eph 2:2 ESV). Jesus propitiates the wrath of God in His sacrifice, but the benefits of this propitiation become the believer's when he comes into

---

8 Francis A. Schaeffer, *Death in the City*, in *The Complete Works of Francis A. Schaeffer*, vol. 4 (Wheaton: Crossway, 1982), 209. I am indebted to Barry Hankins's biography of Schaeffer for pointing out this quote in his treatment of Schaeffer's philosophy of mission. Barry Hankins, *Francis Schaeffer and the Shaping of Evangelical America* (Grand Rapids: Eerdmans, 2008), 114.

union with Christ through belief in the gospel. This faith union is the transition from condemnation to righteousness, from wrath to grace, from the dominion of Satan to the kingdom of Christ (Col 1:13–14).

The cosmic scope of the atonement is a double-edged sword. Jesus grounds the free offer of the gospel in the fact that "all is ready" (Luke 14:16–17). The apostles do not simply instruct unbelievers to believe; they plead with *all* unbelievers to come to Christ (that is, to abandon all other hope of salvation except in the substitutionary death and resurrection of Jesus) on the basis of the provision of the atonement (Acts 2:40; 2 Cor 5:20).

Indeed, the apostles do not merely *invite* all people to come to Christ (though they certainly do that); they also *command* all people to do so (Acts 17:30–31). Those who refuse to come to Christ insist on standing before God without a Mediator. Thus, they bear their own sins (Num 18:22; John 3:18) and receive a heightened condemnation as those who have "trampled" the blood of Christ (Heb 10:26–31). The freeness of the gospel offer means that Great Commission Christians must crucify any hesitation to proclaim the gospel to any sinner in any place at any time. The gospel of the apostles goes to all sinners without distinction.

The *New Hampshire Confession of Faith* (1833) contains a succinct and powerful expression of this biblical truth in its article, "On the Freeness of Salvation." The confession states: "That the blessings of salvation are made free to all by the gospel; that it is the immediate duty of all to accept them by a cordial, and obedient faith; and that nothing prevents the salvation of the greatest sinner on earth except his own voluntary refusal to submit to the Lord Jesus Christ, which refusal will subject him to an aggravated condemnation."[9] This statement resonates with the New Testament mandate for Christians to plead with persuasion and urgency for all sinners—on behalf of Christ Himself—to be reconciled to God through the atoning mission of Jesus (2 Cor 5:17–6:3).

The resurrection establishes the authority and the power Jesus delegates to the church in the Great Commission task. The resurrection of Jesus means that He is the righteous One (Dan 12:2–3). He is the true Israel, who has been raised from the dead (Ezek 37:13–14). He is the propitiation of Yahweh's wrath against rebellious humanity. He has been vindicated as the anointed human king of the cosmos (Rom 1:2–4). This is why the resurrection is so pivotal in the apostolic preaching of the Great Commission,

---

9 William L. Lumpkin, *Baptist Confessions of Faith*, rev. ed. (Valley Forge, PA: Judson Press, 1969), 363.

so much so that Paul was said to be preaching "Jesus and the resurrection" when he stirred the crowds in Athens (Acts 17:18).

The apostles sound less like television evangelists and more like military strategists at Pentecost and beyond. The resurrection of Jesus is good news for Israel (Acts 13:30–32), but very bad news for the cosmic powers and their allies (Acts 2:22–36; 1 Pet 3:21–22). "The resurrection constitutes Jesus as the world's true sovereign, the 'son of god' who claims absolute allegiance from everyone and everything within creation," notes biblical scholar N. T. Wright. "He is the start of the creator's new world: its pilot project, indeed its pilot."[10]

The apostolic preaching of the cross is indeed necessary for the Great Commission mandate. But the preaching of a sacrificial atonement without the bodily resurrection of Jesus is to no avail (1 Cor 15:15–19). Those who come to Jesus for salvation, the Scriptures testify, must "believe in your heart that God raised him from the dead" in order to be saved (Rom 10:9 ESV). This is not simply some sort of test of faith, as though one must believe a seemingly unbelievable miracle in order to "prove" that one is really trusting in Christ. Instead, believing in the resurrection is part of what it *means* to trust Christ. The believer counts the crucifixion of Messiah as the penalty for his sin—and he counts the resurrection of Messiah as his acceptance before the Father. The resurrection is for Jesus the transition from sin-bearing substitute—under the wrath of God—to the vindicated substitute inheriting the blessing of God.[11] When the believer is united with Jesus in His resurrection, his life is now "hidden with Christ in God" (Col 3:3).

This resurrection focus of faith is seen perhaps most clearly in the interchange between Jesus and Martha after the death of Lazarus. When Jesus mentions the resurrection, Martha turns her attention to the eschaton—when the graves of the righteous are opened. Jesus proclaims: "I am the resurrection" (John 11:25), before asking Martha the most soul-penetrating question she had ever heard: "Do you believe this?" (John 11:26). Through His Body the church, Jesus now asks the same question of every sinner on the planet.

---

10 N. T. Wright, *The Resurrection of the Son of God*, Christian Origins and the Question of God, vol. 3 (Minneapolis: Fortress, 2003), 731.

11 For an analysis of the resurrection as the "justification" of Jesus as the righteous new humanity, see Richard B. Gaffin Jr., *The Centrality of the Resurrection: A Study in Paul's Soteriology* (Grand Rapids: Baker, 1978), 116.

Union with Jesus in crucifixion and resurrection is seen also in the baptism mandate of Jesus in the Great Commission. The church is to make disciples of all nations, "baptizing them in the name of the Father and of the Son and of the Holy Spirit" (Matt 28:19b ESV). Baptism is not merely a *Bar Mitzvah* of initiation into Christianity. It is not accidental that baptism is done with water—the element of the wrath of God in the flood judgment of the world (1 Pet 3:20–21) and the element of the seas, which in the Old Testament represent chaos and hostility to the Creator.[12] Jesus speaks of His death under the curse of God as a "baptism" He must undergo (Mark 10:38–39; Luke 12:50). The apostle Paul speaks of the Old Testament Israelites as "baptized" when they passed safely through the waters of judgment (1 Cor 10:1–2).

In the new covenant, baptism signifies the burial of the believer with Jesus in the chaotic waters of death and the resurrection of the believer with Jesus from the grips of the grave (Rom 6:3–9). As such, baptism is itself a call to battle. When believers from every nation go down into the waters, they appeal to God for rescue from the condemnation of the "angels, authorities, and powers" which have been swept away by the resurrection triumph of the warrior Messiah (1 Pet 3:21–22).

THE GREAT COMMISSION AND THE OBEDIENCE OF FAITH

This redemptive plan focuses on the glory of God, but not in an abstract, self-focused sense. Instead, the glory of God finds its expression in the incarnation, atonement, and exaltation of Jesus of Nazareth. The entire sweep of redemptive history finds its goal in the glory of God *in Christ*. God is glorified when His messianic king is recognized as the rightful governor of the entire created universe (Phil 2:7–11). For this reason, the apostle Peter is able to speak of God's glory as focused particularly on the kingdom inheritance of Jesus as Messiah (1 Pet 4:11), a doxological theme that is in line with Old Testament messianic promise (Pss 2:4–12; 110:1–7). In the new covenant,

---

12 This is true from the opening words of Scripture when the Creator Spirit hovers over "the waters" of "the deep" in the formless and void earth. The Old Testament prophets speak of the cosmic warfare as a struggle between God and "the sea" or "the sea dragon" (see, for instance, Isa 27:1). And in the final New Jerusalem in the new earth, the apostle John reveals that "the sea was no more" (Rev 21:1 ESV).

God unveils the identity of the redemptive focus—Jesus of Nazareth—and commands all nations to surrender to His kingship.

This Christocentric focus of the Great Commission is imperiled as perhaps never before. Religious pluralism, now rampant in mainline denominations, insists that Christ is one path among many possible paths to the divine.[13] More subtle, and thus more deadly to the Great Commission fervor of the church, is the emergence among so-called evangelical theologians and missionaries of "inclusivism"—the idea that persons may be saved through Christ without explicit faith in Him.[14] Some argue that the unevangelized may express faith through the testimony of general revelation. Others argue that the Spirit is at work in the other world religions, with a mission of His own that is wider than the proclamation of the name of Jesus.[15] Still others appeal to the example of Old Testament believers, who were saved without knowing the name of Jesus, as hope for the salvation of those who never hear the gospel. And, of course, many of our churches are filled with the popular notion that it would be "unfair" of God to condemn someone who was never confronted with the gospel.

Such notions cut the heart out of the Great Commission, both in terms of its urgency and its focus on the kingship of Christ. After the ascension of Jesus, it would have been quite uncomplicated for the apostles to call for Jews to hope in the future messianic empire, consistent with Old Testament prophetic hope. The apostles could have warned their contemporaries that their works or tribal identities could not save them. They could have pointed to the righteousness of an unnamed Davidic Messiah as the source of salvation.

And yet, their commission from Jesus would not allow for generic sincerity, or even "faith" in a generic Christ. The Book of Acts explodes with a passionate call for explicit faith in "this Jesus whom you crucified" (Acts 2:36). This is precisely what Jesus meant when He compared salvation to Moses' lifting up the bronze serpent in the wilderness (John 3:14–15). Even as the Israelites saved from the venomous bites were to look to the emblem,

---

13 See, for instance, John Hick, *God Has Many Names* (Louisville: Westminster/John Knox, 1986).

14 For a sketch of inclusivist arguments, see Clark H. Pinnock, "Toward a More Inclusive Eschatology," in *Looking into the Future: Evangelical Essays on Eschatology*, ed. David W. Baker (Grand Rapids: Baker, 2001), 249–62. For a critique of the position, see Ronald H. Nash, *Is Jesus the Only Savior?* (Grand Rapids: Zondervan, 1994).

15 See Molly Truman Marshall, *Joining the Dance: A Theology of the Spirit* (Valley Forge, PA: Judson, 2003) and Amos Yong, *Beyond the Impasse: Toward a Pneumatological Theology of Religions* (Grand Rapids: Baker, 2003).

so must those rescued from the death-bite of the serpent of Eden look in faith to this particular One who was sacrificed outside the gates of Jerusalem.

But what if, one may ask, the hypothetical "man on an island" acknowledges the Creator God revealed in general revelation, and is convicted of sin by the Spirit—a sin uncovered by the law written on his heart? What if he then throws himself on the mercy of this God for forgiveness?[16] This is somewhat like asking whether someone would need to call on Christ if that individual never sinned and perfectly obeyed the law of God. Such a situation *never* happens. The apostle Paul anticipates such questions, and answers them decisively—one cannot call on Christ without faith, one cannot come to faith without preaching, and one cannot hear preaching unless the church is faithful to the Great Commission (Rom 10:14–17).

The Spirit does not work independently of God's purpose to glorify Christ through the new covenant witness of the church. It is not unusual that Jesus should tell His disciples that the mission of the Spirit is to testify to His messianic identity and to glorify Him (John 15:26; 16:14), if in fact the goal of God's kingdom purposes is to see to it that Christ "will come to have first place in everything" (Col 1:18).

Calling on Jesus as Lord is not a hoop through which one jumps to reach the goal of eternal life—Jesus Himself is eternal life, and the confession of Jesus as Lord is the goal (Phil 2:9–11). A "sinner's prayer" is a part of coming to faith in Christ, but it is not a formula. The confession of Jesus as Lord is an acknowledgment that Jesus is the Creator God who alone can save (Isa 45:23; Rom 10:9). It is the sinner's bending the knee before the tribunal of God and confessing in the present what one day the entire creation will acknowledge—that Jesus of Nazareth is the just and righteous ruler of the cosmos.

That is why the Great Commission focuses on the identity and mission of Jesus—and why it stirs such controversy from first-century Jerusalem to twenty-first century Baghdad. And that is why the evangelistic task of the church must focus on Christ, not simply on avoiding hell or healing one's marriage or finding purpose in one's life. This is also why the Great Commission centers on preaching and teaching. In the Commission, the proclamation of the gospel comes with the authority of Jesus Himself—and the Bible promises that the Spirit will convict of sin through the preaching of the Scriptures (1 Cor 1:18–25). Effective and compassionate social ministry

---

16 This is the possibility mentioned by Millard J. Erickson, *How Shall They Be Saved? The Destiny of Those Who Do Not Hear of Jesus* (Grand Rapids: Baker, 1996), 143–58.

is part of the Great Commission (Matt 25:31–46), but a social ministry that dispenses with gospel proclamation is no longer Christian, and neither is a preaching ministry that ignores the pleas of the hurting. Videos, musicals, and dramatic presentations may have their place, but they do not carry with them the authority of Jesus—an authority that is present every time the oracles of God are proclaimed in simplicity and in truth.[17]

Where Jesus is announced, though, the Spirit shows up—with power. When marketing a product, a company or sales force might do demographic research to see whether the product "fits" with the already-embedded desires and cultural expectations of a given people group. McDonald's Corporation, for instance, wouldn't put a lot of effort into expanding the hamburger market into a village with a centuries-long devotion to the Hindu reverence for cows as signs of the sacred. A dog meat company isn't going to find many takers in West Frankfort, Illinois. It isn't that way with the gospel, though, since the gospel is itself "the power of God to salvation" (Rom 1:16).

When the good news of the story of Jesus is announced, the Spirit engages the hostile powers. Think about how it is that you came to faith in Christ. Was it primarily a long consideration of the historical or philosophical facts about the Christian religion? For some of you, perhaps it was. For most of us, though, our conversion involved no new argument. Instead, we heard a message we had heard before—Jesus is Lord, He was crucified and raised from the dead for sinners, He calls you to repentance and faith, believe and follow Him—and suddenly this story hit us with a new force. Suddenly it seemed *personal* and scary and exhilarating. We found ourselves wanting to do something we'd never wanted to do before: to *surrender*.

This is what some theologians refer to as "effectual calling," and it sounds more complicated than it actually is. All it means is that when Jesus is announced, the Spirit goes to war. And when the Spirit goes to war against the powers, He frees people from the grip of those powers, and of their own self-delusion. The Spirit assembles the evidence against us—convicts

---

17   Edmund Clowney offers a helpful corrective to the temptation to rely on dramatic gospel presentations as somehow "more effective" than direct proclamation in evangelism: "An actor pleads with the viewer to come to *him* and to trust in *him*," Clowney notes, but "the actor is not Jesus." See Edmund P. Clowney, *Preaching Christ in All of Scripture* (Wheaton: Crossway, 2003), 49, emphasis original. In the proclaimed Word, however, whether in public preaching or personal verbal witness, the oracles of God, inspired by the Spirit of Christ, actually do speak with the voice of Jesus Himself.

us of sin—and He displays Jesus to us in a way that brings "light"—the light that scatters darkness and creates new realities (2 Cor 4:4–6).

There is no people group, then, that is culturally "unreachable" with the gospel. The mission of Christ goes forward even in conditions of religious hostility or political oppression or cultural rejection precisely because we know the gospel is never received by the support of any of these factors. The most enraged hearer of the Word of Christ—the voodoo priestess, the Ku Klux Klan Grand Wizard, the atheist astrophysicist, the half-drunk fraternity pledge—can be, instantly, stopped in his or her tracks with the vision of Christ just as surely as was Saul of Tarsus of old. Indeed, the Spirit loves, it seems, to show up in places and among people the rest of the world sees as marginal or useless or beyond hope.

THE GREAT COMMISSION AND THE COMMUNITY OF THE KINGDOM

A theology of the Great Commission is inextricably tied up with a theology of the church. King Jesus, after all, commands the believing community to baptize the nations and to plant congregations across the planet. Contemporary evangelicals seem to recognize at least this much. What we often miss, however, is the *authority* Christ grants to His church in the Great Commission. At the calling of the apostle Paul, Jesus does not say, "Saul, Saul, why are you persecuting a voluntary association that mentions Me in their constitution and by-laws?" Instead, he asks, "Why are you persecuting *Me*?" (Acts 9:4, emphasis added).

The New Testament presents the union of the Head and His body as a mysterious "one-flesh" union (Eph 5:31–32). What is true of the one is to be true of the other (Matt 18:18–20; cf. Isa 22:22). This means that the church is to mirror the mission of Jesus in seeking the salvation of the world (Matt 18:10–14). A nonevangelistic church is more than just a disobedient body (although it is that). A nonevangelistic church is denying before the nations that Jesus is the Lamb of God who takes away the sins of the world. And that is blasphemy.

The church, however, is to throb with the same evangelistic fervor that fuels its King—and to call, with His authority, the nations to surrender before His coming global reign. Thus, the apostle John sees the universal invitation to Christ coming not only from Jesus, but also from His Spirit and His Bride, the church (Rev 22:16–17). A church that is not enflamed for evangelism, missions, and church growth is not just practically ineffective, it is theologically anemic. A church that prides itself on its pristine confessional statements but is not seeing sinners converted to Christ and is not fueling the global missions endeavor has a defective Christology. It may have some cognitive knowledge of the attributes of God or the *ordo salutis*, but a church that does not long for the expansion of the name of Christ to the nations is at cross-purposes with the Father God (Ps 2:8).

A nonevangelistic church is also in the midst of an identity crisis. This is precisely because the Great Commission is not a "program" of a voluntary association. Instead, the Bible presents both the church and the Great Commission as parts of the sweeping and awe-inspiring unveiling of the mystery of Christ. This is clear in the apostle Paul's appeal for the Roman church's support for the mission to the Gentiles—an appeal we know as the Book of Romans. Paul did not nag or prod the church to fulfill grudgingly its duty. Instead, he pointed them to the climactic eschatological nature of their very existence as the purpose for a global missions thrust. The advance of the gospel is "the mystery that was kept secret for long ages but has now been disclosed and through the prophetic writings has been made known to all nations, according to the command of the eternal God, to bring about the obedience of faith" (Rom 16:25–26 ESV). A congregation that is not ignited for the salvation of the nations doesn't know what time it is.

The New Testament concept of the church is not that of a place to encourage one another in discipleship and to pool together missions offerings. It is a declaration of war. In the church, the triumphant Warrior-King has established an outpost of the kingdom—a colony of the reign that will one day engulf the world (Eph 1:20–23).[18] The New Testament presents the church as a sign to the demonic powers—a sign of their doom (Eph 3:10). This is specifically true in terms of the reconciliation experienced within the church between Jews and Gentiles as the one people of God (Eph 3:6). The gathering of a unified flock means the defeat of the wolves and the triumph of the Shepherd-King. Preaching to the Gentiles is bringing to light the mystery hidden for ages (Eph 3:1–10; Acts 15:14–17), precisely because it is the onset of the triumph of the kingdom (Rom 8:19–23).

---

18   For an analysis of the relationship between Jesus' future role as ruler of the universe and His present role as ruler of the church, see Peter T. O'Brien, *The Letter to the Ephesians*, Pillar New Testament Commentary (Grand Rapids: Eerdmans, 1999), 146–52.

This means that the focus of the church, both in terms of theological conviction and missiological action, ought to be the Great Commission. This Great Commission vision, however, must be rooted in a *theology* of the purposes of God and the mystery of Christ. We have forgotten the big picture. This is why churches that seek to minimize theology cannot long sustain the Great Commission. This is why so many churches—large and small, "traditional" and "contemporary"—are so irrelevant and frankly boring. This is why contemporary gospel ministers too often more resemble attendees at an insurance sales convention than pioneers of a coming global empire. The watching world should identify local congregations as globally engaged in evangelism.

Churches should cultivate peace and unity within the congregation—not just to maintain order, but also to herald the coming kingdom of Christ. Rather than planting congregations based merely on common interests or demographics (most commonly, churches geared toward upwardly mobile young couples), churches should intentionally seek to manifest a commonality in the Spirit of the risen Christ (Gal 6:12–15), not in shared tribal identity or economic status. What would a Jewish-Palestinian Christian congregation on the West Bank say about the gospel? What would a racially mixed congregation in South Africa demonstrate about the triumph of Christ? What would it mean for the Great Commission if a high-powered Wall Street church looked to the leadership of a godly, Spirit-gifted layman, who also happened to be a public school janitor (Jas 2:1–6)? Such things would say precisely what was said in the first century when uncircumcised Gentiles took up offerings to aid their Jewish brothers and sisters in Christ (Rom 15:22–28). It would say: "Jesus is Lord." And human beings aren't the only ones watching.

CONCLUSION

In the end, demonic powers don't tremble before denominational programs or bureaucratic public relations campaigns. What they fear is something more ancient, more mysterious, more personal. What they fear is not a program but a Person—a Person with a name, an authority, and an inheritance. Since the church bears the Spirit of the Anointed One (1 Pet 4:14), the satanic powers lash out violently against it (John 15:25–16:11). The question of the missionary advance of the church, then, is the same question once voiced to the church's King in His hometown synagogue: "Have you come to destroy us?"

Wherever God has put us in His kingdom, we are all to be missionaries and we are all to be theologians. The mission doesn't belong to someone else; it belongs to you (if you belong to Christ). And thinking through what's happening around you—theology—isn't just for academics.

Theology means a word about God. Scripture tells us the definitive *Logos* about our *Theos* isn't a systematic theology text or a Hebrew grammar book, as important as these might be. Theology isn't a "what," but a "Who." He is our brother, and our Lord. He cries for sinners, loves them, warns them of the wrath to come, and promises them the universe itself if they turn to Him.

Theology doesn't just think. Theology walks. Theology weeps. Theology bleeds.

OUTSIDE THE CAMP[1]

David Platt

Hallelujah! Praise God in His sanctuary. Praise Him in His mighty heavens.
Praise Him for His powerful acts; praise Him for His abundant greatness.
Praise Him with trumpet blast; praise Him with harp and lyre.
Praise Him with tambourine and dance; praise Him with flute and strings.
Praise Him with resounding cymbals; praise Him with clashing cymbals.
Let everything that breathes praise the LORD. *Hallelujah! (Psalm 150)*

One purpose: the glory of God. He has created us, He has commissioned us, and He has commanded us to devote our lives and our churches to His glory in all the world. This is our purpose.

I know that as a pastor I have nothing to bring to the table apart from the Word of God, and so I want to go right to Hebrews 13. I want to read from what I believe is a summary statement of the entire book of Hebrews. Then, based on this passage, I want to ask us one question: "Are we going to die in our religion, or are we going to die in our devotion?"

THE CHALLENGE: RETREAT OR RISK?

God's people have had to face this question throughout history. Believers in the book of Hebrews faced this question in the first century, and I believe it is a central question facing the church today.

---

1 This sermon was originally delivered at the Southern Baptist Convention Pastors' Conference, 22 June 2009 (video available from http://www.sbcannualmeeting.net/sbc09/sbcam.asp?cat=home). This chapter has been adapted from the original sermon transcript.

Hebrews 13:11–14 says, "For the bodies of those animals whose blood is brought into the holy of holies by the high priest as a sin offering are burned outside the camp. Therefore Jesus also suffered outside the gate, so that He might sanctify the people by His own blood. Let us then go to Him outside the camp, bearing His disgrace.

For here we do not have an enduring city; instead, we seek the one to come."

Many questions surround the book of Hebrews. Who wrote this book? When was it written? We know that it was most likely written to Jewish Christians in a time when it was not easy to be a Jewish Christian. Full conversion to Christ was costly in the first century, and apparently many believers reading this letter were tempted to shrink back from their faith. In addition, they were tempted to fall away from their mission. They had been given a task to take the gospel from Jerusalem to Judea, Samaria, and the ends of the earth (Acts 1:8), and they were holding back.

Across the whole of Hebrews, the author seems to be addressing two primary struggles in the church. First, they were driven by formalism. Somewhere along the way, *how* they worshipped had become more important than *who* they worshipped. It was style without substance, and the author of Hebrews spends chapter after chapter showing how the religious practices of Judaism pointed to the glory of Christ. Still, the readers were in danger of missing Christ, driven by their formalism.

Second, they were paralyzed by fear. Whether it was the threat of expulsion or persecution from the unbelieving Jewish community, it was costly for these believers to follow Christ. Many of them were trying to figure out a way to stay in the camp of Judaism as Christians. The author of Hebrews, though, was saying that it could not be done. They had been given a mission to declare the glory of Christ to the ends of the earth, and He was saying to them, "You have two options. You can retreat from the mission that you have been given, or you can risk everything for that mission."

I believe God's people throughout redemptive history have had to face these same two options over and over again: Retreat or risk everything.

A STORY OF RETREAT

Much of the background of the Book of Hebrews is the scene at Kadesh Barnea in Numbers 13. The people of God were standing on the brink of the Promised Land, the land God had guaranteed to give them. They sent twelve spies out to look over the land, and they came back with the following report.

Numbers 13:31–33 says, "But the men who had gone up with him responded, 'We can't go up against the people because they are stronger than we are!' So they gave a negative report to the Israelites about the land they had scouted: 'The land we passed through to explore is one that devours its inhabitants, and all the people we saw in it are men of great size. We even saw the Nephilim there.' (The offspring of Anak were descended from the Nephilim.) 'To ourselves we seemed like grasshoppers, and we must have seemed the same to them.'" The story goes on: "Then the whole community broke into loud cries, and the people wept that night. All the Israelites complained about Moses and Aaron, and the whole community told them, 'If only we had died in the land of Egypt, or if only we had died in this wilderness! Why is the LORD bringing us into this land to die by the sword? Our wives and little children will become plunder. Wouldn't it be better for us to go back to Egypt?' So they said to one another, 'Let's appoint a leader and go back to Egypt'" (Num 14:1–4).

They were retreating. With the mission in front of them to take the Promised Land for the glory of God, they were saying, "We want to go back. We don't trust God."

Amidst their rebellion, Moses interceded for them, and God answered Moses' prayer. Listen to how God responded in Numbers 14:20–23: "The LORD responded, 'I have pardoned [them] as you requested. Yet as surely as I live and as the whole earth is filled with the LORD's glory, none of the men who have seen My glory and the signs I performed in Egypt and in the wilderness, and have tested Me these 10 times and did not obey Me, will ever see the land I swore to [give] their fathers. None of those who have despised Me will see it.'"

It got even more severe. In verses 32–35, God said to His People, "But as for you, your corpses will fall in this wilderness. Your children will be shepherds in the wilderness for 40 years and bear the penalty for your acts of unfaithfulness until all your corpses lie [scattered] in the wilderness. You will bear the consequences of your sins 40 years based on the number of the 40 days that you scouted the land, a year for each day. You will know My displeasure. I, the LORD, have spoken. I swear that I will do this to the entire evil community that has conspired against Me. They will come to an end in the wilderness, and there they will die."

Don't miss the gravity of what happened at Kadesh Barnea. God forgave His people. He had bound up His glory in delivering them from slavery in Egypt, and He was not going to let them go back. This is a picture of God's grace and forgiveness. Yet at the same time in Numbers 14, we see a picture of God's discipline, leaving His people to wander in the wilderness until they die.

They had retreated.

The story of retreat is repeated throughout redemptive history. Years later, as the people of God prepared finally to take the Promised Land, they were told to rid the land of the Canaanites and all their foreign gods. Yet in the days to come they retreated from this mission, and in the process they defamed the holiness of God among the nations.

Once established in the land, they rejected God as their King, telling Samuel, "'Look, you are old, and your sons do not follow your example. Therefore, appoint a king to judge us the same as all the other nations have" (1 Sam 8:5). In the process, they defamed the majesty of God among the nations.

Over and over again, this is the story of God's people. As God calls them to the mission of declaring His glory to all nations, they are tempted at every turn to retreat and turn back.

And so we fast forward to the book of Hebrews, and we find a similar picture. We see the church entrusted with the mission of God to declare the glory of Christ to all nations. Once again, the people of God are retreating.

And so I invite us to fast forward a couple thousand years to 2009. Here is what I see:

I see a world suffering from catastrophic natural disasters. Over the last year, cyclones in Myanmar, earthquakes in China and Pakistan, and floods in Nepal and Bangladesh have killed over a quarter of a million people. Most of them had never even heard the gospel. As we know, surviving them are a billion others who at this moment still have not heard His name.

I see a world where half of the population is living on less than two dollars a day, while we sit here extremely rich in comparison.

I see the nation of India, where there are more people living below the poverty line than there are people in the United States all together.

I see a world where today alone, 26,000 children have died of either starvation or a preventable disease.

I see our dogs and our cats eating better than our brothers and sisters in the Sudan.

I see a world where last fall, in one week alone, 50,000 people died of AIDS, over 100,000 children died of hunger-related diseases, thousands of other children were trafficked around the world for human sexual exploitation, and hundreds of men and women died in an earthquake in Pakistan. All of that occurred in one week last fall, and yet for so many, our greatest concern was how our football team played.

On top of all this, I see thousands upon thousands of our brothers and sisters in China and North Korea and Laos and Saudi Arabia imprisoned and killed today because of their faith in Christ.

I see all of these things, and then I look back in the church culture we have created and the church congregations we are leading, and there is so little risk for the mission. We have retreated.

We have retreated into our nice big buildings where we sit in our nice cushioned chairs. Where we are insulated and isolated from the inner city and spiritual lostness of the world. Where we have given a tip of our hats to world missions and evangelism, while we go on designing endless programs that revolve around us. And when we should be in the firing line for God, the majority of our members are still in the nurseries of our churches drinking spiritual milk.

We stand today at our Kadesh Barnea, and we have two options. We can retreat from the mission of declaring the glory of Christ in all nations. We can retreat into a land of religious formalism and wasted opportunity. Or we can risk everything for the mission that we have been created for. And I want to say to you, let's risk it all!

A CALL TO RISK

For the glory of Christ among a billion people who have not even heard His name, let's risk it all!

For the countless millions in your city and my city who do not know Christ and are headed to a Christless eternity, let's risk it all!

For the sake of our lives, our families, our communities, our churches, and our children's lives, let's risk it all!

Let's risk it all! For, if we retreat from this mission, God is gracious. He will forgive us. He will forgive us—but brothers and sisters, He may just leave us to wander in the wilderness until we die. He has done it with thousands of churches in the United States, and He could do it with any one of ours. Are we going to die in our religion, or are we going to die in our devotion?

Maybe you're thinking, "Don't you mean 'live' in our devotion?" Wouldn't that make a better sermon? Are we going to die in our religion, or "live" in our devotion? Possibly, but this is not what Hebrews 13 is saying.

"Let us go to Him outside the camp" (Heb 13:13). We need to put ourselves in the shoes of the original readers here, and we need to envision the images that came to their mind when they heard the phrase, "outside the camp."

Immediately, they thought of the dirty places. Leviticus 16:27–28 tells us that the bodies of the bull and the goat on the Day of Atonement were sacrificed and then burned outside the camp. "Outside the camp" was literally a representation of the sinfulness of God's people.

Leviticus 13:45–46 tells us that if you had an infectious skin disease, then you would go outside the camp. Lepers go outside the camp. It is not only a dirty place; it is a despised place.

And "outside the camp" is a dangerous place. Leviticus 23:13–14 says that blasphemers go "outside the camp" to be stoned.

Needless to say, you don't want to go outside the camp in Judaism. "Outside the camp" represents the dirty, the despised, and the dangerous places.

That is the imagery in verses 11 and 12, and it leads to the profound exhortation in verse 13, "Let us then go to Him." "Him" is Jesus, and the author of Hebrews is reminding us that Jesus Himself went outside the camp.

Jesus went to the dirty, to the despised, and to the dangerous place. He went outside the city gates, where He was cursed on a tree, enduring shame and bearing disgrace. The author of Hebrews says, "Jesus is with the dirty, the despised, and the dangerous. And if we want to be with Jesus, we will be in those places, as well."

Brothers and sisters, in so many ways, we are prone to avoid where Jesus really is. Instead of going to Jesus at the dirty and despised and dangerous place, we craft a much different Jesus. We envision a cleaner, more comfortable Jesus.

A Jesus who does not call us to go to the hard places.

A Jesus who calls us to the easy places where there is little risk involved.

We mold Jesus into our own image so that He looks like us. We create a nice, middle-class American Jesus. And at this point, we need to realize that as long as Jesus looks a lot like us, then every Sunday morning when we sing our songs and practice our worship, the reality is that we are not actually worshiping Jesus. Instead, we are worshiping ourselves.

Meanwhile, Jesus is among the abandoned and the poor and the destitute and the hurting. Jesus is in the places in the world that are most filled with disease and the regions of the world that are most known for terror.

Do we really want to be with Jesus?

I remember having my eyes opened to Jesus when I moved down to seminary in New Orleans. In my first semester, I was in a class where we were paired with a church in the city for evangelism. The church my team worked with was right in the middle of the French Quarter. I remember our first meeting with the pastor of that church. He looked at us and said, "If you can learn to do ministry here, you can do ministry anywhere in the world." Then he put us out in the streets and said, "Have a great semester!"

So we walked down with our eyes wide open into Jackson Square. We saw fortunetellers, tarot card readers, and voodoo queens and kings who had all set up tables on the streets. We decided we wanted to join them in the action. So one day we set up a table of our own, right next to the voodoo queen of New Orleans. We unfolded our table, put a decorative cloth over it, chairs behind it, and a sign in front of it that said, "We'll tell your future for free."

People would come to our table, sit down, and ask, "You will tell me my future for free?""

"Yes," we would respond. Then we would ask them a couple of questions that would establish the fact that they had sin in their lives, and we would look at them and say, "Your future doesn't look very good." Then we would share the gospel with them, telling them how their future could change through Christ.

During the days at that table and the subsequent days that followed, we got to know all sorts of people in Jackson Square, from self-professed pagans to homeless men and women. We entered in to the uneasy, sometimes uncomfortable process of being involved in the details of their lives. One by one, people came to faith in Christ and were baptized. Before Hurricane Katrina hit, about forty to fifty people gathered every Sunday morning in the French Quarter for worship and breakfast together.

I went back to New Orleans not long after Katrina. As I was walking along the street, a man with tattoo-covered arms approached me. This brother had come to Christ and had been baptized through our ministry in the French Quarter. He gave me a strong hug, looked at me with tears in his eyes, and said, "David, I want you to know that I am now leading the ministry in the French Quarter every week." Indeed, Jesus is at work among the dirty places.

He is also at work among the dangerous places. I had the privilege by God's grace to teach at a seminary in the world's largest Muslim-dominated nation, Indonesia. In order to graduate from this seminary, every student is required to plant a church in a Muslim community with at least 30 new baptized believers. As I spoke at their graduation, I looked across the faces of students who had all met this requirement. It was a solemn celebration, for two of their classmates had been murdered in the middle of their church-planting efforts that year.

Jesus is at work among underground house churches in Asia. During my first visit to one particular country, God sovereignly ordained a meeting with two underground house church leaders. They asked me if I would be willing to do some training with them in God's Word. I told them I would, and I prepared a short Bible study to teach them.

We met in a secretive, closed location. As I walked in, these leaders sat quietly around the room with their Bibles open, ready to study it at the risk of their lives. I can't remember where we started, but I do remember that eight hours later we were still going strong. At the end of the day, they said they wanted to do this again—all day the next day!

So the next morning we began studying again. We were walking through the book of Nehemiah, and I explained to them the book's background and history. Then I showed them the importance of the Word of God in the people of God in Nehemiah 8. Afterwards we took a break, and as I looked around the room, I could see that these leaders were gathering in small groups to discuss something specific. After a few moments, one of them came over to me and said, "We have never heard all of that about the Book of Nehemiah, and we would like to learn more. Would you be willing to teach us every book of the Old Testament?"

I laughed. "That would take a long time," I said.

They said, "But we want to know God's Word. We will make whatever sacrifice is necessary to learn it." So for the next ten days, we studied all day every day from Genesis to Malachi. On the last day of training, we had completed the Old Testament, and I began teaching them some more general truths. But about an hour into that last day, one of the brothers in the back raised his hand and said, "We have a problem."

"What is the problem?" I asked.

He responded. "You have taught us the whole Old Testament, but you have not taught us the New Testament." I paused while he continued. "We would like to learn the New Testament today, please." For the next 11 hours, we walked from Matthew to Revelation.

These brothers and sisters love the Word. It means something to them. They risk their lives to know it. Imagine going to a worship service late at night with these believers. You travel by cover of darkness through roads and winding paths to a small house in a village where sixty believers have crammed it full. One small light bulb hangs in the middle of the room as brothers and sisters sit on the floor or on little stools, huddled together with their Bibles open, ready to study God's Word.

We imagine this picture and we think, "What can we do to help these believers? Can we take up an offering? What can we send to them?" Ladies and gentlemen, I want to remind us that the Holy Spirit of God is doing just fine in that country without all of the resources we surround ourselves with. These churches believe that the Word of God with the Spirit of God is enough to accomplish the mission of God, and they are right.

Do we believe this?

I was preparing for a trip to the Sudan, a country where thousands of our brothers and sisters have been killed in a persecution of genocidal proportions over the last twenty years. A couple of months before I was to leave, I received a state Baptist paper in the mail. Two articles lined the front page, side by side. On the left the headline read, "First Baptist Church celebrates new $23 million building." The article went on to talk about all the fine features of this new building. On the right, the headline read, "Baptist relief helps Sudanese refugees." This article talked about how 350,000 refugees in Sudan were dying of malnutrition and might not make it to the end of the year. At the conclusion of this article, the writer said, "Baptists have raised money to send to the Sudanese refugees."

I thought this was wonderful until I read the last sentence. It read, "Baptists have raised $5,000 to send to refugees in Sudan."

Please do not misunderstand. This is not intended to be an indictment of that particular church. It is not even intended primarily to be an indictment of church buildings. Most pointedly, this is an indictment of us. We have prioritized our comforts over the needs of the world around us, and we need to repent. We need to repent and risk it all. We need to repent and join our brothers and sisters in Cuba, India, China, the Middle East, and Central Asia who are giving their lives for the sake of Christ's glory among all peoples.

But why? Why would we risk everything? Why are our brothers and sisters risking everything, and why should we join them? This question leads us to the beauty of Hebrews 13:14: "For here we do not have an enduring city; instead, we seek the one to come."

This is the dominant theme at the end of the book of Hebrews. We are longing for another country, a heavenly one. We do not count this world our home. Brothers and sisters, we risk everything because we are supremely satisfied in Christ, and we are not living any longer for the comforts of the United States of America. We are living for another country, a land where we will see His face and enjoy His beauty. And we desire His glory more than we desire our own safety, our own comforts, and our own lives.

This is why we go. This is why we go to every corner in every inner city in the United States, because there are millions of people in this country right now heading to a Christless eternity, and we long for them to see the glory of God.

This is why we go to Africa, because there are three thousand tribes there worshiping animistic religions that are completely devoid of God, and God is worthy of all their glory.

This is why we go to Japan and Laos and Vietnam, because there are 350 million Buddhists in these countries who are following Buddha's rules and Buddha's regulations, and Buddha is not worthy of their glory. Jesus is worthy of their glory.

This is why we go to India, Pakistan, Bangladesh, Sri Lanka, and Nepal, because there are 950 million Hindus in those countries who are following more gods than you or I could even imagine, and there is only one God who is worthy of all of their glory.

This is why we go to China, North Korea, and Cuba, Communist nations that espouse philosophies that deny the existence of God. We go because there is indeed one God, and He is worthy of all their glory.

This is why we go to the tough places. This is why we go to the Middle East—because there are over 1.3 billion Muslims who are fasting and giving alms and making holy pilgrimages to Mecca and praying five times a day to a false god, but Jesus has died on the cross, risen from the grave, and ascended to the Father in heaven, and He alone is worthy of all their glory.

He is worthy of glory! This is why we go.

CONCLUSION

Brothers and sisters, God will make His glory known. Regardless of whether we retreat or risk everything, God will make His glory known.

He does not need you, and He does not need me. He does not need your church, and He does not need my church. He doesn't need this seminary or that seminary, and He doesn't need this state convention or that state convention. He does not need the North American Mission Board or the International Mission Board. The reality is that the entire Southern Baptist Convention could drop dead and turn to dust, and God will still make a great name for Himself among the nations.

We have this question before us. With the mammoth needs of a lost and dying world in front of us and with a mission to make the glory of God known in all the world, we must ask ourselves, "Are we going to die in our religion, or are we going to die in our devotion?" May God help us, by His grace, to choose the latter.

THE BIG PICTURE OF THE
GREAT COMMISSION[1]

H. Al Gilbert

What is the most important part of a jigsaw puzzle? Some might say the borders. Logically, if you get the borders in place, you can work from the outside in. Personally, I do not have the patience to sit and look at the pieces of a jigsaw puzzle. I mean, come on—it was a perfectly good picture. Why did someone break it?

If you are inexperienced like me, the most important part of a jigsaw puzzle is the "box top"—the picture. Without the picture in mind, we don't know what we are doing. We look at strange colors and shapes that don't fit together; we cannot make sense of all those little pieces without someone helping us know where they fit. We need the "box top"!

GOD HAS THE BIG PICTURE

Did you know that God has a "box top"? God has a *Big Picture* in mind! Life is more than strange shapes and pieces that don't fit together. God has a plan that will one day bring the pieces together for everyone to see. His *Big Picture* will give Him the glory He deserves! He has a global and eternal plan.

Our churches are filled with people searching to make the pieces of life fit together. Most are searching without an understanding of God's plan. Many will spend their lives staring at the pieces and never really discover how things go together. That's why we need to see the *Big Picture* and find ways to lead our churches to discover it!

---

1 This chapter is a revised and expanded version of the author's sermon originally preached in Alumni Chapel, The Southern Baptist Theological Seminary, April 12, 2000.

God's "Big Picture" Is Global

The plan of God includes more than the five percent of the world that lives in the United States. Look at a world map and think about it. We may be the fourth-largest country, but we still need to consider how big the rest of the world is.

Look at the Western Hemisphere. At first glance, we might think this is half of the world—it looks like half the map! Now, look at the other half of the map. See China? The population of this one country is greater than the population of all of the countries in the Western Hemisphere combined. Think about it. More people live in China than live in our hemisphere. The same is true for India. More people live in India than live in the Western Hemisphere! The world is so much bigger than we think.

That's why God's plan has to be big enough to give Him the glory He deserves! And it is bigger than we think. If we are going to find our place, we need to see our lives in the context of the global *Big Picture*.

God's "Big Picture" Is Eternal

From Genesis to Revelation, we see that God has a plan for His creation. In Genesis, He told Abraham that He would bless all peoples. In Revelation, we see all peoples blessed as every tribe and tongue gathers around the throne. This is the plan of God. We see His plan unfold from the beginning of time, and we know that His plan outlasts time.

Throughout the Bible, Creator God is on a mission to bring worshipers to Himself. If we are going to discover how we fit into His *Big Picture*, we have to take a good look at the box top and see how God designed it.

God's "Big Picture" Is Developing through His Church

We cannot understand God's plan for the world without understanding His plan for His Church. God unfolds His plan for the world through His people, the Church. God wants His people to discover His plan to make His glory known among the nations.

But week after week, millions of Americans attend church and miss the point. A consumer mindset has overtaken many churches. Members think that church is about meeting their needs and making them feel better about the life they want to live. This consumer approach to church is not in the Bible. God did not design His Church to feed this hyper-individualistic, self-centered approach to life!

If we really see God's picture and design for His Church, we will repent of our ineffective programs and cry out for His anointing to refocus our churches. We must call every believer to pray for a Great Commission Resurgence that will refocus our churches through God's *Big Picture*. It is not just that God has a mission for His Church—it would be more accurate to say, "God has a Church for His mission!"[2]

Do we really understand this mission? Have we ever really seen the mission of God? Let's take a fresh look at the Great Commission and beg God to open our eyes to see His plan and His *Big Picture*.

When we say "Great Commission," most people begin turning to Matthew 28. Instead, let's turn to Luke 24:44–49 and look at Luke's account of "The Great Commission." Look to the words of Jesus and let Him paint the picture for us:

> *Then He told them, "These are My words that I spoke to you while I was still with you—that everything written about Me in the Law of Moses, the Prophets, and the Psalms must be fulfilled." Then He opened their minds to understand the Scriptures. He also said to them, "This is what is written: The Messiah would suffer and rise from the dead the third day, and repentance for forgiveness of sins would be proclaimed in His name to all the nations, beginning at Jerusalem. You are witnesses of these things. And look, I am sending you what My Father promised. As for you, stay in the city until you are empowered from on high."*

Oh, to have been there that day when Jesus taught this systematic theology to His disciples! He clearly explained the *Big Picture* to them: He is the central person of the *Big Picture*, and He has a comprehensive plan to accomplish His *Big Picture*.

---

2 Christopher H. J. Wright, *The Mission of God: Unlocking the Bible's Grand Narrative* (Downers Grove, IL: IVP Academic, 2006), 62.

THE CENTRAL PERSON OF THE *BIG PICTURE* IS JESUS THE MESSIAH

Don't miss the pronoun used in these verses. Notice, Jesus is talking, and He says: "everything written about Me in the Law of Moses, the Prophets and the Psalms."

Catch this: it is really important! Jesus is explaining God's mission to His disciples. He told them how the Old Testament had promised the Messiah would come and fulfill the purposes of God. He explained to them how He, the Messiah, is the central person in God's plan.

He pointed out, "These are the things written:

- about *Me* in the Law of Moses
- about *Me* in the Prophets
- about *Me* in the Psalms."

Have you ever seen Jesus in the Old Testament? Verse 45 says, "Then He opened their minds to understand the Scriptures." There is only one way for us to understand the *Big Picture*—God has to open our minds to see it. All of His disciples need to see this—Jesus is the promised Messiah! He is the fulfillment of what God has always promised!

Here, in the context of giving His disciples the Great Commission, Jesus uses the Old Testament to explain the plan for the Christ, Messiah. It has always been God's plan for Messiah to suffer and rise again from the dead the third day. It has always been God's plan for forgiveness to be found in His name. The person and work of Christ have always been at the center of the *Big Picture* of God.

I can only imagine that the words of Jesus reminded His audience of their history:

Remember the ram at Abraham's altar? That was about *Me*. It was a picture of how I would be the substitute for your sin and you could be set free. (Gen 22)

Remember the blood that they put over the doorposts in Egypt? It wasn't about the blood of that animal—it was about *Me*. It was about how you can know Me and that My blood will cover your heart, and you can live forever. (Exod 12)

Remember how God gave the instructions on the tabernacle? It wasn't about the animals or the human high priest who would go into the Holy of Holies to sprinkle blood. It was about *Me*! (Heb 9–10)

Perhaps he explained how he was the sacrifice and the High Priest ever living to make intercession for us (Heb 7:25). Or He could have asked,

> Remember when the children of Israel came to the water and it was bitter? What did they do? They threw the tree into the waters, making the bitter waters sweet. That was about Messiah—it was about *Me*! (Exod 15)
>
> Remember the rock Moses struck—and how he was told to strike it only once? The next time Moses was told to speak to the rock. Why? That rock was a picture of *Me*! I was struck once for your sins, and now you speak and ask for the water to flow from me, the Rock of your salvation! (Exod 17; Num 20)
>
> Remember when the serpents were biting people, and they died from the poison? Moses was told to make a serpent of bronze, put it on a pole, and tell them to simply look at it . . . and they would live! That was about Messiah suffering and dying for your sins! "Even as Moses lifted up the serpent in the wilderness, so must the Son of Man be lifted up!" (Num 21; John 3:14–15)
>
> Just as it was then—it is now! All who really look will live.

Jesus is the Christ; Jesus is Messiah; Jesus is the center of salvation history. Take another look at Luke 24. Jesus explained that God has always planned for the person and work of Messiah to be at the center of His *Big Picture* of bringing worshipers to Himself. Then Jesus explained why we proclaim the message of the gospel. Proclaiming this news about Jesus is the way we lead people to repentance and forgiveness.

The *Big Picture* of God demands that we present the message of Messiah. He suffered, died, was raised from the dead, and forgiveness of sins is proclaimed in His name (Luke 24:46–47). This is God's global and eternal plan. We are to point the world to Messiah by proclaiming forgiveness in His name. God has given us the "message of reconciliation" and the "ministry of reconciliation." God uses us to announce His plan. We stand between God and the world and announce, "Messiah has come, and you can be reconciled to God!" (2 Cor 5).

We are His chosen means for presenting His chosen message—the gospel. We are pieces in the puzzle. We fit into God's eternal plan. We cannot bring anyone to salvation on our own. Instead, our assignment is to present the message of Messiah.

THE COMPREHENSIVE PLAN IS PROCLAIMING MESSIAH TO ALL PEOPLES

Notice the connection. This is what flows from God's heart: Jesus is the central person—and now proclaiming Jesus to *all peoples* is the comprehensive plan!

This calls us to respond. God's plan is to bring worshipers to Himself, and He uses all of His people to accomplish this plan. In every generation, disciples of Jesus find meaning for their life by discovering how they fit in God's global and eternal plan. Have you seen it yet?

Look again at these words in Luke's Gospel. In this simple statement, we see the "who," "what," and "where" of the Great Commission: ". . . repentance for forgiveness of sins would be proclaimed in His name to all the nations . . ." (Luke 24:47).

Who? *We* are His witnesses. What? We proclaim *the message* of repentance and forgiveness through Messiah. Where? We proclaim Him to the ends of the earth—to *all the nations*. When we see this, really see it, the *Big Picture* of God starts coming into focus. I sure know that's how it happened to me! I knew something about the "who" and the "what," but never really understood the scope of the "where." That is why I didn't understand just how big His plan really is.

I had studied the Bible for years before I ever caught a glimpse of God's *Big Picture*. Mainly, I missed it because I did not understand the meaning of one of the words. It is a word found here and many other places in the Bible, but I had never really seen it—that is, I had never understood it.

So many times, I looked at these passages and saw the word "nation," but missed the heartbeat of God. Are you like me? When you hear the word "nation," does your mind immediately see a geopolitical entity with borders? Do you see a country on a map?

If we look behind this word, we notice the term "nation" is not really about countries at all. It translates the Greek word *ethnē*. You don't have to be a Greek scholar to hear the meaning and passion of the word. It means so much more than countries on a map. It is about language, customs, and the things that make people unique and special in their differences.

The central person, the Lord Jesus, has a comprehensive plan. He desires and deserves worship by all the *ethnē*—by all the peoples of the world. Don't miss it! He is the worthy one! He deserves worship as the King of Kings, the Lord of Lords, and the Governor of Governors. He deserves to be worshiped by *panta ta ethnē*—all the peoples. This has always been God's plan.

Don't forget the context! This was not a plan Jesus came up with *after* the resurrection. Jesus showed them (and us) this picture of salvation from the Old Testament. This always was, and still is, the plan of God—to proclaim Messiah to all the *ethnē* . . . all the peoples (and that's not just countries on a map).

Every time we open the Word of God, we should look to see how it applies to our lives. "What is my response?" If we see the *Big Picture*, it should move us to ask, "How do I fit? What should I do?" Let me explain it this way, looking at the "A B C's of the Great Commission."

"A" Stands for ALL Peoples

As we just read in the words of Jesus, God has a plan for ALL the peoples of the world to worship Him. This passage in Luke is just one of many places where we see God's heart for the peoples of the world. Jesus explained it from the Old Testament, but I first discovered it in another place in the New Testament.

I remember the first time God overwhelmed me with the scope of His plan . . . the first time I really understood "ALL Peoples." Here's how it happened to me. I was teaching through the book of Galatians, verse by verse, and came to Galatians 3:8. It reads: "Now the Scripture saw in advance that God would justify the Gentiles by faith and told the good news ahead of time to Abraham, saying, All the nations will be blessed through you."

I reached for my Greek New Testament to look at the meaning of the words in the original language. That's when the word for "nations" finally found its way into my heart. I was so surprised to see how the text reads:

"*the Scripture*"—the Old Testament
"*saw in advance*"—looking ahead to the *Big Picture* of God
"*God would justify the Gentiles*"—the *ethnē*, the nations
"*told the good news*"—the good news of Messiah

"*ahead of time*"—God, not limited by time, has an eternal plan
"*to Abraham*"—Messiah is the promised seed of Abraham
"*saying All the nations*"—*ethnē*, same word as "Gentiles"
"*will be blessed through you*"—the blessing comes through Messiah

It still makes my heart beat fast as I see it. Our English translations try to give the sense of Paul's illustration and the point he is making. But, to do this, our English Bibles translate the same Greek word *ethnē* by using two different English words ("Gentiles" and "nations"). Somehow, because of this, I had missed the heartbeat of God.

The word "Gentile" means so much more than "not a Jew," just like the word "nations" means so much more than countries on a map. To understand the Great Commission fully, we need to see God's heart for the Gentiles, for the nations, for ALL the peoples of the world!

God told Abraham that He had a plan to justify the peoples (the *ethnē*) by faith. God is looking through time telling Abraham about His (eternal) plan. At this point in history, God is looking forward to the time when He will bless ALL the *ethnē* through Messiah. It is about the global and eternal glory of Messiah. This is for ALL peoples.

That day, when I first caught a glimpse of the *ethnē* in Galatians, the picture of God's plan started coming into focus. I started seeing it in so many other places in the Bible. I had to admit that most of my life I had read the Bible with a self-centered focus and not a God focus.

How many times had I read and heard the truth of Psalm 46:10? But I had misquoted it for years: "Stop your fighting—and know that I am God, exalted among the nations, exalted on the earth." Like most Americans, I thought that was the entire verse, and it's not! Why had I never realized that was just the first part of the verse? Could it be that I had missed the *Big Picture*?

There is a second part to that verse. Right here in a verse that had often brought me comfort I began to see that I had missed the heart of God. The rest of the verse reminds me that it is not about my comfort: "Be still——and know that I am God . . ." (Ps 46:10).

Wow! That's what's on God's heart! The *Big Picture*! If we will stop and focus on who God is, we will see what is on His heart. He plans to be exalted among ALL Peoples . . . exalted in ALL the earth!

From God's promise to Abraham, to the climactic scene in the Revelation, Messiah is God's plan for every tribe, tongue, nation, and people. But we miss it. I missed it! Like the children of Israel, we have too small a vision. God said this about Messiah:

> "It is not enough for you to be My Servant raising up the tribes of Jacob and restoring the protected ones of Israel. I will also make you a light for the nations, to be My salvation to the ends of the earth." Isaiah 49:6

Oh, that God would give us greater vision to understand that Jesus desires and deserves worship by ALL peoples! See it. Admit it. Believe it. Live it.

How can we live this out? Think about the times we go into a convenience store, and the clerk speaks English . . . but with a heavy foreign accent. Do we see this as an inconvenience or as a reminder to stop and pray for the nations? This is a reminder that God's plan is bigger than our frame of reference. Jesus deserves worship by people who are just like us, and by people who are different from us! He deserves worship in ALL languages by ALL people groups!

What comes to mind when we watch the evening news? Do we view the world through the eyes of the US economy or through the economy of God? Do we look at wars between nations or do we see the conflict in the heavenlies? God is at work in the affairs of humanity, and He wants His Church to see the need to make Jesus known among ALL peoples. Ethnic rivalry should remind us of the difficulty of our task. Because of sin, the gospel does not flow freely. We must be intentional to see that this message of Messiah crosses all barriers. The gospel is to be proclaimed to ALL peoples!

Oh, that God would help us see His *Big Picture!* He plans to be worshiped by ALL peoples, with every tribe, tongue, nation and people declaring, "Jesus, Lamb of God, You are worthy!" (Rev 5)

In the ABC's of the Great Commission, "A" stands for *All Peoples*, and . . .

"B" Stands for BLESSING

We are blessed to be a blessing! When we start understanding the plan and purposes of God, we begin to see why He blesses His people. Throughout the Bible, we see that God has a people of His own. Consistently, He tells them that He is blessing them for the glory of His name. Consistently,

He makes it known to His people—He is blessing them to make them a blessing.

Do we really understand how blessed we are? Once we are gripped by the global and eternal purposes of God, we will fall on our knees in repentance. We will confess our self-centeredness. We will repent of our materialism. We will confess our ungratefulness.

Ungratefulness really is the root of so much of our sin. We are a blessed people. We have multiple copies of the Bible on our shelves while there are still places on earth where people have never seen a Bible. It may be hard to believe, but it is true!

We have so much access to the gospel—Christian bookstores, Christian radio, and Christian television stations—while there are still places in the world where entire people groups have never heard the name of Jesus. Think about that! We are blessed!

Oh, that God would open our eyes to see what we have—and what others don't have! A true Great Commission Resurgence will be a revival of gratefulness. Self-centeredness and the Great Commission can never go hand in hand.

Some have said, "We don't need a Great Commission Resurgence— we need revival!" As I see it, they are connected. Revival always turns our hearts toward others. If we will let God break our hearts and turn our attention toward the lost, we will experience revival. If there is revival, it will turn our hearts to the nations.

Jesus deserves worship by **(A) ALL** peoples, and He has **(B) BLESSED** us to make us a blessing. Are you beginning to see it now? Can you see the *Big Picture*? What will it take to move you? What motivates you? What keeps you from being moved into action? Maybe you still can't imagine that God has a plan to make your life fit into His *Big Picture*.

We need to look at the **"C"** of the Great Commission. How does God plan to accomplish His mission of bringing worshipers to Himself? He does this work through the Church.

"C" Stands for CHURCH

Jesus did not give the Great Commission to a mission board. He gave these marching orders to His disciples and through them to His Church. The picture will never come into focus if we keep thinking the job of missions belongs to someone else. We have to get it straight: God does His work through His CHURCH!

As a little boy in Baptist Sunday School, I was taught a rhyme. We put our hands together a certain way and said:

"Here's the church and here's the steeple.
Open the door and see all the people."

It was easy to memorize with the hand motions, but there is something seriously wrong with this little rhyme. It is terrible theology!

The church is not a building. And even if it meets in a building, it may or may not have a steeple! We must teach our children to look beyond the building and see the church—the people. We need to remind ourselves often that the Great Commission was not given to a building, an organization, or a mission board. The challenge of telling the world about Jesus was given to people—all of God's people—His CHURCH.

In 1974, believers from around the world gathered at the Lausanne Congress on World Evangelization. As they discussed sharing Christ with the entire world, one thing became very clear. World evangelization requires "the whole Church taking the whole gospel to the whole world."[3]

We will never understand the *Big Picture* until the "whole Church" gets it. If we keep thinking that "missions" is only the assignment of the missionary, we will miss our place in God's *Big Picture*. We have to look at the missionary task differently. That may sound strange to you, but think about it! Is missions the job of the missionary or the job of the church? The responsibility of telling the whole world belongs to the CHURCH—the whole CHURCH!

Our passion and our lifestyle must demonstrate that we all really believe that. We must put every skill and gift on the altar . . . every resource, every life submitted to the Lordship of Christ . . . every person willing to go anywhere!

With our hearts set on Jesus, the Author and Finisher of our faith, we will gladly submit to this responsibility given to His Church. We are ready to go anywhere. We long for the message of hope to go everywhere. And if we aren't the ones who leave our homeland, that doesn't mean that we only care about our homeland. Some are sent; all are to

---

3 See Article 6, "The Church and Evangelism," of *The Lausanne Covenant* (available online from http://www.lausanne.org/covenant).

be involved in spreading the message. Some come face-to-face with ethnicity on foreign soil; all must seize every opportunity to see that all peoples worship Jesus.

A–All peoples
B–Blessed to be a blessing
C–Church

Imagine what could happen if the whole Church were committed to sharing the gospel with the whole world! What could happen if we took the challenge to find our place in God's *Big Picture*? We would discover that we are not simply a misplaced piece of a puzzle. We really do fit into God's global plan. We are part of God's Church, and, therefore, strategically part of His plan of bringing worshipers to Himself.

Seeing the *Big Picture* opens our eyes to see a lost world and moves our hearts to care. Recognizing our blessing and our calling moves us to find our place in telling the world—the whole world.

The whole Church owning the Great Commission? How does this really work *in* the church? How does this work *through* the church? Can the whole Church really get involved? Here are some first steps to consider:

Sent Ones and Senders

Some are "sent"—and the rest of us are "senders." By definition, if there are "sent ones," somebody had to do the "sending." We may use agencies to facilitate and focus the work of missionaries, but we must not separate our lives from theirs as they go out from our churches. We must hook our lives to those who go and do everything in our power to serve them as they go. We shouldn't simply throw money in the offering plate once a year. We should examine our lives in the light of their going and adjust our lives to align with theirs as they go.

We really do hold the ropes as they go out to the edge with the gospel. Our children should know their children. We should talk about them in our homes and church gatherings. We should pray for them at the dinner table and at the Lord's Table. They are family. They are sent; we are senders.

Some will hear God say: "I've called you to be one of those with beautiful feet who take the message." Others will hear Him say, "You need to buy the shoes for those beautiful feet so they can make the trip." Either way, our hearts will be hooked to the message because we want all peoples to worship the Messiah. He desires it—He deserves it—Lordship demands it!

It is rightly said that we have only three choices when it comes to world evangelization: we are either sent, a sender, or sinning. The *Big Picture* does not demand that everyone "go." But it does clearly expect that those who stay will give their lives caring, praying, and supporting those who go. We should all share the same commitment to the gospel. The "senders" hold the ropes for the "sent ones."

Welcomers and International Connections

When our hearts have been gripped with the Great Commission, we will serve the international families that have moved into our city. We will help these new families find their way around in a new place, serve as tutors so they can learn English, and open our homes and lives to use every means possible to love them and find ways to lead them to Christ. As we all see the *Big Picture*, we are all moved to care for the peoples of the world who have come to live in our own communities.

Our international business leaders will look for ways to use their influence to share Christ in places where missionaries are not welcome. Business owners will find ways to facilitate believers with jobs that will strategically place them where the gospel is not.

Our campus ministries will reach out to international students and share Christ. Then, we will pray for and train our new fellow believers, joining them as they take the message of Christ back to their homeland.

What would happen if the whole Church fell on its knees and prayed, "God, You have blessed me! What can I do to be part of your plan to tell the world about Jesus?"

Making Disciples and Mobilizing

For some, the Great Commission means selling everything and moving to a distant land. For others, it is learning how to hold every possession in an open hand. This will never happen unless we faithfully teach God's heart for the nations and challenge every believer to lay up treasure in heaven. Discipleship demands being controlled by the Great Commission and not by the American dream.[4]

---

4 See Al Jackson, "The American Dream or the Great Commission Resurgence?", in this volume.

God's Word does not allow us to set our affection on the comforts of this world. The Scripture is not given to help us find ways to make life easy and comfortable. Faithful teaching of the Bible will move us to explain the global and eternal purposes of God to every disciple. We will begin to understand what the Bible teaches about suffering and sacrifice. This will be clearly taught (and caught) in our homes, discipleship groups, and church gatherings. This *Big Picture* really is God's plan, and faithful disciple-making must present the whole counsel of God.

In Matthew's Gospel, Jesus commands us to make disciples of all the nations (*ethnē*). It is interesting that the words for "making disciples" and "all the nations" are side by side. When Jesus says "all nations," is He just suggesting a possible extent? No, He is announcing an expected intent! It is not just possible—it is expected, and it will happen! But we have to keep asking, "Do our churches really understand this dimension of disciple-making?" We must examine our vision for making disciples! A Great Commission Resurgence will move us to teach every believer that God expects His Church to take the gospel to the nations (*ethnē*). True disciples must see the *Big Picture*!

How can we talk about the Great Commission and not humble ourselves before the Lordship of Christ? When was the last time we told God that we are willing go anywhere, anytime for His glory? If we truly understand the Lordship of Christ, how else can we respond? Do you see the *Big Picture*? Is your life on the altar with no strings attached? Can you pray this prayer?

> *"Lord, I see the Big Picture. You deserve worship by ALL peoples. You have BLESSED me to make me a blessing, and You do Your work through the CHURCH. Since I am part of your Church, I will go anywhere, any time for Your glory."*

Perhaps the greatest test comes when we have to add our children to that prayer. Are we willing to pray this prayer?

> *"Lord, I will go anywhere, any time for Your glory. And, if it's not me, it would be a great honor if You would send my children!"*

Over 30 years ago, my wife and I met Miss Bertha Smith, who had been a missionary to China. At that time my wife was expecting our fourth child. Miss Bertha looked at our three children and challenged my wife,

"Pray that God would send half of your kids to the mission field and enable the other half to support them." Miss Bertha's words found their way into my wife's heart and shaped the way she prayed for our children.

My wife began praying that God would send our children and then added: "and send me." God finally softened my heart enough to see His *Big Picture*, and I joined my wife in praying a simple prayer: "Lord, we will go anywhere anytime for Your glory, and if You don't send us—send our children!" Years later, we watched our oldest daughter and son-in-law as they walked away with our little grandson to board a plane for the Middle East. We could say nothing for a few minutes, but then we were able to pray, "Lord, it's such an honor that our little girl wants people to know Jesus!"

"Anywhere, anytime, for God's glory!"

Anywhere? Our town? The inner city? The great population centers of America? The Northwest? The ends of the earth?

Anytime? When I finish college? While my kids are young? When I retire? Right now, in the middle of my career?

For God's glory? It's not about me—it is about God's *Big Picture* and His global and eternal plan.

What would happen if everyone in our churches caught a glimpse of the *Big Picture*? What if we all were stirred by the global and eternal glory due Messiah? What if the pieces of our lives were focused by the *Big Picture*? Perhaps we would all be praying, "Lord, I will go anywhere, any time for Your glory . . . and, if it's not me, send our best! If it's not me, it would be a great honor if You would send our children!"

"Pray to the Lord of the harvest to send out workers into His harvest" (Matt 9:38). Until every tribe, tongue, nation, and people gather around and the throne and give Him the praise that He deserves . . . Amen!

THE GREAT COMMISSION TENSION
GOD'S WORK AND OURS

Thomas K. Ascol

As a young pastor, William Carey took up the challenge to propose a topic for discussion among his colleagues who had gathered for an associational ministers' meeting in Northampton, England. The burden that had been growing in his heart led him to suggest that they discuss "the duty of Christians to attempt to spread the gospel among heathen nations." An older pastor was incredulous at such a suggestion and rebuked him saying, "Young man, sit down. When God pleases to convert the heathen, He will do it without your aid or mine!"[1]

Carey went on to become the "Father of Modern Missions" and a few years after this incident sailed to India, where he spent the rest of his life making disciples for Christ. His confrontation with the older pastor dramatically illustrates the controversy that has often swirled around the relationship between divine sovereignty and human responsibility in the work of evangelism and missions. If God is absolutely sovereign, then what difference does it make whether or not we evangelize? Do our efforts to spread the gospel even matter? How can unbelievers still be held

---

1 Timothy George, *Faithful Witness: The Life and Mission of William Carey* (Birmingham, AL: New Hope, 1991), 53. The rebuke has traditionally been attributed to John Ryland Sr., but his son, John Ryland Jr., repudiated that claim. See Iain Murray, *The Puritan Hope* (London: Banner of Truth, 1971), 139, 280. For a helpful overview of the primary resources addressing this event, see Michael Haykin, *One Heart and One Soul: John Sutcliffe of Olney, His Friends and His Times* (Durham, England: Evangelical Press, 1994), 193–96. Thomas J. Nettles argues that this exchange is best understood as arising from questions surrounding the latter day glory with which many Baptist leaders of the day were concerned. He argues his point in "Baptists and the Great Commission," in *The Great Commission: Evangelicals and the History of World Missions*, ed. Martin I. Klauber and Scott M. Manetsch (Nashville: B&H Academic, 2008), 89–92.

accountable for their sin or Christians be responsible to make disciples if salvation is wholly God's work?

The questions that emerge from the sovereignty of God and responsibility of man are not idle speculations of ivory tower theologians. They bear directly on every aspect of Christian living. Failure to integrate all that the Bible says on this subject results in stunted faith and diminished witness, as history can sadly verify. When God's sovereignty is held in such a way that human responsibility is eclipsed, the nerve of evangelistic compassion is inevitably cut. This old doggerel attributed to an unbalanced stream of Particular Baptists demonstrates what can happen.

> We are the Lord's elected few,
> Let all the rest be damned;
> There's room enough in hell for you,
> We won't have heaven crammed![2]

The opposite mistake is no less deadly. After the influence of the revival theology of Jonathan Edwards waned in nineteenth-century America, emphasis shifted to "the human side of religious experience" largely influenced and popularized by the views of Charles Finney. Conversion was often reduced to a personal decision that an individual could make at any time. A popular tract produced in the nineteenth century was designed to look like a ballot with 2 Peter 2:10 printed at the top, "Make your calling and election sure." After the question, "Will you be saved?" the ballot showed that God has voted yes while Satan has voted no. Then, next to the third and last box—left blank so that the reader can complete it—were these words: "A TIE! Your vote must decide the issue."[3]

Any resurgence in living out the Great Commission must tenaciously avoid the deadly errors that result from misconstruing the relationship between God's sovereignty and human responsibility in salvation. Rather, to avoid being doctrinally hijacked or spiritually distorted, such resurgence must dogmatically insist on carefully integrating all that the Bible teaches about God's work and ours in the great work of saving sinners.

---

2 Cited in Timothy George, *Theology of the Reformers* (Nashville: Broadman, 1988), 233.

3 George M. Marsden, *Fundamentalism and American Culture: The Shaping of Twentieth-Century American Evangelicalism, 1870–1925* (New York: Oxford University Press, 1980), 99–100. See also Iain Murray, *Revival and Revivalism: The Making and Marring of American Evangelicalism 1750–1858* (Edinburgh: Banner of Truth, 1994), 242–50.

The questions cannot be avoided. What is God's responsibility and what is ours? What has He done and promised to do? What can we do and what must we do?

While believers may not always state their answers in precisely the same way, *how* we answer them must be governed by what the Bible teaches. Only to the degree that we are faithful to Scripture can we be confident in our theological explanations about God's part and our part in the work of evangelism and missions. Such is what many of our forebears have helpfully done, and it is what we must do if we hope to move aggressively toward a true Great Commission Resurgence that brings glory to God.

BIBLICAL TEACHING

In the very words of the Great Commission, we find the sovereignty of God wedded to the responsibility of man. Before challenging us with the imperative, Jesus reassures us with an indicative. Before He commands, He asserts, and what He asserts is His unmitigated sovereignty. As the risen Lord, He declares, "All authority has been given to Me in heaven and on earth" (Matt 28:18).

The authority that Jesus claims for Himself includes both the right and power to rule over people and situations as He sees fit. He demonstrated His divine authority during His earthly ministry by commanding evil spirits to do His bidding and granting His twelve apostles the power to do likewise (Matt 10:1; Mark 6:7; Luke 9:1). He also displayed His command of the weather (Matt 8:26–27; Mark 4:39–41; Luke 8:24–25) and even an ability to control people and circumstances (Mark 14:1–2, 43–50; Luke 4:28–30).

In the preface of His final charge to His followers, Jesus makes a claim of comprehensive and sovereign authority. As A. T. Robertson noted, Christ speaks "as one already in heaven with a world-wide outlook and with the resources of heaven at his command. His authority or power in his earthly life had been great (7:29; 11:27; 21:23f.). Now it is boundless and includes earth and heaven."[4] Obviously, Jesus wants to remind His disciples that they are receiving orders from the sovereign Lord of the universe.

---

4   A. T. Robertson, *Word Pictures in the New Testament*, 6 vols. (New York: Harper & Brothers, 1930), 1:244.

As the almighty Lord, Jesus lays the responsibility for making new disciples squarely on the shoulders of His apostles and the church that will be built on their foundation. "Go, therefore, and make disciples of all nations, baptizing them in the name of the Father and of the Son and of the Holy Spirit, teaching them to observe everything I have commanded you. And remember, I am with you always, to the end of the age" (Matt 28:19–20). No one doubts that this commission requires the followers of Jesus both to baptize and to teach those who become His disciples. These two duties are readily accepted as the responsibility of the church. Yet, the work of baptizing and teaching actually begins with and extends from the work of making disciples.

Jesus obligates His followers to make disciples of all nations. It is our responsibility to turn unbelievers into believers, to lead those who do not know God to a saving knowledge of Him through faith in the risen Lord.

Immediately, questions that arise from the tension between God's sovereignty and human responsibility suggest themselves from this passage. If Jesus has comprehensive and sovereign authority, then does He really need anyone to go and make disciples for Him? If He is not lacking in power to change the hearts of men and women, turning them into His disciples, then why does He call on others to do what He could do without their involvement? Since He commissions His followers to make disciples, does that mean that He is in some way dependent on us?

Matthew's record of Jesus' last words before He ascended into heaven paints a portrait that forces us to recognize the operation of both sovereignty and responsibility in the Great Commission. We must believe both with equal fervency and at the same time. God is absolutely sovereign in the work of salvation, and we are absolutely responsible. Whatever else might be said in our effort to understand God's part and ours in the work of evangelism, those two truths must never be separated or diminished in our thinking. Rather, we must integrate and honor both truths in the way we trust and obey the Lord Jesus.

God Is Absolutely Sovereign

If Genesis 1:1 were the only verse in the Bible, it would suffice to establish the sovereignty of God: "In the beginning, God . . ." Nothing was before Him. Nothing was beside Him. Everything has come from Him (Acts 17:24). Few people who regard the Bible as the Word of God dispute His sovereignty in creation. More would have questions about His sovereignty in providence—at least with regard to how meticulous it is.[5]

Our concern in this chapter, however, is more narrowly focused on the sovereignty of God in salvation and therefore in evangelism. Scripture teaches that God plays a three-part role in the salvation of sinners: (1) He planned it, (2) He accomplished it, and (3) He applies it. The apostle Paul celebrates all three aspects of God's work in salvation in the first chapter of Ephesians.

Salvation planned. Ephesians 1:3 introduces a symphony of praise to the glorious grace of God. This grace is manifested first through God's work in salvation that began in eternity past: "He chose us in Him, before the foundation of the world, to be holy and blameless in His sight. In love He predestined us to be adopted through Jesus Christ for Himself, according to His favor and will" (Eph 1:4–5). Paul informs his Christian readers that their salvation began with God. God initiated it before the world was created, by choosing them to be renewed in holiness in Christ. He predestined them to be adopted into His eternal family.

It is not incidental that the treatment of this topic in the 2000 *Baptist Faith and Message* statement is entitled "God's Purpose of Grace" (Article V). As that article states, "Election is the gracious purpose of God, according to which He regenerates, justifies, sanctifies, and glorifies sinners."[6] In other words, God's election of sinners to be saved is His gracious work of planning every aspect of their salvation.

The prolific twentieth-century Southern Baptist theologian, W. T. Conner, elaborates this point:

> To put the matter another way, election is saying that what God does in saving men he does because he purposed to do it. We are arguing on the assumption that as a God of wisdom he has a purpose that is being carried out in the history of the world, and that as a God of power he does all that he purposes to do. If these two propositions are accepted, election must be accepted.[7]

---

5 It is beyond the scope of this chapter to deal with the sovereignty of God in providence—a subject that necessarily includes the problem of pain and evil. A brief, helpful treatment is found in Bruce Ware, *God's Greater Glory: The Exalted God of Scripture and the Christian Faith* (Wheaton: Crossway, 2004), 67–78. For evaluations of various models of providence, see Terrance Tiessen, *Providence and Prayer: How Does God Work in the World?* (Downers Grove, IL: InterVarsity Press, 2000).

6 The complete text of the current *Baptist Faith and Message* (2000) statement is available online from the Southern Baptist Convention's Web site at http://www.sbc.net/bfm/bfm2000.asp.

7 Walter Thomas Conner, *Christian Doctrine* (Nashville: Broadman, 1937), 161.

God's purpose to save sinners, manifested through His gracious election of them before the foundation of the world, is His work of planning salvation.

Salvation accomplished. Just as a blueprint never built a house, so also election has never saved a sinner. That which has been planned and purposed must be accomplished. Ephesians 1:7–11 celebrates God's work in doing just that through the person and work of Jesus. "In Him we have redemption through His blood, the forgiveness of our trespasses, according to the riches of His grace" (v. 7). The reference to blood is theological shorthand for the atoning death of Jesus on the cross.

In the first century "redemption" described delivery that resulted from payment. Both prisoners of war and slaves were redeemed when a ransom price was paid. This accords with Old Testament redemption laws that prescribe the payment of a set price in order to gain the freedom of first-born sons and male animals (Exod 13:12–13; Num 3:40–49). What Paul asserts, then, is that Jesus' death on the cross ("His blood") is the means whereby our redemption is accomplished.

The salvation that God planned from eternity past was accomplished two thousand years ago when Jesus substituted His life for ours, enduring divine wrath on the cross. Scripture consistently describes this *fait accompli* as God's work, as in Romans 3:25, "God presented Him as a propitiation through faith in His blood, to demonstrate His righteousness," and Isaiah 53:6, 10, "The Lord has punished Him for the iniquity of us all" and "was pleased to crush Him." God planned the salvation of sinners. Through Christ, He accomplished the salvation of sinners. The only thing still needed is the application of salvation to individuals.

Salvation applied. It is at just this point that some get confused. Obviously, no one helped God plan salvation and no one assisted Jesus in atoning for sin on the cross, but people are involved in getting the good news of salvation to those who need it. Our participation, however, does not mitigate divine sovereignty in changing unbelievers into believers. A careful reading of Scripture reveals that God is just as sovereign in the application of salvation as He is in the planning and accomplishment of it.

Paul refers to this work of application when he writes about being "sealed with the promised Holy Spirit" who is also the "down payment on our inheritance" that we have received through the redemption that is in Christ (Eph 1:13–14). A few verses later, he elaborates the sovereignty of God in applying salvation by describing the nature of life without Christ as spiritual death (Eph 2:1–3). Then he reminds Christians of the great work that God performed in their lives in order to rescue them from that condition: "But God, who is abundant in mercy, because of His great love that He had for us, made us alive with the Messiah even though we were dead in trespasses. By grace you are saved!" (Eph 2:4–5). Making a dead person live is a work that only divine power can accomplish.

This notion fits perfectly with Jesus' teaching in John 3:1–8 where He tells Nicodemus, "You must be born again" (v. 7). The new birth is necessary before a person can "see," much less "enter" the kingdom of God (vv. 3, 5). To underscore the sovereignty of God in the Spirit's work of giving spiritual life (being "born again") Jesus compares it to the wind. "The wind blows where it wishes, and you hear its sound, but you do not know where it comes from or where it goes. So it is with everyone who is born of the Spirit" (v. 8).

Paul makes precisely the same point in Titus 3:5–6. After describing his condition and that of his readers before they became Christians he writes, "But when the goodness and love for man appeared from God our Savior, He saved us—not by works of righteousness that we had done, but according to His mercy, through the washing of regeneration and renewal by the Holy Spirit." Regeneration, or the new birth, is God's work. He is the author of it, and Christians are people who have received it.

The same can be said for other aspects of the application of salvation, as Paul makes plain in his reminder to the Roman Christians of what God has done for them: "Those He predestined, He also called; and those He called, He also justified; and those He justified, He also glorified" (Rom 8:30). In each case God is the subject—the actor—and Christians are the ones on whom He has acted. Even repentance and faith by which sinners turn from sin and entrust themselves to Christ are said to be given by God (Acts 11:18; 2 Tim 2:25; Phil 1:29; Eph 2:8). The Lord is sovereign in applying salvation.

Salvation's purpose. Why does salvation exist? Why does God save anyone? Why did He purpose to save before the foundation of the world? Why did He accomplish salvation by sending His Son to live and die on the earth? Why does He call, regenerate, justify, adopt, and convert sinners today? Paul gives the answer three times in his explanation of the planning, accomplishment, and application of salvation in the first fourteen verses of Ephesians: God saves sinners for His own glory. Everything that God does in providing salvation is designed to evoke praise from us for the glory of His grace. He chose and predestined us to be adopted "to the praise of His glorious grace" (Eph 1:6). He redeemed us through the blood of Christ by lavishing His grace on us in forgiveness, so that we who hope in Christ "might bring praise to His glory" (Eph 1:12). He sealed us with the Holy Spirit and gave Him to us as a down payment on the inheritance that is ours in Christ "to the praise of His glory" (Eph 1:14).

God is determined to glorify Himself through the salvation of sinners. This reality means that the manifestation of His glory is inextricably bound to the work of evangelism.

We Are Absolutely Responsible

If God's part is to plan, accomplish and apply salvation, then what role is left for us? If He is absolutely sovereign in salvation, then in what sense can we say that people bear legitimate responsibility for either their own salvation or the salvation of others? We insist on this point on the same basis that we insist on God's sovereignty—the Bible clearly teaches it.

Those who hear the gospel. Jesus teaches that those who have greater opportunity to know the salvation God has provided bear a greater responsibility to repent and believe than those who have less opportunity. This fact is why He denounced the towns "where most of His miracles were done because they did not repent" (Matt 11:20). What they had witnessed made them accountable to God and obligated to repent and trust His Messiah. Their failure to turn from sin and become His disciples invoked a public denunciation by Jesus, "Woe to you, Chorazin! Woe to you, Bethsaida! For if the miracles that were done in you had been done in Tyre and Sidon, they would have repented in sackcloth and ashes long ago! But I tell you, it will be more tolerable for Tyre and Sidon on the day of judgment than for you" (Matt 11:21–22). They had seen and heard but had not repented and their culpability will be made evident at the final judgment.

When Paul went to Corinth, he first went to the Jews in the synagogue. Despite his best efforts to persuade them to believe the good news of salvation in Christ, he met with severe opposition. When their opposition rose to the level of blasphemy, Scripture records that "he shook out his clothes and told them, 'Your blood is on your own head! I am clean. From now on I will go to the Gentiles'" (Acts 18:6). Paul's statement indicates that they were completely responsible for their unbelief.

What this means is that no one who lives in unbelief and impenitence can justify his condition with arguments that God is sovereign in salvation. Everyone is obligated to be reconciled to God. Those who hear the gospel are responsible to turn from sin and believe it. Scripture allows no other conclusion.[8]

Those who have the gospel: commands. It is hard to imagine how anyone could question the Bible's teaching on the responsibility that believers have to work for the salvation of others. Throughout the Old Testament, God declares that His purpose is to be known among all the nations of the earth, the fulfillment of which will take place through the efforts of His people (Gen 12:3; 22:18; 1 Chron 16:24, 31; Pss 22:27–28; 67; 72:17; 96; Isa 42:6; 49:6, etc.) In the New Testament, this commitment becomes even more apparent in the many commands that are given to Christians to engage in the work of evangelism:

> "You are the light of the world. . . . Let your light shine before men, so that they may see your good works and give glory to your Father in heaven." (Matt 5:14–16)
>
> "Go, therefore, and make disciples of all nations, baptizing them in the name of the Father and of the Son and of the Holy Spirit, teaching them to observe everything I have commanded you." (Matt 28:19–20)
>
> "Go stand in the temple complex and tell the people all about this life." (Acts 5:20)
>
> "He commanded us to preach to the people, and to solemnly testify that He is the One appointed by God to be the Judge of the living and the dead." (Acts 10:42)
>
> "Proclaim the message. . . . Do the work of an evangelist." (2 Tim 4:2, 5)

These commands, which are given both to particular individuals and to Christ-followers in general, leave no doubt that evangelism—declaring

---

8 A classic treatment of this question is Andrew Fuller's *The Gospel Worthy of All Acceptation*, in *The Complete Works of the Rev. Andrew Fuller: With a Memoir of His Life, by Andrew Gunton Fuller*, edited by Joseph Belcher, 3 vols. (Philadelphia: American Baptist Publication Society, 1845), 2:328–416. Fuller lays the foundation for addressing the larger question of the duty of everyone to believe the gospel because of the universal obligation given by the law to love God with all the heart. Such love, Fuller argues, includes loving Him "*in every character in which he has made himself known; and more especially in those wherein his moral excellencies appear with the brightest lustre.*" This necessarily leads to the duty to love God in the way that He has revealed Himself as "*saving sinners through the death of his Son*" (Ibid., 2:351).

the message of God's salvation in Christ—is indeed the responsibility of Jesus' disciples.

Those who have the gospel: examples. The first-century Christians certainly saw things this way. As John Stott rightly notes, "The early church understood its task to be the diligent and systematic proclamation of a message. If God's part was to give the power, their part was to give the word."[9] Even a cursory reading of the book of Acts proves this point.

When the Holy Spirit was poured out on the church at Pentecost, not only did Peter stand and preach the gospel to a crowd of thousands, but the other disciples also began to declare the "magnificent works of God" (Acts 2:11). The apostles, who were the leaders, obviously engaged in the work of spreading the gospel, but the task was not relegated to them exclusively. Stephen (Acts 6:8–7:60) and Philip (Acts 8:5–13, 26–40) were deacons who boldly evangelized. When persecution broke out against the church in Jerusalem, all the membership "except the apostles were scattered throughout the land of Judea and Samaria" (Acts 8:1). Luke tells us what they did as they traveled: "So those who were scattered went on their way proclaiming the message of good news" (Acts 8:4).

The word used for "proclaiming the message of good news" is *euangelizomenoi*, which D. Martyn Lloyd-Jones describes as "gossiping the gospel."[10] These believers incorporated into their daily conversations the good news of what God has done in providing salvation in Jesus Christ. Nor was this effort sporadic on their part, because six years later they are described as continuing in the work of spreading the gospel: "Those who had been scattered as a result of the persecution that started because of Stephen made their way as far as Phoenicia, Cyprus, and Antioch, speaking the message to no one except Jews. But there were some of them, Cypriot and Cyrenian men, who came to Antioch and began speaking to the Hellenists, proclaiming the good news about the Lord Jesus" (Acts 11:19–20).

Evangelism was built into the DNA of the churches of the New Testament. The church at Jerusalem, after seeing thousands come to Christ locally through their witness, was providentially compelled through persecution to send out members into Judea and Samaria spreading the gospel. The church at Antioch, after prayer and fasting, sent out workers to preach the gospel and plant churches throughout the Roman Empire (Acts 13:1–4; cf. 15:36–41). Within the first three years of the Ephesian church's

---

9 John Stott, *The Meaning of Evangelism*, rev. ed. (London: Falcon, 1973), 4.

10 D. Martyn Lloyd-Jones, *Preaching and Preachers* (Grand Rapids: Zondervan, 1971), 24.

existence, Luke could write that through them "all the inhabitants of the province of Asia, both Jews and Greeks, heard the word of the Lord" (Acts 19:10). The Roman church's faith was "being reported in all the world" (Rom 1:8). Paul commends the Philippian church for their partnership with him "in the defense and establishment of the gospel" (Phil 1:7). He describes the Thessalonian church as having become "an example to all the believers in Macedonia and Achaia" because "the Lord's message rang out" from them in "every place" that their faith had gone out (1 Thess 1:7–8).

The Christianity of the first century spread rapidly because the early believers accepted their responsibility as disciples of Jesus to make the gospel known far and wide. They saw their evangelistic efforts not as a mere discharging of duty, however. They also recognized that their evangelism was necessary.

Those who have the gospel: necessity. The apostle Paul teaches the indispensability of evangelism to the salvation of sinners. In the tenth chapter of his letter to the Romans, Paul states that the reason that his fellow Israelites are not saved is because they do not believe the gospel and one reason they do not believe is because they have never heard: "But how can they call on Him in whom they have not believed? And how can they believe without hearing about Him? And how can they hear without a preacher? And how can they preach unless they are sent?" (Rom 10:14–15). These rhetorical questions make the point that people will not—indeed, cannot—be saved unless someone proclaims the gospel to them.

Repentance and faith are, according to the *Baptist Faith and Message*, "inseparable experiences of grace" (Article IV, "Salvation"). They are two sides of the one response to the gospel that is necessary for salvation: "The one who believes in the Son has eternal life, but the one who refuses to believe in the Son will not see life; instead, the wrath of God remains on him" (John 3:36). No faith, no salvation. Similarly, Jesus said to His disciples, "Unless you repent, you will all perish as well" (Luke 13:3, 5). No repentance, no salvation.

How do repentance and faith arise in the heart of a person, turning him from a state of being unconverted to conversion? Again, here is how the *Baptist Faith and Message* answers this question:

> Regeneration, or the new birth, is a work of God's grace whereby believers become new creatures in Christ Jesus. It is a change of heart wrought by the Holy Spirit through conviction of sin, *to*

which the sinner responds in repentance toward God and faith in
the Lord Jesus Christ (Article IV, "Salvation," emphasis added).

Repentance and faith are created through the regenerating work of the
Holy Spirit. The Spirit, however, does not do this work apart from the
Word, as the apostle Peter testifies: "You have been born again—not of
perishable seed but of imperishable—through the living and enduring
word of God" (1 Pet 1:23).

The Spirit owns the Word as it goes forth and wields it as a sword to
destroy strongholds and fortresses of resistance in the minds of unbelievers, convincing and convicting them of sin, righteousness and judgment,
enabling them to see and enter the kingdom of God through repentance
and faith. Thus, the gospel must be proclaimed to people if they are going
to be saved: "Faith comes from hearing, and hearing through the word of
Christ" (Rom 10:17 ESV).

How will the word of Christ get to unbelievers unless believers bring it
to them? Indispensible to the salvation of sinners is the preaching, teaching, spreading, sharing, or "gossiping" of the gospel.

Those who have the gospel: urgency. The understanding that God is
working for an eternal purpose, coupled with the recognition that included
in that purpose is the necessary means of evangelism through which He
accomplishes His divine plan, led the New Testament believers to have a
sense of urgency about them regarding the proclamation of the gospel.
The evangelistic passion exhibited in Paul's life and letters arose from both
a love for God and commitment to His glory as well as a love for people
and commitment to their eternal welfare. Thus he was so deeply burdened
for the salvation of his fellow Jews that he could wish that he himself were
cursed and cut off from Christ if thereby they would be saved (Rom 9:1–3;
10:1). It was why he counted his life as not worth preserving if only he
could finish his course and the ministry that he had received from Jesus,
"to testify to the gospel of God's grace" (Acts 20:24). It was why he was
willing to become all things to all people so that by any means he might
save some (1 Cor 9:22). It was why his spirit was provoked by all the idols
he saw on the streets of Athens, and why he could not be silent before the
intellectual elites of his, but rather called them to repent and trust the risen
Lord (Acts 17:16–31).

Paul consistently saw himself as an ambassador for Christ, as one who
had entered into the very mission of Jesus to bring glory to God through

the salvation of sinners. As such he was unashamed to persuade and plead with people on behalf of Christ to be reconciled to God (cf. 2 Cor 5:11, 20).

In the work of salvation, only God can bring people to Christ, but we must do what we can to bring Christ to people. A right appreciation of this balanced biblical perspective will save us from the twin pitfalls of thinking either that "there is nothing that we can do" (an apathetic passivism) or "if it is to be, it is up to me" (an assertive pragmatism). As the truth of Scripture is integrated more fully into our lives, we will become increasingly liberated and motivated to proclaim boldly the finished work of Christ as the only hope of salvation for everyone who believes. John Stott helpfully summarizes the way that such biblical integration works itself out in our belief and practice:

> God finished the work of reconciliation at the cross, yet it is still necessary for sinners to repent and believe and so "be reconciled to God." Again, sinners need to "be reconciled to God," yet we must not forget that on God's side the work of reconciliation has already been done. If these two things are to be kept distinct, they will also in all authentic gospel preaching be kept together. It is not enough to expound a thoroughly orthodox doctrine of reconciliation if we never beg people to come to Christ.[11]

THEOLOGICAL REFLECTION

The intellectual tension created by belief in God's absolute sovereignty and humanity's absolute responsibility is nothing new. Paul addressed it head-on in the most famous chapter in the Bible referencing the sovereignty of God, Romans 9. After elaborating God's sovereign prerogative to show mercy to whom He will and to harden whom He will, the apostle anticipates a question that naturally arises from such teaching, "You will say to me, therefore, 'Why then does He still find fault? For who can resist His will?'" (Rom 9:19). Paul's rhetorical response both refutes the complaint and rebukes the questioner, "reminding him that the real relation of every man to God . . . is that of created to Creator, and hence not only has he no

---

11   John Stott, *The Cross of Christ* (Downers Grove, IL: InterVarsity Press, 1986), 201.

right to complain, but also God has the Creator's right to do what He will with those whom He has Himself moulded and fashioned."[12]

Such is surely the right starting point—a reminder to us of the proper posture that we, as creatures, are to have when seeking to understand the ways of our Creator. Yet the same does not mean that we are not to seek to understand the relationship between truths as profound as divine sovereignty and human responsibility. Rather, it reminds us that our quest for understanding should be characterized with the kind of humility that befits a creature.

Antinomy and Compatibilism

Belief in both the absolute sovereignty of God and absolute responsibility of man seems irrational, but no more so than belief in the Trinity or in the complete deity and full humanity of Jesus Christ. The reason these latter two doctrines are received as true is that they are taught in Scripture. We submit our understanding to them not as an expression of irrationality but in recognition that they are suprarational—that they are revealed. In the exact same way, God's sovereignty and our responsibility, as we have seen, are revealed in Scripture. Therefore, we must equally embrace them both.

J. I. Packer calls this tension an "antinomy"—that is, the sovereignty of God and responsibility of people appear to be contradictory without actually being so:

> It is an *apparent* incompatibility between two apparent truths. An antinomy exists when a pair of principles stand side by side, seemingly irreconcilable, yet both undeniable. There are cogent reasons for believing both of them; each rests on clear and solid evidence; but it is a mystery to you how they can be squared with each other. You see that each must be true on its own, but you do not see how they can both be true together.[13]

---

12 William Sanday and Arthur Headlam, *A Critical and Exegetical Commentary on the Epistle to the Romans*, 5th ed., International Critical Commentary (Edinburgh: T&T Clark, 1977), 259.

13 J. I. Packer, *Evangelism and the Sovereignty of God* (Downers Grove, IL: InterVarsity Press, 1961), 18–19. Packer draws an analogy from physics: "There is cogent evidence to show that light consists of waves, and equally cogent evidence to show that it consists of particles. It is not apparent how light can be both waves and particles, but the evidence is there, and so neither view can be ruled out in favor of the other; the seemingly two incompatible positions must be held together, and both

For the true believer, the fact that God's Word teaches both sovereignty and responsibility is a cogent enough reason to believe them both together. Consequently, we must resist the temptation to alleviate the tension between these two truths by diminishing either one. Failure at this point will inevitably result in a reductionism that will inhibit a true understanding of the Bible's message.

D. A. Carson goes into greater detail in his reflections on this question by articulating two propositions that the Bible specifically and generally teaches to be true:

1. God is absolutely sovereign, but His sovereignty never functions in such a way that human responsibility is curtailed, minimized or mitigated.
2. Human beings are morally responsible creatures—they significantly choose, rebel, obey, believe, defy, make decisions, and so forth, and they are rightly held accountable for such actions; but this characteristic never functions so as to make God absolutely contingent.[14]

Carson labels this view *compatibilism*, as the two ideas are both taught in the Bible and are mutually compatible, even if our finite minds have difficulty grasping the precise nature of that compatibility.

The cross as a paradigm. Whether we use the language of Packer, Carson, or someone else, the point that we cannot escape is that the Bible forces us to recognize the reality and operation of God's sovereignty and human responsibility in every aspect of our relationship to our Creator. Nowhere is this more poignantly displayed than in the crucifixion of Jesus, which, when seen in the light of the issue at hand, provides a paradigm to help us maintain a balanced perspective.

In his sermon at Pentecost, Peter indicted his hearers for the death of Jesus. They were responsible because of their participation in calling for His crucifixion. Yet, in the very same breath, Peter also attributes the death of Jesus to God, highlighting in one sentence God's sovereignty and human responsibility in the crucifixion of Jesus. "This Jesus, delivered up

---

must be treated as true. Such a necessity scandalizes our tidy minds, no doubt, but there is no help for it if we are to be loyal to the facts" (Ibid., 19).

14 D. A. Carson, *How Long, O Lord?: Reflections on Suffering and Evil* (Grand Rapids: Baker, 1990), 201.

according to the definite plan and foreknowledge of God, you crucified and killed by the hands of lawless men" (Acts 2:23). In Peter's understanding the death of Jesus was both the sinful act of lawless men and the exact fulfillment of God's plan of salvation at the same time.

This compatibilist view of the issue also informed the prayers of the early Church. After being released from the Jewish leaders who had arrested them, Peter and John returned to their fellow believers and led them in prayer. How they prayed reveals an understanding of the compatibility of God's sovereignty and human responsibility. "For, in fact, in this city both Herod and Pontius Pilate, with the Gentiles and the peoples of Israel, assembled together against Your holy Servant Jesus, whom You anointed, to do whatever Your hand and Your plan had predestined to take place" (Acts 4:27–28). Herod, Pilate, the Gentiles, and the Jews were complicit in the horrendous crime of murdering Jesus. They were responsible and therefore guilty. Yet, their actions fulfilled the sovereign purposes of God.

Sovereignty establishing responsibility. Not only are divine sovereignty and human responsibility compatible, the former establishes and provides the motivation for the latter. This is true not only in the work of evangelism, but in every area of Christian living. Paul makes this point in Philippians 2:12–13: "So then, my dear friends, just as you have always obeyed, not only in my presence, but now even more in my absence, work out your own salvation with fear and trembling. For it is God who is working in you, enabling you both to will and to act for His good purpose." The responsibility given to Christians in this passage is to cultivate energetically the new life that they have received in Christ (they are to work *out*, not *for*!). Doing so involves choices, effort, discipline, obedience, commitment, and determination, and it extends until the end of a believer's life.

Believers are obligated to work out their salvation in this way, but it is God who sovereignly works in them. Paul makes an astounding claim here. Not only does God give us the ability to "act for His good purpose," he also enables us to "will" to do so. Even the desire to do His will comes from God. Every inclination to obey God and live for His honor is the result of God's work in a person, granting Him that desire.

Even more astounding is the connection between God's working in us and our working out the responsibilities of the Christian life. The fact that we are completely dependent on God even for the desire to do His will in no way lessens our responsibility to do it. On the contrary, Paul charges the Philippians to be diligent in working out their salvation *because* God is working in them: "Work out your own salvation . . . *For* it is God who works in you. . . ." (emphasis added). God's absolute sovereignty is not a hindrance to energetic Christian living. It is a strong motivation for such living.

Whatever else might be said about the mystery of sovereignty and responsibility, one thing should be patently clear: if your view of the issue does not result in sincere, energetic Christian obedience to God, then your understanding is woefully deficient. It falls far short of the apostle Paul's view and, therefore, needs to be rehabilitated by the Word of God.

HISTORICAL EXAMPLES

Ours is not the first generation to grapple with the questions arising from the relationship between divine sovereignty and human responsibility. There are many who have gone before us that have seen the issues clearly and whose testimonies of faithfulness have been sealed by history. Even among those whose beliefs separated them ecclesiastically we find great unity in their commitment to the Great Commission under the sovereignty of God. Though hundreds of noteworthy examples could be studied with profit, the testimonies of the following three men can certainly point the way forward for us today.

John Calvin

The leading magisterial reformer of the sixteenth century was a man whose very name has come to be associated with exalted views of God's sovereignty. John Calvin is best known today for his theological writings and those writings are best known for advocating the sovereignty of God over all life.[15] What is not as well-known about Calvin is his evangelistic and missionary zeal.

Calvin's passion for the glory of God motivated him to desire that all people should come to a saving knowledge of God. In a sermon from Deuteronomy he said, "When we know God to be our Father, should we not desire that he should be known as such by all? And if we do not have this passion, that all creatures do him homage, is it not a sign that his glory

---

15   Benjamin Warfield wrote concerning Calvin, "No man ever had a profounder sense of God than he," in *Calvin and Augustine* (Philadelphia: Presbyterian & Reformed, 1971), 24.

means little to us?"[16] Love for God and a desire to see Him glorified leads to a love for people and a desire to see them experience salvation to the praise of God's glory.

Beyond this, Calvin understood and taught that God desires His gospel to be spread to the nations. He interprets the miracle of tongues at Pentecost as proof of this divine desire, noting that God enabled the gospel to be heard in many languages so that it might "break out" as the apostles "spread that abroad amongst all people which was delivered to them."[17] In his book, *Concerning the Eternal Predestination of God*, Calvin argued, "Since we do not know who belongs to the number of the predestined and who does not, it befits us so to feel as to wish that all be saved." This burden to see everyone saved should make us so evangelistic that "whoever we come across, we shall study to make him a sharer of peace."[18]

This burden for the unconverted worked itself out so dramatically in Calvin's ministry that Philip Hughes has called him a "Director of Missions" and refers to sixteenth-century Geneva as "a dynamic centre of missionary concern and activity."[19] During Calvin's ministry in Geneva hundreds of men were trained and sent out to preach in nations beyond Switzerland. "Records indicate missionaries . . . were sent to Italy, the Netherlands, Hungary, Poland and the free Imperial city-states in the Rhineland" and even across the Atlantic to Brazil.[20] Of utmost concern to Calvin was his native France. Under his leadership, the church at Geneva helped provoke what became a church planting movement that saw more than 2,100 Protestant churches started in France between 1555 and 1562. These churches had between two and three million people attending them. From correspondence between Calvin and the men he helped commission to the work in France we learn that among the congregations that were

---

16 Sermon 196, on Deuteronomy 33:18–19 (*Ioannis Calvini Opera*, 29:175), quoted from Michael Haykin, "Calvin on Missions—'A sacrifice well pleasing to God': Calvin and the Missionary Endeavor of the Church," *Founders Journal* 75 (Winter 2009): 24.

17 *Commentary upon the Acts of the Apostles by John Calvin*, ed. Henry Beveridge, trans. Christopher Fetherstonel, reprint ed. (Grand Rapids: Baker, 1981), 1:75.

18 John Calvin, *Concerning the Eternal Predestination of God*, trans. J. K. S. Reid (London: James Clarke, 1961), 9. For more on this point see Ray Van Neste, "John Calvin on Evangelism and Missions," *Founders Journal* 33 (Summer 1998): 15–21.

19 Philip E. Hughes, "John Calvin: Director of Missions," in *The Heritage of John Calvin*, ed. J. H. Bratt (Grand Rapids: Eerdmans, 1973), 40; idem, ed. and trans., *The Register of the Company of Pastors of Geneva in the Time of Calvin* (Grand Rapids: Eerdmans, 1966), 25.

20 Frank James, "Calvin the Evangelist," *Founders Journal* 75 (Winter 2009): 5.

planted some quickly became mega-churches with as many as nine thousand members—and this during a time when it was a capital crime to be a Protestant in France.[21]

Such energetic devotion to the Great Commission is nearly unprecedented in the history of Christianity. Calvin's ministry, with all of the deficiencies that Baptists would appropriately critique, demonstrates the positive impact that can be made on God's kingdom when personal responsibility remains wedded to God's sovereignty.

William Carey

A man of equally balanced views though possessing different gifts and a different calling from those of Calvin is William Carey. Despite the cold reception with which his missionary burden was met by an older pastor in his association, Carey was not deterred by such attitudes. Beginning in 1784 he joined with fellow pastors Andrew Fuller, John Ryland Jr., and John Sutcliff (and, after a few years, Samuel Pearce) on a monthly basis for eight years to pray for revival. The answer to those prayers was the beginning of the modern missionary movement.

During this time Carey began relentlessly to share his burden for the nations with his prayer partners until they, too, came to embrace it. On May 30, 1792, at the spring meeting of the Northamptonshire Association of Baptist Churches, he preached a moving sermon from Isaiah 54:2–3, "Enlarge the place of your tent, and let them stretch out the curtains of your habitations; do not despair; lengthen your cords and strengthen your stakes. For you shall expand to the right and to the left, and your descendants will inherit the nations, and make the desolate cities inhabited." From this text Carey developed two points: "Expect great things. Attempt great things." The impact was immediate and lasting. Four months later the "Particular Baptist Society for the Propagation of the Gospel amongst the Heathen" was duly formed. Thus began the modern foreign missions movement.[22]

Earlier that year Carey published a small book entitled *An Enquiry into the Obligations of Christians to Use Means for the Conversion of the Heathens* that became the manifesto of this movement. In it he argued that

---

21 See James, "Calvin the Evangelist," 3–6.
22 George, *Faithful Witness*, 25–33.

Christians are indeed to be actively engaged in seeking the conversion of the lost, and he called on believers to pray, plan, give, and go to that end. Less than a year later, Carey and his wife and four children set sail for India, where he would live out the remaining forty-one years of his life making Christ known to unreached people groups. He helped translate the Scriptures into twenty-four languages, produced several grammars in native Indian languages, and rendered the Word of God accessible to one-third of the world.[23] In addition, he "ran a publishing house, founded a college, organized scores of schools, planted numerous churches, sent out hundreds of Indian evangelists, worked tirelessly for human rights including the abolition of both slavery and the horrible practice of widow-burning, worked for prison reform, and more."[24]

In assessing the lessons that Carey's legacy can teach us today, Timothy George puts at the top of the list, "The sovereignty of God":

> Carey knew that Christian missions was rooted in the gracious, eternal purpose of the Triune God, Father, Son, and Holy Spirit, to call unto Himself a redeemed people out of the fallen race of lost humankind. As a young pastor in England he confronted and overcame the resistance of those Hyper-Calvinistic theologians who used the sovereignty of God as a pretext for their do-nothing attitude toward missions. It was not in spite of, but rather because of, his belief in the greatness of God and His divine purpose in election that Carey was willing "to venture all" to proclaim the gospel in the far corners of the world.[25]

Confirming this evaluation was the "Serampore Compact," which Carey and his fellow missionaries drew up on October 7, 1805 as a summary of guiding principles for their work. They agreed that three times each year this compact would be read aloud at each mission station. The first part of that document declares their understanding of God's sovereignty in salvation.

---

23 William Cathcart, *Baptist Encyclopedia*, 1881 ed., s.v. "William Carey."

24 Timothy George, *Amazing Grace: God's Initiative—Our Response* (Nashville: LifeWay, 2000), 95.

25 George, *Faithful Witness*, 171.

We are firmly persuaded that Paul might plant and Apollos water, in vain, in any part of the world, did not God give the increase. We are sure that only those ordained to eternal life will believe, and that God alone can add to the church such as shall be saved. Nevertheless we cannot but observe with admiration that Paul, the great champion for the glorious doctrine of free and sovereign grace, was the most conspicuous for his personal zeal in the work of persuading men to be reconciled to God. In this respect he is a noble example for our imitation.[26]

For Carey and those who served with him in that pioneer missionary effort, it was a clear vision of God's sovereignty and human responsibility that led them to expect great things from God and attempt great things for Him.

Adoniram Judson

An American colleague of Carey's, Adoniram Judson, gave his life to preach Christ to the people of Burma (modern Myanmar). Commissioned as a Congregationalist missionary when he left America on February 19, 1812, by the time he arrived in Calcutta on June 17 and met Carey, Judson had become convinced of Baptist convictions. Shortly after his arrival he was baptized. This turn of events meant that American Baptists had their first missionary on the field before they had formed any board or agency to serve him. Within a year Judson settled in Rangoon, Burma, the land that would receive the benefit of his gospel labors for the next thirty-eight years. He saw over one hundred churches started with eight thousand Burmese converts. He also translated the Bible into Burmese and wrote a Burmese grammar and a Burmese-English dictionary. He buried two wives and eight children, nearly went insane with despair, was brutalized in prison as a spy, and experienced a very difficult death.

No one can question Judson's sense of personal responsibility to the Great Commission. Even before he left the shores of his homeland his commitment was demonstrated in the honest way he appealed to John Hasseltine for his daughter's hand in marriage. In a letter to his prospective father-in-law he writes,

---

26   This document is available from Christian History Institute, Box 540, Worcester, PA 19490.

> I have now to ask whether you can consent to part with your daughter early next spring, to see her no more in this world; whether you can consent to her departure for a heathen land, and her subjection to the hardships and sufferings of a missionary life; whether you can consent to her exposure to the dangers of the ocean; to the fatal influence of the southern climate of India; to every kind of want and distress; to degradation, insult, persecution, and perhaps a violent death? Can you consent to all this for the sake of Him who left his heavenly home, and died for her and for you; for the sake of perishing immortal souls; for the sake of Zion and the glory of God? Can you consent to all this hope of soon meeting your daughter in the world of glory, with a crown of righteousness, brightened by the acclamations of praise which shall redound to her Saviour from heathens saved, through her means, from eternal woe and despair?[27]

The absolute sovereignty of God in salvation was not merely compatible with his missionary zeal; in Judson's mind it was the driving force of evangelism. The only English sermon he ever preached in Burma was on John 10:1–18. In it he argues that because those whom God has chosen must be called to faith in Christ, Christian pastors must be faithful in going to the lost and indiscriminately calling them to Christ.

> We come now to consider the main duty of a Christian pastor. First he must call his people. Though enclosed in the Saviour's electing love, they may still be wandering on the dark mountains of sin, and he must go after them; perhaps he must seek them in very remote regions, in the very outskirts of the wilderness of heathenism. And as he cannot at first distinguish them from the rest, who will never listen and be saved, he must lift up his voice to all, without discrimination, and utter, in the hearing of all, that invitation of mercy and love which will penetrate the ears and the hearts of the elect only.[28]

---

27 Quoted in Arabella Stuart, *The Three Mrs. Judsons* (Springfield, IL: Particular Baptist Press, 1999), 7–8.

28 Francis Wayland, ed., *A Memoir of the Life and Labors of the Rev. Adoniram Judson, D.D.* (Boston: Phillips, Sampson, & Co., 1853), 2:490.

Judson labored over six years before seeing anyone converted to Christ. After four years on the field, in a letter he wrote to "Rev. Dr. Baldwin," he tells of the disappointments he had met in his evangelistic efforts. Those who had shown real interest in the gospel quit speaking with him out of fear of being persecuted. This widespread fear among his Burmese contacts provoked two thoughts in Judson. The first was that "God can give to the inquirers that love to Jesus, and that resolution to profess his religion, which will overcome their fears."[29] God is sovereign over the hearts and minds of those to whom he was witnessing.

His second thought involved going to the Emperor to explain his efforts to introduce the gospel of Christ to the Burmese people. Such a course of action could result in his immediate execution, but it could also result in the alleviation of any persecution among future Burmese converts were he to find favor with the Emperor. Judson's reasoning on this point demonstrates the balanced grasp he had on God's sovereignty in salvation and our responsibility in the evangelistic task.

> It is true that God will call those whom he has chosen; but since he has made means necessary to the end, since it is by the gospel of his Son that he calls his people, it is certainly as much the duty of his servants to endeavor to avert such persecution as would effectually prevent the use of means as it is to use any means at all; and we may reasonably conclude that, when God has a people whom he is about to call, he will direct his servants in such a course.[30]

The final paragraph of his letter exudes an exemplary, Spirit-given hope and confidence that is born of a right grasp of God's work and ours in fulfilling the Great Commission.

> I have no doubt that God is preparing the way for the conversion of Burmah [*sic*] to his Son. Nor have I any doubt that we who are now here are, in some little degree, contributing to this glorious event. This thought fills me with joy. I know not that I shall live to see a single convert; but, notwithstanding, I feel that I would not leave my present situation to be made a king.[31]

---

29   Ibid., 1:191.
30   Ibid., 1:192.
31   Ibid.

CONTEMPORARY APPLICATION

The fact that we cannot finally explain to everyone's (or anyone's!) satisfaction just how the doctrines of divine sovereignty and human responsibility are both equally true is no justification for disbelieving one in preference of the other. Charles Haddon Spurgeon, the great soul-winning pastor, emphasized this point in his sermon on Romans 9:15, "Jacob have I loved, but Esau have I hated":

> "How," says some one, "do you reconcile these two doctrines?" My dear brethren, I never reconcile two friends, never. These two doctrines are friends with one another; for they are both in God's Word, and I shall not attempt to reconcile them. If you show me that they are enemies, then I will reconcile them. "But," says one, "there is a great deal of difficulty about them." Will you tell me what truth there is that has not difficulty about it? "But," he says, "I do not see it." Well, I do not ask you to see *it;* I ask you to believe it. There are many things in God's Word that are difficult, and that I cannot see, but they are there, and I believe them. I cannot see how God can be omnipotent and man be free; but it is so, and I believe it.[32]

If, with Spurgeon, we also believe it, then we will acknowledge that because God is sovereign in salvation, only He can do what must be done to bring a person who is enslaved in sin into the joy of new life in Christ. God must regenerate. He must justify. He must forgive. He must adopt. He must grant repentance and faith. No one becomes a disciple of Jesus apart from the sovereign work of God.

If we share Spurgeon's view we will also acknowledge that as followers of Christ we are responsible for making disciples of others and therefore we must do what can be done to bring this about. We must proclaim the gospel. We must pray. We must live in ways that demonstrate that having Jesus Christ is more valuable than having health, wealth, ease, comfort, or any of the benefits that are so often associated with "the good life." We must so live that the mission of making disciples of all nations and baptizing and teaching them—the mission that our Lord and Savior has given

---

32 *The New Park Street Pulpit*, 6 volumes, reprint ed. (Pasadena, TX: Pilgrim Publications, 1981), 5:120.

us—shapes our thinking and influences our decisions. We must be willing to go to the people groups (nations) where Christ is not known, or to send those who will.

It is the sovereign authority of Jesus that impels us to go and gives us confidence that in our going the mission of making disciples of the nations will not fail. It is the weight of the commission itself that will not allow us to mask disobedience, laziness, or lack of love for people under the sanctimonious pretense of resting in the sovereignty of God. We obey because we have been commanded. We obey with joy and hope because the One who has given us the command possesses "all authority in heaven and on earth."

This truth, as John Stott rightly notes, is the "fundamental basis of all Christian missionary enterprise":

> If the authority of Jesus were circumscribed on earth, if he were but one of many religious teachers, one of many Jewish prophets, one of many divine incarnations, we would have no mandate to present him to the nations as the Lord and Saviour of the world. If the authority of Jesus were limited in heaven, if he had not decisively overthrown the principalities and powers, we might still proclaim him to the nations, but we would never be able to "turn them from darkness to light, and from the power of Satan unto God" (Acts 26:18). Only because all authority on earth belongs to Christ dare we go to all nations. And only because all authority in heaven as well on earth is his have we any hope of success. It must have seemed ridiculous to send that tiny nucleus of Palestinian peasants to win the world for Christ. For Christ's church today, so hopelessly outnumbered by millions who neither know nor acknowledge him, the task is equally gigantic. It is the unique, the universal authority of Jesus Christ which gives us both the right and the confidence to seek to make disciples of all the nations. Before his authority on earth the nations must bow; before his authority in heaven no demon can stop them.[33]

Our responsibility is clear. Our Commander, who is with us, is unlimited. The nations are waiting. Why are we?

---

33   John R. W. Stott, "The Great Commission," in *One Race, One Gospel, One Task*, ed. Carl F. Henry and W. Stanley Mooneyham (Minneapolis: World Wide Publications, 1967), 1:46.

SECTION 3
FOR THE WORLD

A THEOLOGICALLY DRIVEN MISSIOLOGY FOR A GREAT COMMISSION RESURGENCE

Bruce Riley Ashford

One of the most significant challenges facing the Southern Baptist Convention (SBC) today is the imperative to allow her evangelical theology to shape her actual ministry practices. For three decades now since the Conservative Resurgence, the churches of the SBC have declared their belief that the Christian Scriptures are *ipsissima verba Dei*, the very words of God.[1] What we declare, however, is not always consistent with what we do. In reality, we sometimes ignore Scripture when forming our strategies, methods, and practices. It is as if we are saying that what we believe about God is important, but how we practice is not.

If the SBC is not careful, these fissures between belief and practice will leave the Conservative Resurgence incomplete and derail the Great Commission Resurgence (GCR) we now seek. A faulty doctrine of God, for example, will lead us to a wrong definition of success. A poor hermeneutic will lead to an aberrant definition of God's mission and of our mission. A misguided soteriology will neuter our attempts at evangelism and discipleship. A reductionist ecclesiology will result in anemic churches that fail to disciple their members or reach their communities. In order to foster a healthy GCR, therefore, we must seek carefully, consciously, and

---

1   In fairness, not all Southern Baptist churches would affirm the full inspiration and inerrancy of the Scriptures. The majority of Southern Baptist churches clearly do, however, and this reality is reflected in confessional statements such as the 2000 *Baptist Faith and Message* and in numerous representative publications.

consistently to rivet missiological practice to Christian Scripture and its attendant evangelical doctrine.[2]

In other words, sound doctrine must take the "driver's seat" in our missiology. In the following pages, this chapter will provide summaries of the classical loci of Christian theology along with practical examples of how each one bears upon the church's practice in general and upon missiology in particular.

REVELATION

The 2000 *Baptist Faith and Message* affirms that "the Holy Bible was written by men divinely inspired and is God's revelation of Himself to man." We believe that Scripture is given supernaturally by God; indeed, it is the very breath of God (2 Tim 3:16). Again, we believe that Scripture is *ipsissima verba Dei*, the very words of God.

Because the Christian Scriptures are indeed the very words of God, we will want to shape our strategies and methods according to its teachings. And while, for most evangelical Southern Baptists, this might seem to be a yawningly obvious observation, we must pay careful attention in light of the fact that we sometimes *do not* allow the Scriptures to inform and shape our evangelism, discipleship, church growth, and church planting. We sometimes speak loudly about inerrancy, while undermining that same conviction by our practices.

One cannot craft a truly evangelical missiology by means of proof-texting. Many of the practical ministry challenges waiting to be met are not explicitly addressed in isolated passages of Scripture. In the absence of clear statements on some particular methodological or strategic initiative, we must call forth the deep-level principles in the Bible and allow them to speak with propriety and prescience to the issue at hand. Further, as our global, national, and cultural contexts change from era to era, we must rework and rewrite our missiology afresh for every generation.

Nor can we craft our missiology without taking into account general revelation. While God provides certain knowledge (e.g., the Trinity, the Incarnation, and salvation by grace through faith alone) through special revelation alone,

---

2 Thom Rainer's *The Book of Church Growth* is an example of one Baptist missiologist's conscious and careful reflection on the connection between theology and missiology. He devotes one third of the book to showing how each locus of systematic theology comes to bear upon church growth principles and practice. Thom Rainer, *The Book of Church Growth* (Nashville: Broadman, 1993), 71–168.

He provides other (nonsalvific) knowledge through our human faculties. God Himself created us with the capacities for reason and imagination. Therefore, we benefit from studying history, philosophy, linguistics, anthropology, sociology, marketing, and other disciplines. In other words, God is the giver both of Scripture and of the created order, and the two are not in conflict with one another. When properly interpreted, they agree.[3]

How, then, might a missiologist view extra-biblical disciplines such as history, philosophy, anthropology, sociology, and marketing? How should they be positioned in light of Christian Scripture? Here are four of the ways that they might be helpful.[4]

First, extra-biblical disciplines may be helpful in the apologetic task of pointing to God's existence and some of His attributes (Rom 1). We may make ontological, teleological, cosmological, and moral arguments for the existence of one God based upon what we may learn in philosophy, anthropology, sociology, or other disciplines.

Second, knowledge from these disciplines may be helpful for proclaiming the gospel and planting churches in an appropriate manner contextually. Reading widely in history and current affairs, for example, helps us to understand the cultural and social contexts of those to whom we minister. Cultural anthropology and sociology may also be helpful in studying the way God's image bearers live in their diverse contexts, assisting us in the task of contextualization. Linguistics and communication theory are helpful in showing us how to proclaim the gospel across linguistic and cultural barriers.

Third, these disciplines are sometimes useful in illustrating theological truths. One might illustrate such concepts as God's love and fatherhood, or man's sin and its consequences, using insights gleaned from anthropology and sociology.

Fourth, they may be helpful in subverting false theologies. We may use philosophy and the social sciences to defend the truth, goodness, and

---

3 This is not to say that theologians and natural or social scientists never disagree. Often they do, but the disagreement is not found in any inherent conflict between Scripture and the natural world, but rather in theologians' and scientists' interpretations of the two. Either group might err, and either group is therefore subject to correction. To sharpen the point, our will is bent toward idolatry, and therefore our attempts at interpreting Scripture and the natural world will be affected by our idolatry. God's grace, by His Spirit and Word, corrects our interpretations of both Scripture and nature. For further reflection, see John M. Frame, *Apologetics to the Glory of God* (Phillipsburg, NJ: P&R, 1994), 22–26.

4 For further reflection on the relation of theology to other disciplines, see David K. Clark, *To Know and Love God: Method for Theology* (Wheaton: Crossway, 2003): 259–317.

beauty of the gospel, in response to those who attack us. We may use them to "take the roof off" opposing worldviews, philosophies, and religions, showing them to be unable to deliver what they promise.[5]

This, then, is a very limited exploration of how the doctrine of revelation comes to bear upon the church's practice.[6] In riveting missiological practice to the doctrine of revelation, we must beware of at least two dangers. The first is to allow the insights gleaned from general revelation (in particular, anthropology, sociology, and business marketing) to take the driver's seat in missiology. The second danger, however, is that we will not only give theology the driver's seat but also demand that no other discipline be allowed a seat.[7] To do so, I believe, is to reject the great gift that God has given us in allowing us to study and interact with His good world.

GOD

The doctrine of God is central to all of the church's life although, ironically, we seem to have difficulty allowing this doctrine to drive our practice. How does such a lofty and majestic doctrine speak to concrete and even mundane practices? How do God's Trinitarian nature, His creativity, and His sovereignty affect our strategies and methods?

God as Trinity

God is Triune. Scripture reveals this truth (Matt 3:16–17; 28:19), and the church has taught it across the centuries. But what does this doctrine have to do with missiology? One oft-overlooked example of the relevance of Trinitarian doctrine for missiology is hermeneutics and cross-cultural communication. The task of proclaiming the gospel across cultures is no

---

5 Francis Schaeffer spoke of "taking the roof off" a person's worldview in order to reveal that it is unlivable. For a brief description, read Bryan Follis, *Truth with Love: The Apologetics of Francis Schaeffer* (Wheaton: Crossway, 2006), 40–42. Also, see James W. Sire, *The Universe Next Door: A Basic Worldview Catalog*, 3d ed. (Downers Grove, IL: InterVarsity Press, 1997).

6 This chapter provides further reflection on Christian Scripture below, under the doctrine of the Spirit.

7 This latter danger is perhaps presently the greater challenge. Southern Baptists have discovered and put to use many concepts gleaned from business marketing, anthropology, psychology, and other disciplines. The problem, however, is that many of the theories and practices recommended within these disciplines arise from, and are shaped by, false worldviews and therefore are at odds with the gospel and its implications.

longer limited to international missionaries, as church planters and pastors in North American contexts now confront a diverse array of cultures and subcultures. Countless books, articles, and essays on cross-cultural communication and contextualization have been written, but many of these publications fail to recognize that the success of this enterprise rests squarely on the shoulders of the Triune God.

Kevin Vanhoozer makes this point, arguing that the Trinity is not only the foundation for a faithful hermeneutic, but also a model of accomplished communication. The Triune God is God the Father (the one who speaks), God the Son (the Word), and God the Spirit (the one who illumines and guides and teaches). God the Father speaks through His Son, and His Spirit enables us as humans to hear and understand that communication. The Trinity is a demonstration that accomplished communication is possible.[8] In communicating across cultures and subcultures, the North American or international church planter is assured that the gospel can be communicated accurately precisely because of the God who called him to do so.

God as Creator and King

As creator, God brought into existence the world in which we now live, and it is a *good* world (Gen 1–2). God's world is ontologically good and—although it is morally corrupt as a result of the Fall—we may use any and all aspects of God's world to bring Him glory. A robust doctrine of creation emphasizes the biblical teaching that God created man in His image and likeness (Gen 1:26–27), endowing him with spiritual, moral, rational, relational, and creative capacities. It does not ignore the cultural aspect of our Christian witness, but encourages us to bring the gospel to bear upon all aspects of the created order, including the arts, the sciences, and the public square.[9] It urges us to live out the implications of our faith in the midst of multiple callings—workplace, family, church, and community.[10]

---

8 See Kevin J. Vanhoozer, *Is There a Meaning in This Text? The Bible, the Reader, and the Morality of Literary Knowledge* (Grand Rapids: Zondervan, 1998), 455–68.

9 Abraham Kuyper, the famous theologian and former prime minister of the Netherlands, is perhaps best known for his work on this aspect of our Christian witness. See Abraham Kuyper, *Lectures on Calvinism* (Grand Rapids: Eerdmans, 1931); Peter Heslam, *Creating a Christian Worldview: Abraham Kuyper's Lectures on Calvinism* (Grand Rapids: Eerdmans, 1998).

10 A concise and helpful treatment of vocation is Gene Edward Veith Jr., *God at Work: Your Christian Vocation in All of Life* (Wheaton: Crossway, 2002), which is based on Martin Luther's sermons and teachings on the topic.

Our salvation includes being remade into the image of our Creator (Col 3:10) and conformed to the image of the Son (Rom 8:29) who is Himself *the* image of God (Col 1:15). The gospel, therefore, affects all aspects of man in the image of God, and these aspects ought to be used to minister in God's world for His glory.

Finally, the doctrine of creation reminds us that God claims sovereignty over every tribe, tongue, people, and nation—over every type of person who has ever lived throughout the span of history and across the face of the globe. In short, a biblical doctrine of creation teaches us to use every aspect of our created being to give God glory in every dimension of human culture and across the fabric of human existence, among every tribe, tongue, people, and nation.

God and His Name

God the Creator, in all of His blazing glory, stands at the center of the universe. He is the fountainhead of all truth, all goodness, and all beauty. God's ultimate goal and man's ultimate purpose is the increase of His glory and His kingdom.[11] Scripture describes how God does all that He does for the sake of His name, for His renown, for His glory. He created man for His glory (Isa 43:7) and chose Israel for His glory (Isa 49:3). God delivered Israel from Egypt for His name's sake (Ps 106:7–8) and restored them from exile for His glory (Isa 48:9–11). He sent our Lord Jesus Christ so that the Gentiles would give Him glory (Rom 15:8–9) and then vindicated His glory by making propitiation through His Son (Rom 3:23–26). He sent the Spirit to glorify the Son (John 16:14) and tells us to do all things for His glory (1 Cor 10:31). He will send His Son again to receive glory (2 Thess 1:9–10) and will fill the earth with the knowledge of His glory (Hab 2:14; Is 6:1–3). Indeed, all of this is "so that at the name of Jesus every knee should bow . . . and every tongue should confess that Jesus Christ is Lord, to the glory of God the Father" (Phil 2:10–11).

One implication of this for mission is that we have the great joy of proclaiming that God's goal to be glorified enables man's purpose, which

---

11 Jonathan Edwards, in his *The End for Which God Created the World*, gives the most well-known and extended reflection upon this doctrine. Technically, *The End* is the first part of a two-part book by Edwards entitled *Two Dissertations*. See Paul Ramsey, ed., *Two Dissertations, Ethical Writings*, The Works of Jonathan Edwards, vol. 8 (New Haven: Yale University, 1989). It should be noted, however, that it is not only Reformed Christians who would affirm this doctrine.

is to be truly satisfied. The psalmist writes, "God, You are my God; I eagerly seek You. I thirst for You; my body faints for You in a land that is dry, desolate, and without water" (Ps 63:1). Man's deepest thirst turns out to be resonant with God's highest goal for him. The road toward pleasing God and giving Him glory and the road toward knowing deep happiness are not two roads; they are one. The message we bring to the nations is one of profoundly good news.[12]

Another implication is that if our ultimate goal is God's glory, then we are set free from unbridled pragmatism. Our ultimate goal is to please God, not to manipulate or coerce professions of faith, church growth, or church multiplication. And so, we are directed away from the temptation to engage in evangelism and discipleship that subverts the gospel or the health of the church, and are free to proclaim the gospel God's way and leave the results to God.

God's Mission

Finally, and this point will be expanded upon later, mission finds its origin in God. Mission is God-centered, being rooted in God's gracious will to glorify Himself. God defines mission. It is organized, energized, and directed by God. Ultimately, it is accomplished by God. The church cannot understand her mission apart from the mission of God.

CHRIST

It is said that a Hindu once asked E. Stanley Jones, "What has Christianity to offer that our religion has not?" Jones's answer: "Jesus Christ."[13] Indeed, Jesus Christ, central to Christian belief and practice, is the driving force in our missiology.

Jesus Christ Is Supreme

Jesus Christ is preeminent—all things were created by Him, through Him, and for Him (Col 1:16). It is only through Him that people are saved

---

12 John Piper, *Let the Nations Be Glad: The Supremacy of God in Missions*, 2nd ed., rev. and exp. (Grand Rapids: Baker, 2003).

13 Paul Borthwick, *Six Dangerous Questions* (Downers Grove, IL: InterVarsity Press, 1996), 48.

(Acts 4:12) and only through Him that the church is built (Matt 16:18). It is in Christ, writes Ajith Fernando, that "the Creator of the world has indeed presented the complete solution to the human predicament. As such it is supreme; it is unique; and it is absolute. So we have the audacity in this pluralistic age to say that Jesus as He is portrayed in the Bible is not only unique but also supreme."[14]

Scripture in its entirety proclaims none other than Christ Himself. Both the Old and New Testaments are Christocentric—Christ is the axis of the testaments, the linchpin of the canon. The purpose of the Scriptures is to present Christ (Luke 24:27). The central promise of the Old Testament is that God would send the Messiah (Gen 3:15). Riveted to that promise is the further promise that this Messiah would win the *nations* unto Himself and indeed reconcile *all things* unto Himself. From Genesis 3 onwards, we see the triumphant march of God to fulfill that promise in the crucified and resurrected Jesus who will come again and bring with Him a new heavens and a new earth where His redeemed people will live in His presence.

He Has Commissioned Us to Make Disciples of All Nations

From His supreme authority comes the commission Christ has given His church (Matt 28:18–20). We proclaim this Great Commission, but sometimes we overlook the particulars of the command. In the first phrase, "All authority has been given to Me in heaven and on earth," it is made clear that the follower of any other lord must repent and follow Jesus, and do so on the basis of the supreme authority of the Lord of the universe. He has authority over Satan, evil spirits, the forces of nature, the human race, and indeed all of the created order. We go in confidence, even as we pray for a Great Commission Resurgence.

Next, our Lord gives the imperative, "Go, therefore, and make disciples of all nations, baptizing them in the name of the Father and of the Son and of the Holy Spirit." In this command, we are instructed to make *disciples*, and not merely professions of faith. Moreover, we are to do so through baptism (and therefore in the context of His church) and in the name of

---

14 Ajith Fernando, *The Supremacy of Christ* (Wheaton: Crossway, 1995), 262.

the Triune God (who alone can save), teaching believers to obey everything He has commanded us.

The missiological implications of this are manifold, but two demand our attention. First, the "commands of Christ" are contained in the *Christian Scriptures*. There is no true evangelism or discipleship apart from the proclamation of the Word of God. Any other tools that we may use, such as philosophical apologetics or Qur'anic points of contact, are preliminary and are for the sole purpose of engaging that person with the Word of God.

Second, the commands of Christ are not limited to those statements in the New Testament in which Jesus speaks in the imperative. Indeed, the entirety of Christian Scripture, including Old and New Testaments, teaches us what God has done through Christ. All Scripture is inspired by God (2 Tim 3:16), and hence also bears the insignia of Christ. Our evangelism and discipleship, therefore, will include the clear teaching of the entire canon of Scripture.

In the final phrase of Matthew 28:20, our Lord promises, "And remember, I am with you always, to the end of the age." This promise is our confidence; we go under the authority of Christ and in the very presence of Christ. *Missiology is at its heart Christological.* There is perhaps no better picture of this than in Revelation 5:9–10, where the Lion of the Tribe of Judah receives the worship of the nations: "You are worthy to take the scroll and to open its seals; because You were slaughtered, and You redeemed [people] for God by Your blood from every tribe and language and people and nation. You made them a kingdom and priests to our God, and they will reign on the earth."

Missiology is also inextricably linked with suffering. Just as the Lion of Judah suffered as the Lamb who was slain, we are called to be willing to suffer on behalf of the gospel. Paul hints at this "missiological suffering" when he writes, "Now I rejoice in my sufferings for you, and I am completing in my flesh what is lacking in Christ's afflictions for His body, that is, the church" (Col 1:24). There is a sense in which Paul's suffering makes up what is lacking in Christ's suffering, and the only thing lacking is Christ's sufficient renown among the nations.[15] Thus, we now proclaim His name to all people, living in anticipation of His Second Coming when we will worship Him as the king of the nations.

---

15 For further reflection on missiological suffering, see Piper, *Let the Nations Be Glad*, 71–107.

HOLY SPIRIT

Christians acknowledge that Father, Son, and Spirit live in eternal and unbroken communion with one another. The unified nature of their fellowship lies not only in Their shared attributes and perfections but also in Their shared mission. The Triune God's mission is equally that of the Father, the Son, and the Spirit. Though the persons of the Trinity may play different roles, They nonetheless are working as one. Scripture presents the Spirit as He who empowers us for mission (Acts 1:8) and gives us the words to say in time of need (Matt 10:17–20). It is He who convicts souls (John 16:8–11) and grows the church both in number (Acts 2:14–41) and in maturity (Eph 4:7–13). Again, the application of this doctrine is significant.

The Spirit Reveals

Throughout the ages, Christians have recognized that God reveals Himself through His Word by His Spirit. Indeed, the human writers of Scripture wrote as they were moved by the Spirit (2 Pet 1:21) so that Paul could make clear that all Scripture is *theopneustos*, or "God-breathed," and is "profitable for teaching, for rebuking, for correcting, for training in righteousness" (2 Tim 3:16). Scripture is the very breath of God.

This teaching has manifold and serious implications for our missiology. For example, there are entire people groups who are oral learners unable to read Scripture. Christian workers must (1) make every effort to communicate the Scriptures orally to them; (2) equip them to share the gospel and build the church; (3) pray for and support Bible translation just as we do church planting; (4) pray and work for the development of literacy among the leaders of these people groups;[16] and (5) pray, work, and even fight to have the Scriptures translated accurately.[17]

---

16 Some missiologists reject the call to translate the Bible for, and introduce literacy to, a society of oral learners. This rejection, however, is misplaced. Although cultures have a fair degree of internal consistency, they are always changing because of either internal developments or external introductions. Change is not bad in and of itself. While the missionary should not seek to be colonial (seeking to export Western culture) or to build his missiology upon Darwinist anthropology (seeing Western culture as inherently farther along on the evolutionary scale), he should seek to be a change agent by introducing the gospel immediately and the written Scriptures eventually.

17 Some Bible translators, in their desire to provide contextualized translations, have mistranslated the Scriptures and in so doing have undermined doctrines central to the gospel. For example, some translators working in Islamic contexts have sought to remove the phrase "son of God" from

The Spirit Empowers, Convicts, Teaches, and Illumines

The Spirit empowers us to proclaim the Word (1 Thess 1:5; 1 Pet 1:12), to pray effectively (Rom 8:26), and to have power over the forces of evil (Matt 12:28; Acts 13:9–11). He convicts of sin, righteousness, and judgment (John 16:8–11). He teaches all things (John 14:26) and opens the eyes of our hearts that we might understand (1 Cor 2:12; Eph 1:17–19). With this in mind, we must not rely exclusively on our human efforts such as communication models, demographic studies, or people-group profiles. Rather, we should undergird our mission in any context with prayer, in reliance upon the Spirit who will enable us to interpret the Scriptures rightly and bring understanding and conviction to our audience.

The Spirit Gives Gifts and Enables Fruit

The Spirit gives gifts to each person (1 Cor 12:11) and enables believers to bear fruit (Gal 5:22–23). This truth suggests that church planting is probably best done in teams, as the multiple members of a team use their spiritual gifts together and bear fruit together in the context of Christian community.[18] The result is that those who are watching will see more clearly what Christ intends for His church. It also suggests that a new convert can immediately be considered a "new worker," a part of the team, already gifted by the Spirit and capable of bearing fruit. Immediately he can give testimony to Christ and edify the believers.

The Spirit Restrains

The Spirit works providentially, restraining evil (2 Thess 2:6–7). After the Fall, sin entered the world with devastating consequences. Man's relationships with God, with others, with the created order, and even with himself were broken. Sin fractured the world at all levels. It is only by the restraining power of the Spirit that the world is not an utter horror. God has given to the entire world this common grace that allows us to act and interact in family, workplace, and community. It allows us to use our relational,

---

translations in an attempt not to offend Muslims. To do so, however, is to remove a central biblical teaching and to neuter the gospel itself.

18 For further reflection on a "team model" for international church planting, see Daniel Sinclair, *A Vision of the Possible* (Waynesboro, GA: Authentic, 2006).

rational, and creative capacities, even though they are distorted by sin and are bent toward idolatry.[19]

MAN

Apart from the Christian Scriptures, one cannot make sense of humanity. Absent the Christian doctrine of God and the *imago Dei*, one cannot account for the unique nature, capacities, and ends of human existence.

Man's Creation

Inevitably, other worldviews tend toward either enthronement or denigration of humanity, unable to strike a proper balance.[20] Scripture, however, strikes a balance, making clear that man has both a great humility and a great dignity. His great humility, on the one hand, is that *he is not God*; indeed, he is created for the express purpose of worshiping God. His great dignity, on the other hand, is that unlike the animals and the rest of the created order, *he is created in God's image*.

At creation, man possessed a four-fold excellence in his relational capacity. He was in right relationship with God, with others, with the created order, and with himself. He experienced *shalom*—a universal human flourishing, a right ordering of things, a divine peace. It was in this state of *shalom* that God instructed man to work the ground, to change and even enhance what God had made. Further, He instructed man to multiply and fill the earth. Man, therefore, is made to be both productive and reproductive.[21]

---

19   For further reflection, see Michael S. Horton, *Where in the World is the Church?* (Phillipsburg, NJ: P&R, 2002).

20   Naturalism is exemplary in this respect. On the one hand, the atheists of the Humanist Manifestos enthrone man, speaking of him as if he is a god. On the other hand, contemporary pagans such as Peter Singer denigrate man, speaking of him as a mere animal. "By 2040," Singer writes, "it may be that only a rump of hard-core, know-nothing religious fundamentalists will defend the view that every human life, from conception to death, is sacrosanct." Peter Singer, "The Sanctity of Life," *Foreign Policy* (September–October 2005): 40.

21   G. K. Beale views the Great Commission as the fulfillment of God's original command to fill the earth. According to Beale, Adam was to expand the Garden of Eden, which is presented in Genesis as a temple, and thereby expand God's presence "to the ends of the earth." Therefore, in the Great Commission, "Jesus is empowering his followers . . . with spiritual empowerment to do what

Man's Fall

After the Fall, however, man experienced the cataclysmic consequences of his rebellion; he was no longer in right relationship with God, with others, with the created order, or with himself. Beginning with Adam and Eve, every member of the human race has taken up arms and rebelled against God. The aftermath has been devastating, with sin wreaking havoc across the entire fabric of human life. Man's sin has caused a deep and pervasive distortion of God's good creation.

Because of the Fall, our relationship with *God* is broken. We are serial idolaters, enemies of God, seeking goodness and happiness on our own, apart from Him. We are *homo incurvatus in se*, or man "turned in on himself" (Luther) and, thus, are not "fully alive" (Irenaeus).[22] Our wills are bent toward sin; we are dead in our trespasses (Eph 2:1). As a result, we must recognize that such idolaters need something deep and powerful in order to be saved. In other words, if man is corrupted by sin "through and through," then salvation is not a matter merely of intellectual assent. Therefore, we must avoid reductionist methods of evangelism and discipleship. We must proclaim the gospel according to the Scriptures as we seek to see God break up the ground of hard hearts.

Second, our relationship with *others* is broken. Rather than serving and loving our fellow man, our relationships are marked by interpersonal and societal ugliness. There is hardly a more easily proven fact than human badness—consider the abuse, divorce, rape, war, incest, gossip, slander, murder, and deceit that abound. The church should take note that her mission includes the modeling of a more excellent way; a watching world should know us by our love one for another (John 13:35). Our life together, in mutual love for one another and Christ, is a sign of God's kingdom, a foreshadowing of the unbroken harmony that we will experience on a new heavens and earth.

Third, our relationship with the *created order* is broken; rather than unbroken harmony and delight, we experience pain and misery. This brokenness of the created order provides an opportunity for the church to

---

Adam and others had failed to do." G. K. Beale, *The Temple and the Church's Mission* (Downers Grove, IL: InterVarsity Press, 2004), 199.

22 Luther argues that man is *incurvatus in se*, "curved in on his own understanding." See Jaroslav Pelikan, ed. *Luther's Works* (St. Louis: Concordia, 1955–1986), 25:426. For Irenaeus, there is no "complete" or "perfect" man without the Spirit. Christ, through his Incarnation, bestows the Spirit and enables man to be truly alive. See Irenaeus, *Against Heresies* 5.6.1; 5.9.2.

minister. Natural disasters are signposts that point to the brokenness of the natural order. We can use this signpost to proclaim the gospel, by teaching the gospel according to the Scriptures. In other words, we do not simply tell hurting and suffering people "Jesus loves you." In addition, we describe how God created the world without such evil, that such evil entered the world because of sin, and that one day there will be a new heavens and earth where there is no more sin and no more evil. We also act upon the privilege of ministering to the physical needs of our fellow image-bearers, demonstrating the love about which we speak.

Fourth, we are alienated even from *ourselves*. This alienation is another signpost that points to the brokenness of God's good creation. Again, we can use this signpost to declare the gospel. Take, for example, the despair that many experience at the apparent meaninglessness of life. The person who despairs may be an American materialist, a Thai Buddhist, a philosophical nihilist, a victim of sexual abuse, or merely a person who senses that his life lacks meaning and purpose. The gospel answers this concern by showing man that he is created in the image of God, that his purpose in life is to glorify God, and that this purpose is not at odds with his own deepest satisfaction. Happiness, in its deepest and most profound sense, comes from being conformed to the image of the Son (Rom 8:29), who Himself is the image of God (Col 1:15).

In light of man's holistic corruption, we are driven to minister holistically. We must work hard, therefore, to bequeath to the churches we plant a vision for the deep, broad, and powerful impact that the Christian faith can and should have on the various sociocultural dimensions of life. We may use all of our human capacities to minister to man in the wholeness of his humanity. We may seek to glorify God in the arts, the sciences, education, and the public square, as well as inside the four walls of a church meeting. We must teach our children to devote their intellectual and creative capacities, and not merely their spiritual and moral capacities, to Christ. We must teach them that "pastor" and "missionary" are not the only honorable callings for a godly child; science, education, law, and journalism are also honorable callings. In so doing, our churches will bear witness from within every arena of human society and culture.

SALVATION

The doctrine of salvation receives as much attention as any of the classical loci of Christian doctrine. It is central to missiological method and yet, ironically, we have a difficult time making a "full connect" between the doctrine and our methods and strategies.

Salvation is God's work from beginning to end (Ps 3:8; Heb 12:2). At the beginning, we see God's hand in election, the gracious decision by which He elects people to salvation. We see God's hand also in calling sinners back to Himself (Gen 3:9), and in calling preachers who are an instrument of others' salvation (Rom 10:14–15). God is also at work as people repent and place their faith in Christ. Human beings are converted as God regenerates them, renewing them inwardly, and imparting eternal life to them.

Salvation is by grace alone, through faith alone, in Christ alone. We seek to form missiological practices that recognize all aspects of God's work of salvation. Because of the limited scope of this chapter, I will choose only a handful of the many facets of soteriology and give a limited exposition of their implication for missiology.

We Must Recognize That It Is God Who Calls

In the *ordo salutis*, we see God drawing people to Himself (Gen 3:9; Luke 15:1–7). While we will never have sure or final knowledge of who God is drawing, we may pray that God will bring across our paths those men and women whom he is drawing to Himself. These may very well be individuals through whom He will declare His glory to an entire city or people group. We may pray for particular people, asking God to begin drawing them to Himself. We do evangelism God's way, without compromising sound biblical theology, and leave the results to God who calls.

We Must Call Nonbelievers to Repentance and Not Merely Mental Assent

We must work hard to form evangelism and discipleship practices that recognize the entire salvific process. One of the most oft-ignored aspects of salvation is repentance. Therefore, we seek to form testimonies, gospel presentations, Bible-study sets, and sermons that call people to repentance rather than merely to mental assent. This means that they must turn their backs on false saviors, repudiate tribal gods and witch doctors, reject their belief that the Qur'an is God's revelation and that Muhammad is His prophet, cease to worship in spirit temples and ancestral shrines, and turn their back on the worship of sex, money, power, and other metaphorical idols.[23]

We Must Preach Salvation by Grace through Faith in Christ, and Do So in a Way That Is Faithful, Meaningful, and Dialogical

We must work hard to preach justification by grace alone, through faith alone, in Christ alone. We must do so in a contextually appropriate manner, communicating faithfully, meaningfully, and dialogically. We do so *faithfully* by remaining true to the authorial intent of the biblical writers and *meaningfully* by communicating in such a way that the audience understands our message in the way we intend it. [24] We must be very careful, as we face cross-cultural and cross-linguistic challenges, to work hard not only to interpret the Word properly, but also to proclaim the Word clearly.

---

23   This doctrine of repentance, premised upon the Lordship of Christ and crucial to biblical teaching about salvation, disallows "insider movements" (IM) as a mission strategy for reaching Muslims. Proponents of IM say that such movements contain Muslim background believers who choose to remain within Islam as a means of reaching Muslims. In response to the IM movement, we must respond by saying that IM ideology transgresses biblical bounds and misunderstands the nature of Islam. Islam is a religion custom-built to subvert and overthrow orthodox Christianity. Its merely human Jesus and its doctrines of tawhid and shirk make clear that the worst possible sin for a Muslim is to believe in the Christian doctrines of Trinity and Incarnation. Although Muslim background believers face persecution and even death, and although we understand that it will take God-given courage to stop attending the mosque and confessing that Muhammad is God's prophet, we must reject IM strategy because of its subversion of the doctrines of Lordship and repentance. For two insider descriptions of IM, see Kevin Higgins, "The Key to Insider Movements: The 'Devoted's' of Acts," *IJFM* 21 (Winter 2004): 155, and Rebecca Lewis, "Promoting Movements to Christ within Natural Communities," *IJFM* 24 (Summer 2007): 75.

24   For a concise and helpful discussion of the concepts of "faithfulness" and "meaningfulness," see David J. Hesselgrave and Edward Rommen, *Contextualization: Meanings, Methods, and Models* (Pasadena: William Carey, 2000), 199–211. Perhaps this is the best place to comment on the current debate about using the term *Allah* in Bible translations in Arab contexts. Sometimes the term *Allah* is the most appropriate word for the deity, as it predates Islam and is the only serious term used to refer to God. See Irfan Shahid, "Arab Christianity before the Rise of Islam," in *Christianity: A History in the Middle East*, ed. Habib Badr (Beirut: Middle East Council of Churches, 2006), 441–42. Christians may use the term, therefore, but must define the term consciously, carefully, and consistently according to Christian Scripture, just as John did in using logos and as Moses did in using elohim.

Finally, we communicate the gospel *dialogically*.[25] The gospel must be proclaimed and embodied. There is an ever-present danger that Christian preachers, missionaries, and communities will equate the gospel with a cultural context, the consequence of which is devastating. In an attempt to communicate the gospel meaningfully within a culture, and in an attempt to affirm whatever in a culture can be affirmed, Christians find it easy to lose sight of the effects of depravity on that same culture. The gospel stands in judgment of all cultures, calling them to change. It does not condemn all of a culture, but it is always and at the same time both affirming and rejecting.

For example, a married Hindu-background believer will cease to have his primary relationship with his mother, and it will now be with his wife. This is contrary to Hindu tradition. A married Muslim-background believer will cease beating his wife. When an animist-background believer comes to Christ, he may see eventually that the Bible answers but also reframes his questions about "power." The gospel answers that Jesus Christ has defeated Satan and his forces, but the gospel also reframes the animist's worldview by teaching him that he need not constantly be in fear, that he need not constantly think in terms of "power."

When a Buddhist background person is confronted with the gospel, he may see "shame and honor" as the central categories in life. The Bible affirms those categories, but adds a new set of questions concerning guilt, sacrifice, and forgiveness. If the gospel loses this prophetic edge, it loses its power. Much has been made about contextualization, but often the discussion emphasizes the need to make the gospel meaningful while neglecting or de-emphasizing the need to teach it faithfully and dialogically. To do so, however, almost ensures that one's proclamation will distort the gospel and one's church plant will not adequately represent the gospel.

We Must Beware of Mechanical or Magical Understandings of Salvation

One of the greatest hindrances to missions is the tendency to present a "magical" or "mechanistic" view of salvation.[26] We must correct the tendency to view salvation as mere mental assent, mere verbal profession of

---

25 For a concise and helpful discussion of the dialogical nature of contextualization, see David K. Clark, *To Know and Love God: Method for Theology*, Foundations of Evangelical Theology (Wheaton: Crossway, 2003), 99–131.

26 I owe this idea to a conversation I had with a long-time mission leader in Central Asia.

faith, or mere repetition of a prayer of salvation. If a person holds to such a reductionist view of salvation, he will have a wrong goal: the maximum number of people who have prayed a prayer or made a verbal profession. Further, he will give false assurance of salvation to people who are not saved, and a false testimony to the church and the broader community. Third, he will create methods of evangelism that are reductionist and harmful to the progress of the gospel and the planting of healthy churches.[27]

We Must Beware of Both Reductionism and Complexification

One who holds to a mechanical or magical understanding of salvation will likely create methods of evangelism, discipleship, leadership training, and theological education that are reductionist to the extreme, that misunderstand what we are saved *from* and what we are saved *for*. Another, however, may run the opposite risk of crafting methods that are unnecessarily complex. The tendency is to attempt to dump one's historical, systematic, and philosophical theology on the new convert's head. Instead, we need to teach new believers the gospel in a manner that they are capable of understanding and reproducing in their present context. We must resist, therefore, the twin errors of reductionism and complexification.

We Must Make Sure That Our Methods Are Grace- and Gospel-Centered

Because only the gospel saves, our methods should be gospel-centered. Since salvation is by grace through faith, our methods should center on grace. Take, for example, various methods of "obedience-based teaching"

---

27 Many proponents of insider movements (IM) in Islamic contexts hold to an overly privatized and reductionist view of salvation which leads to a warped and reductionist ecclesiology. IM proponents promote a "churchless Christianity." However, the persecuted believers of the New Testament baptized, gathered for worship, and refused to recognize Caesar as a god. Theirs was not a churchless Christianity. Although the (commendable) aim of IM proponents is to help new converts maintain familial and communal connections, they undermine the role of the church in nurturing faith, building community, and bearing witness to the kingdom. It is my hope that this treatment of IM does not appear to be insensitive to the massive challenges that Muslim-background believers confront as they face persecution and even death.

which are popular in international missions.[28] Although we must teach obedience, these methods can quickly become legalistic and works-oriented if "obedience to Christ" is not carefully and consistently put in the context of what Christ has already accomplished through His death.

It is not that obedience-based teaching is inherently legalistic or works-oriented. The point is that teaching "obedience to Christ" can be lifeless legalism that does not differ essentially from Islam or any other works-based religion. It is not only justification that comes by grace through faith, but sanctification also.

We Must Learn How to Disciple

One of the significant challenges any pastor or church planter faces is how to create an environment in which the church makes robust disciples of its members. Discipleship is the process of being conformed into the image of Christ and therefore involves much more than a once-a-week Bible study. Discipleship at its best is immersion in the life of a healthy local church, and when such a church does not yet exist, discipleship is best accomplished through deep relationships formed with whatever believers the disciple might know.

Americans who seek to plant churches outside of the deep South of the USA will likely find themselves in non-Christian, pre-Christian, and post-Christian contexts. In such contexts, the church planter confronts the massive challenge of discipling a person who has little or no knowledge of the Bible or Christ, and little or no experience watching others live their lives in a truly Christian manner.[29] In such instances, we find it particularly urgent and necessary to allow a robust soteriology to inform our discipleship.

---

28   One prominent paradigm for obedience-based teaching is George Patterson, *The Church Multiplication Guide* (Pasadena, CA: William Carey, 2002). Another is Ying Kai, *Trainers: Establishing Successful Trainers*, 2nd ed. (Ying Kai, 2005).

29   Church planters face many additional challenges, especially in persecution-heavy environments. The disciple who publicly professes faith in Christ faces the possibility of losing his job and family and perhaps even his life. He must decide how (and how soon) he will make public his faith in Christ. He may deal with second thoughts about his faith and must do so without the support network of his family and community, and without the benefit of a biblical upbringing. In one Middle Eastern country, our workers ask fearful new converts to list the two hundred people they know best—family, friends, colleagues, etc. Once these new disciples have come up with a list of two hundred friends and acquaintances, our workers ask them to pick five names of those who are least likely to kill the new disciple if he shares the gospel. Armed with those five names, the new disciples begin to share their faith. For further reflection on discipleship in persecuted contexts, see Sinclair, *A Vision of the Possible*, 139–57.

Such a soteriology demands several responses. First, we must teach the entire redemptive narrative, refusing to teach isolated passages of Scripture divorced from their context. We teach the broad sweeping redemptive story, beginning at creation, leading through to the first coming of Christ, and concluding with His second coming and the new heaven and earth. We do not need months or years to do this; it may be accomplished in fifteen minutes, in an hour, or in a twenty-lesson Bible study set. Second, we must teach biblical commands regarding Christian living. Third, we must model what we teach by practicing "life on life" discipleship. Such discipleship is not accomplished merely by information dissemination. We must roll up our shirtsleeves and get involved in people's lives, eating with them, laughing with them, and weeping with them. We must *show* a man what it means for him to love his wife and children, *show* him what it means to carry himself with the grace and love of Christ, and *show* him how to remain faithful in the midst of adversity.

In sum, the doctrine of salvation is a most precious doctrine, displaying for us the salvation that we have found in Christ Jesus, to the glory of God the Father. It is our responsibility and high privilege to proclaim that gospel in a manner worthy of our Lord. Because whatever we model for new believers we disciple and for churches we plant will likely be copied for generations to come, nothing less than the purity of the gospel and the health of the church is at stake.

THE CHURCH

Missiology is inextricably intertwined with ecclesiology; one cannot be discussed properly without the other. It is probably for that reason that there are so many controversial issues at the intersection of the two disciplines. At the beginning of this section, we will give a cursory overview of some of the main themes of ecclesiology. This concise biblical ecclesiology will give us a "place to stand" as the latter part of the section will speak to some significant and controversial ecclesiological issues in contemporary missiology.

Being the Church

Scripture does not give a dictionary definition of the nature of the church. What it does instead is provide images and analogies that help us to understand the nature of the church. The church cannot be defined apart from its relationship to God, which is evident especially in the following three images.

In 1 Peter 2:9–10, the church is described as the *people of God*, reminding us that we are God's possession, and that we are a community rather than a collection of individuals. Second, Paul instructs us that we are the *body of Christ*. Sometimes he uses this image to refer to the church universal (Eph, Col) and sometimes to the church local (Rom, 1 Cor). This image helps us to understand that we are many members but one body (unity and diversity) and that each of us belongs to the other members of the body (mutual love and interdependence). Third, we are the *temple of the Spirit*. Our body is a temple of the Spirit (1 Cor 6:19); we are living stones built into a spiritual house (1 Pet 2:5). This image evokes not only the memory of Christ who "tabernacles" with us, but also the idea of relationship. We are held together by the Spirit.

As the Church Fathers and the Reformers reflected on the Scriptures, they came to identify the church with certain marks. The Fathers spoke of the church as one, holy, catholic, and apostolic. As evangelicals and Baptists, we accept these marks, but we understand these somewhat differently from the way Roman Catholics or Eastern Orthodox do. We are *one*, in that the same Spirit indwells all of us. We are *holy*, in that we seek to allow as members only those who profess faith in Christ and show visible signs of regeneration. We are *catholic*, in that the gospel is universally available for all people, in all places, at all times. We are *apostolic*, in that we hold to the same gospel proclaimed by the apostles. Moreover, the Reformers noted that the church is marked by the right preaching of the *gospel*, the right administration of the *ordinances*, and a commitment to church *discipline*.

These marks, however, are not exhaustive. There are many ways we can describe the church. For example, as John Hammett has pointed out, the church (1) is organized and purposeful; (2) is primarily local; (3) is by nature living and growing; (4) is centered on the gospel; and (5) is powered by the Spirit.[30]

The Scriptures teach that the church is composed of regenerate members (1 Cor 1:2; Eph 1:22–23). This belief is the center of Baptist ecclesiology,

---

30 John Hammett, *Biblical Foundations for Baptist Churches* (Grand Rapids: Kregel, 2005), 67–77.

and is directly linked to the purposes of the church.[31] While, on this side of eternity, we will never know for sure the state of another person's soul, we may keep diligent watch over the church, discipling and disciplining toward the goal of faithfulness and holiness.

Doing Church

The Scriptures speak of churches that meet in houses (Rom 16:5) as well as house churches that were connected to one another as city churches (Acts 13:1). Further, the Scriptures speak of these churches, together, as a sort of regional church (Acts 8:1) and the church universal (1 Cor 1:2). The universal church includes believers both living and dead; is not synonymous with any one institution, denomination, or network of churches; and is not entirely visible at any time.

The way that the church functions is a direct outworking of what the church is. Scripture gives us specific guidance as to how we are to live as the church. Because the church is defined by its relation to Christ, its members are actually connected to one another. Our union with Christ connects us not only to God but also one to another.

This relational dimension is evident especially in the Eucharist and in the "one another" commands. For example, we must live in harmony with one another (Rom 12:16; 15:5), forgive and bear with one another (Col 3:13), and must not pass judgment on one another (Rom 14:1). We must admonish and encourage one another (1 Thess 5:14), care for one another (1 Cor 12:25), and comfort one another (2 Cor 13:11). Perhaps all of the many "one another" commands could be summed up in 1 Thessalonians 5:15: "Always pursue what is good for one another and for all."

These commands, which are given to all of the members of the church, show that we are all responsible to one another and ultimately to Christ. The church is congregational (Acts 6:3; 13:2–3; 15:22), recognizing the congregation as the human authority but Christ as the ultimate divine authority. We follow Christ as He leads the church.

---

31 Ibid., 81. See also J. D. Freeman, "The Place of Baptists in the Christian Church," in *The Baptist World Congress: London, July 11–19, 1905, Authorised Record of Proceedings* (London: Baptist Union Publication Department, 1905), 27; Justice C. Anderson, "Old Baptist Principles Reset," *Southwestern Journal of Theology* 31 (Spring 1989): 5–12; and Mark Dever, *Nine Marks of a Healthy Church* (Wheaton: Crossway, 2000), 136.

This understanding is not at odds with the appointment of pastors, to whose leadership we submit unless for doctrinal or moral reasons their leadership is forfeited. Scripture teaches that the church has two leadership offices, the bishop/elder/pastor and the deacon. The officers are chosen by the congregation (Acts 14:23). The bishop/elder/pastor must be able to administrate (bishop), teach and nurture (pastor), must be mature in the faith (elder), and must meet the requirements laid out in Scripture (1 Tim 3, Titus 1). The deacon is a servant (Acts 6:1–6) and must meet the requirements laid out in Scripture (1 Tim 3:8 13). Pastors, in particular, are to equip the saints for the work of ministry (Eph 4:11–12).

The church's ministries are manifold and may be summarized in five categories. Hammett points out that these five ministries may be seen together in Acts 2:42–47. Those ministries are teaching, fellowship, worship, service, and evangelism.

Ecclesiology and Missiology

It is difficult to overstate the significance of ecclesiology for Christians in general and for missiologists in particular. We must agree with Mark Dever, who writes,

> The enduring authority of Christ's commands compels Christians to study the Bible's teaching on the church. Present-day errors in the understanding and the practice of the church will, if they prevail, still further obscure the gospel. Christian proclamation might make the gospel audible, but Christians living together in local congregations make the gospel visible (John 13:34–35). The church is the gospel made visible.[32]

In the coming decades, at least four issues will continually surface at the intersection of ecclesiology and mission, demanding theologically sound and missiologically savvy answers. These four issues are (1) what counts as a *church*, (2) how to evaluate *house* churches, (3) how to plant *indigenous* churches, and (4) how to remain faithful to biblical ecclesiology and at the same time pray for church planting *movements*.

---

32 Mark E. Dever, "The Church," in *A Theology for the Church*, ed. Daniel L. Akin (Nashville: B&H Academic, 2007), 767.

Bible study or church? One of the first questions that a fledgling church planter often faces is, "When does a group of believers become a church?" This is another way of asking, "What are the marks of the church?" In the previous section, we affirmed the patristic and Reformation marks of a church.

There is, however, yet another challenge that causes us to inquire about the true marks of a church once again. That challenge is world evangelization. This is the case today as the International Mission Board and other like-minded agencies seek to bring the gospel to, and plant churches among, every unreached people group in God's creation. In an eagerness to do so, though, some well-intentioned missionaries have counted as churches groups that are not churches. For example, Bible studies or small clusters of believers who know one another are sometimes improperly counted as churches.

So, how do we know when a group has become a church? First, we should say that churches can be placed legitimately on certain spectrums, such as mature and immature, healthy and unhealthy, developed and undeveloped. A group of believers can be a church without being a fully developed, mature, or healthy church. Second, we must affirm certain minimum standards in order for a group to qualify as a church. There must be a group of baptized believers, consciously committed to one another under the headship of Christ, partaking of the Lord's Supper. They may or may not have a pastor, but at the very least they must be praying for the Lord to raise up among them a pastor. Such a group may be called a church even if it is a very small group.

Church in a house? The church is not a building; the church is the people of God, the body of Christ, the temple of the Spirit. We do not need a temple because we are the temple. Therefore, where the people meet is less significant, perhaps, than we tend to think. In many of the contexts in which we are seeing the gospel go forth and churches planted, conversion to Christianity is illegal—and therefore the purchase of a building is also illegal. In these cases, of course, a church meets in a house. This raises two questions.

Is a house church un-Baptist? Is it in some way an inferior type of church? It absolutely is not, although believers in the United States might tend to think so. A church is a church, no matter where it meets. It has the same nature and is held to the same standards as any other church. There is precedent in the Scriptures for churches meeting in a house (Rom 16:5), and such churches are never treated as inferior. A house church is, in every sense of the word, a church. Further, a Baptist church is a Baptist church, whether it meets in a wooden chapel, a brick auditorium, or a neighborhood home.

Is, then, house church the superior model for church? Although those who are involved in house churches are sometimes tempted to speak as if churches that meet in houses are superior in every way, this is not the case. While a church in a house might tend to fulfill better one of the ministries of the church (e.g., fellowship), it might also tend to lag behind in another ministry (e.g., teaching).[33]

An indigenous church? Much has been made, in the past century, about the "indigenous" church. Henry Venn, Rufus Anderson, John L. Nevius, Roland Allen, and others have argued for a church that is self-supporting, self-governing, and self-propagating, and few Baptists would disagree, at least in principle.[34] Based on our doctrine of the church, especially our views on regenerate membership and congregational rule, we affirm these principles. In practice, however, we struggle to implement what we believe.

Concerning *self-support*, often our stateside churches subsidize overseas pastors and fund overseas churches in a way that undermines the health of those same pastors and churches. While it is acceptable to give special gifts for specified needs, we must be careful with other types of well-intended financial offerings. Supporting national pastors tends to sever accountability between the pastor and the church, and supporting national churches on a regular basis can foster the mindset that an expensive building is necessary for a church to be formed. Setting a finance-heavy model for church life and church multiplication will unnecessarily hinder or kill the spontaneous expansion of the church. Short-term help, in this instance, may handicap long-term growth.

---

33 Wolfgang Simson is a leading house church proponent and influential missiologist who argues that house church is a superior model. A fair-minded and helpful Baptist response to Simson's argument is James A. Atkinson, "House Church: A Biblical, Historical, and Practical Analysis of Selected Aspects of Wolfgang Simson's Ecclesiology from a Southern Baptist Perspective" (Th.M. thesis, Southeastern Baptist Theological Seminary, 2006).

34 Max Warren, ed., *To Apply the Gospel: Selections from the Writings of Henry Venn* (Grand Rapids: Eerdmans, 1971); R. Pierce Beaver, ed., *To Advance the Gospel: Selections from the Writings of Rufus Anderson* (Grand Rapids: Eerdmans, 1967); John L. Nevius, *The Planting and Development of Missionary Churches* (Hancock, NH: Monadnock, 2003); Roland Allen, *The Spontaneous Expansion of the Church* (Grand Rapids: Eerdmans, 1962).

Concerning *self-governance*, the churches we plant must submit to the leadership of Christ, who is their head. We must not unintentionally set up a hierarchy with the church planter (or the mother church or the church planting agency) as the "Pope." Long and Rowthorn describe the missiological context in which Roland Allen proclaimed the need for an indigenous church: "In missionary work overseas, concern for 'traditions' made missionaries reluctant to hand over real responsibility to indigenous leaders and often confused the Tradition of the gospel with the particular traditions of the church and society from which the missionaries came."[35] We must love and care for, exhort and admonish, and even hold them accountable, but we must not control the congregations that we plant.

Concerning *self-propagation*, we must consciously seek to plant churches whose members understand their responsibility to reach their own people group. We must plant sound, healthy churches that will grow over the long run and not just in the short term, and we must remove anything that unnecessarily hinders the growth and multiplication of the church. They must not see the Westerner as the "key" to the evangelization of their people group; they must see that they have the God-given privilege of winning their own people. It is, in fact, appropriate that we lovingly allow the churches we plant to grow without being dependent on us.

Church Planting Movements? In recent days, much has been said about Church Planting Movements (CPM), and rightly so. David Garrison defines a church planting movement as "a rapid multiplication of indigenous churches planting churches that sweeps through a people group or population segment."[36] Evangelicals, including Southern Baptists, have long been praying for and working toward the birth of CPMs among the unreached people groups of the world, and indeed, even in our own country. But there is much work left to be done to ensure that our methodology is driven by the Scriptures. It must be biblical theology that gives church planting methodology its starting point, trajectory, and parameters.

Of the many substantial missiological issues that cluster around CPM theory, two must be treated. The first issue relates to CPM as a goal. Our ultimate goal, above all others, is the increase of God's glory and kingdom; no goal that we have should subvert this goal. For this reason, we are

---

35 Charles Henry Long and Anne Rowthorn, "The Legacy of Roland Allen," in *International Bulletin of Missionary Research* 13, no. 2 (April 1989): 67.

36 David Garrison, *Church Planting Movements* (Midlothian, VA: WIGTake, 2004), 21.

concerned not only with rapidity of multiplication, but also with the purity of the gospel and the health of the church.

On the one hand, if the church multiplies rapidly but is not healthy, the long-term picture is bleak. An inordinate emphasis on rapidity will likely lead to reductionist methods of evangelism and discipleship and a reductionist view of the church that will harm the church in the long term and actually curb its growth. On the other hand, if the church is doctrinally pure but not seeking to multiply, the long-term picture is also bleak. Maybe it would be better to say that a church cannot be doctrinally pure without praying for, and working toward, the healthy and rapid growth of God's church.[37]

The second missiological issue is *leadership development*. The rapid reproduction of the church will lead to challenges in leadership identification and development. If multiple churches are planted in a short period of time, they are faced with the question of how soon a believer might be recognized as an elder. Further, in a context where the church is persecuted, how might elders train for pastoral ministry? In addition, how will they be discipled if they are not able to read? These are not hypothetical scenarios—they are church planting situations faced globally at any given time. We must take seriously the biblical teachings concerning the church, discipleship, and elder qualifications and work hard to apply them in challenging situations such as the ones listed here. [38] A Great Commission Resurgence assumes first a Great Commission *church*.

---

37 A final note regarding CPM as a goal: CPMs are not the only worthwhile missiological accomplishment. In Hebrews 11, we read of men and women of great faith whose reward was not a CPM; instead, their reward was torture, destitution, affliction, and martyrdom (11:35b–38). Many faithful workers who labor in prayer and in deed, hoping with all that is within them to see a CPM, never see the birth of a CPM. This does not mean that their labor is in vain. If they have labored for the glory of God, then He is pleased with their efforts. Rodney Stark, in fact, shows how it took several centuries of faithful witness for an obscure and marginal "Jesus movement" to become the dominant religious force in the Western world. Rodney Stark, *The Rise of Early Christianity* (San Francisco: Harper SanFrancisco, 1997).

38 These are only a few of the methodological issues connected to the doctrine of the church. The challenges are many and though they are not easily met, we may conclude with J. L. Dagg that, "Church order and the ceremonials of religion, are less important than a new heart; and in the view of some, any laborious investigation of questions respecting them may appear to be needless and unprofitable. But we know, from the Holy Scriptures, that Christ gave commands on these subjects, and we cannot refuse to obey. Love prompts our obedience; and love prompts also the search which may be necessary to ascertain his will. Let us, therefore, prosecute the investigations which are before us, with a fervent prayer, that the Holy Spirit, who guides into all truth, may assist us to learn the will of him who we supremely love and adore." J. L. Dagg, *Manual of Church Order*, reprint ed. (Harrisonburg, VA: Gano, 1990), 12.

THE END TIMES

Eschatology, as much as any other doctrine, undergirds the theory and practice of mission. Indeed, "all of Christian theology points toward an end—an end where Jesus overcomes the satanic reign of death and restores God's original creation order."[39] The doctrine of the end times is broad-ranging, and therefore this section will address only three aspects of this doctrine, followed by pointing the way toward a missiological appropriation.

The Great Divide

The Christian Scriptures instruct us about death, heaven, and hell. To be concise to the extreme, we may say that death entered the world because of sin (Rom 5:12) and is a tool of Satan (Heb 2:14–15). It is appointed to man once to die, and then the judgment (Heb 9:27). After death, he enters into either eternal damnation or eternal bliss. Eternal torment waits for those who die apart from Christ (Matt 5:22; 8:12), while eternal bliss is the reward of those who are in Christ (Rev 21:2–4).

This is a difficult doctrine, but a necessary one as the Scriptures clearly teach it. Furthermore, it is a great motivator for the Christian and for the church. The Christian must hold three truths together in tension. (1) There is no name other than Christ by which people are saved, and all those who die apart from Christ abide in eternal torment. (2) Countless millions of people have practically no access to the gospel, many of whom could search for days, weeks, and months, and never find a Bible, a Christian, or a church. (3) We, as believers, have the awesome privilege and responsibility of proclaiming to them the good news. More to the point, those of us in the United States have greater financial and personnel resources to proclaim the gospel than Christians in any other part of the globe or at any other time in history.[40]

---

39 Russell D. Moore, "Personal and Cosmic Eschatology," in Akin, *A Theology for the Church*, 858. Moore writes, "In Scripture the eschaton is not simply tacked on to the gospel at the end. It is instead the vision toward which all of Scripture is pointing—and the vision that grounds the hope of the gathered church and the individual believer. In the face of death, we see faith, hope, and love. This is what we mean when we speak of Christian eschatology—the study of the last things or ultimate matters."

40 This, of course is changing, as the Christian faith is experiencing explosive growth in certain areas of sub-Saharan Africa, East Asia, and South America. Increasingly, these regions of the world will

If we apprehend and affirm these three truths, we should find it difficult to remain apathetic. Once we hold these truths in tension, we face a decision. Will we act on their implications? Many people have never heard the gospel; without Christ, they will go to a Christless eternity; we are able to take the gospel to them. Our response likewise tends to fall into one of three categories. (1) We may change our belief system by rejecting the biblical teaching that salvation comes through Christ alone in order to ease our conscience. (2) We may simply ignore these truths, so that our conscience may rest more easily. (3) We may take these truths to heart by working to take the gospel to the nations. This latter choice means building Great Commission churches and seminaries, raising up believers who will take the gospel to the nations, and praying for and supporting those who go.

The Nations

The Scriptures also reveal, as a point of focus, the destiny of the nations. The teaching of Christian Scripture is that the gospel will be proclaimed to the whole world: "This good news of the kingdom will be proclaimed in all the world as a testimony to all nations. And then the end will come" (Matt 24:14). But it is not only that the gospel will be *proclaimed*. It is also that this gospel is *powerful to save* worshippers from among all people: "Worthy are you . . . for you were slain, and by your blood you ransomed people for God from every tribe and language and people and nation" (Rev 5:9 ESV).

The ingathering of the nations is not an add-on to Christian doctrine; it is at the heart of God's promises. The central promise in the Scriptures is that God would send Messiah, and tightly riveted to it is the promise that Messiah would win the nations unto Himself. God put His Son on the cross in order to purchase the nations. The ingathering of the nations is not an issue merely for the missiologists to write about, for professional missionaries to care about, or for churches to nod toward once a year during the Lottie Moon Offering emphasis. Rather, it is central to all who are Christian because it is central to the work of Christ.

We are to be instruments in God's hands as He makes clear to the world that He is not a tribal deity. He is the Creator, King, and Savior of the

---

have more personnel resources for engaging the unreached people groups of the rest of the world. See Philip Jenkins, *The Next Christendom* (Oxford: Oxford University Press, 2002).

nations, and we will not know Him in His full splendor until we know Him as the King of the nations.

The New Heaven and New Earth

Finally, the Scriptures declare God's promise of a new heavens and a new earth. Peter states that "we wait for new heavens and a new earth, where righteousness will dwell" (2 Pet 3:13). John sees a vision in which there is a new heaven and a new earth, where there remains no pain or tears (Rev 21). And although this teaching does not get much airtime in evangelical circles, it is no insignificant doctrine. Indeed, it is the doctrine of creation come full circle. The God who gave us the good creation of the Genesis narrative is the God who will give us a new heavens and a new earth.

In this new universe, God's image bearers will experience neither sin nor its consequences. No longer will we use our rational capacities to speak false-hoods, or our creative capacities to construct idols. Never again will we use our relational capacities to suppress others and promote ourselves, our moral capacities to slander, rape, or murder. No longer will we live in an environment where tsunamis and floods destroy or where pollution poisons the ground and air. Never again will there be war or rumors of war.

Instead, we will live in unbroken relation with God, with others, with the new universe, and with ourselves. We will be "man fully alive," worshipping God in spirit and truth. But what does this doctrine of a new heavens and earth have to do with the mission of the church? Of the many implications, here are three.

First, as noted earlier, we may use our God-given human capacities to glorify Him in human culture, as a sign of what the new heavens and new earth will be like. We may teach our children that it is honorable to be an artist (writer, composer, singer, painter, graphic designer, etc.), a scientist (biologist, chemist, physicist, sociologist, anthropologist), or a participant in the public square (journalist, lawyer, politician, ethicist, educator). In so doing, we will see God glorified from every conceivable dimension of human society and culture. Second, we may seek to glorify God in all of our callings. May we speak and live the gospel in all of those contexts so that the glory of God is not limited to the four walls of a church building, but instead is broadcast across every square inch of His universe.

Third, we may demonstrate that if there is anyone who should care about God's good creation, it is the evangelical Christian. We do not care about it inordinately, or in the wrong way, but we do care. We have a different motivation than do most "environmentalists." We recognize the creation as *God's* good creation. We do not take the gift that God has given us and trash it recklessly. To do so would be an insult to the God who made it and gave it to us to have dominion over it.

In the doctrine of the end times, therefore, we confess that the promised Messiah has come, and that He will come again to win the nations and reconcile all things to Himself. He will do this because He loves the world (John 3:16–17). In His first coming, He provided the first fruits of that redemption; in His second coming, He will provide the consummation of it.

We find ourselves living between those two comings, and the ramifications of this are multiple and significant. We must proclaim the gospel not only in Jerusalem, Judea, and Samaria, but also to the ends of the earth (Acts 1:8). We must also seek to glorify Christ in every facet of creation and culture, and in all of our multiple callings. Our worship of God should not be limited or reduced to what happens once a week on Sunday mornings. Moreover, we look toward, and hope for, the day when we can join the chorus around the throne and declare, "The Lamb who was slaughtered is worthy to receive power and riches and wisdom and strength and honor and glory and blessing!" (Rev 5:12).

CONCLUSION: A THEOLOGICALLY DRIVEN MISSIOLOGY

Southern Baptists are more than merely an indiscriminate collection of congregations who practice believer's baptism by immersion. We are churches who stand by conviction in the Baptist tradition of historic Christianity, and therefore *what* we believe should affect *how* we practice.

One of the most significant imperatives facing the SBC today is to ensure that her evangelical Baptist theology drives her actual ministry practice. In so doing, we allow the Conservative Resurgence to issue forth into a healthy Great Commission Resurgence. This chapter has been an attempt to join the conversation, drawing attention to the great doctrines of the Christian faith and some of their implications for our missiological strategies, methods, and practices. May we seek carefully, consciously, and consistently to rivet missiological practice to Christian Scripture and its attendant evangelical doctrine and in so doing, bring glory to Christ who gave us both the doctrine and its attendant mission imperative.

TO ALL PEOPLES
THE GREAT COMMISSION AND THE NATIONS[1]

Jerry Rankin

It is encouraging that the Southern Baptist Convention is embracing a call for a Great Commission Resurgence and renewing its focus on the priority of missions. The denomination was formed to facilitate taking the gospel to the lost, particularly in pagan lands around the world. W. B. Johnson was instrumental in the beginnings of the Southern Baptist Convention and the Foreign Mission Board. Three decades earlier, he had advocated the formation of a Baptist body "for the purpose of organizing a practical plan on which the energies of the whole Baptist denomination may be elicited, combined and directed in one sacred effort for sending the word of life to idolatrous lands."[2] The implication of a "resurgence" is recovering an impetus that once surged but has been neglected or become latent. Are we seeking to reclaim the basic purpose that united our cooperative efforts over 165 years ago? Is this a resurgence of the compelling mission passion of the New Testament church? How we answer these questions significantly affects our future course of action.

Perhaps this compelling theme has reference to an era of post-World War II growth when the number of foreign missionaries actually tripled in just fifteen years. Americans came back from the front in Europe and the Pacific with an expanded worldview. It was a world that was hurting and suffering, open to spiritual needs as well as the government

---

1   This chapter is a revised and expanded version of the author's original article, "The Great Commission and International Missions," in Thom Rainer et al., *Great Commission Resurgence* (Nashville: LifeWay, 2008), 51–63.

2   W. B. Johnson, quoted in T. Bronson Ray, *Southern Baptist Foreign Missions* (Nashville: Sunday School Board, 1910), 264.

supplied foreign aid for recovery and rebuilding. Southern Baptists were stirred beyond their traditional rural provincialism to reach out with the life-saving hope of the gospel. Giving to missions escalated, and a heart for evangelism was expressed in the generally successful theme of "A Million More in '54."

So what are the expectations of such a resurgence as we move further into the twenty-first century? The opinions and speculations encompass a broad spectrum. Many would see a Great Commission Resurgence as a renewed emphasis on evangelism, or improved church health, or reversing the trends to restore a growing denomination that would have greater cultural impact on our own communities and nation. Whether or not we effectively implement a renewed commitment to the Great Commission is dependent on how we define it.

Bold Mission Thrust was launched in 1976 with a vision to share the gospel with every person in the world by the year 2000. But instead of sending more missionaries and investing resources in this auspicious goal of evangelizing the massive numbers of unreached peoples of the world, the emphasis became a banner for anything and everything Southern Baptists did. Everything from Sunday school growth to food pantries was identified as BMT.

A later emphasis on Empowering Kingdom Growth had the obvious potential of renewed focus on extending the kingdom of God geographically to the nations. That concept was somewhat captured in the "Acts 1:8 Challenge" of reaching our Jerusalem, Judea, Samaria, and the ends of the earth. Some felt that the mission aspects of EKG distracted from the simple emphasis on the Lordship of Christ in our lives and in our churches, which was a needed precursor to more practical areas of ministry and outreach. Not only was the fact that denominational entities existed to empower the local church largely ignored, but there was also failure to recognize that real kingdom growth would occur only when God's reign resulted in a systemic, grassroots movement of church members and a growing network of local churches empowered to fulfill God's mission.

We are vulnerable to losing the momentum of a Great Commission Resurgence from the very beginning by a failure to identify and define the task. The potential of failure and futility is enhanced by the fact that "Great Commission" is not itself a biblical term and is therefore open to a variety of subjective interpretations. For that reason, we will begin with a look at biblical teachings about the Great Commission.

THE GREAT COMMISSION IN THE BIBLE

We have traditionally understood the Great Commission as that final mandate Jesus gave to His disciples at the conclusion of His earthly ministry before ascending to the Father (Matt 28:18–20). Assuring them that He would be with them in all power and authority, even to the end of the age, He told them to make disciples of all nations.

Other parallel Scripture references with variations in wording are identified with this mandate, subsequently labeled the "Great Commission" apparently because it was to become preeminent and supersede other activities and concerns among Jesus' followers. Luke records it in Luke 24:46–49 and Acts 1:8 as expressing the basic purpose for which we have received the power of the Holy Spirit—to be Jesus' witnesses to the ends of the earth.

We tend to make a local, practical application of the Acts 1:8 passage, justifying our witness in our hometown and the area where we live as if that responsibility were more important and preempted the task of crossing geographic and cultural barriers to reach all peoples. In fact, Jesus was outlining the geographic progression of the gospel reflected in the rest of the book of Acts. After the Day of Pentecost and an initial evangelistic thrust in Jerusalem and Judea, the gospel then spread to Samaria and a harvest began among the Gentiles. That is historic fact, and it now remains to reach the ends of the earth—which of course includes the people of America as well as those of other nations, languages, and ethnicity.

To understand and refocus our efforts on the Great Commission, it is necessary to see it essentially as the mission of God. We must not neglect the implicit fact that the verb "make disciples" in Matthew 28:19 requires an object, and that object is "all the nations." Jesus was not referring to geopolitical countries; the expression He used, *panta ta ethnē*, means the ethnic and linguistic people groups throughout the world.[3]

Ultimately, the origin of the Great Commission was not the final words of Jesus on a mountaintop in Galilee. Instead, it represents the heart and mission of God for His people from the foundation of the world.

God's purpose to be glorified among the nations is a prominent thread woven throughout Scripture from Genesis to Revelation. It was reflected

---

3 John Piper, *Let the Nations Be Glad: The Supremacy of God in Missions*, rev. ed. (Grand Rapids: Baker Academic, 2003), 161–67. See also D. A. Carson, *Matthew*, in vol. 8 of *The Expositor's Bible Commentary*, ed. Frank E. Gaebelein (Grand Rapids: Zondervan, 1984), 596.

in His call to Abraham to leave his home and family: "I will bless those who bless you, I will curse those who treat you with contempt, and all the peoples on earth will be blessed through you" (Gen 12:3). This covenant with Abraham was referring to the promise of a redeemer who would come providing the blessing of salvation for the nations. God's renewal of this covenant promise is recorded in Genesis 22:18, "And all the nations of the earth will be blessed by your offspring because you have obeyed My command."

The nation of Israel realized that God had chosen them, not because they deserved His special favor and blessing, but because they were to be an instrument to declare His glory among the nations. The occasion of bringing the Ark of the Covenant into the tabernacle in 1 Chronicles 16 was a day of celebration and praise. The ark represented the presence of God in the midst of His people. The people rejoiced in having a special relationship with God, but they recognized their responsibility to declare His glory and make Him known among all peoples: "Give thanks to the LORD; call on His name; proclaim His deeds among the peoples. Sing to Him; sing praise to Him; tell about all His wonderful works!" (1 Chr 16:8–9). God's purpose clearly extended beyond them as His chosen people: "Sing to the LORD, all the earth. Proclaim His salvation from day to day. Declare His glory among the nations, His wonderful works among all peoples. For the LORD is great and is highly praised. . . . Worship the LORD in the splendor of His holiness; tremble before Him, all the earth" (vv. 23–30).

As God's people, they were to proclaim His salvation and tell of His mighty works. They were to declare His glory among the peoples of the earth so that all nations would sing His praise. In fact, this was the purpose for their location. Generations earlier when God called Abraham "to the land that I will show you" (Gen 12:1) and eventually led His descendants to possess the land of Canaan, that location was related to His glory among the nations. God had a Great Commission motive in growing their numbers to be a great nation for four hundred years in Egypt and then giving them a land where they would prosper. He was acting on their behalf not only out of concern for their welfare to give them a land flowing with milk and honey; rather, He was positioning them on the trade routes of the world, in the heart of civilization, to be a witness to His glory. Ezekiel reminds them of this aspect of God's providence: "This is what the Lord GOD says: I have set this Jerusalem in the center of the nations, with countries all around her" (Ezek 5:5).

His glory among all peoples is a theme that resonates throughout the Psalms. "Know that I am God, exalted among the nations, exalted on the earth" (Ps 46:10). Psalm 117:1 says, "Praise the LORD, all nations! Glorify Him, all peoples!" Is there a people, created by God, anywhere on the planet among whom He does not desire to be worshipped and exalted? That day revealed in Revelation is foreseen in Psalm 22:27–28, "All the ends of the earth will remember and turn to the LORD. All the families of the nations will bow down before You, for kingship belongs to the LORD; He rules over the nations." Again, His glory among the nations is affirmed: "All the nations You have made will come and bow down before You, Lord, and will honor Your name. For You are great and perform wonders; You alone are God" (Ps 86:9–10). As the Book of Psalms approaches its conclusion, we are told: "Praise the LORD from the earth . . . kings of the earth and all peoples, princes and all judges of the earth, young men as well as young women, old and young together. Let them praise the name of the LORD, for His name alone is exalted, His majesty covers heaven and earth" (Ps 148:7a, 11–13).

Solomon recognized this twofold purpose of God—to bless and prosper Israel, but also for that blessing to result in the nations exalting God. As he dedicated the temple he prayed regarding Israel, "So that they may fear You all the days they live on the land you gave our ancestors" (1 Kgs 8:40). But he continued in the following verses: "Even for the foreigner who is not of Your people Israel but has come from a distant land because of Your name—for they will hear of Your great name, mighty hand, and outstretched arm" (vv. 41–42). When Solomon's reputation for wisdom began to spread, "people came from everywhere, sent by every king on earth who had heard of his wisdom, to listen to Solomon's wisdom" (1 Kgs 4:34). What they heard was that the fear of the LORD is the beginning of wisdom! (Prov 9:10). David reflected a similar consciousness of their witness among the nations in his song of deliverance after being rescued from the hand of his enemies: "Therefore I will praise You, LORD, among the nations" (2 Sam 22:50).

It is not uncommon for us to focus on specific aspects of the narrative history of Israel and miss the big picture, the macro-perspective of God's providence. His intervention in the lives of His people was not just to hover over them dispensing blessings. His presence among them was not to get them beyond a local challenge with timely deliverance. In manifesting His sovereignty and power, He was focusing on the greater goal of bringing the nations and peoples of the earth to the point of exalting and fearing His name.

When Israel turned back from entering the Promised Land in faithlessness and rebellion against God's will, He threatened to destroy them and create another nation greater and mightier than Israel. But Moses reminded God that Israel was already known as His chosen people; if He rejected them and they were defeated or destroyed, then it would reflect upon His reputation. "If You kill this people with a single blow, the nations that have heard of Your fame will declare, 'Since the Lord wasn't able to bring this people into the land He swore to give them, He has slaughtered them in the wilderness'" (Num 14:15–16). God relented, being "slow to anger and rich in faithful love, forgiving wrongdoing and rebellion" (Num 14:18). He declared that His power would be manifested, and "the whole earth is filled with the Lord's glory" (Num 14:21). That is an early radical affirmation of what the Great Commission is all about.

After forty years in the wilderness had passed and the faithless generation had been replaced, Joshua led Israel across the Jordan River. He reminded them that God had demonstrated His power to deliver them from Egypt, had rolled back the waters of the Red Sea, and now had dried up the waters of the Jordan River that they might cross over. But the miracles were not just for their sake, but as a testimony to all the nations: "For the Lord your God dried up the waters of the Jordan before you until you had crossed over, just as the Lord your God did to the Red Sea, which He dried up before us until we had crossed over. This is so that all the people of the earth may know that the Lord's hand is mighty, and so that you may always fear the Lord your God" (Josh 4:23–24).

God's heart and mission is that all peoples know Him, and our mission can be no less. The Great Commission is why God called Israel as His chosen people. In Psalm 67:1 they prayed, "May God be gracious to us and bless us; look on us with favor." We often use words like these at the conclusion of our worship service as a benediction, say, "Amen," and go home. But the next two verses say, "so that Your way may be known on earth, Your salvation among all nations. Let the peoples praise You, God; let all the peoples praise You " (vv. 2–3). God blessed Israel and favored them so they would be His instruments to fulfill His purpose and make His way known throughout the earth.

Just as God's miraculous intervention in the affairs of His people was a testimony to the nations, so it was in other individual incidents. We should not miss the fact that the outcome of some of our favorite Bible stories was a testimony to the nations that they might recognize God's power and glory. Note David's defiance of Goliath in 1 Samuel 17:45–47 and the fact that the victory God would give was to be a testimony to the world. David so told the giant: "You come against me with a dagger, spear, and sword, but I come against you in the name of the LORD of Hosts, the God of Israel's armies—you have defied Him. Today, the LORD will hand you over to me. Today, I'll strike you down. . . . Then all the world will know that Israel has a God, and this whole assembly will know that it is not by sword or by spear that the LORD saves, for the battle is the LORD's."

Following Daniel's deliverance from the lions' den, King Darius issued a decree that all the peoples within his royal dominion should fear and worship the God of Daniel. "Then King Darius wrote to those of every people, nation, and language who live in all the earth . . . I issue a decree that in all my royal dominion, people must tremble in fear before the God of Daniel: for He is the living God, and He endures forever" (Dan 6:25–26). Even the pagan king recognized the power and protection of Daniel's God, and he proclaimed that decree to all peoples.

If this is God's desire and purpose, should not God's people, called by His name, be diligent to proclaim His glory among the nations and bring all the peoples of the earth into His kingdom that they might give Him worship and honor and praise? God's glory among the nations is the compelling task of missions and the primary objective for which He calls to Himself a people to serve Him and be His possession. Peter quotes several Old Testament passages in reminding us, "You are a chosen race, a royal priesthood, a holy nation, a people for His possession, so that you may proclaim the praises of the One who called you out of darkness into His marvelous light" (1 Pet 2:9). Becoming the people of God is not just for our blessing and benefit; it is to declare His glory and to be an instrument of praise so that all the earth will exalt His name. David so declared: "I will praise You, Lord, among the peoples; I will sing praises to you among the nations. . . . God, be exalted above the heavens; let your glory be over the whole earth" (Ps 57:9, 11).

The apostle Paul argued that the Messiah came to the Jews for this same purpose of bringing God glory among the nations, or Gentiles—the peoples of the world who were not ethnic Jews—in fulfillment of this Old Testament expectation:

> Now I say that Christ has become a servant of the circumcised on behalf of the truth of God, to confirm the promise to the

fathers, and so that Gentiles may glorify God for His mercy. As it is written:

> Therefore I will praise You among the Gentiles,
> and I will sing psalms to Your name.

> Again it says: Rejoice, you Gentiles, with His people! And again:
> Praise the Lord, all you Gentiles;
> all the peoples should praise Him!

And again, Isaiah says:

> The root of Jesse will appear,
> the One who rises to rule the Gentiles;
> in Him the Gentiles will hope.
> (Rom 15:8–12)

Because of this understanding, Paul expressed the conviction that Christ had called him to "preach the gospel to the regions beyond you" (2 Cor 10:16). Paul had a vision and calling to take the gospel to the Gentiles, the non-Jewish peoples and nations of his day. In fact, we look to him as a prototype of a cross-cultural missionary. He testified to this calling and mission throughout his epistles and in the book of Acts. He described his kingdom vision this way: "For I would not dare say anything except what Christ has accomplished through me to make the Gentiles obedient by word and deed" (Rom 15:18). In his testimony before King Agrippa, he quoted Jesus who called him on the road to Damascus: "For I have appeared to you for this purpose, to appoint you as a servant and a witness of things you have seen, and of things in which I will appear to you. I will rescue you from the people and from the Gentiles, to whom I now send you, to open their eyes that they may turn from darkness to light and from the power of Satan to God, that they may receive forgiveness of sins and a share among those who are sanctified by faith in Me" (Acts 26:16–18). The compelling passion of Paul's life was "to evangelize where Christ has not been named, in order that I will not be building on someone else's foundation, but, as it is written: 'Those who had no report of Him will see, and those who have not heard will understand'" (Rom 15:20–21).

Paul observes in Romans 15:19 that his work was done "by the power of miraculous signs and wonders, and by the power of God's Spirit." The power of God is what enabled Paul to proclaim the gospel and plant churches all the way from Jerusalem to Illyricum. It is only as Christ's followers are engaged in being His "witnesses in Jerusalem, in all Judea and Samaria, and to the ends of the earth" (Acts 1:8) that they are promised the power of God. We can pray for God's blessing on our church programs, and He will bless them if they are in accord with His will and for His glory—but witnessing to a lost world is the reason He has given us the power of the Holy Spirit in our lives.

We must never forget that the Great Commission in Matthew 28:19–20 is preceded by the claim of Christ, "All authority has been given to Me in heaven and on earth" (v. 18). It is because of the authority that has been given to Him that we are expected to disciple the nations. He promises to go with us when we go to fulfill His mission. The realization of the vision of the kingdom of God reaching all peoples, even to the most remote part of the earth, is contingent on His power.

God's ultimate purpose is to be glorified through the redemption of the nations. He alone is worthy of all praise and honor. His purpose is that all the nations and peoples of the earth would know and exalt Him in worship, and this purpose will be fulfilled. The culmination of His divine activity in the world is expressed in the book of Revelation: "Our Lord and God, You are worthy to receive glory and honor and power, because You have created all things, and because of Your will they exist and were created" (Rev 4:11). We are told of that coming day when there would be:

> . . . a vast multitude from every nation, tribe, people, and language, which no one could number, standing before the throne and before the Lamb. They were robed in white with palm branches in their hands. And they cried out in a loud voice: Salvation belongs to our God, who is seated on the throne, and to the Lamb! All the angels stood around the throne, the elders, and the four living creatures, and they fell on their faces before the throne and worshiped God, saying: Amen! Blessing and glory and wisdom and thanksgiving and honor and power and strength, be to our God forever and ever. Amen. (Rev 7:9–12)

Everything that exists in the world does so for God's glory. Every activity and endeavor should be to glorify Him, not only in our lives and community but also among all peoples, even to the ends of the earth.

THE GREAT COMMISSION IN OUR LIVES

Unfortunately, we seldom understand our needs in the perspective of God's glory and purpose beyond our own provincialism and self-centered concern. We seldom see the trials and adversity we encounter as an opportunity to prove our faith and for God to be glorified through divine intervention. For example, there is a concerted appeal to pray for America to return to God and for a restoration of Judeo-Christian values in our society. We pray that we might be relieved from a volatile and uncertain economic situation so that we can be assured of security and prosperity. God delivered Israel from many similar trials, but it was for a greater purpose. Deliverance had to do with His plan for the nations and His desire to be exalted among the peoples of the earth.

As we are going to see, perhaps we do not experience the divine intervention we yearn for because we think "renewal" is only about us, our needs, and our country rather than an impetus for the mission to which God has called us. We need to recognize that, in God's providence, all He allows us to experience is to result in a testimony to the nations.

We tend to have an egocentric theology. If most Christians were asked why Jesus died on the cross, they would reply, "To save me from my sin." That is correct; He did die for all. When we come to Jesus in repentance and faith today, His death on the cross is for the penalty of our sin, and we are saved through faith. But note the answer to this question in the words of Jesus Himself as He explains to His disciples why He died on the cross. In Luke 24:46–47 Jesus said, "Thus it is written, and was necessary for the Christ to suffer and to rise again, that repentance and remission of sins would be preached in His name among all nations beginning in Jerusalem." His death was not just for us. He died and rose again to give us a message of forgiveness and salvation that we are to proclaim among all nations.

We have had a tendency to dilute the Great Commission to mean whatever we do in witnessing, evangelism, and ministry. Many have taken this entire thrust of Scripture to interpret our task in terms of winning individuals in order to populate heaven with as many born-again souls as possible. Certainly, people groups must be discipled through winning and discipling individuals as followers of Christ, but we must not lose the biblical perspective on nations or peoples. "Peoples" may not seem to be grammatically correct, as the word "people" is already a collective plural noun. But Jesus was not talking about evangelizing all people, that is, all the individuals in the world. The word He used, *ethnē* (the plural of *ethnos*), is the source of our word "ethnic," those distinct cultural and racial characteristics that distinguish some people from others.[4] Jesus was commissioning His disciples—and that includes us today—to bring into the kingdom of God and make disciples (that is, Christ-like followers) members of every ethnic, cultural, and language group in the world.

Due to accelerating evangelistic efforts in recent years, we are told that approximately 10 percent of the world's population—around 700 million people—now profess to be born-again believers.[5] When we think of one out of ten people having come to saving faith in Jesus Christ, the task of reaching everyone seems doable; all it would take is every Christian sharing the gospel with nine others. However, the problem is a matter of proportion. Unfortunately, most of those believers are clumped together in America and other places where the church has been established while hundreds of people groups, some numbering in the millions, have yet to hear the name of Jesus. Researchers estimate 1.7 billion people are "Last Frontier" people who have no access to the gospel almost 2000 years after Jesus sent His followers to make disciples of all nations.[6] That means they are isolated culturally and geographically in places where there are no churches and no Christian believers as a witness. They have no Scripture in their own language, and no missionary enterprise has yet to confront them with the claims of Christ.

Why should we expect God to bless us and prosper our church programs if it is not for the sake of proclaiming His salvation among the nations, those peoples who live around us and at the ends of the earth? God's desire is for all the peoples to know Him and praise Him. He is worthy of all honor and glory and praise, but He is being deprived of the praise of the people groups that do not yet know Him and have not yet come to faith in Jesus Christ.

One of the first passages of Scripture I remember learning as a child in Vacation Bible School was Psalm 100, which begins, "Make a joyful noise unto the LORD, all ye lands" (KJV). Psalm 96:1 says, "Sing to the LORD, all the earth." But how can that ultimate objective of all the lands

---

4 See Jim Slack, "A 'Ta Ethne' Ethnolinguistic People Group Focus as Seen in The Scriptures," accessed at http://images.acswebnetworks.com/2015/51/Slack_Ta_Ethne_Doc.pdf.

5 David B. Barrett, Todd M. Johnson, and Peter F. Crossing, "Christian World Communions: Five Overviews of Global Christianity, AD 1800–2025," *International Bulletin of Missionary Research* 33, no. 1 (Jan. 2009): 32.

6 "Fast Facts," accessed at http://imb.org/main/page.asp?StoryID=4452&LanguageID=1709; "Glossary," accessed at http://imb.org/main/news/page.asp?StoryID=4837&LanguageID=1709.

and all the earth praising His name be realized? The verses that follow tell us how: "Proclaim good tidings of His salvation from day to day. Tell of His glory among the nations, His wonderful deeds among all the peoples" (Ps 96:2–3). That was clearly God's purpose for His people throughout the Old Testament and was reinforced when Jesus, having purchased redemption for a lost world, sent us to be witnesses to the ends of the earth and to make disciples of all nations.

We are constantly encouraged to be witnesses and lead people to salvation where we live, but we tend to ignore the rest of this admonition of Scripture to proclaim God's wonderful deeds to all peoples. We are told of the power of the gospel in Romans 10:13, "Whoever will call upon the name of the Lord will be saved." But then we are confronted with the question, "How then shall they call upon Him in whom they have not believed? And how shall they believe in Him whom they have not heard? And how shall they hear without a preacher? And how shall they preach unless they are sent?" (Rom 10:14–15).

Often churches draw a circle around their community and see their mission simply as reaching the people where they live. The excuse is made that we must give priority to our church programs in order to have a base for doing missions, but seldom do we move on to engage a world beyond our own. Certainly, God wants us to witness where we live and minister to the people around us, but if we do not carry the gospel to those who have never heard, who will? How can we expect people to confess Jesus as Lord in places where there are no churches to be a witness of the gospel if we consider ourselves and our church exempt from the task? God said to Israel in Isaiah 49:6, "It is too small a thing that you should be My Servant to raise up the tribes of Jacob and to restore the preserved ones of Israel; I will also make you a light of the nations so that My salvation may reach to the end of the earth." Because God has given us the privilege of knowing Him, we have a responsibility to share that with which we have been entrusted—the light of the gospel—with the nations, until news of His salvation literally reaches every people group to the end of the earth.

All peoples coming to faith in Jesus Christ is obviously God's desire and purpose, but that is not our mission; it is God's mission. "Missions" is the activity of God in the world and through His people to fulfill His mission. And He is seeking to involve us in His mission and what He is doing in the world.

For years, we prayed for those behind the Iron Curtain in Communist countries where people lacked religious freedom and the government persecuted believers. In all of our long-range planning and mission strategies, no one projected the possibility of having missionary personnel witnessing freely in the former Soviet Union or once again serving in China. Yet today, literally thousands of missionaries and volunteers have swept into those countries. That did not happen as a result of our strategic planning or Western diplomacy, but because of the power and providence of God.

When the walls began to crumble and the doors began to open to the Communist world in the early 1990s, we recognized that there was still one formidable barrier to global evangelization remaining: the Muslim world across Northern Africa, the Middle East, and Central Asia. However, following the tragic events of September 11, 2001, personnel began reporting that people throughout that region were expressing disillusionment with their Islamic faith. They were questioning a religion that would be used to justify terrorist activity. They were asking questions that reflected a search for hope and security that only Jesus can provide.

God is using social upheaval, political disruption, economic uncertainty, natural disasters, and wars—so prominent throughout our world today—to stir a search for spiritual answers. People all over the world living in despair and hopelessness are looking for comfort and security that they can find only in Jesus Christ. God said through the prophet Haggai, "I am going to shake the heavens and the earth. And I will overthrow the thrones of kingdoms and destroy the powers of the nations" (Hag 2:21–22). It appears this prophecy is being fulfilled as nations are disintegrating and fragmenting in ethnic conflict, and totalitarian powers are being overthrown. God is manifesting His power in global events so that His kingdom might be extended.

We have long made the assumption that if we make people aware of the needs of a lost world, they will respond by giving and praying, and maybe even going as a missionary. We do not have to have a parade of missionaries coming to our churches describing emaciated refugees in Africa or the masses of people in China in bondage to a Godless Communist dogma to understand lostness. We can see it every day on television newscasts and in newspaper headlines. We see live video feeds of Muslim terrorists and suicide bombers as they seek to destroy life. We witness the despair of victims of earthquakes and natural disasters and the genocide of ethnic conflicts. But we turn off those images in our minds and any sense of responsibility as easily as we turn off the television commentator.

Southern Baptists have taken pride in now having more than five thousand international missionaries. Yet that number represents less than

.03 of one percent of our church membership. Is that all God would call into the fields that are white unto harvest around the world (John 4:35)? Does He choose only one out of every three thousand faithful church members to go and witness to 95 percent of the world's population, while allowing the rest of us to live contentedly among the remaining 5 percent that have abundant opportunity to hear the gospel?

Over 6,800 ethnic linguistic people groups are identified as unreached, and hundreds of them have no access to the gospel whatsoever.[7] In spite of modern communication and technology in which we can witness events from all over the world as they occur on our television newscasts, more than one billion people have likely never heard the name of Jesus; they are isolated culturally and geographically from a Christian witness. The task cannot be dependent on the limited number of missionaries alone. Only as every church and every believer catch a vision for God's purpose and are mobilized to be on mission with God can a lost world be reached and the kingdom of God extended to the ends of the earth. That is what a Great Commission Resurgence must be.

I wonder to what extent the apostles and that first generation of Christians understood the scope of their Lord's mandate to disciple the nations. What represented the "ends of the earth" to which they were to be witnesses? The birth of the Syrian church reflected the witness of some of the apostles. There is historical evidence that Thomas made it all the way to India. But it was a new generation beginning with Paul and Barnabas and the vision of a multi-ethnic church at Antioch that God used to convey the scope of His mission. God called subsequent believers to bring the gospel out of a narrow, Jewish context. The expanding church in Acts saw the gospel as applicable to all cultures and endeavored to spread the message of "the way" (Acts 9:2), as it began to be called, to all nations.

Paul responded to the Macedonian vision and swept across the civilized provinces of Europe planting churches. He envisioned going to Rome and beyond to Spain, reflecting a view of the world broadened by Roman roads and maritime commerce. It is doubtful the followers of Christ knew anything about an oriental culture that was already flourishing in what is now China or the barbaric tribes of Northern Europe. Yet they pressed forward to penetrate the world they knew with the life-saving message of God's love.

---

7 "Fast Facts."

Today we are without excuse in our lack of awareness of the nations and peoples that need Jesus. Modern sociological research gives us an intimate knowledge of the languages, cultures, and locations of every people group in the world. But have we become content in our own salvation and allowed an egocentric provincialism to cause us to dismiss the imperative of God's mission to the nations?

Why did Isaiah sense God's heart for a lost world and respond with a willingness to go? It was not a personal call. God did not single out Isaiah, calling him to go to a people in darkness. No, it was a generic call. Isaiah heard God saying, "Who should I send? Who will go for Us?" (Isa 6:8). He did not wait for God to tap him on the shoulder and say, "You're the one." Isaiah took the initiative and invited God to send him. In essence, he said, "Lord, if you need someone to go to people in darkness, well, here I am. Let me be the one to go."

Why did Isaiah hear God's heart for the people and respond with a submissive spirit? We read in the earlier verses of Isaiah 6 that he had a vision of God high and exalted (6:1–3). He had an experience of coming into God's presence, and he recognized God's lordship and claim on his life. Having entered into that intimate relationship with God, Isaiah felt and shared the passion of God's heart. The motivation for our involvement in God's kingdom plan will not come from denominational programs and church promotion. Putting people on a guilt trip will not result in fulfilling the Great Commission. It will only come from an intimate relationship with God that results in our being filled with His passion for all peoples.

CONCLUSION

God's passion is for all the peoples of the earth to know and praise Him. He has a passion to be exalted among the nations. Should not God's passion be ours as well? Is there anything other than God's glory among the nations that is worthy of our devotion? His passion for the nations led Him to leave the glories of heaven in order to provide redemption for a lost world. He called Israel to tell of His glory among the nations and He has commissioned us to extend His kingdom by making disciples of all nations. We will be motivated to obedience only when we come into such a relationship with God that we know His heart and share His passion for the Great Commission task.

NORTH AMERICA AS A MISSION FIELD
THE GREAT COMMISSION
ON OUR CONTINENT[1]

Jeff Iorg

Context shapes perspective. My life's context for the past twenty years has been the edge of the Southern Baptist Convention, both geographically and spiritually. Our family has lived near Portland, Oregon and San Francisco, California, sharing the gospel, planting a church, and leading in Baptist denominational roles. Without a doubt, my perspective on the future of the Great Commission in North America is impacted—positively and negatively—by my vantage point. This chapter is written from the perspective of living the gospel, raising a family, planting a church, and ministering in two of the most secular cities in the Unites States outside the mainstream of Southern Baptist life.

Our family has thrived in these environments. When we arrived in Oregon, we clearly remember feeling, "We're finally home!" We had an immediate affinity for Northwest people. We made friends, enrolled our children in public school, joined community sports organizations, and became Blazers, Seahawks, and Mariners fans. We loved people as they were, and in turn they accepted us into their community. We started a new church that grew to significant strength—a Northwest-style church full of native Oregonians with no concept of the "southern" part of being a Southern Baptist. No potlucks, no visitation without calling first, no Southern gospel music, and little interest in SEC football!

---

1 This chapter is a revised and expanded version of the author's original article, "A Perspective on a Great Commission Resurgence in North America," in Thom Rainer et al., *Great Commission Resurgence* (Nashville: LifeWay, 2008), 37–49.

Now we live near San Francisco. We have had a similar experience, albeit shaped by a ready-made Christian community because of Golden Gate Seminary. Once again we have made friends, enrolled our children in public school, joined community sports programs, and switched allegiance to the Giants, A's, and 49ers. We are still working, however, on our feelings about the Raiders!

We are learning the nuances of living in this community, accepting people as they are, and communicating the gospel in new ways. And once again, we are finding people open to the gospel. Our current assignment seems more spiritually challenging than our Oregon assignment, but we are not dissuaded in our belief that the gospel is efficacious in every cultural setting. From this perspective, I offer some observations about accelerating the fulfillment of the Great Commission in North America, particularly for Southern Baptists who are praying for a Great Commission Resurgence.

THEOLOGICAL FOUNDATIONS FOR FUTURE SUCCESS

Baptists believe ministry practices should emerge from biblical convictions. We take the Bible seriously as a guide to life and work. While a comprehensive doctrinal foundation is essential for effective ministry, our generation faces unique challenges requiring us to consult Scripture and emphasize certain doctrinal realities for this current season of ministry. In our day in North America, Southern Baptists need first to affirm and celebrate two theological foundations.

First Theological Foundation: Affirm the Gospel

We must not compromise the gospel, in any measure, as a supposed means to accelerate the fulfillment of the Great Commission. It's a fool's errand to do so. The temptation to compromise the gospel, to minimize it for easier acceptance, is very real. We must resist this temptation, no matter how much people accuse us of being intolerant.

Tampering with the gospel has been a problem since the beginning of the church. The Jerusalem church resisted the gospel spreading among the Gentiles at Antioch (Acts 11:22, 15:1–2), which resulted in the Jerusalem Council. The problem was that Gentiles were becoming Christians without first becoming Jews—a heritage that had been symbolized by their submission to circumcision. This frustrated some people in the Jerusalem church. They sent preachers to Antioch to proclaim, "Unless you are circumcised according to the custom prescribed by Moses, you cannot be saved!" (Acts 15:1).

When Barnabas and Paul heard this heresy, they immediately engaged these false teachers in "serious argument and debate" (Acts 15:2). Paul later labeled these men "false brothers smuggled in" to disrupt the church (Gal 2:4). When Peter fell under their influence and stopped having table fellowship with Gentile believers, Paul opposed him "in front of everyone" (Gal 2:14). Paul was resolute in teaching that salvation was "by grace . . . through faith" (Eph 2:8) with no human agency or addition—not even the historic, covenant-making act of circumcision. The purity of the gospel has been under attack since the first generation of the Church's existence. We must be ever vigilant to preserve the gospel.

The gospel has always been and will always be convicting to all, controversial to many, and offensive to some (Acts 17:32). Despite our best efforts to live and speak the gospel winsomely, the message itself creates backlash (Acts 14:19). My sense is that the intensity of the backlash will increase in the coming years across North America. Still, we must not compromise the gospel.

One key aspect of preserving the gospel is keeping the person and work of Jesus Christ central in our preaching, teaching, and witnessing. Jesus' exclusivity as the only Son of God and the only Way of salvation (John 14:6) is the core issue that makes the gospel controversial. Most North Americans do not object to interjecting God as a generic concept into almost any life situation—but Jesus is another matter. I was once asked to lead the invocation at a prominent event. After I had been asked, the organizers reminded me of the ecumenical nature of the gathering and the need for an "appropriate" prayer. I knew what they meant—no Jesus. My response was simple, "I am a Christian who prays in the name of Jesus. If that isn't acceptable, I won't be offended, but you will need to ask someone else."

Jesus is controversial. But we must share Him, His life, death, resurrection, and return in His fullness. We must not compromise the gospel. Jesus is our message (John 12:32).

Second Theological Affirmation: Celebrate the Church

The Church—local, covenanted, organized as churches—is God's plan for making disciples (Matt 16:16–19, 28:18–20) and advancing His kingdom. While some may question this conviction, historical evidence and biblical promises underscore the effectiveness and durability of the Church (Eph 3:10–12).

Granted, many churches in North America today are not healthy. They have lost their mission, identity, focus, and in some cases, their credibility. But do not dismiss the Church too quickly. God will sustain the Church and churches, both universally and locally (Rev 5:9–10). Some churches need to repent to rediscover spiritual power. Some need methodological overhaul to return to usefulness. Some may need to close and give their assets to a new wave of church planters with vision, strategy, and passion for the coming generation. But do not allow ineffective churches to undermine your confidence in God's design. Do not give up on the church. God has not, so we must not.

Great Commission churches in the future will have high standards for membership, practice appropriate church discipline, demand doctrinal integrity, be resolutely missional, and model community in ways our increasingly urbanized and technologically isolated population craves. Effective churches in the future will also be more diverse in methodology than ever before—more entrepreneurial, more creative, and more malleable than many churches have been in recent history.

Increased methodological diversity makes some Christians fearful of possible compromise of their church's theological integrity and missional focus. Some leaders, in fact, may have compromised sound ecclesiology in pursuit of methodological effectiveness, whether inadvertently or intentionally. When this happens, it must be pointed out and resisted. But we must not let the mistakes of the few hinder our continued quest for ecclesiastical vitality in every culture and generation.

The most effective churches for this century have not yet been started; the most innovative methods have not yet been discovered; and the most effective disciple-making processes have not yet been created. Our best and brightest leaders must be encouraged to pioneer church forms for this century without undue criticism simply because they are different, unique, or a challenge to the status quo. Theological soundness must be coupled with innovative methodology to lead us forward.

STRATEGIC CHANGES FOR FUTURE EFFECTIVENESS

Many other doctrines are, of course, significant to our faith, but a proper theology of the gospel and of the Church are foundational for expansion of the Great Commission in North America. Resting on this theological base are four strategic changes for improved evangelistic effectiveness by Southern Baptists. These strategic—not programmatic—changes must permeate our evangelistic approaches, shaping them to become more relevant and effective in this generation if we really want to see a Great Commission Resurgence.

We Must Humble Ourselves and Seek God's Power

The Southern Baptist denomination is large, powerful, and rich. We have significant, influential institutions and agencies. We have capable leaders and proven programs. We speak often of our successes, our growth, and our leadership in the evangelical world.

Our triumphal rhetoric makes it sound like God is obligated to use us because of our size or influence. He is not. God resists the proud and gives grace to the humble (1 Pet 5:5b). We typically begin any discussion of improved evangelistic effectiveness by analyzing data, debating methods, proposing programs, and challenging Southern Baptists to greater effort. This approach is proving less and less effective, and we need another starting place.

Our declining effectiveness in evangelism is, at the root, a spiritual problem. It calls for a spiritual solution. We must begin with a collective admission to God that we are powerless. We begin by acknowledging not how much we have to offer God, but how desperate we are for Him to work through us. We must humble ourselves and ask God to use us to bring the gospel to others.

While the Bible has many "one another" instructions, such as to serve one another, forgive one another, encourage one another, and love one another (Gal 5:13; Col 3:13; 1 Thess 4:18; 1 John 3:23), there is no biblical instruction to "humble one another." Instead, the Bible tells us to humble *ourselves* (Jas 4:10, 1 Pet 5:6). We must make the choice, individually and collectively, to confess our weaknesses, admit our inadequacies, and cry out to God for His power. A Great Commission Resurgence will coincide with intensification of two specific spiritual realities: increased intercession for people to be saved and fresh dependence on the power of the Holy Spirit for witnessing. Both of these are lagging in Southern Baptist life.

When was the last time you were in a prayer meeting and the *primary and most frequent* prayer requests were for the salvation of specific individuals? Our prayer meetings tend to focus on health concerns, financial provision, missionary support, and church needs. To be sure, any subject is worthy of prayer, and these issues deserve appropriate attention. But we seem to have lost our passion, our focus, on praying for the most important thing—the salvation of friends and family members.

God delights in prayers related to the conversion of others (Rom 10:1). Whether you are praying for divine appointments to happen, a gospel presentation to be well received, or individuals to be converted, God delights in answering these prayers because finding the lost is His passion (Luke 15; 1 John 5:14–15). We will increase our evangelistic effectiveness when we consistently, humbly cry out to God for the salvation of friends and family.

Southern Baptists must also rediscover dependence on the power of the Holy Spirit. Again, when was the last time you heard someone cry out in prayer for the filling, anointing, or unction of the Holy Spirit for witnessing? Charismatic excesses have made us fearful of seeking the Holy Spirit's power. The Holy Spirit is the power for Christian witness (Acts 1:8). His dual work of empowering witnesses and converting unbelievers is essential for evangelistic success (Rom 8:14–17).

While there is no biblical formula for experiencing the filling of the Holy Spirit (Eph 5:18), there are aspects of spiritual life connected to this process. First, you must be saved (Rom 8:14–16). At conversion, the Holy Spirit permanently indwells every believer. Being born again conjoins and commingles your spirit and the Holy Spirit in ways we experience but have difficulty explaining (Rom 8:9–13).

Second, you must surrender control of your life regularly and intentionally to God (Rom 12:1–2). To be filled with the Spirit means to be controlled or empowered by the Spirit. Relinquishing control of your life and confessing your lack of power is a precursor to experiencing God's power. Daily prayer, including fresh surrender or submission to God, facilitates the filling of the Spirit.

Third, you must stop sinful behavior and confess known sin. We are warned not to "grieve God's Holy Spirit" (Eph 4:30). The warning about grieving the Spirit is in the context of a passage on ethical behavior among believers (Eph 4:17–5:5). This means whenever our actions contradict God's instructions, they limit the Spirit's work through us. Thankfully, sinful actions and attitudes can be stopped, confessed, and forgiven (1 John 1:9), restoring our capacity as a channel for spiritual power.

Fourth, we are also cautioned, "don't stifle the Spirit" (1 Thess 5:19). The warning about stifling the Spirit is in the context of a passage encouraging spiritual disciplines (1 Thess 5:16–22). Failure to maintain devotional practices limits the Spirit's influence through us. Restoring habits like Bible reading, prayer, journaling, Scripture memory, fasting, and almsgiving facilitates the Spirit's control of your life.

Finally, the Spirit's power will be evident through your actions when you move forward by faith (Jas 2:14–26). Being filled with the Spirit is about maintaining a submissive attitude while you are working as hard as possible at the task God assigns. The believer usually experiences the Spirit's filling during spiritual service, not as a precursor to it. For example, when you pray for the Spirit's filling for witnessing, the empowering is experienced about the time your mouth opens and the conversation starts—not before!

We must humble ourselves and pray for evangelistic effectiveness. We must seek the filling of the Holy Spirit for witnessing. We must cry out to God for the salvation of sinners and our empowerment as believers. To use good methods is wise, but to *trust* in any method is futile. We need God's power for evangelistic effectiveness, and we need it now.

We Must Deploy Believers through Infiltration Strategies

North American churches today largely focus on "attraction" and "engagement" strategies to communicate the gospel. An attraction strategy is a Christian event or program designed to accommodate unbelievers and introduce them to Jesus Christ. An engagement strategy is an event or program designed to involve unbelievers and introduce them to Jesus Christ. Both of these types of strategies have their place and should not be abandoned. But they are inadequate for gospel penetration of a post-Christian or never-Christian culture across North America. Churches must develop and celebrate an *infiltration* strategy.

An infiltration strategy is the deployment of believers throughout the culture to introduce unbelievers to Jesus Christ in their context. For example, starting a church-sponsored softball league for the community is an attraction strategy. Creating a church-sponsored softball team and playing in a community-sponsored league is an engagement strategy. Joining your company's softball team—practicing, playing, and staying for the after-game refreshments—is an infiltration strategy. Inviting a friend to Sunday school is an attraction strategy. Organizing a Bible study at your workplace and inviting friends is an engagement strategy. Volunteering as a corporate chaplain and seeking opportunities to share the gospel in the workplace is an infiltration strategy. Another attraction strategy is starting a children's home. An engagement strategy is developing a church-sponsored mentoring program for at-risk children. An infiltration strategy is becoming a foster parent through the state children's services division.

Infiltration strategies are more difficult than attraction or engagement strategies for several reasons.

First, Christians cannot control the venue or the conversation. This is a problem because secularization intimidates many Christians.

Second, Christians are afraid of being tainted by the culture. We are uncomfortable hearing profanity, sharing meals where alcohol is served, sitting in the smoking section, hearing off-color humor, or socializing with secular people. We prefer insulation from the culture rather than infiltration of it.

Third, many Christians have poor spiritual esteem. In essence, we are not sure about the Christian faith's legitimacy in the marketplace of competing religions and ideologies. We feel threatened when unbelievers share gut-honest, critical opinions of our church or Christianity.

Fourth, Christians often lack a robust faith capable of standing up in the marketplace. What passes for "discipleship" today has too often produced insipid, weak-willed believers without the spiritual stamina to make a difference in their communities and workplace. Our faith is a "greenhouse" faith, capable of thriving only in controlled environments.

Finally, church and denominational leaders do not celebrate Christians who adopt an infiltration lifestyle. We celebrate what happens in church buildings (e.g., attendance, baptisms, and offerings received) rather than church members who devote significant time to infiltrating the community with the gospel.

We must send Christians with a robust faith to infiltrate public schools, sports programs, Chambers of Commerce, factory floors, country clubs, foster care systems, and countless other venues with the gospel. Believers who choose this path must be celebrated, not criticized, by church leaders and viewed as missionaries with an apostolic mandate. These believers are not merely social workers or spiritual activists; they are gospel-tellers who seek intentional ways to introduce Jesus to every person. They talk about Jesus, win converts, and make disciples.

One thing that troubles some leaders about empowering church members for infiltration strategies is that they may attend church functions less often. Time demands mandate that no person can keep adding more and more activity to his or her schedule. Frankly, many Christians are too busy with church activities to consider meaningfully engaging their communities. When we planted our church in Oregon with an intentional infiltration strategy, one member (a pastor's daughter) told me, "I am going to church less than at any time in my life. I am also doing more of what the church is supposed to be doing than at any time in my life. Thanks for setting me free."

Our churches have the money for an infiltration strategy because it costs very little to implement. The current institutional church model in North America is too expensive for rapid replication in many areas. Land costs alone make traditional church planting in major cities virtually impossible. Infiltration strategies require limited funding since they are not building-dependent, program-centered, or employee-intensive. These strategies equip people to share the gospel in existing systems, companies, schools, and organizations (usually funded and supported by others) with little actual expense incurred by the sending churches.

The reality is that believers are already dispersed throughout the culture, embedded in schools, companies, and communities where they study, work, and live. Since many are already there, why are not more people coming to faith in Jesus through our presence? The answer is Christians are dispersed, but they are not *deployed*. Military units are not dispersed overseas; they are deployed. They are sent on a mission, with purpose, to get a job done. Believers must adopt a similar spiritual mindset. We must intensify discipleship efforts to produce believers with a robust faith, a passion for God's mission, and a genuine love for people that prompts them to live and share the gospel, taking advantage of their networks as opportunities for the gospel.

Once again, attraction and engagement strategies should not be abandoned. But they will, by themselves, be more and more inadequate in an increasingly secularized culture giving less and less credence to church activities and programs. We need an infiltration strategy deploying millions of Southern Baptists, and we need it now.

We Must Learn to Communicate with Secular People

Christians, including Southern Baptists, speak in Christian code not easily understood by the typical unbeliever in North America. We assume unbelievers have at least some biblical or ecclesiological frame of reference.

When we use terms like "saved," "born-again," or "repentance," we think people know what we mean. Increasingly, these are faulty if not arrogant assumptions on our part.

Consider two friends of mine, both named Steve. The first Steve was the first convert in our church plant in Oregon, where our church met in a public school. He was a salesman, in his mid-thirties, married with two children. After he had been a Christian for a few months, he accompanied me to a conference in a nearby Baptist church. When we entered the auditorium, he stopped and slowly gazed around the room. I said, "Steve, everything okay?" He replied, "So . . . this is what a church looks like." "Yeah," I tentatively replied, somewhat confused by his behavior. His next comment explained everything, "This is the first time I have ever been in an actual church building."

Do you grasp the implications of that statement? Steve had never been inside a church building—not even once in his life. Not for Vacation Bible School, Sunday school, or a Christmas musical. Not even for a wedding or funeral. His entire Christian/church frame of reference was what he had learned since conversion and experienced in our portable church. Dozens of people like Steve were part of our ministry in Oregon—and across North America, more and more people are like him. They don't know the songs, service decorum, or the seating chart!

The other Steve, along with his wife Michelle, was among the last people I baptized as a pastor. This Steve was also a businessman, with two children, and a wife who also had her own small business. After they attended our church a few times, they invited me to their home to answer some questions about the experience.

During my visit, Michelle asked, "When you get up to give the talk [note the absence of Christian jargon] on Sunday, you say 'Open your Bible to the New Testament.' My first question is 'What's a testament?'" I answered by saying, "Before I answer, can I ask you one question? Before you came to our church, had you ever read the Bible?"

Steve and Michelle smiled sheepishly. Steve said, "No. But we know you like to use the Bible. So I went to bookstore today and bought three." He pulled them from under a shelf on his coffee table and continued, "Did you know there are lots of different kinds of Bibles? I hope one of these will work." Steve and Michelle had never, prior to coming to our church, read (much less studied) the Bible.

Communicating with people who have little or no concept of the gospel, the church, or the Bible requires a skill set many believers have lost because of their immersion in the Christian subculture. Our vocabulary becomes over-spiritualized, and we unintentionally communicate arrogance by our unwillingness to help unbelievers patiently to understand what we are trying to say. Nothing ends a relationship more quickly than communicating subtle disdain or bemusement when a person asks a question or does not understand a biblical concept.

One implication of increased biblical illiteracy is that communicating the gospel often takes more time today than it did in previous generations. Sure, God still works so dramatically that some persons are converted the first time they hear the gospel. We should share as much of the gospel as possible with as many people as possible and expect immediate results. What happens, though, when a person is not ready to commit immediately to Jesus? Often people—particularly adults—need to be taught the gospel, have their questions answered, consider its implications over time, and come to the moment of conversion through a process of gradual insight and understanding. This requires patient, loving, time-consuming work.

Another implication is the need for believers to develop better listening skills and dialogical approaches to sharing the gospel. Much of our witness training has been about speaking a memorized presentation and getting an immediate response, but what happens if this approach does not work? Some of my most significant witnessing relationships have been going on for years, sustained by friendship based on common interests or community activities. Sharing the gospel in these relationships is more than a one-time, "read-a-tract-and-hope-they-get-saved" event. It is a patient process of living the gospel, sharing it incrementally, openly discussing it, and patiently praying and working toward the person's conversion.

No Southern Baptist would require an international missionary to go to the field without adequate language training. We need the same passion for learning effective communication skills for our domestic witness. We need improved communication skills about the gospel, and we need them now.

We Must Affirm Methodological Pluralism

In the not too distant past, there was a generally recognized "Southern Baptist way" of doing church. Sunday school format and literature, mission promotion and offerings, worship services and revival meetings all had a comfortable feel to them. There was an easy familiarity about "what it means to be a Southern Baptist." That day is gone. Forever. We now live in a church world of methodological pluralism.

The loss of methodological unity has been a difficult experience for many Christians. Their comfort level with church form and function has been lost. Some now fear a loss of Southern Baptist identity as churches have names, schedules, worship styles, organizational structures, and dress codes unknown a generation ago. It would have been easier to assimilate this paradigm shift if the older forms had simply been exchanged for a new normal. But that did not happen. Instead, new forms of church have proliferated, mutated, and morphed into an ever-changing kaleidoscope of methodological pluralism.

New forms of Southern Baptist churches have emerged for several reasons, including generational changes among leaders, expansion of Southern Baptists outside the South, the emergence of rapidly growing churches in dozens of ethnic cultures, the willingness of seminaries to challenge students to consider globally effective methods, and the influence of successful, non-Baptist churches on Southern Baptist church methodology. All of these, and more, are shaping the form of Southern Baptist churches today.

This has been particularly challenging for state conventions and associations that attempt to resource churches. In past generations, denominational bodies worked with churches on the basis of common denominators of similar church programs and approaches. Seminaries also struggle with this problem as students come from a variety of churches and expect to be prepared for the new milieu, not for operating the programs of the old. Effective denominational bodies in the future will transform their work to consulting and coaching church leaders (and churches) toward common outcomes rather than promoting one particular set of church programs.

Our corporate effectiveness in accelerating the fulfillment of the Great Commission will be largely determined by our capacity to embrace methodological pluralism. We must stop criticizing Southern Baptists who do their ministry differently simply because we do not like their methods. We must develop the spiritual maturity to celebrate innovators who are breaking new ground by attempting new approaches. Our failure at this point has already pushed many young leaders to the edge of (or out of) our denomination, unsure if there is a place for them in our work. We can and must stop this trend.

We must also do more to embrace ethnic churches in our denomination. We accept these churches, and their leaders, as long as they support our existing programs and processes. The next important step will be encouraging these churches and leaders to participate in reshaping the definition of church life and the form and structure of our denominational entities. If we are unsuccessful at this point, ethnic churches will continue to flourish, but we will lose the contribution they could have made to Southern Baptist identity and structure.

Part of embracing methodological pluralism is accepting the inevitability and the desirability of the denominational change this will produce. One of the enemies of future effectiveness is past success. Our denomination has had some evangelistic success in the past. We can experience renewed evangelistic success, but not by doing better what we have always done. The coming generation of leaders needs the blessing of the waning generation to explore and develop new models of evangelism.

Young leaders will find ways to fulfill the Great Commission. They are too passionate not to do this. The real question is whether we will be flexible enough to assimilate the changes they introduce and enjoy the benefits of their efforts.

Methodological pluralism creates significant theological concern for some. They correctly observe that some methods compromise sound doctrine. Tension on this point is inevitable as new methods are pioneered. Some innovations can lead, of course, to theological compromise, but many do not. The problem is not, though, an unwillingness to evaluate new methods; many leaders are willing to do this important task. The problem is broad-brushing all innovation as inherently theologically suspect. Many young leaders are passionately committed to sound doctrine and make more mistakes of omission than commission in creating new ministry methods. Wise, veteran leaders must coach and counsel rather than critique and condemn.

But even then, the tension between doctrinal soundness and methodological innovation will be ever-present. Our task is to manage this tension for the advance of the gospel. The stakes are high. God's grace is sufficient. We must embrace healthy methodological pluralism, and we must do it now.

PRIMARY VENUES FOR MAXIMUM IMPACT

While resting on the theological foundations of the gospel and the Church and adjusting our evangelistic strategies to reflect current challenges, we must also take the difficult step of focusing resources (human and financial)

237

in the most effective venues for gospel expansion and cultural impact. This is a controversial recommendation because, on the surface, it seems to exclude some constituencies. Focusing limited resources, however, is not without biblical precedent.

The First Primary Venue Is Major Cities

The missiological strategy in Acts was teams traveling *through* smaller towns and *centering* their evangelistic and church starting work in major cities. The length of this chapter permits only one example of this principle. Stated succinctly, Paul's team "traveled through Amphipolis and Apollonia and came to Thessalonica, where there was a Jewish synagogue" (Acts 17:1). The text makes it clear that one reason Paul went straight to Thessalonica was to visit the synagogue in hopes of sharing the gospel with the Jews there. But a logical question is, "Didn't God want the gospel shared and churches planted in the small towns the early missionaries traveled through?" The answer is, of course, "yes." But how was this to take place given the limited resources (human and financial) of the missionary teams in the first century?

First-century missionaries focused their work in major cities in their world—centers of thought, transportation, and cultural influence—as the best way to initiate a gospel movement with broad impact. They knew that if they successfully planted in cities, within a relatively short time the city's influence would spread the gospel to the surrounding areas. The natural transportation and communication pipelines that spread commerce, governmental influence, and cultural development would also spread the gospel. The early missionaries took the long-term view, looked a generation or two down the line, and realized the most effective way (in terms of both money and, more importantly, their time) to grow the gospel across a region was to plant it in the largest cities.

Southern Baptists have not generally followed this methodology. We have been a rural people who have generally learned to work effectively in suburbs. We have not been successful in sharing the gospel, planting churches, and building ministries in the urban core of large cities. We are somewhat successful in the suburban rings around cities, but we have not developed many successful truly urban strategies.

This must change for at least three reasons. First, we want to emulate the biblical pattern and structure our plans around timeless principles.

Second, cities are where the vast majority of North Americans live.[2] Third, we need to take advantage of the cultural impact we can have by influencing the moral fiber of large cities.

Why have we done poorly reaching cities and why do some resist a city-based strategy? Cities, since biblical times, have often been equated with perversion and sin. They are seen as foreboding and inhospitable. They are also expensive, which contravenes our typical church growth plans requiring large tracts of property and huge buildings. When land is several million dollars an acre, it is easier to feel "God's leading" to stay in the suburbs or the country. We also have rural and suburban leaders who resent denominational funding—most of which comes from their churches—being focused on efforts in major cities. "What about us?" they lament, "and what about the lost people in less populated areas?"

Every person, family, church, and denomination (even Southern Baptists) has limited resources. All of us make allocation decisions based on priorities. The challenge for Southern Baptists is to allocate personnel and money in the most strategic way possible for Great Commission advance. Focusing resources on cities does not negate or deny our responsibility to reach the entire continent. Focusing resources in this way is simply the best strategic choice for maximizing our effectiveness in the long run.

We must discipline ourselves to invest our resources wisely for maximum generational impact. We must prioritize evangelism, church planting, church development, and ministry initiatives in major cities. When we do this, even if the short-term impact is negligible, the long-term impact of gospel expansion and cultural change will make a significant difference across our continent.

The Second Primary Venue Is Campuses

The second venue for strategic advance across North America is public schools and university campuses. When Paul arrived in a city in Acts, he went either to the synagogue (center for religious learning) or to the public square (center for intellectual debate). The closest parallels in contemporary culture to the latter are school campuses.

---

2 According to the North American Mission Board, about 168 million people (58 percent) of the total population now live in the 50 largest metropolitan areas of the United States. "Southern Baptist Churches & Baptisms and the 50 Largest Metropolitan Areas," accessed at http://www.namb .net/site/apps/nlnet/content3.aspx?c=9qKILUOzEpH&b=1715025&ct=2535431.

Public schools in North America are the center of community life in small towns and urban centers alike. Schools are found in almost every neighborhood and are the organizing center for younger families—parents who are stressed by multiple life demands and children who are forming their worldview. Public schools often serve families without the educational background to home school or the financial resources for private school. These secular families are the primary people that churches are trying to reach. Connecting with, serving the needs of, and communicating high value to public schools is the most direct way to connect a church to its community in North America today.

Some Christians react negatively to involvement in public schools because of the schools' secular mindset and promulgation of values contradicting the Christian worldview. Because of this concern, many Christians prefer to educate their children at home or in Christian schools. Removing children from public school does not mean, however, that Christian adults should abandon ministry to and through public schools. Public schools are struggling, often understaffed and underfunded, while trying to deal with the results of the collapse of the family structure in North America. The fact that public schools collectively exemplify the struggles in the communities they serve is the very reason churches should engage them aggressively.

Churches are serving schools by repairing and painting buildings, providing school supplies, placing volunteers like tutors and crossing guards, donating meals and other expressions of appreciation to teachers, hosting worship events to honor school employees, providing release time and after school programs (including Bible study), and opening church buildings for school programs and events. Churches engaged in these ministries gain credibility with people and an entrée into the homes of people in their communities. Thus, a primary channel to community contact and evangelistic success for the typical church is serving local schools.

Beyond this, Baptist colleges and universities must redouble their efforts at producing graduates committed to teaching and administrating in public schools. Many Baptist colleges were initially founded to train ministers and teachers, professions that Baptists considered callings and closely connected because of their potential to produce life change. Many institutions now have well-developed schools of education that must recapture their missional intent of training leaders not only to educate, but also to shape the worldview of the next generation in the public square. Christian colleges and universities must refocus on their mission of producing educational leaders who view their career as a calling to be deployed on mission to campuses across our nation.

Besides public schools, the other campus venues requiring intensified effort from Southern Baptists are secular college and university campuses. The overwhelming reason for this is the large number of students—more than 19 million in the United States—currently enrolled in colleges and universities.[3] This includes about 600,000 international students who are usually cream-of-the-crop young adults selected and sent to the United States to obtain a degree before returning home to become governmental and business leaders.[4] When Christians conduct effective evangelism, discipleship, and ministry on a university campus, the results change a generation, multiple cultures, and the world.

Campuses are also prime venues because of the openness of students to radical life change. College-age adults are the adults most open to the gospel, most open to developing new worldview convictions, most open to making life-shaping career choices, and most open to responding to the challenge of devoting themselves to worthwhile causes. Every survey of the age of conversion among adults shows a decline in the percentage of converts as age increases. Thus, adults who do convert to Christianity tend to do so as younger adults. Unfortunately, while young adults are the most likely to convert and most likely to make life-directing decisions, Southern Baptists have retreated from collegiate ministry by defunding ministry positions and defaulting campus ministry leadership to various parachurch organizations.

While we should celebrate the success of any sound campus ministry, by neglecting this fertile mission field we are missing a significant opportunity to further Baptist work. Of the students who enroll at Golden Gate Seminary with an undergraduate degree, more than 90 percent come from secular colleges and universities. They often became Christians during college, were influenced by a Baptist leader, sensed God's call to ministry, and have come to train for missionary or pastoral leadership. Some of these are international students now preparing to return to their country of origin as missionaries rather than as business or governmental leaders. In every way, intensive ministry on college and university campuses is a strategic

---

3 "Facts for Features, Back to School: 2009–2010," accessed at http://www.census.gov/Press-Release/www/releases/archives/facts_for_features_special_editions/013847.html.

4 "International Students at US Campuses at All-Time High" (November 2008), accessed at http://opendoors.iienetwork.org/?p=131590.

venue for the advancement of God's kingdom that deserves the best effort of Southern Baptists.

A COORDINATED MISSION EFFORT

Southern Baptists are a cooperative people—most of the time! We work jointly through the Cooperative Program. Sadly, for many this has come to be only about money for missions (in a narrowly defined way). We have forgotten that the Cooperative Program is a comprehensive strategy to do our work jointly in a coordinated fashion, with intentionality and the force multiplier of working together rather than individually. We continually debate the funding aspects of the Cooperative Program, which are the results of cooperation rather than the cause. The real discussion needs to take place at a much deeper level as it relates to a coordinated strategy for North American and international missions and for training leaders through our seminaries to support this effort more effectively.

Southern Baptists have two mission boards—the International Mission Board (IMB) and the North American Mission Board (NAMB). The strategic design of these two boards is dramatically different. The IMB is a sending agency. It sends missionaries and other workers among people who have never heard the gospel and usually in a context largely devoid of Christian entities or influence (churches, schools, hospitals, etc.). For that reason, its missionaries operate by necessity with a large amount of autonomy, although that changes as local Christian infrastructure emerges.

NAMB, on the other hand, is a coordinating agency. Its missionaries work in the context of a developed infrastructure of Christian culture and organization (stronger in some parts of the continent than others but still greater, on the whole, than almost anywhere the IMB works). Specifically, Southern Baptist churches, associations, state conventions, colleges, universities, hospitals, children's homes, retirement facilities, etc., dot the landscape where NAMB works. For that reason, a chief role of NAMB must be coordinating the efforts of various expressions of Southern Baptist denominational life toward the goals of evangelism, church planting, and mission ministries.

Do you realize there is a significant difference between the Southern Baptist *Convention* and the Southern Baptist *denomination*? The Convention is a national denominational body comprised of messengers from churches with an annual meeting each summer. It owns and operates mission boards, seminaries, and organizations for publishing, ministerial support, and influencing public policy. The denomination, on the other hand, is a multi-faceted, de-centralized collaboration of the national convention, state conventions, associations, churches, ethnic fellowships, and all the various entities owned and operated by all of the above. Our cherished Baptist principle of autonomy and our disdain for centralized control means the denomination is a collaborative network, led by influence rather than command and control.

Our future effectiveness depends on a fresh approach, initiated by NAMB but embraced by denominational partners, to a coordinated strategy for national evangelism, church planting, and mission ministries. Our future depends on a fresh commitment to cooperation, to a bedrock conviction we can do more working together than we can individually. While this has financial ramifications, we must rediscover a definition of the Cooperative Program that entails more than giving money. It must also include a commitment to be cooperative in the way we approach each other, a willingness to compromise organizational agendas for kingdom advance, and support for shared strategies whether or not there is something "in it for us."

We are dangerously close, perhaps closer than we want to admit, to reshaping the Cooperative Program into merely a societal mission-funding plan rather than the comprehensive plan for coordinating Southern Baptist denominational life it was originally designed to be. We must discover fresh ways to coordinate our total efforts and to remember the financial expression of our unity is the result—not the cause—of our cooperation.

CONCLUSION

God's mission is clear—the gospel to the nations and the Church prepared for eternity with Him. God resources any people who pursue these ends. Southern Baptists, deep in our denominational soul, share God's passion for His mission. We can experience a Great Commission Resurgence. We can accelerate effectiveness in evangelism, church starting, and church strengthening.

To do so, we must prioritize the gospel and the Church. We must prepare ourselves spiritually, infiltrate the culture intentionally with the gospel, learn fresh ways to communicate with secular people, and embrace the multi-faceted future God has for the churches of our denomination. We must prioritize cities and campuses as fertile fields for missional advance. We must learn afresh, with new methods and expressions created by a new generation of leaders, what it means to coordinate our efforts and work cooperatively. We can do these things if we make a denomination-wide commitment to missional effectiveness no matter the cost.

May God give us the grace to move forward, united in His mission for His glory!

THE AMERICAN DREAM OR THE
GREAT COMMISSION RESURGENCE?[1]

Al Jackson

In June 1979 I was at the Southern Baptist Convention annual meeting in Houston, Texas, when the Conservative Resurgence's opening shot was fired with Adrian Rogers's election as our convention president. There was a shock in the room when his election was announced. Those who were in control of our denomination in those days thought this would be a short-lived rebellion that would be put down the next year or the year following. In the providence of God, however, the unprecedented occurred. The Southern Baptist Convention, which had taken a decided turn toward a neoorthodox and liberal theology, began to change course. This Conservative Resurgence took place over twelve or thirteen years before significant changes were made in our institutions, boards, and agencies. I'm grateful that God allowed me to be a foot soldier in that battle.

Now we face another challenge as Southern Baptists. In recent days President Johnny Hunt has challenged us to a Great Commission Resurgence. We have been reminded that while we have had a conservative theological resurgence, we now need a Great Commission Resurgence. My heart resonates with anything and everything done by anybody anywhere to get the gospel to all the nations who desperately need to hear the good news of salvation through Christ Jesus.

---

1 This chapter is a revised and expanded version of the author's sermon originally preached in Alumni Chapel, The Southern Baptist Theological Seminary, September 15, 2009 (audio available from http://www.sbts.edu/media/audio/fall2009/20090915jackson.mp3); and in Binkley Chapel, Southeastern Baptist Theological Seminary, October 13, 2009 (audio available from http://apps.sebts .edu/chmessages/resource_2522/10–13–09_Dr_Al_Jackson.mp3).

But there is an obstacle to the Great Commission Resurgence that we need to face. We must face it head on, and face it humbly before our Holy God. That obstacle is not theology. Our theological concerns have been addressed and corrected. We need to be eternally vigilant so that what happened in past generations, who denied the trustworthiness and inerrancy of the Bible, will never happen again.

Neither is that obstacle the lack of missionary candidates. We are in an unprecedented time with large numbers of men and women both young and old who are presenting themselves to our International Mission Board to go to the ends of the earth with the gospel of salvation. In fact, there are Southern Baptist men and women who are qualified, trained, prepared, equipped, and ready to go to the mission field, but who are on hold because of the lack of funds.

The biggest obstacle to the Great Commission Resurgence is not our doctrine. It's not a lack of men and women who will say, "Here am I, Lord, send me" (cf. Isa 6:8). I am persuaded that the greatest obstacle to the Great Commission Resurgence is the American Dream. Last year in Southern Baptist churches, for all of our churches together for all causes— budget, building fund, missions—all the income received last year totaled approximately $11.1 billion. Only 2.77 cents out of every dollar of that money made its way to our International Mission Board. In other words, we are spending over 97 cents out of every dollar we give to take the gospel to the United States and less than 3 cents out of every dollar to take the gospel to the nations of the earth.[2]

We are an affluent people. Even in these days of economic recession we remain an affluent people. Let me ask this question: Do you have an automobile? Are you aware that most people in the world do not have an automobile? Are you aware that they will never have an automobile? Perhaps someday they may own a bicycle. Most walk where they need to go. In comparison with the rest of the world we Americans are wealthy, even if we think we are not. Furthermore, we have bought into the American dream, perhaps unwittingly, but nonetheless we have done so. As a result, we are suffering the consequences of our being enamored with the American Dream. Ralph Winter, founder of the US Center for World Mission, has noted:

---

2 Mark Kelly, "IMB Budget Shortfall Could Affect 600 Positions," *Baptist Press*, 12 November 2009 [article on-line]; accessed 17 November 2009; available from http://bpnews.net/bpnews .asp?id=31674; Internet.

America today is a "save yourself" society if there ever was one. But does it really work? The underdeveloped societies suffer from one set of diseases: tuberculosis, malnutrition, pneumonia, parasites, typhoid, cholera, etc. Affluent America has virtually invented a whole new set of diseases: obesity, heart disease, strokes, lung cancer, venereal disease, cirrhosis of the liver, drug addiction, suicide, murder. Take your choice.[3]

As Southern Baptists, we are an affluent people. Southern Baptists are no longer a poor denomination. We now share in the bounty of the American wealth. If you make at least $25,000 per year, you are richer than 90 percent of the people in the world. If you make at least $50,000 per year, you are richer than 98 percent of the people in this world. Like our fellow Americans, Southern Baptist are stuffed with stuff. We are overflowing with material possessions. We have so much stuff that we find it difficult to get into our closets. We are no longer able to park our automobiles in our garages because we have so much stuff in them that we have to park our cars on the street or in the driveway. We are stuffed with stuff.

Furthermore, where other than the United States of America do you have businesses that rent empty rooms for us to store our surplus stuff? Only here. The American Dream is spelled with four letters: M-O-R-E. That's the American way. More. More of whatever. Whatever we have, we want more. We are a consumer society adding more and more stuff to our already over-stuffed lives.

Scott Wesley Brown's song "Things" exposes the emptiness of the American dream. Read the words slowly:

Things upon the mantle
Things on every shelf
Things that others gave me
Things I gave myself
Things I've stored in boxes
That don't mean much anymore
Old magazines and memories
Behind the attic door,

---

3 Ralph D. Winter, "Reconsecration to a Wartime, Not a Peacetime, Lifestyle," in *Perspectives on the World Christian Movement*, ed. Ralph D. Winter and Steven C. Hawthorne, 3rd ed. (Pasadena, CA: William Carey Library, 1999), 706.

Things on hooks and hangers
Things on ropes and rings
Things I guard that blind me to
The pettiness of things
Am I like the Rich Young Ruler
Ruled by all I own
If Jesus came and asked me
Could I leave them all alone?

Oh Lord, I look to heaven
Beyond the veil of time
To gain eternal insight
That nothing's really mine
And to only ask for daily bread
And all contentment brings
To find freedom as Your servant
In the midst of all these things

For discarded in the junkyards
Rustling in the rain
Lie things that took the finest years
Of lifetimes to obtain
And whistling through these tombstones
The hollow breezes sing
A song of dreams surrendered to
The tyranny of things.[4]

I write, not as a role model, but a pilgrim on a journey, battling in my own soul the American Dream. I do not have all the answers, but I do have a deep conviction that until we get over our love affair with the American Dream, we will never—no never—fulfill the Great Commission. The Great Commission Resurgence will just be another Southern Baptist slogan that we talked about for a few years, but never took seriously.

The time has come for Southern Baptists to become radical like Jesus was during the days of His earthly ministry. I have a deep conviction that the bottleneck in getting the gospel to the nations in our Southern Baptist

---

4 Cited in Paul Borthwick, *How to Be a World-Class Christian* (Waynesboro, GA: Authentic Media, 2003), 96–97.

life is not found in our missionaries. Our Southern Baptist missionaries are some of the most splendid men and women that God ever raised up. The problem does not lie in Richmond. The problem doesn't lie with the ladies who make up our Woman's Missionary Union. I believe that the problem lies for the most part with those who are pastors of our Southern Baptist churches. I believe our Southern Baptist church members will rise up with renewed missionary fervor and passion when the pulpits of our churches are aflame with a holy zeal to pay any price to get the gospel to all nations. But first we must repent of our love affair with the American Dream.

Will we have a Great Commission Resurgence, or will we give mere lip service to world evangelization while pursuing the American Dream? It will be either one or the other. If Southern Baptists will find this to be their finest hour, it will be because we renounced the American Dream in order to release the resources that God has already put in our pocket books to mobilize our God-called missionaries to take the gospel to the nations.

Jesus spoke to this very pointedly. Jesus was and is counter-cultural. The message of Jesus is counter to the American culture. But the message of Jesus is counter to every culture in every generation and in every century. Jesus said in Matthew 6:19–24:

> Don't collect for yourselves treasures on earth, where moth and rust destroy and where thieves break in and steal. But collect for yourselves treasures in heaven, where neither moth nor rust destroys, and where thieves don't break in and steal. For where your treasure is, there your heart will be also. The eye is the lamp of the body. If your eye is good, your whole body will be full of light. But if your eye is bad, your whole body will be full of darkness. So if the light within you is darkness—how deep is that darkness! No one can be a slave of two masters, since either he will hate one and love the other, or be devoted to one and despise the other. You cannot be slaves of God and of money.

TWO INVESTMENTS—EARTH OR HEAVEN

We have only two options for the investment of our resources. In verse 19 Jesus said, "Don't collect for yourselves treasures on earth." In verse 20 Jesus said to "collect for yourselves treasures in heaven." Either we invest in earth or we invest in heaven. We invest our resources in the American

Dream or we invest those resources in the kingdom of God. Jesus was always quite clear. You never had to guess where you stood with Jesus.

When Jesus said in verse 19, "Don't collect for yourselves treasures on earth," He was saying, "Do not do that because if you store up treasures on earth, you're going to lose that treasure." He said that the moth or rust will destroy and corrode, or if not, then thieves perhaps will break in and steal. Everything that we invest in this world we lose forever. We leave it behind. It's not that Jesus doesn't want us to have treasure. He wants us to have treasure, but He wants us to have eternal treasure, treasure in heaven. Jesus commands us to treasure up treasures for ourselves in heaven, because treasure stored up in heaven is safe. It is secure. There are no moths in heaven. There is no rust in heaven. There are no thieves in heaven. What you and I store up in heaven we have forever.

Now the American Dream is just the opposite. The American Dream is to store up treasure on earth. The American Dream calls for the accumulation of more and more possessions. More of everything—more clothes, more possessions, more stocks, more bonds, more real estate. The American Dream is to have whatever I want when I want it. When asked what his dream was one Christian university student responded, "To be able to buy whatever I want whenever I want it without having to worry about running out of money." To which I would ask this question: Is that why Christ died? You and I know that's not the answer. We shouldn't blame this Christian student. Somehow he managed to grow up in a Christian home, attend a Christian church, get a Christian education at a Christian university, and never had the whole idea of the American Dream being challenged at any level. How could he have missed the counter-cultural message of Jesus?

Jesus said, "Don't store up for yourselves treasures on earth, but store up for yourselves treasures in heaven." There are only two things eternal—the Word of God and the souls of human beings. Everything that you and I invest in, other than the Word of God and human souls, we lose eternally. And everything that we invest in the Word of God and in human souls we gain eternally. So the choice is ours. There are two and only two investment opportunities: earth or heaven.

Some years ago I was alone in my study on a Saturday evening. I heard someone at the far end of the hall of the office area. I assumed it was one of our other pastors so I did not give it any thought. My study was located at the end of the hall. There was a series of cabinets in the hall leading down to my study. I heard movement down the hall. I heard cabinet doors opening and closing. This person was slowly making his way down the hall. My door was opened, so I knew someone was there. I just didn't know who. When he came to my study door and looked in, he was surprised. I was surprised. He was not a fellow pastor as I had assumed. He was a stranger. He froze for a moment. Then, he turned and ran down the hall. I jumped out of my chair and began to chase him. I shouted, "I rebuke you in the name of Jesus." I chased him down the hall. He ran outside. I chased him across the church lawn. I chased him down the street. I chased him through the neighborhood. He managed to elude me in the darkness.

I returned to my office and called the police. I said, "Someone has come in our office and I want to report an attempted burglary." The police came and I began to fill out a report of the attempted burglary. Forty-five minutes later the police called to inform me that they had caught the burglar. They asked me to come and identify him. The man they had in custody was the man I had chased. The police officer asked, "Do you want to press charges?" I thought to myself, "I've never had to press charges. I'm not sure if I should." So, I asked, "If I don't press charges, what are my options?" I was angry, but I wanted to be merciful. The police officer said, "If you don't press charges, we're going to let him go." Immediately I said, "I want to press charges."

Once I decided to press charges, the police officer informed me that I would need to meet him at the police station. The burglar had a paper sack in his hand at the time of his arrest. While filling out forms at the police station, I asked the officer, "What's in the sack?" To which he replied, "Go take a look." I poured out the contents of the sack on the table. This is what was in the sack: dried flowers, an empty Coca-Cola bottle, a paper cup, some junk mail, and a transistor radio that didn't work. That was it. Now as I found out later, this man didn't have all of his mental facilities. But the whole time I was chasing him, he was holding on tightly to this paper sack that contained absolutely nothing of value.

I thought, "What a parable of the American Dream." All of the things that we cherish and treasure, all of the things that we purchase for ourselves and for our families, all the things that we consume, the gold and the silver, the wool, the linen, the jewels, the investments, the houses, the land, the wardrobe—it's all going to be destroyed one day. We're clinging on to it as if we're going to have it forever. The American Dream is the accumulation of more. We want more stuff, more and more and more! But Jesus said, "Do not store up for yourselves treasures on earth . . . but store up for yourselves treasures in heaven." The only avenue for storing up treasure in heaven is to invest in the Word of God and the souls of human beings.

What about Southern Baptists? How are we doing? Are we like the burglar holding onto his sack of worthless junk? Are we just holding on to our stuff for ourselves in our own churches? The statistics say we are. When less than three cents out of every dollar given in Southern Baptist offering plates makes its way to our International Mission Board, we are guilty of misplaced priorities.

In verse 21 Jesus said, "For where your treasure is, there your heart will be also." Where we put our money is where our heart goes, and based on Jesus' criteria if you find yourself not caring for the nations, one way to deal with that is to start putting more and more of your treasure in getting the gospel to the nations. As you do, you will find that you will follow your treasure to the nations.

The contrast is stark but real. There are two and only two investment possibilities. One is heaven. The other is earth. Everything we invest in earth we lose eternally. Everything we invest in heaven we gain forever.

TWO PERSPECTIVES–TEMPORAL OR ETERNAL

Jesus talks about two perspectives. The two perspectives are the temporal perspective and the eternal perspective: "The eye is the lamp of the body. If your eye is good, your whole body will be full of light. But if your eye is bad, your whole body will be full of darkness. So if the light within you is darkness—how deep is that darkness! "(Matt 6:22–23).

Jesus is using the example of physical sight to illustrate for us the importance of spiritual sight. Jesus speaks of a good eye and a bad eye. Taken in context it's obvious that the good eye has an eternal perspective and the bad eye has a temporal perspective. Jesus is saying we are nearsighted at times. We can see really well up close. We can see our immediate needs for ourselves, our families, our local churches, but we don't see much beyond our local area. Jesus is calling us to see with spiritual sight, with eternal perspective.

It's not easy to do, because we are here and not there. We're in Kentucky or Alabama, not Kenya or India. So we don't see. If you could go with me and walk through the vast cities of Asia or to the dusty villages in Africa and go from hut to hut, and see how the people live and see their desperation, you would have eyes to see. It's hard to see from here, but we must see.

In Africa today there are multitudes in bondage to witchcraft and fetishes and charms. They live in fear. They do not have the gospel of the grace of the Son of God. Six thousand will die today in Africa of HIV/AIDS. In India there are hundreds of millions who bow down daily before idols. In the Muslim world you will find some of the most devoted religious fanatics you will ever meet. Five times a day when the call to prayer is issued they bow down toward Mecca and pray to a god who doesn't exist. They are in spiritual bondage and Jesus is saying, "We need to see these people. They are harassed and helpless like sheep without a shepherd. And it is our responsibility and our privilege to get the gospel of salvation through Christ Jesus to these who dwell in spiritual darkness.

If you only have a temporal perspective, if you have the bad eye, you're going to say, "I need this possession and I need that one. I need to go to the mall in order to take advantage of the sale prices." We buy stuff we do not need simply because we can afford to do so. Contrast this pursuit of the American dream with what the apostle Paul writes to Timothy. According to Paul, "But godliness with contentment is a great gain. For we brought nothing into the world, and we can take nothing out. But if we have food and clothing, we will be content with these. " (1 Tim 6:6–8). You say, "What about shelter?" The Bible does not say shelter. It simply says food and clothing. If it takes more than food and clothing and a relationship with God, something about our relationship with God is lacking.

I write that with a full awareness that I personally have far more than food and clothing. I'm an affluent man. I have far more than most people in the world, as do most Americans. As disciples of the Lord Jesus, we are to use the surplus we have by investing it in the Word of God and in people's souls so that God-called missionaries can be sent to the ends of the earth with the message that Jesus saves. We must have God's eternal perspective for that to take place.

TWO MASTERS–MONEY OR GOD

After declaring to His disciples the wisdom of storing up treasure in heaven that results from having an eternal perspective, in verse 24 Jesus identifies two masters. He says it's either money or God. It's not money and God. It's money or God. Jesus said, "No one can serve two masters. Either he will hate the one and love the other, or he will be devoted to the one and despise the other. You cannot serve both God and Money." Jesus didn't say you *should not* serve both God and money. He just said you *cannot* do it. He said it was impossible. You serve one or you serve the other, but you don't serve both. It's a choice. Either we serve God and we use money, or we serve money and we use God. Both cannot be our master. If God is our master, then money is our servant. But if money is our master, then Jesus is not Lord over us.

The 2.77 cents out of every dollar given in Southern Baptist's offering plates for international missions is a very good barometer that reveals where our heart is. We are pursuing the American Dream and the Lord Jesus says, "Stop! Don't go there. Don't lay up treasures on earth because you're going to lose it. The moths will get it. The rust will corrode it. Thieves will break in and steal it. Stop! Don't go there!" Instead, He says, "lay up for yourselves treasures in heaven."

How much stuff do we need? I have had to ask myself—how much stuff do I need? How many suits do I need? How many neckties? How many shirts? How many pairs of shoes? How many fishing rods? How many hunting rifles? How many shotguns? How many bass boats? How many sets of golf clubs?

Or, to move to less expensive items, how many T-shirts do you need? Where I serve as pastor we cannot have any event without having a T-shirt to commemorate it. We have T-shirts for our mission trips. We have T-shirts for Vacation Bible School. We have T-shirts for the children's musical, T-shirts for youth camp, T-shirts for retreats, T-shirts for disciple now weekends, T-shirts for the prayer ministry. Every time we print a new T-shirt, they get one for the pastor and give it to me! I have enough T-shirts to last me for years and years.

Now, a T-shirt is not an expensive item, but how many T-shirts do we need? Is there not a limit where somewhere along the way we say, "Enough"? Let's release some of these funds to mobilize our people who have been called to take the gospel to the nations. Let's use our surplus for the Great Commission. That's the issue before us. It's not a matter of let's just divide up the pie in different ways so we can get some of the pie that is spent here to be spent overseas. It's an issue of releasing from the purses and checkbooks and bank accounts of Southern Baptist church members those resources to get the gospel to the nations. Jesus said, "No man can serve two masters. Either he will hate the one and love the other, be devoted to the one and despise the other. You cannot serve both God and money." D. A. Carson expands further, "Either God is served with single-minded devotion or he is not served at all. All attempts at divided loyalty betray, not partial commitment to discipleship, but a deep-seated commitment to idolatry."[5]

Is he right? Are we worshipping our stuff? Have we put money before God? I am persuaded that we will never have a Great Commission Resurgence until we have pastors who are willing to lead their churches to be Great Commission Christians. I have spent the better part of my life calling young men and women to go to the nations with the gospel of salvation. Now we are seeing in Southern Baptist life an extraordinary response like never before. It's time for Southern Baptists to step up and pay the way of those who have been called by God.

Sadly, I have little hope for my generation. For the most part, my generation of Southern Baptists has bought into the American Dream. But I do have hope for this generation of seminarians. My prayer is that in the providence of God some of them will be led of the Holy Spirit to put down deep roots in one community and in one church and fight the battles and pay the price to mobilize God's people to do great exploits for the glory of God among the nations.

My friend, Michael Johnson, is a surgeon in Nairobi. He works with the poorest of the poor. Twenty years ago when the Lord called him to Africa, he went to his pastor to share the good news that he'd been called as a missionary to Kenya. Thinking that his pastor would rejoice with him, instead his pastor said, "Mike, you don't want to go to Africa. Mike, if you go to Africa, you'll never be able to buy your Jag." When Mike told me that, I said, "Mike, your pastor wasn't concerned about you never having a Jaguar to drive. He was concerned that he was about to lose the tithe of your income as a surgeon in his church budget." He said, "I know." How many pastors are like that? How many want to hold on to as much as they can? How many want to build empires in our local churches to the neglect of the multitudes without Christ?

Approximately 4.5 billion people on the planet do not confess faith in the Lord Jesus Christ. Yet we say, "I'm going to do something great for the Great Commission someday, but first we have to get the Family Life Center paid for. Then we have other local needs we must address." We add and add locally while giving very little to get the gospel to the nations. Where are the pastors who will stand before God's people and call them to give

---

5   D. A. Carson, *Matthew*, in vol. 8 of *The Expositor's Bible Commentary*, ed. Frank E. Gaebelein (Grand Rapids: Zondervan, 1984), 179.

generously and sacrificially to mobilize the church of the Lord Jesus Christ, to declare his glory among all nations?

We are an affluent people. We have at our disposal all the financial resources we need to send every God-called missionary through our International Mission Board. Yet we refuse to release those resources. I believe it is not so much the fault in the pew. I believe our people are waiting to be led. They are waiting for someone to blow the bugle and wave the banner and say, "This is the way for us to go! We can be used of the Spirit of God to mobilize ourselves to reach the nations with the gospel of Christ." That means we need to say no to the American Dream. That may mean downsizing our standard of living. An increase in your salary should not call for an increase in your standard of living. It ought to call for an increase of your standard of giving.

Jesus is our example. Perhaps we don't want Jesus as our example. Do you remember when Jesus was on His way to Jerusalem? Beginning in Luke chapter 9 we have the account of Jesus traveling from Jericho to Jerusalem and all the events that happened along the way. In one of those encounters a man came up to Jesus and said, "I will follow you wherever you go." Jesus said, "Foxes have holes and birds of the air have nests, but the Son of Man has no place to lay his head." Jesus was homeless during the days of his public ministry. He was dependent upon the hospitality of people like Mary and Martha and Lazarus and others. Sometimes Jesus slept under the open sky. I'm not advocating homelessness as something you ought to pursue. I am saying Jesus was not the kind of preacher whom the Chamber of Commerce would have elected "Clergyman of the Year." He was homeless. Apparently it is possible to have a fulfilled satisfying life and walk with God and not have many material possessions, if Jesus is our example.

We have a choice to make. Jesus said, "No one can serve two masters." He is not saying you should not do it. He is saying you cannot do it. It is either God or money. We can choose either the American Dream or we can choose the kingdom of God. It is one or the other but not both.

During my early years as pastor of Lakeview Baptist Church, I grew to appreciate Mr. and Mrs. A. L. Pate. Mr. Pate was a retired sawmill hand who had spent his working years at a local lumber yard. He never made more than minimum wage. He had a limited formal education, having completed only the eleventh grade. Mr. Pate served faithfully as a deacon over many decades. He and Mrs. Pate were prayer warriors and soul winners. Mrs. Pate was "Mrs. Missions" at Lakeview Baptist Church. Like few people I have known her heart's desire and passion was to declare the gospel to the ends of the earth. Their only regular source of income in retirement was a small Social Security check. When Mr. Pate died, Mrs. Pate's limited income became ever more limited.

Some of the ladies in her Sunday school class were concerned that Mrs. Pate did not have enough money to buy food. The teacher of her Sunday school class took up an offering and converted it into a $100 bill. She came to see me and said, "Pastor, we're concerned that Mrs. Pate does not have enough to eat. The members of this class have taken up an offering. Would you give this $100 bill to Mrs. Pate? Do not tell her where it came from. Just say it came from an angel." I said, "I'll be happy to."

All this happened during the Christmas season. Like all Southern Baptist churches, during December we take up the Lottie Moon Christmas Offering. When Sunday came, I put that $100 bill in my coat pocket. Before the service, I went up to Mrs. Pate, who always sat center section, second row. I leaned across the front pew and I held out the $100 bill and I said, "Mrs. Pate, an angel told me to give you this money." She took the $100 bill. She looked at it. She looked at me, and said, "Brother Al, do you think that angel would mind if I gave this to the Lottie Moon Christmas Offering?" I said, "Mrs. Pate, I think that angel would be pleased." She needed that money, but more than that, she had an opportunity to do something very, very significant. That opportunity was to invest in the Word of God and in the souls of human beings through the Lottie Moon Offering for international missions. Her sacrificial gift paralleled that of the poor widow who was commended by Jesus when she gave two small copper coins.

On the other end of the economic spectrum from Rosa Lee Pate is Milton Scott. In his excellent book, *Fields of Gold*, Andy Stanley describes Milton Scott as a fearlessly generous man:

> I wish every Christian were as fearless as Milton Scott. He gave about as fearlessly as anyone I've ever known. For the most part, "Mr. Milton" blended quietly into the landscape where I grew up. But beneath the surface, his story had the makings of folklore.
>
> By the time he died at the age of 106, Milton Scott had experienced more of life than then ten average men. Born in 1895, he lived in three different centuries. He saw a demonstration by the Wright brothers with their first airplane. He attended a parade for Admiral Dewey, hero of the Spanish-American War. He commanded a US unit of black soldiers during World War I and

was given the French Legion of Honor, France's highest national award. He had a loving wife and four daughters. He took daily walks throughout old age, and when confronted one evening by a mugger with a gun, he told the thug to go ahead and shoot because he didn't intend to cooperate. (The mugger fled.) During his lifetime, he watched transportation advance from horse and buggy to the space shuttle.

In business, Mr. Milton also had his share of opportunities. As a young man, he became related to Atlanta's Candler family by the marriages of two Scott sisters to two Candler brothers. Mr. Milton looked on unimpressed while investors were sought for the marketing and distribution of a new drink Asa Candler was marketing. Whenever he told the story later in life, he would shrug casually and explain, "I didn't want none of Asa Candler's Coca-Cola."

Milton Scott had his own life to live. He operated a successful textile mill from age 25 until he was 102, when he sold the company to a British conglomerate. Even when he was no longer involved in the day-to-day operations of the business, he prayed regularly for the company.

Perhaps the most remarkable thing about Mr. Milton was how uncompromising he was about his kingdom calling. He was born to give. More specifically, he felt called to put God's Word in the hands of people who were eager to absorb it. And he knew no greater joy than finding a new Bible distribution opportunity to fund; he called these distributions his "projects."

For himself, Mr. Milton allotted a very meager lifestyle. He typically kept four suits, four pairs of shoes and half a dozen white shirts in his closet. He drove a basic American car, replacing it every ten years. He lived out his days in the same house he had built for his bride in 1920. No modern kitchen. No Jacuzzi tub. He didn't even have air-conditioning until he was in his nineties when a live-in nurse required a window unit to stay comfortable.

On a typical day, Mr. Milton would eat a bacon breakfast and then sit in his favorite chair reading the Bible for one or two hours. On average, he would read through the entire Bible four or five times per year, a pace he maintained for eighty years. After Bible reading, he took the short ride to work where he tended the mill and his prayer closet. He enjoyed hamburgers, Georgia Bull-dog football, and telling jokes. Masterfully, he balanced simple living with a zest for life.

Unlike most people with a growing income, Mr. Milton didn't elevate his lifestyle in turn. Nor did he fumble for a twenty-dollar bill when the offering plate was passed. For Milton Scott, funding the work of ministry was a priority. And fund he did. In vigilant secrecy, he went about the task of dividing his sizeable earnings among God's interests around the world. Along the way, he amassed a list of accomplishments many charities only dream about.

He helped to smuggle thousands of Bibles into Russia before the Iron Curtain fell. He single-handedly funded a ministry that equipped lay preachers across South America. By himself, he was one of the largest sources of aid to the country of Bangladesh for two years in a row. He was personally responsible for the printing and distribution of more than thirty Wycliffe Bible translations. In China, Egypt, India, Central America, and countless other places, innumerable people got their first glimpse of Scripture because of his vision and generosity. He also took literally the call to care for widows and orphans, supporting a widow ministry and paying the college tuition for several children of deceased parents.

Mr. Milton sent his assistants to investigate the inner work-ings of the ministries he was considering helping. As soon as God placed a suitable project on his desk and the money in his account, he would get to the task of giving. It was not uncom-mon for him to clean out his account two or three times a year. In his later years, a nephew in charge of his estate would often have to notify him when the money had run out. Whenever his account was replenished again, his giving would resume.

Mr. Milton seemed impervious to the "what ifs" most of us fear. Not that they weren't familiar. He had lived through the Great War. He survived the Great Depression. He raised a large family. But despite all those invitations to worry about himself, he was much too enraptured in the joy of giving to notice. He didn't amass a reserve fund. He didn't watch the stock market. He just gave and gave.

Because of his commitment to secrecy during his lifetime, no one knows exactly how many millions passed through his hands. Conservative estimates suggest he gave at least 70 to 80 percent of his income. At least. And all along, he maintained a lifestyle that barely qualified as middle-class.[6]

John Drummond, a Florida layman serving on the SBC Great Commission Task Force, reminds us:

We expect our career missionaries to abandon their families and the comforts of home to engage lost people groups around the world, yet somehow we fail to see that we as laity are called to the same level of commitment to the unreached. Whether at home or abroad, we must be willing to make the necessary sacrifices and forgo certain comforts and pleasures for the sake of reaching those who do not know Christ. This must not be something that we attempt to do once a week from the safety of a church sanctuary— it must become our very lives, no matter how difficult, complicated or messy it may be. Such a dramatic wholesale change in lifestyle must be rooted in a profound love of our Savior.[7]

Famed missionary to China, Lottie Moon, confronted Southern Baptists of her generation when she wrote in the January 1888 issue of *Foreign Missions Journal*:

It does seem strange that when men and women can be found willing to risk life, or at least, health and strength–in order that these people may hear the gospel, that Christians withhold the means to send them. Once more I urge upon the consciences of my Christian brethren and sisters the claims of these people among whom I dwell. It fills one with sorrow to see these people so earnest in their worship of false gods, seeking to work out their salvation by supposed works of merit, with no one to tell them of a better way. Then, to remember the wealth hoarded in Christian coffers! The money lavished on fine dresses and costly

---

6   Andy Stanley, *Fields of Gold* (Carol Stream, IL: Tyndale House Publishers, 2004), 22–27. Used by permission.

7   John Drummond, "A Great Commission Resurgence Must Penetrate the Heart of All Southern Baptists," Pray4GCR.com Blog, entry posted October 26, 2009, http://www.pray4gcr.com/2009/10/a-great-commission-resurgence-must-penetrate-the-hearts-of-all-southern-baptists/ (accessed November 17, 2009).

living! Is it not time for Christian men and women to return to the simplicity of earlier times? Should we not press it home upon our consciences that the sole object of our conversion was not the salvation of our own souls, but that we might become co-workers with our Lord and Master in the conversion of the world?[8]

We are an affluent people. Are we going to continue to pursue the American Dream? Or are we going to be radical like Jesus and say, "I'm not going to buy everything I can afford. I'm going to give far beyond the tithe. I'm going to invest in the Word of God and the people's souls for the glory of the name of our great God among the nations." We stand at a crossroads. We can continue to spend most of our reserves upon ourselves or we can obey the Lord of the harvest who said, "It is more blessed to give than to receive." The time is now for us to adjust our lifestyles and thereby free up our resources for the evangelization of the world in this generation.

---

8   Cited in Keith Harper, ed., *Send the Light: Lottie Moon's Letters and Other Writings* (Macon, GA: Mercer University Press, 2002), 225–26.

SECTION 4
VIA THE CHURCH

THE GREAT COMMISSION LEADER
THE PASTOR AS PERSONAL EVANGELIST

William D. Henard

When one considers the meaning of the pastor's role as a Great Commission leader, one needs only to review the sobering statistics to reveal the lack of commitment to evangelism by the church as a whole. Many of these statistics have already been addressed in this book by Ed Stetzer and Thom Rainer, among others. The statistics could go on almost without stopping. The bottom line is that the church as a whole does not seem to be making the impact that it should. The church appears to be losing ground when it comes to reaching the world.

Think for a moment, though, if one person really developed a passion for Great Commission evangelism. This individual makes a commitment to win one person to Christ, disciple that individual for that year, teaching him/her how to be a follower of Jesus and how to personally share his/her faith. The next year, these two individuals go out and each win one person to Christ, following the same pattern. The next year, the four believers each win one person to Christ and disciple those individuals. Each succeeding year the process continues. If that fact happened, America would be reached in 28 years (268,425,440 converts). The world would be won in 33 years (8.5 billion converts). The question remains, who will be that one?

This chapter intends to lay out a strategy for how the pastor should be the catalyst for a Great Commission Resurgence. If pastors do not catch the vision, most probably the church will not. How will they do that, though, if they do not possess the gift of the evangelist? The answer comes in the words of the apostle Paul to young Timothy. Second Timothy 4:1–5 records a very familiar passage to most pastors, probably the one preached at most ordination services and in many seminary chapel messages. Yet the importance of the passage is almost unparalleled.

The apostle Paul wrote from incarceration in which he was chained (2 Tim 1:16), "languishing in a Roman prison and treated like a criminal (2:9)—with little light to read or write by, no sanitation, and no prospect of relief except by death."[1] The circumstances of the imprisonment probably occurred sometime around AD 66, some five or six years after his initial house arrest in Rome. Many theologians believe that the heightened persecution of Paul was illustrative of the greater persecution that had begun in 64 under Nero. Tacitus, a Roman historian, wrote:

> But all human efforts, all the lavish gifts of the emperor and the propitiations of the gods did not banish the sinister belief that the conflagration was the result of an order by Nero. Consequently, to get rid of the report, Nero fastened the guilt and inflicted the most tortures on a class of hated for the abominations, called Christians by the populace.[2]

Based on an examination of Acts 13:4–14:27, Paul probably met Timothy during his first missionary journey, an encounter that may have led to Timothy's conversion. When Paul returned to Lystra during his second missionary journey, he found that Timothy had grown in his faith and had the respect of other believers (Acts 16:1–2). At this point, Paul asked Timothy to accompany him on his journeys. As Timothy traveled with Paul, he gleaned great insight through the mentoring wisdom of Paul, who showed his confidence in Timothy by giving him important ecclesiastical and missional leadership responsibilities. About these opportunities Thomas Lea and Hayne Griffin write:

> Paul sent Timothy on several important assignments in ministry. The assignment mentioned in 1 Thess. 3:1–10 was an effort to encourage a congregation that faced serious persecution. Following this assignment, Paul sent him to Corinth to remind the believers there of Paul's teaching (1 Cor. 4:17; 16:10–11). He later sent him to an unspecified ministry in Macedonia (Acts 19:22) and to a special visit to Philippi (Phil. 2:19–24). At the time of the writing of 1 Timothy, Timothy was still on assignment in Ephesus (1 Tim. 1:3), and he was apparently still at the same tasks in 2 Timothy.[3]

---

1 John MacArthur, *2 Timothy*, MacArthur New Testament Commentary (Chicago: Moody, 1995), x.

2 Quoted in ibid.

3 Thomas D. Lea and Hayne P. Griffin Jr., *1, 2 Timothy, Titus*, New American Commentary 34 (Nashville: Broadman, 1992), 52.

As Paul wrote young Timothy, he offered his final thoughts and encouragements. One can imagine how discouraging it might have been to Timothy for Paul to have left him in Ephesus. The city served as a center for the worship of Diana, the patroness of sexual immoralities of various kinds (Acts 19). Timothy followed Paul's three-year ministry in Ephesus (Acts 19:10), which also added to his stress. Warren Wiersbe insightfully says, "It was not easy for Timothy to follow a man like Paul!"[4] It is in this context that Paul wrote the verses in chapter 4.

Obviously, Paul did not specifically mention a Great Commission Resurgence or even the Great Commission. He did tell Timothy, however, to "do the work of an evangelist." As one examines the text, the verses present a clear picture on how pastors are to accomplish that task.

A GREAT COMMISSION RESURGENCE AND AN UNDERSTANDING OF THE JUDGMENT

In these verses, Paul first reminded Timothy that the judgment of Christ was a certainty. He said, "Before God and Christ Jesus, who is going to judge the living and the dead, by His appearing and His kingdom." These words express the certainty of an impending confrontation with Christ as Judge.

Two Judgments to Consider

According to Scripture, at least two judgments await humanity.[5] The first is the judgment of nonbelievers. Revelation 20:11–15 speaks of the Great White Throne Judgment, in which those who are not Christians will give account of themselves before God. The purpose of this judgment is not for unbelievers to justify their behavior with the hope of God making an exception for them, but for them to receive the divine judgment of God. The final place of judgment will be a place that the Bible calls hell, or the lake of fire (Rev 20:15).

---

4 Warren W. Wiersbe, *Be Faithful: How to be Faithful to the Word, Your Tasks, and People Who Need You* (Wheaton: Victor Books, 1988), 15.

5 One might also speak of a third judgment, the Separation of the Sheep and the Goats (Matt 25:31–33), in which Christ separates believers from nonbelievers.

Fewer people today believe in a literal hell. One poll by Beliefnet.com found that 35 percent of their respondents did not believe in hell.[6] When one examines the words of Jesus, a different conclusion is drawn.

The primary word that Jesus used to describe a place of punishment or judgment was the word *Gehenna*. This word originates out of a transliteration of the Hebrew expression *Gehinnom*, which means "Valley of Hinnom" or the "Valley of Lamentations." During the days when Ahaz was king, altars were erected to various pagan gods. The Old Testament recounts how Ahaz was enamored with what he saw on a visit to Assyria (2 Kgs 16:10). One altar he erected was to Molech, the Canaanite fire god (2 Kgs 16:3, 13). It is thought that some Jews practiced child sacrifice on this altar, including Ahaz himself. One can imagine the wailing of the mothers, as their babies were taken from them to be sacrificed. One can also visualize the babies themselves, as they screamed for life and from the pain they suffered as they were burned alive.

Under Hezekiah, reforms were instituted, and the altars were torn down. By the time of Jesus, this valley had been turned into a garbage dump, where people would bring their refuse, waste, and the bodies of dead animals. Fires would burn there twenty-four hours a day. Eleven different times in the New Testament, Jesus referenced a place of judgment as Gehenna.[7] It provided a picturesque visual of what was awaiting those who refused to follow Christ. Outside of the southern gates, which furnished some of the more prominent entrances to the Temple complex, one would find the valley of Gehenna. Every time a Jew would enter the gate to go to Temple, if he looked over his shoulder, he would see this valley. If he had heard the words of Jesus, he would have had a constant reminder of the choice awaiting him and his family.[8] Jesus used this valley as a call to repentance and faith, for one did not want to find oneself there.

The word "Hades" occurs ten times in the New Testament, four times in sayings of Jesus in the Gospels.[9] Luke 16 records one of the most memorable uses, as he records Jesus' story of the rich man and Lazarus. Whether or not this story was a parable, Jesus' description presupposes that Hades

---

6   Religious Tolerance, "Poll Results on Heaven and Hell" [on-line]; accessed 20 October 2009; http://www.religioustolerance.org/chr_poll3.htm; Internet.

7   Matt 5:22, 29, 30; 10:28; 18:9; 23:15, 33; Mark 9:43, 45, 47; Luke 12:5.

8   The Gospel of John records at least four times that Jesus was in Jerusalem.

9   In its contextual use, the word *hades* is employed five times as a reference to the dead, twice as the place of the departed wicked, and four times as a general reference for death.

is a very terrible place. The rich man finds himself in torment there, crying out for just a taste of water. So great is his suffering that he wishes someone would go and warn his living brothers about this place. Elsewhere, Jesus also uses very vivid language to describe a place of eternal torment. He described this place as "the furnace of fire" and as the "outer darkness," and described the reactions of those cast into it as "weeping and gnashing of teeth" (Matt 8:12; 13:42, 50; 22:13, 25:30).

John 3:16 is perhaps the most memorable verse in all the Bible, one that is known more than any other, even by those outside of Christ. Yet this verse includes a caution about judgment. People remember the first part of the verse, "For God loved the world in this way: He gave His One and Only Son, so that everyone who believes in Him." We forget, however, the last phrase of the verse, "will not perish but have eternal life." The world likes to hear about the "eternal life" part. Not as much confidence stands with the "perish" statement, though.

CHRISTIANS AS CLOSET UNIVERSALISTS

In evaluating the response and attitude of many evangelical Christians, it appears that many are probably closet universalists. They believe that the most evil of people go to hell when they die. Hell is the place for murderers, rapists, and thieves. Hitler is there, along with Saddam Hussein. Charles Manson will also find himself there one day.

Christians make exceptions, though, when it comes to family and friends. They recognize that bad people go to hell, but then they rationalize that "their dear sweet Granny, though she never gave her heart to Jesus, He had to have an exception for her. She always did good, taking care of her neighbors and friends. She never had an unkind word to say about anyone. She was the one who let me sleep on her feather bed. She served me Grape Nuts for breakfast. I did not like Grape Nuts, but it was her favorite cereal. She let me get by with things, and even kept Dad from spanking me when I got caught. I know hell is real, but my Granny cannot be there."

The fact remains, though, that Christians will never gain a true passion for evangelism until they realize the reality of hell for all unbelievers, including those among their family and friends. When believers understand that their unbelieving spouses, children, parents, friends, and relatives will spend an eternity in this terrible place, it will help motivate them to share Christ with others.

The judgment of believers provides the second judgment that must be considered and that should encourage Christians to share their faith. Paul told Timothy to fulfill his ministry. The word "fulfill" carries with it the idea of bringing it to its full completion. Timothy did not need to stop, get discouraged, or quit. He did not need to leave some things out. Lea and Griffin describe this act as "filling his work to the brim with those tasks on which Paul had urged him to focus. The Greek word for 'ministry' refers to 'service for the Lord,' a general reference to all kinds of work in the name of Christ and for the help of believers."[10]

The word "judge" as it is used in the first verse of this passage probably references Christians more than it does non-Christians. E. M. Blaiklock comments that "it is the word of First Timothy 5:21. Our responsibility must be exercised in view of inevitable judgment, a thought to which Paul often returned (Acts 17:31; Rom. 2:16; 1 Cor. 4:5). And the responsibility is the Gospel committed to our care."[11] At least three times in the New Testament, the idea of a personal judgment for the Christian's labor and work is specifically mentioned (1 Cor 3:11–12; 2 Cor 5:10; Rom 14:10). In the 2 Corinthians and Romans passages, the words "judgment seat of Christ"[12] are mentioned. Robert Mounce explains:

> The judgment will not entail a decision regarding one's salvation because according to John 5:24 the believer has already crossed over from death to life. Eternal life is a present possession (cf. 1 Cor. 3:10–15). There will, however, be for every believer a judgment of the quality of his or her life. . . . This will be a judgment based on works (cf. Matt 16:27; Rom 2:6; Rev 22:12).[13]

The concept of the judgment seat of Christ provides a very vivid understanding of the Christian's responsibility and obligation toward faithfulness in ministry and service. John MacArthur provides an excellent description at this point:

---

10 Lea and Griffin, *1, 2 Timothy, Titus*, 246.

11 E. M. Blaiklock, *The Pastoral Epistles*, Bible Study Commentary (Grand Rapids: Zondervan, 1972), 118.

12 The Romans passage probably says "God" instead of "Christ." For an explanation of the distinctions in these readings, see Leon Morris, *The Epistle to the Romans*, Pillar New Testament Commentary (Grand Rapids: Eerdmans, 1988), 483.

13 Robert H. Mounce, *Romans*, New American Commentary 27 (Nashville: B&H, 1995), 254.

Judgment seat translates *bema*, which, in its simplest definition, describes a place reached by steps, or a platform. The Septuagint (the Greek translation of the Old Testament) uses it that way in Nehemiah 8:4. In Greek culture *bema* referred to the elevated platform on which victorious athletes received their crowns, much like the medal stand in the modern Olympic games. In the New Testament it was used of the judgment seats of Pilate (Matt 27:19; John 19:13), Herod (Acts 12:21), and Festus (Acts 25:6, 10, 17). There was also a *bema* at Corinth, where unbelieving Jews unsuccessfully accused Paul before the Roman proconsul Gallio (Acts 18:12, 16, 17). A person was brought before a *bema* to have his or her deeds examined, in a judicial sense for indictment or exoneration, or for the purpose of recognizing and rewarding some achievement.[14]

While it is clear that the believer's own salvation is not at risk at this judgment, that person's reward will certainly be scrutinized. Christians must remember that they will stand before God and give an account of themselves individually. If one connects these passages together, an obvious judgment stands in the realm of evangelism. Believers are accountable for how and if they have witnessed to others. While a person stands ultimately responsible for his or her personal decision in accepting or rejecting Christ, Christians must also recognize their accountability in the realm of witnessing. Giving an account to Christ provides a good motivation for being faithful in evangelism.[15]

---

14   John MacArthur, *2 Corinthians*, MacArthur New Testament Commentary (Chicago: Moody, 2003), 177, emphasis original.

15   Mark D. Liederbach, Associate Professor of Christian Ethics at Southeastern Baptist Theological Seminary, cautions, "The idea that believers should practice evangelism because unbelievers will go to hell if they do not tell the good news . . . [is] utilitarianism. . . . Clearly, however, the motivational tool employed is concern for the consequences of failing to join the 'harvest team.' . . . The subtle and most insidious nature of this utilitarian motivation is the implication that instead of a sinner being guilty of their own damnation, it is the lazy Christian's fault. . . . Each encounter with a lost person becomes one in which the eternal destiny of their soul depends upon the believer's actions. One wonders if the good news at this point is really good because it offers someone else an opportunity to know their Creator or because telling it assuages the potential guilt of failing to do so. . . . Christians must understand that the purpose of the Great Commission is directly linked to the very nature and fabric of the universe and was the reason it was created in the first place—to spread the worship of God to the ends of the earth and magnify the glory of God in all places and times! . . . The utilitarian assessment is exactly right—the lost will perish without Christ. But the energy to seek and to save them does

A GREAT COMMISSION RESURGENCE AND A LOVE FOR PEOPLE OUTSIDE OF CHRIST

Once the theological basis has been determined with regard to the eternal destiny of those outside of Christ, another perspective must be considered. If the church is going to reach those outside of its walls, then the church must recapture, once again, a love for those who do not know Christ as their Savior. Take a look at Jesus for a moment. If there is one thing that could be said about Him, it was that He had a deep love for people. People were attracted to Him because of His divinity. The Jews marveled at His wisdom, saying, "How does He know the Scriptures, since He hasn't been trained?" (John 7:15). Individuals like Nicodemus were probably drawn to Christ through the works that He did, specifically the cleansing of the Temple (John 2:13–25). Yet, there was more to Jesus than just these things. He loved people.

In Mark 10, Jesus was headed down the eastern side of the Jordan River, making His way to Jerusalem. He traveled through the region of Perea and stopped along the way, perhaps in one of the villages, although Mark does not identify which one. At this point, parents began bringing their children to Jesus for a blessing. It was customary that a rabbi bless a Jewish child by his or her first birthday, and who better to do the blessing than the rabbi Jesus?[16] The disciples, however, were not so inclined, and rebuked the parents.

Mark records Jesus' response: "When Jesus saw it, He was indignant and said to them, 'Let the little children come to Me'" (Mark 10:14). The word "indignant" means that He was aroused to anger. Interestingly enough, the Bible portrays Christ as angry at least four different times: at the cleansing of the Temple, which happened twice (John 2:13–17; Mark 11:15–17); at the Pharisees concerning the man with the withered hand (Mark 3:5); again at the Pharisees in Matthew 23; and here in Mark 10.[17] His anger toward most

---

not primarily rest in the fact that they are lost, but that their lostness robs God of the glory He alone is due. . . . We are commanded to evangelize because evangelism's primary function is to promote the glory of God and the worship of the King of the universe! . . . By commanding us, God is instructing us on how to have the fullest and best life now!" See Mark D. Liederbach, "Ethical Evaluation of Modern Motivations for Evangelism," *Journal of the Evangelical Theological Society* 48 (2005): 2–11.

16 Herschel H. Hobbs, "Mark," in *An Exposition of the Four Gospels* (Grand Rapids: Baker, 1970), 154.

17 One might also assume Christ's anger when He rebuked Simon Peter (Matt 16:23), when He rebuked the demons (Mark 1:25), and when He cursed the fig tree (Mark 11:14).

of these people had to do primarily with their treatment of others, especially as their actions originated out of a cold or hard heart.

Jesus, however, loved people. He visited with hated Zacchaeus in his home (Luke 19:1–10). He restored the woman caught in adultery by the Jews (John 8:1–11). He had His feet washed with the tears of a sinful woman who found forgiveness in Him (Luke 7:36–38). And He loved children. While He never compromised with sin, He was able to communicate a love even for sinful people . . . and they knew it.

A Biblical Mandate

Paul wrote, with regard to ministry, that it must be done "with great patience and teaching"(2 Tim 4:2). The word translated as "great patience" in this context refers to the patience the pastor is to show with people. The primary application would be with the church, as MacArthur explains that this patience is shown "with members of a flock who may have been persistently stubborn and were resisting their pastor's admonitions. But the shepherd is not to become angry, remembering that he himself is firmly but lovingly and patiently held accountable by the Great Shepherd."[18]

This "great patience" can also apply to the pastor's attitude toward those outside of Christ. Since Paul admonishes Timothy to "do the work of an evangelist," one can see how important patience is to be effective in evangelism. Many Christians, especially those who serve in some form of full-time vocational service, experience a unique bias toward those who do not know Christ. Christian people who are trying to grow in their faith surround themselves with other Christian people. They read Christian books, listen to Christian radio, and have Christian symbols displayed on their person and workspace, if possible. For those in Christian service, their primary responsibility lies in taking care of the flock of God. They work with Christians, have a Christian coffee mug from which to drink, have Christian paraphernalia decorating their offices, and fellowship primarily with other Christians. As a result, most Christians have very little contact with those who do not know Christ.

Truthfully, most Christians probably do not like being around non-Christians. Once Christ has transformed an individual, that person will often become very aware of the behavior of others. People outside of Christ

---

18   MacArthur, *2 Timothy*, 178.

become offensive in the language they use, in the attitudes they demonstrate, and in the behaviors they accentuate. As a result, many Christians isolate themselves from non-Christians.

If one truth can be communicated at this point, it is this: *the reason that lost people act the way they do is because they are lost.* That statement is not intended to be pejorative. It is meant, however, to arouse Christians to examine their lifestyles and to discover why they are not more engaged with people outside of Christ. Evangelism must become a priority for believers if a Great Commission Resurgence is to take place. For pastors, that level of primacy must begin with them.

The argument is made that, since there are several primary functions of the church, one can pick and choose which one is most dear to that person's heart. Both Rick Warren and Gene Mims identify five purposes or functions of the church: worship, discipleship, evangelism, ministry, and fellowship.[19] While these functions are indeed all essential for church growth and health, I would propose that one of those purposes stands out over against all of the others.

It would seem to be a cruel joke if God saved people and then left them here on this sinful earth without a real purpose. The best thing that could happen to a new Christian would be to die immediately and go to heaven, unless God had a reason for leaving that new believer in the fleshly realm. It is my opinion that the primary purpose for our continued mortal life as believers is evangelism. While worship and the glory of God serve as our ultimate purposes, in that believers will spend eternity in fellowship and in worship of Christ, we are mandated to witness and to see people come to Christ so that they, in turn, will become His worshipers.

Think of it this way. While worship provides an essential element of Christian growth and existence (Heb 10:25), believers will never perfectly worship the Savior on this earth. The only way that Christians achieve perfection in worship occurs when heaven becomes a reality for them. Discipleship serves as a necessary segment of the Christian life, but no one on this earth will become perfect in discipleship. John said that "when He appears, we will be like Him, because we will see Him as He is" (1 John 3:2). Fellowship is necessary for Christian growth, but Christians do not fellowship perfectly. In fact, if anything demonstrates the imperfection of

---

19 See Rick Warren, *The Purpose-Driven Church: Growth Without Compromising Your Message and Mission* (Grand Rapids: Zondervan, 1995), and Gene Mims, *Kingdom Principles for Church Growth* (Nashville: Convention Press, 1994).

Christianity, it is fellowship. Many Christians, churches, and Christian organizations do not like each other, much less fellowship with each other. True fellowship will not happen until God fully glorifies believers in the presence of Christ. Finally, ministry must happen in the Christian community, but no matter how hard the church tries, it really does not perfectly meet the needs of people. Our needs as believers will be ultimately met when we find ourselves in the presence of God.

Therefore, one reason remains as to why God has left us here on this earth, and that reason is evangelism. While it is true that our evangelism is not perfect and never will be, the acts of proclamation and evangelism are tasks given specifically to the church and to believers. Angels are not sent as evangelists. Angels delivered Christians from prison (Acts 5:19). Angels direct Christians where and with whom to share Christ (Acts 8:26). Angels can even guide non-Christians to one who can share the message of Jesus with them (Acts 10:7). They can minister (Heb 1:7), they have power (Rom 8:38), and they stand in the presence of God praising Him (Ps 148:2), but they do not evangelize. Evangelism remains a responsibility for Christians and them alone.

Thus, it is for that purpose that God has left us here on this earth. Believers are to worship, disciple, fellowship, and minister, but none of those things will ever be complete on this side of heaven. God intends that followers of Jesus, while they are still here, will commit themselves to the priority of a Great Commission evangelism, whereby they "go . . . and make disciples of all nations, baptizing them in the name of the Father and of the Son and of the Holy Spirit, teaching them to observe everything I have commanded you" (Matt 28:19–20).

A CALL TO RESPOND

As Paul encouraged Timothy to "encourage with great patience and teaching," he did so with the instruction to "proclaim the message, persist in it whether convenient or not; rebuke, correct, and encourage" (2 Tim 4:2). In fact, in this passage, Paul utilized nine different imperative verbs to instruct Timothy with regard to his role as a pastor.[20] Therefore, the demands that Paul placed on Timothy serve not as mere suggestions but

---

20 These imperatives include "proclaim," "persist," "rebuke," "correct," "encourage" (verse two); "keep a clear head," "endure," "do," "fulfill" (verse five).

constitute those activities that are essential to his success and well-being as a pastor.

The word "encourage" (*parakaleō*) occupies one particular important concept in Paul's definition of pastoral responsibilities. R. Alan Streett explains that this word is "used 108 times in the New Testament. . . . Five times *parakaleō* is used in the New Testament in relation to evangelistic preaching. . . . In sixty-one of its 108 appearances, *parakaleō* means 'to beg or to plead' or 'to express an urgent request.'"[21] Streett quotes Paige Patterson, who said, "I have frequently translated it [*parakaleō*] as 'give an invitation.' Any time you come across the word 'exhortation' on the pages of the New Testament, you have, in effect, an appeal made for people to come and stand with the speaker in whatever it is that he is doing."[22] Streett applies these thoughts to Acts 2:38–41, concluding, "If Dr. Patterson's definition of *parakaleō* is correct, Peter actually called for his listeners to respond publicly to his message by presenting themselves to him. The record makes it clear that Peter's invitation elicited an overt response, for approximately three thousand people openly indicated their desire to repent and submit themselves for baptism."[23]

Now apply these ideas to Paul's words to Timothy. The word "encourage" could quite possibly be related to what Paul says in verse five, "do the work of an evangelist." Therefore, Paul admonishes Timothy to invite people, to urge people, to plead and to beg with them with regard to their spiritual condition. This pleading and begging do not presuppose the work of the Holy Spirit in conversion. It emphasizes, however, that the effect that evangelism has on the heart of the pastor is passion. Do we really believe in heaven and in hell? Do we really believe that a person who dies without Christ does not receive a second chance to be saved? Do we believe in eternal punishment? If we do, then a passion to see people come to Christ provides the only proper response to the lostness of humanity.

---

21 R. Alan Streett, *The Effective Invitation: A Practical Guide for the Pastor* (Grand Rapids: Kregel, 2004), 62–65. The five instances of the use of *parakaleō* with evangelism are Acts 2:38–41; 11:23; 2 Cor 5:20; 2 Tim 4:2; Titus 1:7–9. A sixth occurrence could be 2 Cor 6:1–2.

22 Ibid., 63.

23 Ibid.

A GREAT COMMISSION RESURGENCE AND A
COMMITMENT TO PERSONAL EVANGELISM

In verse five, Paul offered one final exhortation to Timothy to "do the work of an evangelist." Note that Paul does not use the definite article "the" with the word "evangelist." The call of Timothy to do the work of *an* evangelist indicates that "the type or quality of work is being stressed, rather than some official position. In his pastoral duties, he is not to forget the unsaved, but must always be concerned with announcing the good news of man's redemption through Christ."[24] Lea and Griffin explain further:

> Although it is true that some Christians have the gift of evangelism more obviously than others, the fact must not discourage active sharing of the gospel by all believers. The Great Commission (Matt 28:19–20) and the example of the Book of Acts make clear that witnessing is not simply a responsibility for the ordained leaders but for all believers. No single spiritual obligation is more natural for committed believers or more important than the practice of this conviction.[25]

In order for a Great Commission Resurgence to take place, the pastor must make a personal commitment to evangelism. Evangelism is not the only thing that the pastor does, but it must become a priority. Pastors must pursue evangelism with intentionality.

TOO MANY ACTIVITIES

One of the problems that most pastors face that stifles most evangelism is busyness. We have many things to do in pastoral ministry. All of them are important, and we must accomplish all of them. The problem, though, is that evangelism typically falls to the bottom of our list and therefore is rarely done. This explains why in a recent survey 53 percent of Southern Baptist pastors indicated they had not personally shared their faith with anyone within the last six months.

---

24 Homer A. Kent, Jr., *The Pastoral Epistles*, rev. ed. (Chicago: Moody, 1982), 286.

25 Lea and Griffin, *1, 2 Timothy, Titus*, 245–46.

One of the reasons pastors are not witnessing is because they are responsible for a plethora of activities. They have administrative duties to handle including budgeting, staffing, planning, and programming. They have ministry to be done, from visiting Aunt Susie because her bunions are hurting to ministering to a family who has suffered an untimely death. They have visits to make, from hospitals, to nursing homes, to the home-bound, and to new members. They have discipleship to accomplish, from prayer groups, to personal mentoring, and to preparation for weekly Bible study. And they have sermons to prepare . . . lots of sermons. Every week they write sermons; most times, they have to prepare for at least three sermons a week. Every pastor has some sugar sticks, but one cannot preach old sermons and stay at a church for very long. Therefore, the pastor literally spends hours preparing to preach on a weekly basis. Even sermons. com and the latest Rick Warren series do little to stem the homiletic tide. If one prepares properly, then countless hours are spent getting ready for Sundays and Wednesdays.

In the end, little time is left for evangelism. The most unfortunate issue in this entire scenario comes from the fact that the pastor will be criticized if he does not visit Aunt Susie, or if he misses seeing a church member who just needed a visit, or if his sermons are not as exciting or uplifting as that guy on television who smiles a lot. Rarely do people become upset if he has not done any evangelism. Thus, the pastor finds it easy to put evangelism on the back burner and to concentrate on doing the things that keep people happy and secure his job. Then we wonder why we are not winning the world and seeing a Great Commission Resurgence take place!

This resurgence challenges all Christians to re-evaluate the purpose of the pastor and the church. Does the church exist in order to take care of itself, or did Jesus die for the church so that it will charge the gates of hell and change the world? If we really believe in evangelism, then churches must release their pastors from activities that members of the church can accomplish and allow their pastors to practice evangelism and to empower and equip their flocks to do "the work of ministry" (Eph 4:12) and to share their faith with others.

TOO LITTLE INTENTION

Coupled with evangelism occupying the bottom of the priority list is the fact that too many pastors have little contact with people who do not know Christ. On a personal note, when someone visits my office, that person will discover that 99 percent of my books are Christian books and that I drink out of a cup that has a Christian logo on it (unless I have gone out for lunch to a restaurant that gives me a "to go" cup to bring back to the office). Most of the stuff in my office has some kind of Christian label or connection (except for my Tennessee Volunteers helmet signed by Peyton Manning, but I think he is a Christian). All of the people I hang out with are Christians. My friends are Christians. Most of the pastors on my staff are Christians! My problem is that I do not know anyone who is not already a Christian.

The answer is simple. If we are going to engage in a Great Commission Resurgence, it has to start with the pastor committing himself to personal evangelism. Evangelism must be *intentional.* We have to make it a priority. Evangelism must be *relational.* We must be willing to go outside our normal activities to establish real relationships with real people who do not know Jesus. And evangelism must be *confrontational.* It is not confrontational in the sense that it is arrogant or abrasive, but in the sense that we must come to the point that we confront people about their need for Christ. We must invite them to a saving relationship with Jesus through repentance from sin and trusting in Christ through faith.

As pastors, we must make that personal commitment to do the work of an evangelist. Even if we are not gifted evangelists, we must still accomplish the task. Without that level of commitment, a Great Commission Resurgence will never take place. We have exegeted the texts, we have read the commands, and we have understood the obstacles. The bottom line with regard to evangelism and a Great Commission Resurgence is this thought: *pastors must make the commitment to do evangelism.* We can make the excuses and offer the apologies, but the crux of the need to reach the world lies in commitment. To do evangelism requires simply that the pastor commit himself to do the work . . . regardless!

CONCLUSION

One of my favorite pastimes is playing golf. It serves as a great source of relaxation but it also opens doors for witnessing. I have discovered that, most of the time, if I am going to play and do not have a playing partner or partners, the golf course will automatically put me in a foursome. Here is what I do. I do not mention that I am a pastor or seminary professor during the first nine holes. If the guys in my foursome are not believers, telling them that I am a preacher will scare them off, and they probably will make other plans when we make the turn after the ninth hole. On the back nine, I will then ask them what they do for a living. In turn, they will also ask me the same question. That one question then provides the opportunity, oftentimes, to share Christ with them.

Several things have to take place, though. First, I have to remember why I am on the golf course that day. If I cannot hold my temper when I make a bad shot or if I would rather enjoy a so-called "adult beverage" with the gang, my witness is pretty much shot. Those with whom I play must see that a genuine change exists in my life. It is my conviction that righteousness and transformation are essential to elements in witnessing, not trying to conform to culture or argue the merits of whether a particular behavior or activity is strictly condemned in Scripture. Individuals who do not know Christ sense that type of hypocrisy.

The people to whom I witness must also know that I am honestly concerned and interested in them. They will see right through me, quite rapidly, if they notice that I am just looking to put another notch in my spiritual belt. People are not numbers or projects. They are individuals who matter to Christ. I must communicate that idea through my actions and words.

When I have been successful in demonstrating the love of Christ and the transformation he affords, the opportunity to share my faith arises. It may not be that everyone with whom I share accepts God's gift of eternal life, but I know that I am in the business of sowing the seeds of the gospel. As a result, when I am out practicing Great Commission evangelism, I gain the passion and focus that allow me to encourage others to do the same. I can start with the one, win that person to Christ, and provide discipleship so that, in turn, the two of us will share our faith and each win one person each to Christ . . . and so a Great Commission Resurgence begins.

PREACHING FOR A GREAT COMMISSION RESURGENCE

David L. Allen

INTRODUCTION

Why is preaching important to the fulfillment of the Great Commission? If the mission of the church is the evangelization of the lost and the equipping of the saved, then of all things the church does, preaching must be at the apex. A careful study of the Great Commission given by Jesus indicates precisely that. The Great Commission appears in all four Gospels in some form, and in the first chapter of the book of Acts.

> "Go, therefore, and make disciples of all nations, baptizing them in the name of the Father and of the Son and of the Holy Spirit, teaching them to observe everything I have commanded you." (Matt 28:19–20)
>
> "Go into all the world and preach the gospel to the whole creation." (Mark 16:15)[1]
>
> "This is what is written: the Messiah would suffer and rise from the dead the third day, and repentance for forgiveness of sins would be proclaimed in His name to all the nations, beginning at Jerusalem." (Luke 24:47)
>
> "As the Father has sent me, I also send you." (John 20:21)

---

1 This is, of course, part of the longer ending of Mark, which most scholars doubt was a part of the original. See the succinct discussion of this complicated issue in Bruce Metzger, *A Textual Commentary on the Greek New Testament*, 2nd ed. (Stuttgart: German Bible Society, 1994), 102–06. If Mark's Gospel ends at verse 8, then one should disallow Mark 16:15 as evidence.

From these accounts, we observe the following: (1) Jesus has been given all authority in heaven and on earth. (2) On this authority, the apostles and by implication all Christians are sent forth to make disciples. (3) The gospel message is to all the nations, hence a worldwide endeavor. (4) New believers are to be baptized and taught. (5) Preaching is the primary means of making disciples. (6) This preaching is grounded in Scripture ("thus it has been written," Luke 24:46). In the Greek text of Luke 24:47, the aorist passive infinitive translated "should be proclaimed" stands first in the clause for emphasis. Obviously preaching plays a paramount role in the church's mandate to fulfill the Great Commission.

THE ROLE OF PREACHING AND THE GREAT COMMISSION IN ACTS

Preaching is at the heart of church growth in Acts. In fact, Acts is actually a book about preaching, since 30 percent of the book is composed of sermons. Preaching is the principle strategy for church growth in Acts. Note the five summary statements that Luke places at key points in Acts exemplifying the importance of preaching: Acts 6:7; 9:31; 12:24; 16:5; 19:20. We are told in Acts 6:4 that prayer and preaching were the priorities of the apostles. Acts 4:8 illustrates the role of the Holy Spirit and preaching in the early church. Throughout Acts, preaching is the seed of church planting and the tool for church growth.

The nature of the church requires that preaching be paramount in the fulfillment of her mission. The church was birthed in preaching according to Acts 2. Paul says in Romans that "faith comes from what is heard, and what is heard comes through the message about Christ" (Rom 10:17). Evangelistic preaching grows the church. Biblical preaching edifies the church. The New Testament itself testifies to the foundational nature of preaching for the mission and purpose of the church. In his swan song, Paul tells young Timothy "Preach the Word" (2 Tim 4:2 NIV). You cannot have a church without preaching, and you cannot have church growth without preaching. Preaching is fundamental to New Testament ecclesiology. Preaching must be foundational in the mission of the church for theological reasons.

Preaching is the strategy for both evangelism and discipleship in the book of Acts. Key words for preaching in Acts include "preach," "speak," "say," "announce good news," "herald," "exhort," "persuade," "teach," "publically proclaim," "reason/debate," and "solemnly testify." Notice the key places where preaching occurs in Acts: the temple, council chambers, a desert road, Cornelius's house, synagogues, market places, jails, courtrooms, on board ships, in schools and lecture halls. Likewise, Satan's strategy is ever an attempt to silence the preaching of the apostles and early Christians primarily by means of persecution.

Acts does not leave us in the dark concerning the content of this preaching. Its primary focus was the person and work of Christ (2:36), salvation in Christ alone (4:12), and the necessity of repentance and faith in Christ (2:38; 20:21). Eternity and judgment were frequent subjects as well (2:20; 17:30–31). Acts reveals the manner of preaching: constant appeal to the conscience about sin (2:23), admonishing people with warnings (2:40; 28:23–28), intensity and boldness (4:13,31), and compassion and tears (20:19,31). Preaching in Acts regularly called for a response from the hearers as in Acts 2:38 and 16:31.

Finally, Acts informs us about the results of preaching: three thousand were saved at Pentecost after Peter's sermon (2:41), Stephen the preacher was martyred after his sermon (7:54–60), and frequent references occur in Acts of people's response to preaching as either obedience or rejection (28:23–28). Jews and Gentiles alike heard the gospel, repented of sin, and believed in Jesus as a result of the preaching of the early church. According to Acts, the early church, with laser-like intensity, understood the Great Commission of Jesus and sought to carry the gospel to the ends of the earth. The early Christians' understanding, vision, and commitment to the Great Commission should be the pervasive pattern today.

In light of this importance attached to preaching in the book of Acts, it is astounding to see the way much of the modern church growth literature marginalizes preaching. Since 1971, myriad dissertations and books have been written on the subject of how to grow a church. Many of these books and the principles behind them are less theological and more pragmatic in nature. The church growth movement has been a mixed bag. One of the most surprising things about the books produced by this movement is the lack of emphasis placed on the role of preaching in church growth. Many do not even mention preaching. David Eby wrote a book in 1996 entitled *Power Preaching for Church Growth: The Role of Preaching in Growing Churches.*[2] As far as I know, this was the first book to treat the subject

---

2 David Eby, *Power Preaching for Church Growth: The Role of Preaching in Growing Churches* (Dublin, Ireland: Mentor, 1996).

in book-length format and Eby is not even in the church growth movement. His two chapters analyzing the church growth movement are must-reads. Eby read every book in the church growth movement and charted where they talk about preaching. His conclusion was startling: the movement paid very little attention to preaching as the means of growing the church. The church growth movement has emphasized marketing and de-emphasized preaching. To the extent that preaching is downplayed in the church, to that extent the Great Commission suffers.

Paul states that it is the "foolishness of the message preached" that God is pleased to use in the salvation of the lost (1 Cor 1:21). Paul's mandate to Timothy to "preach the Word" (2 Tim 4:2) makes it clear that preaching is God's program for the church.

THE ROLE OF PREACHING AND THE GREAT COMMISSION IN THE EPISTLES

In the New Testament epistles, preaching serves as the means to motivate and equip the church to fulfill the Great Commission. The epistles of Paul, Peter, and John, along with James, Jude and Hebrews, are all examples of how these early Christian authors used preaching to fulfill the Great Commission's mandate of teaching the church all things. Right doctrine is absolutely necessary for the health and growth of the church. All true evangelism and missions must be built on the foundation of sound doctrine. Much of the New Testament epistles are essentially written sermons and constitute what their authors believed the early church needed to be taught so as to be equipped to fulfill the Great Commission.

PREACHING, CHURCH CONFESSIONS, AND THE GREAT COMMISSION

The necessity of preaching for the mission of the church is illustrated in the history of the church. Many of the confessions of faith developed by the Anabaptists,[3] magisterial reformers, and other post-Reformation groups speak about the primacy of preaching for achieving the mission

---

3 See Abraham Friesen, *Erasmus, the Anabaptists, and the Great Commission* (Grand Rapids: Eerdmans, 1998), 98–99.

of the church. The church cannot be the church unless she is the preaching church. The Reformers, by their own preaching and writing, show they considered preaching to be critical to the establishment and ongoing growth and health of the church.

PREACHING, PASTORAL CARE, AND THE GREAT COMMISSION

Another reason why preaching is necessary for the mission of the church is the pastoral reason. The classical definitions of pastoral care throughout church history speak of preaching as the primary method of doing pastoral care.[4] Only as Christians are in a healthy state spiritually will they be effective in fulfilling the Great Commission. Thomas Oden has contributed a significant body of work on the importance of pastoral care and the necessity of preaching as a primary means of doing pastoral care.[5] Preaching to the church plays a crucial role in preparing and maintaining Christians spiritually to fulfill the Great Commission.

---

4   See the classic work on this subject by Gregory the Great, *The Book of Pastoral Rule*, in *Nicene and Post-Nicene Fathers*, Second Series, ed. by Philip Schaff and Henry Wace, vol. 12 (Grand Rapids: Eerdmans, 1997 repr.), 69, where Gregory argued that preaching must be used in pastoral care. This work is probably the single most influential book in the history of pastoral care. Lisa Kaaran Bailey's dissertation, "Preaching and Pastoral Care in Late Antique Gaul: The Eusebius Gallicanus Sermon Collection" (Ph.D. diss., Princeton University, 2004), argued that preaching was a crucial aspect of pastoral care during this period and was one of the foundations for the success of the late Patristic church in integrating itself into Western European culture. This anonymous sermon collection from fifth-century Gaul was compiled into a preaching resource for the sixth century and continued to be used into the early medieval period. See also A. C. A. Hall, *Preaching and Pastoral Care* (New York: Longmans, Green and Co., 1913); Arthur Teikmanis, *Preaching and Pastoral Care* (New York: Prentice-Hall, Englewood Cliffs, NJ, 1964); Francesca Tinti, ed., *Pastoral Care in Late Anglo-Saxon England* (Woodbridge: Boydell, 2005).

5   Thomas Oden, *Pastoral Theology: Essentials for Ministry* (San Francisco: Harper, 1983); *Care of Souls in the Classic Tradition* (Philadelphia: Fortress, 1984); and *Ministry through Word and Sacrament*, Classical Pastoral Care 2 (Grand Rapids: Baker, 2000).

PREACHING AND THE GREAT COMMISSION AMONG THE ANABAPTISTS, ENGLISH BAPTISTS, AND SOUTHERN BAPTISTS

One of the most surprising, even shocking, things concerning the Reformation is the almost total lack of missionary vision on the part of the magisterial reformers. This state of affairs no doubt occurred, at least in part, to the standard interpretation of Matthew 28:18–20 that had been held since Augustine: namely, the Great Commission was intended solely as a command to the apostles and not to the church after the apostolic age.[6] This interpretation continued to dominate Protestant churches until the end of the eighteenth century. Until that time, missionary zeal was a scarce commodity within Protestantism.

However, the Great Commission via Erasmus's interpretation became crucial for the theological orientation of the Anabaptists, and was, in fact, the "key to understanding the movement as a whole," according to Friesen.[7] Following Erasmus, Anabaptists believed the Great Commission applied to all Christians at all times. As Franklin Littell pointed out, within Anabaptist confessions, there are no texts more frequently cited than the Great Commission texts in Matthew 28 and Mark 16.[8] Additionally, the preaching and missionary focus of Anabaptism found its impetus from

---

6 Harry R. Boer, *Pentecost and Missions* (Grand Rapids: Eerdmans, 1961), 22–23. Gustav Warneck noted that not only was there a lack of missionary activity among the magisterial Reformers, but the very presence of the missionary idea was lacking among them (G. Warneck, *Abriss einer Geschichte der protestantischen Missionen: von der Reformation bis aus die Gegenwart* [Berlin: Martin Warneck, 1900]), 9. Leonard Verduin remarked that the notion "that the Great Commission was intended for the pre-Constantinian era" only was a "theological absurdity" brought on by Augustine's promulgation of the so-called "Constantinian innovation" that the church after the apostolic era would function differently (L. Verduin, *The Reformers and Their Stepchildren* [Grand Rapids: Eerdmans, 1964], 66)." Other related aberrations concerning the Great Commission included Calvin's belief that missionary work should be under the jurisdiction of the "Christian" government and not the church. Glenn Sunshine has sought to nuance the harsh verdict concerning the magisterial Reformers' lack of missionary zeal ("Protestant Missions in the Sixteenth Century," in *The Great Commission: Evangelicals and the History of World Missions*, ed. M. Klauber and S. Manetsch [Nashville: B&H, 2008], 12–22), but the general consensus remains intact, as David Bosch has argued in *Transforming Mission: Paradigm Shifts in Theology of Mission*, American Studies of Missiology Series 16 (Maryknoll, NY: Orbis, 1991), 239–61, especially pp. 245–48.

7 Friesen, *Erasmus, the Anabaptists, and the Great Commission*, 98.

8 Franklin Littell, *The Origins of Sectarian Protestantism: A Study of the Anabaptist View of the Church* (New York: Macmillan, 1964), 109.

these texts.[9] To commit oneself to Christ as Lord was, for the Anabaptists, a commitment to work toward the fulfillment of the Great Commission. Unlike their magisterial Reformer counterparts, Anabaptists went everywhere preaching the gospel in an attempt to be faithful to Christ's command in Matthew 28:18–20.[10] Hans Kasdorf, in writing about the Anabaptists during the Reformation and their view of the Great Commission, succinctly stated the reason for their missionary zeal: "The essence of the Christian life, as the Anabaptist understood it, is *being a disciple*. This, in turn, means multiplication of that very life by making disciples who enjoy the privileges and share the responsibilities that such life entails."[11]

Though the Anabaptists were in many ways the spiritual ancestors of the earliest Baptists, most historians do not trace Baptist origins directly to the Anabaptists, but rather to England in the early seventeenth century with the rise of English Baptists. English Baptists, though mired in hyper-Calvinism early in the eighteenth century, broke free through the strong leadership of such men as Andrew Fuller and William Carey. Both Fuller and Carey stressed the necessity of the Great Commission as the foundation for their missionary endeavors.[12] Each preached now-famous sermons that served as catalysts for the modern missions movement.

On April 27, 1791, Fuller preached at an association ministers' meeting at Clipstone. His text was Haggai 1:2 and his title was "Instances, Evil, and Tendency of Delay, in the Concerns of Religion."[13] This sermon, when first preached and later in published form, proved important in the founding of the Baptist Missionary Society one year later. A key portion of the sermon

---

9   Friesen, *Erasmus, the Anabaptists, and the Great Commission*, 99.

10   See Paige Patterson, "Learning from the Anabaptists," in *Southern Baptist Identity: An Evangelical Denomination Faces the Future*, ed. David Dockery (Wheaton: Crossway, 2009), 137, for a summary of Anabaptist practices which our Southern Baptist churches should emulate today. Consult also Malcolm Yarnell, *The Formation of Christian Doctrine* (Nashville: B&H Academic, 2007), 73–106, for an excellent overview of the theology of the believers' church over against the magisterial reformers using the Anabaptist Pilgrim Marpeck as a benchmark, and David Bosch, *Transforming Mission*, 243–47, who contrasts the missionary work of the Anabaptists with that of the magisterial reformers.

11   Hans Kasdorf, "Anabaptists and the Great Commission in the Reformation," *Direction*, vol. 4, no. 2 (April 1975): 307, emphasis original.

12   See Peter Morden, "Andrew Fuller as an Apologist for Missions," in *'At the Pure Fountain of Thy Word': Andrew Fuller as an Apologist*, Studies in Baptist History and Thought 6, ed. Michael Haykin (Waynesboro, GA: Paternoster, 2004), 236–55.

13   Andrew Fuller, *The Complete Works of the Rev. Andrew Fuller, with a Memoir of His Life by the Rev. Andrew Gunton Fuller*, ed. A. G. Fuller; rev. ed., J. Belcher (Harrisonburg, VA: Sprinkle Publications, 1988 [1845]), 1:145–51.

concerns Fuller's direct challenge to his hearers to be involved in world missions based on the Great Commission in Matthew 28:19–20. Listen to these pungent words:

> When the Lord Jesus commissioned his apostles, he commanded them to go and teach "all nations," to preach the gospel to "every creature;" and that notwithstanding the difficulties and opposition that would lie in the way. The apostles executed their commission with assiduity and fidelity; but, since their days, we seem to sit down half contented that the greater part of the world should still remain in ignorance and idolatry. Some noble efforts have indeed been made; but they are small in number, when compared with the magnitude of the object. And why is it so? . . . The truth is, if I am not mistaken, we wait for we know not what; we seem to think "the time is not come, the time for the Spirit to be poured down from on high." We *pray* for the conversion and salvation of the world, and yet *neglect the ordinary means* by which those ends have been used to be accomplished. It pleased God, heretofore, by the foolishness of preaching, to save them that believed; and there is reason to think it will still please God to work by that distinguished means. Ought we not then at least to try by some means to convey more of the good news of salvation to the world around us than has hitherto been conveyed? The encouragement to the heathen is still in force, "*Whosoever shall call upon the name of the Lord shall be saved*: but how shall they call on him in whom they have not believed? and how shall they believe in him of whom they have not heard? and how shall they believe in him of whom they have not heard? and how shall they hear without a preacher? and how shall they preach except they be sent?" . . . Were every true minister of the gospel to make a point of preaching as often as possible in the villages within his reach; and did those private Christians who are situated in such villages open their doors for preaching, and recommend the gospel by a holy and affectionate behaviour, might we not hope to see the wilderness become as a fruitful field? Surely, in these matters, we are too negligent.[14]

---

14   Fuller, *Works*, 1:147–48, emphasis original.

Oh, that such preaching were common in our SBC churches today!

Interestingly, some of the language found in this sermon is also found in Carey's now famous *An Enquiry into the Obligations of Christians to Use Means for the Conversion of the Heathen* that was published only one year later. This similarity of language indicates that Carey was most likely drawing upon Fuller's Clipstone sermon. However, since Fuller had read an early manuscript of Carey's *Enquiry*, published in 1792, it is also possible that Carey influenced Fuller.[15] It was Carey's pamphlet that paved the way for the beginning of the Baptist Missionary Society and thus the beginning of the modern missions movement.

On May 30, 1792, William Carey preached his celebrated sermon "Expect Great Things; Attempt Great Things" at the annual Association Meeting at Nottingham.[16] Isaiah 54: 2–3 was the text, and Fuller was in attendance. Carey's sermon was electrifying as he pleaded for the formation of a missionary society, but the following morning during the business meeting attended by only the pastors, it appeared nothing would be done. Walker relates the spine-tingling tale:

The following morning the ministers met alone for their usual conference, and

> Carey's proposal to form a missionary society came up for discussion. But the enthusiasm kindled by the previous day's sermon had passed and the cold logic of practical difficulties seemed overpowering. That little band of comparatively insignificant preachers felt the task to be beyond their strength. They came to the conclusion that Carey's proposal was for the time being impossible; they turned it down, and the gathering prepared to break up. In distress, Carey seized Fuller by the arms and asked whether they were once more to separate without doing something definite. Then a change came over the company, and after further discussion, and passionate exhortation from Carey, it was decided to place on their minutes a resolution that: "A plan be prepared against the next ministers' meeting for forming a Baptist Society for propagating the gospel among the heathens."[17]

---

15 P. Morden, "Andrew Fuller as an Apologist for Missions," 245.

16 F. Deaville Walker called the sermon "nothing short of epoch-making," in *William Carey: Missionary Pioneer and Statesman* (Chicago: Moody, 1951), 78–79.

17 Ibid., 80.

Thus was born what was to be called the Baptist Missionary Society, with Carey serving as its first missionary and Fuller its secretary. Carey ultimately succeeded in dismantling the false interpretation of the Great Commission in his *Enquiry*[18] that he published shortly before his famous sermon. He rightly concluded that Christ's Great Commission was, in effect, Christ's missionary mandate and marching orders for the church for all time. From the late eighteenth century on, Baptists were firmly committed to missions.[19]

The lesson for us today from these two sermons is clear. One man with a heart for God and the souls of the lost, willing to deliver a sermon with pathos urging Christians to the task of missions, can stir people to action in such a way that changes the world. These two sermons furnish us with stellar examples of the kind of preaching we need today to challenge SBC churches to fulfill the Great Commission. Once again, the necessity of passionate preaching to the church on the Great Commission is evident.

On the American front, the formation of the Southern Baptist Convention in 1845 had as its primary goal the reaching of the world for Christ.[20] Throughout our 165-year history, Southern Baptists have sought to place missions and evangelism at the forefront of everything we do. Preaching and church planting have gone hand in hand in our missionary endeavors. Although we have always been a mission-minded people, something is wrong today in our denomination. We seem to be losing the battle when it comes to evangelism in many of our local churches. One thing on which we can all agree: we need a Great Commission resurgence, and preaching will play a crucial if not preeminent role in that resurgence.

HINDRANCES TO PREACHING AND THE GREAT COMMISSION

In light of the above, if preaching is hindered, the fulfillment of the Great Commission will be hindered. In this section I will address some of the

---

18 William Carey, *An Enquiry into the Obligations of Christians to Use Means for the Conversion of the Heathen*, ed. J. Pretlove (Dallas, TX: Criswell Publications, 1988).

19 For a brief but helpful historical survey of Baptists and Missions, see Thomas Nettles, "Baptists and the Great Commission," in *The Great Commission: Evangelicals and the History of World Missions*, 89–107.

20 "Preamble and Constitution of the Southern Baptist Convention, 1845" [on-line]; available from http://baptiststudiesonline.com/wp-content/uploads/2007/02/constitution-of-the-sbc.pdf.

theological and practical hindrances to preaching that negatively impact the Great Commission.

First, preaching that does not communicate the gospel at all or that communicates it unclearly hinders the Great Commission. No one will come to Christ through preaching that does not have the gospel in it, since only the gospel saves. Many evangelical churches are "gospel lite" today. Likewise, preaching that does not clearly communicate the gospel makes it difficult for people to understand exactly what God has done for them in Christ and how they must respond in repentance and faith to receive salvation. It is incumbent on preachers to be crystal clear concerning exactly what the gospel is and what people must do to respond to it. As with all things in preaching, clarity has to be crafted; it will not happen accidentally. The process of sermon construction and delivery needs careful thinking to make sure the gospel is in no way discarded or distorted.

Second, an "easy believeism" fostered by a pragmatic approach to preaching and church growth hinders the Great Commission. There is a growing recognition within our SBC that we must recover, as Nathan Finn put it, "a robust understanding of the gospel."[21] I agree completely. We must preach the gospel and present it with theological integrity, with public invitations to obey the gospel through repentance of sin and faith in Christ. Though some within the Calvinistic tradition reject the use of altar calls, while others in the same tradition view them as optional, I am persuaded that altar calls are a wise course of action given the nature of the gospel, but they should be extended with integrity as well.[22]

Third, we must recognize that our theology impacts our preaching, which in turn impacts the Great Commission. Let us return to consider the case of one of our most famous and celebrated Baptist forefathers, Andrew Fuller. Growing up amidst the stifling influence of eighteenth-century hyper-Calvinism, Fuller saw firsthand its debilitating effects on preaching, evangelism and missions. Through a careful study of the Scriptures

---

21 Nathan Finn, "Priorities for a Post-Resurgence Convention," in *Southern Baptist Identity*, 265.

22 I highly recommend every pastor read R. Alan Streett's *The Effective Invitation*, 2nd ed. (Grand Rapids: Kregel, 2004). This is the single best book on the subject of the public altar call and Streett is a moderate Calvinist.

and influenced by John Bunyan and Jonathan Edwards,[23] Fuller moved away from hyper-Calvinism and developed two key theses that he argued brilliantly in his famous work *The Gospel Worthy of All Acceptation.*[24] First is the duty of all sinners to believe the gospel. All sinners should be encouraged through preaching to believe in Christ. Second, Fuller argued that it is the duty of preachers to offer the gospel to all people. Thus, preachers should make every effort to exhort everyone to believe in Christ.[25] Key to understanding Fuller's two theses is the influence of Jonathan Edwards concerning the natural ability of sinners to respond to the gospel but their moral inability to do so.[26] This Edwardsean distinction provided Fuller with the theological groundwork for his *Gospel Worthy.*

One of the most fascinating aspects of Fuller's *Gospel Worthy* concerns the influence of the General Baptist Dan Taylor on Fuller's view of the extent of the atonement. In the first edition of Fuller's *Gospel Worthy*, published in 1785, it is evident that he was committed to particular redemption (limited atonement) in the Owenic sense of that term.[27] However, following his debates with Dan Taylor, Fuller was persuaded that particular redemption in the sense of limited substitution did not comport with Scripture. Taylor had argued the case for universal atonement and that the only proper ground for universal invitations for sinners to believe

23   Incidentally, both Bunyan and Edwards were moderate Calvinists with respect to the extent of the atonement. See my essay, "The Extent of the Atonement: Limited or Universal?" in *Whosoever Will: A Biblical-Theological Critique of Five-Point Calvinism,* ed. David L. Allen and Steve W. Lemke (Nashville: B&H Academic, 2010), 61–107.

24   *The Gospel Worthy of All Acceptation, or the Duty of Sinners to Believe in Jesus Christ, with Corrections and Editions; to which is Added an Appendix, on the Necessity of a Holy Disposition in Order to Believing in Christ,* in *Fuller's Works,* 2:328–416. Fuller's *Gospel Worthy* was first published in 1785, but a second edition with his revisions was published in 1801. The second edition appears in *Fuller's Works.*

25   Peter Morden, *Offering Christ to the World: Andrew Fuller (1754–1815) and the Revival of Eighteenth Century Particular Baptist Life,* Studies in Baptist History and Thought (Waynesboro, GA: Paternoster, 2003), 8:26–27. This work is an excellent biography of Fuller. As Morden noted, Fuller followed Jonathan Edwards's concept of natural and moral inability in sinners. All the unregenerate have natural ability to respond to the gospel, but none has the moral ability to respond to the gospel. Fuller believed no one can respond apart from electing grace and the regenerating work of the Spirit (Morden, *Offering Christ,* 44).

26   Ibid., 49. By "moral inability," Edwards and Fuller meant that no one would come to Christ apart from the work of the Holy Spirit. Morden correctly noted the "natural" and "moral" distinction has been criticized even by some in the Reformed tradition (ibid., 61).

27   See *Gospel Worthy,* 1st ed., 132–39. "Owenic" has reference to John Owen's famous *The Death of Death in the Death of Christ,* the classic volume on the subject of particular redemption (limited atonement).

the gospel is a universal provision in Christ's death.[28] Taylor continued to point out that if limited atonement were true, then there is no provision at all for the nonelect in the death of Christ. God could not command something of sinners that is naturally impossible for them to do. Fuller felt the brunt of this argument and could not answer it. He later confessed in 1803: "I tried to answer my opponent . . . but I could not. I found not merely his reasonings, but the Scriptures themselves, standing in my way."[29] Morden pointed out how Fuller, in his reply to Dan Taylor, "stated his revised position on the atonement clearly and openly."[30] Morden's conclusion is striking and important for the discussion to follow: Fuller's view of the extent of the atonement "could now properly be called 'general.'"[31] As a Calvinist, Fuller's concept of redemption was still "particular" in the sense that the particularity was now located not in the *extent* of the atonement, but in the *design* and *application* of the atonement. Fuller believed the elect were determined in the elective purpose of God in eternity past. For Fuller, a universal atonement "safeguarded the basis upon which the all-important universal calls to repentance and faith could be made."[32] Everyone has the natural ability to respond to the gospel call "because not only did they have the natural powers enabling them to do so, but there was, potentially, provision for them in the death of Christ."[33]

Proof of Fuller's shift on the extent of the atonement can be found in his *Reply to Philanthropos* where he admitted he had been mistaken about the terms "ransom" and "propitiation" being applied only to those who were among the elect. Now these terms were "applicable to all mankind in general," an admission that clearly shows Fuller had abandoned limited substitution/atonement.[34] Additional proof for Fuller's shift can also be found in a comparison of the first and second editions of *Gospel Worthy*

---

28 Morden, *Offering Christ*, 69. It should be noted that Fuller did register his praise for Owen, however this does not argue for any continued agreement with Owen's limited substitution perspective.

29 *Six Letters to Dr. Ryland Respecting the Controversy with the Rev. A. Booth*, in *Fuller's Works*, 2:709–10; cited also in Morden, *Offering Christ*, 70.

30 Morden, *Offering Christ*, 70. For Fuller's reply, see *Reply to Philanthropos*, in *Fuller's Works*, 2:488–89.

31 Morden, *Offering Christ*, 70.

32 Ibid., 72.

33 Ibid. Morden's statement is clarified when one understands him to mean that the potentiality is in the application, not the provision. This is the point he is arguing in the paragraph.

34 Ibid. See *Reply to Philanthropos*, in *Fuller's Works*, 2:496 and 2:550, respectively.

where he discusses particular redemption.[35] I own both of these works and have compared them carefully. The section on particular redemption in the first edition is almost completely rewritten in the second edition.[36] All references to particular redemption in the sense that Christ suffered only for the sins of the elect are excised by Fuller. Fuller abandoned his Owenic pecuniary (commercial) argument that Jesus' death was a literal debt payment. This commercial argument by Owen is one of the linchpin arguments for limited atonement. As Morden correctly noted, Fuller now argued against Owen's concept of Christ's death as a literal debt payment: if Christ's death were a literal debt payment, "then it would be inconsistent, not only with 'indefinite invitations' but also with 'free forgiveness of sin', for sinners in the Bible were directed to apply for forgiveness as supplicants rather than claimants."[37] Fuller believed, as Morden confirmed, that no inconsistency ensued from this "special design" in the death of Christ in its application to the elect and that all people everywhere were under obligation to repent and believe the gospel. Only if limited atonement in the Owenic sense is maintained is there an inconsistency.[38]

This theological issue is of immense importance to our discussion of preaching and the Great Commission. The death of Christ for the sins

---

35 Morden, *Offering Christ*, 73–74, illustrates some of the substantive changes.

36 See *Gospel Worthy*, 1st ed., 132–39 and *Gospel Worthy*, in *Fuller's Works*, 2:373–75.

37 Morden, *Offering Christ*, 73–74. The well-known nineteenth-century Calvinistic Baptist Andrew Broaddus also rejected the pecuniary understanding of the atonement. Following his statements expressing his viewpoint on the subject, Broaddus continued: "These remarks on the *nature* of the atonement, lead to the question as to its *extent*. And here I take occasion to say, that a consistent and scriptural view of this subject appears to lead to the conclusion, that the atonement is *general* in its *nature* and *extent*. As opening a way for the salvation of sinners, considered *as sinners*, it is general in its nature; and as being of sufficient value for the salvation of the world, it is general in its *extent*. At the same time, it may be proper to remark, that *redemption*, considered as the result and application of the atonement, is limited, of course, to those who actually become the subjects of grace; in other words; to those who become believers in Jesus." Andrew Broaddus, "The Atonement," in *The Sermons and Other Writings of the Rev. Andrew Broaddus*, ed. A. Broaddus (New York: Lewis Colby, 1852), 109.

38 Ibid. Michael Haykin has observed this shift in Fuller's view on the extent of the atonement as well. See his "Particular Redemption in the Writings of Andrew Fuller," in *The Gospel in All the World*, Studies in Baptist History and Thought 1, ed. by D. Bebbington (Waynesboro, GA: Paternoster, 2002), 128. When Haykin says, "Fuller did not surrender his commitment to particular redemption" (128), I presume he means that Fuller, like all Calvinists whether Moderate or High, believed that the atonement was "particular in the sense that God the Father intended to extend its benefits only to the elect" (126). Fuller did indeed surrender his commitment to particular redemption *in the Owenic sense of the term*, since he had come to believe that the death of Christ satisfied for the sins of all people, not just the elect.

of all people and not just the elect becomes the ground for the indiscriminate preaching of the gospel and the "bold proclamation" to the whole world. Morden also noted that Fuller's second edition of *The Gospel Worthy* contained "a new note of boldness, indeed urgency, as he pressed the practical consequences of his thesis on his readers. In the first edition, Fuller gave several notes of caution concerning preaching. Concerned to guard against careless evangelistic preaching, he urged that hearers should 'pray to God for an interest in his salvation.'"[39] Morden continued by noting that Fuller eliminated these cautions in the second edition. Now Fuller wrote about the danger of preachers being too reticent in preaching the gospel. "By 1801 he was clear that the need of the hour was not caution—rather it was committed gospel preaching."[40] Morden concluded: "Fuller both clarified and modified his theology of salvation between the years 1785 and 1801, years in which this theology was a crucial motor for change in the life of the Particular Baptist denomination."[41]

Carey's *Enquiry* was "deeply indebted" to Andrew Fuller.[42] Both men viewed Matthew 28:19–20 as the key biblical text for missions. As a result of their vision and commitment, the "Particular Baptist Society for Propagating the Gospel Among the Heathen" was founded in October 1792. Fuller's *Gospel Worthy* provided the theological foundation for a worldwide missionary outreach that would characterize Baptists to this day.

Fuller believed, as all Southern Baptists do also, that God Himself sincerely desires the salvation of all people and thus God Himself is offering salvation to all, as made clear in many places in the Bible, especially John 17:21, 23; 1 Tim 2:4; 2 Pet 3:9; and 2 Cor 5:18-21. To deny this will invariably place a stranglehold on preaching and missionary endeavor and will be deleterious to the fulfillment of the Great Commission. The point to be noticed here is not just our making the offer of salvation to all by means of our preaching, but the fact that God Himself makes the offer to all through us (2 Cor 5:20). Without the universal saving will of God and

---

39 Morden, *Offering Christ*, 75–76.

40 Ibid., 75.

41 Ibid., 75–76. Morden adds that "the most important change was his shift from a limited to a general view of the atonement during his dispute with the Evangelical Arminian Dan Taylor."

42 See Brian Stanley, *The History of the Baptist Missionary Society 1792–1992* (Edinburgh: T&T Clark, 1992), 12–13; and Michael Haykin, "Andrew Fuller on Mission: Text and Passion," in *Baptists and Mission: Papers from the Fourth International Conference on Baptist Studies*, ed. Ian Randall and Anthony Cross, Studies in Baptist History and Thought 29 (Bletchley, Milton Keynes, UK: Paternoster, 2007), 28.

a universal extent in Christ's sin-bearing, there can be no well-meant offer of salvation from God to all who hear the gospel call.[43] We should engage in preaching as a vital means of doing missions and evangelism because of the direct commands of Christ as seen clearly in Matt 28:19–20. Christ's actual sufficiency to save all men should also form a basis for our preaching, missions, and evangelism. All preachers should be careful to make sure they do not inadvertently undermine the well-meant gospel offer. We are to evangelize because God desires all people to be saved and has made atonement for all, thus removing the legal barriers that necessitate their condemnation. Our Great Commission preaching should be a way of conforming ourselves to the very heart of God's own missionary interests.

CONCLUSION

The mission of the church to fulfill the Great Commission cannot be accomplished without preaching. Preaching that does not communicate the Gospel clearly and that does not explain the meaning of the text of Scripture to Christians to equip them to fulfill the church's mission will result in a spiritually dwarfed church and a truncated witness to the world. Preaching that does not inform and challenge all believers to understand that the very crux of what it means to be a Christian is to be someone who is committed lock, stock, and barrel to the Great Commission will fail to build Great Commission Christians and Great Commission churches. As the case of Andrew Fuller demonstrates, one's theology can have immense repercussions for preaching, evangelism, and missions. What lessons does the case of Andrew Fuller have for preaching in the Southern Baptist Convention and our efforts to experience a Great Commission Resurgence? One's theology does indeed impact in a practical way one's evangelistic preaching, which in turn impacts evangelism and missions. If there is to be a Great Commission Resurgence among us, and it is most certainly needed, preaching is going to play a key role locally and around the world.

---

43   See the excellent discussion in Kenneth Keathley, "Salvation and the Sovereignty of God: The Great Commission as the Expression of the Divine Will," in *The Mission of Today's Church*, ed. R. Stanton Norman (Nashville: B&H Academic, 2007), 179–93; and his *Salvation and Sovereignty: A Molinist Approach* (Nashville: B&H Academic, 2010), 42–62. See also David L. Allen, "The Atonement: Limited or Universal?" in *Whosoever Will: A Biblical-Theological Critique of Five-Point Calvinism*, ed. David L. Allen & Steve W. Lemke (Nashville: B&H Academic, 2010), 61–107.

The moving story of Samuel Pearce's 5 a.m. sermon to two hundred farm laborers in Guilsborough, Northhamptonshire, in May 1794, should give all of us pause to reflect on our preaching commitment and its relationship to the Great Commission. Here is the account as related by Cox in his two-volume *History of the Baptist Missionary Society.* Following the sermon, Pearce was seated at the breakfast table with a few people, including Andrew Fuller. Fuller remarked to Pearce, his dear friend, how pleased he was with the sermon. But, he went on to add that it appeared Pearce's sermon was poorly structured in that it seemed Pearce did not close when he had finished, but he appeared to begin again at the end of the sermon. Pearce responded tersely, acknowledging the accuracy of the observation but stated he had his reason. In a "jocular manner," Fuller kept urging Pearce for the reason. When he finally responded, Pearce said:

> Well, my brother, you shall have the secret, if it must be so. Just at the moment I was about to resume my seat, thinking I had finished, the door opened, and I saw a poor man enter, of the working class; and from the sweat on his brow, and the symptoms of his fatigue, I conjectured that he had walked some miles to this early service, but that he had been unable to reach the place till the close. A momentary thought glanced through my mind—here may be a man who never heard the gospel, or it may be he is one that regards it as a feast of fat things; in either case, the effort on his part demands one on mine. So with the hope of doing him good, I resolved at once to forget all else, and, in spite of criticism, and the apprehension of being thought tedious, to give him a quarter of an hour.[44]

The words of Cox following his relating this anecdote speak volumes to all of us in the SBC today.

> It cannot be supposed that such a man could be lukewarm, while others were feeling for the distant heathen, and planning a missionary enterprise. No; he was just the individual to kindle at once. His reason, his heart, his conscience, his every power and passion, became consecrated to the cause. The materials for the

---

44 F. A. Cox, *History of the Baptist Missionary Society, from 1792–1842* (London: T. Ward & Co. and G. and J. Dyer, 1842), 1:52–53.

sacred fire were all ready in his mind; it was only to apply the torch, and he blazed forth, till his zeal consumed him.[45]

May God deliver us all from our lukewarmness and may the Holy Spirit "apply the torch" and empower us to fulfill conjointly our Lord's Great Commission and Paul's admonition to "Preach the Word!" Let us join with the very heart of God and our Lord Jesus Himself, who as Paul says, *through us* pleads with all people to be saved on the basis of Christ's shed blood for *all* men:

> "Everything is from God, who reconciled us to Himself through Christ and gave us the ministry of reconciliation: That is, in Christ, God was reconciling the world to Himself, not counting their trespasses against them, and He has committed the message of reconciliation to us. Therefore, we are ambassadors for Christ, certain that God is appealing through us. We plead on Christ's behalf, 'Be reconciled to God.'" (2 Cor 5:18–20)

---

45   Ibid., 53.

THE GREAT COMMISSION AND
THE URBAN CONTEXT

Troy L. Bush

Southern Baptists are not known as urban people. In 1980 it could be said "that Southern Baptists are over-represented in non-metropolitan areas and severely under-represented in the fifty largest SMSAs."[1] In 2000, twenty years later, the situation was almost unchanged. One of every four Southern Baptist churches was located in the fifty largest metros where 58 percent of the US population (162 million) lived. Looking at the ten largest metros in 2000, Southern Baptists' presence thins even more, with only one of eight churches located there.[2]

In the last ten years I am confident the picture has improved, at least some. Through the North American Mission Board's (NAMB) Strategic Focus City efforts, Southern Baptists have started churches in twelve metros. Recently, the NAMB formed the Metropolitan Missions Team, and the International Mission Board (IMB) now provides an urban training experience for some new personnel. In 2008 The Southern Baptist Theological Seminary launched the Dehoney Center for Urban Ministry Training, which I am now privileged to direct.[3] Despite these advances, the city remains a distant universe to many Southern Baptists.

A Great Commission Resurgence must embrace the cities of the world. Southern Baptists will need to become comfortable in the city, and urban

---

1   C. Kirk Hadaway, "Learning from Urban Church Research," in *Planting and Growing Urban Churches: From Dream to Reality*, ed. Harvie M. Conn (Grand Rapids: Baker, 1997), 38. The United States Census Bureau defines a SMSA as a standard metropolitan statistical area.

2   Richie C. Stanley, *America's 50 Largest Metropolitan Areas: Population and Southern Baptist Presence, 1990–2000* (Alpharetta, GA: North American Mission Board, 2002), 5.

3   See http://urban.sbts.edu for more information about the ministry of the Dehoney Center.

missions will need to be one of our highest priorities in the US and around the world. So, let's go to the city!

OUR URBAN WORLD

In 2008 the majority of people in the world for the first time in history were living in urban areas.[4] Every day, the world's urban population increases by 193,107 people.[5] During the next four decades, modest estimates indicate the world's population will increase by 2.5 billion, reaching 9.2 billion inhabitants. During the same period, urban areas will increase in size by 3.1 billion people, a rate greater than the exploding global population.[6] In 2018 or 2019, the world's rural population will climax at 3.5 billion people and begin declining.[7] China, Indonesia, Japan, the Russian Federation, and the US have the fastest declining rural populations.[8] Our world is moving to the city.

Urban areas come in all shapes and sizes. Megacities (at least 10 million inhabitants) receive regular attention in the media, and it would seem most of the world's population lives in them. These behemoth metros usually encompass large urban areas, including adjacent cities and towns. For example, the Tokyo metro includes 87 cities and towns around it.[9] As of 2009, there are 26 urban agglomerations with at least 10 million people. Change the criteria to 1 million people or more, and the total climbs to 476 cities with as many as 200 of them in China.[10] Compare that to 1975 when 181 cities had a population of at least 1 million and there were three agglomerations having a population of 10 million or more.[11] Further, 75 percent of the world's urban population is concentrated in just 25 countries.[12]

---

4 United Nations, *World Urbanization Prospects: The 2007 Revision, Highlights* (New York: United Nations, 2008), 2 [on-line], accessed 28 July 2009; available from http://www.un.org/esa/population/publications/wup2007/2007WUP_Highlights_web.pdf; Internet.

5 UN-Habitat, *State of the World's Cities 2008/2009: Harmonious Cities* (New York: United Nations, 2008), 11.

6 United Nations, *World Urbanization*, 1.

7 Ibid., 4.

8 Ibid., 8.

9 Ibid., 11.

10 Thomas Brinkhoff, "The Principal Agglomerations of the World," City Population [on-line], accessed 28 November 2009; available from http://www.citypopulation.de; Internet.

11 United Nations, *World Urbanization*, 220.

12 Ibid., 5.

In order to understand better our urban world, I will survey three regions: Asia, Africa, and North America. Asia and Africa represent the developing world, while North America represents the developed world.

Asia

It would be hard to overstate the dramatic urban growth in the developing world. During the last two decades, the urban population increased by an average of 3 million people per week. At this rate, it would take less than three years of urban growth to populate the entire US. Asia plays a leading role in the urban expansion. In 1950 Asia was only 17 percent urbanized. In 2005 it was 40 percent urbanized and it is projected to be 54 percent urbanized in 2030, with an increase of 1.25 billion urban inhabitants in the 25 years between 2005 and 2030.[13]

Two-thirds of the 100 fastest growing cities in the world with a population of at least 1 million are located in Asia, and 33 of these are located in China. Furthermore, Asia is home to the majority of the largest cities found in the developing world. Of the 140 big (1–5 million people) and large (5–10 million people) cities to emerge in the world since 1990, 111 are located in Asia.[14]

China and India are leading the way in Asian urbanization. If we were to force China's future urban population increase through 2020 into new cities, we would need to build about 40 new Beijings or 80 new Nanjings.[15] Extraordinary growth of some cities in China, such as Chongqing, Xiamen, and Shenzhen, has exceeded 10 percent per year.[16]

Slums comprise a large urban population in Asia, with Southern Asia and Western Asia experiencing significant growth in slums during the last 15 years.[17] In the greater Mumbai metro are 6.48 million slum-dwellers, and in the Delhi metro there are 1.85 million.[18] In Bangladesh, 71 percent of the

---

13   United Nations, *World Urbanization*, 80, 81; UN-Habitat, *State of the World's Cities*, 15, 19.

14   UN-Habitat, *State of the World's Cities*, 20, 21.

15   Xuemei Bai, "The Urban Transition in China: Trends, Consequences and Policy Implications," in *The New Global Frontier: Urbanization, Poverty and Environment in the 21st Century*, ed. George Martine, Gordon McGranahan, Mark Montgomery, and Rogelio Fernández-Castila (London: Earthscan, 2008), 336. Bai cites Chinese Government projections.

16   UN-Habitat, *State of the World's Cities*, 19.

17   Ibid., 22.

18   S. Chandrasekhar and Abhiroop Mukhopadhyay, "Socioeconomic Heterogeneity in Urban India," in *The New Global Frontier*, ed. Martine et. al., 320.

urban population lives in slum housing. On the other end of the spectrum, less than 2 percent of the urban population of Thailand, Malaysia, China, Democratic People's Republic of Korea, and Singapore live in slums.[19]

Africa

Urban growth in Africa is greater than in any other region of the world. From 2000 to 2005 urban growth was 3.3 percent annually. Annual growth of at least 3 percent is expected to continue in urban areas through 2030.[20] In 1950 Africa was 15 percent urbanized. In 2005 it was 38 percent urbanized and projected to be 50 percent urbanized in 2030.[21] Though sub-Saharan Africa is the least urbanized region of the world, its urban population is already greater than that of North America.[22] Seventeen of the world's 100 fastest growing cities with a population of 1 million or more are in Africa.[23]

African populations have experienced a number of forces that contribute to urbanization, including drought, famine, ethnic conflicts, and war. For example, Khartoum, Sudan, grew from 2.3 million in 1990 to 3.9 million in 2000 as a result of conflict. Kinshasa, the capital of the Democratic Republic of the Congo, grew from 3.6 million to 5 million from 1990 to 2000. Cities in other countries, including Somalia and Liberia, have had similar experiences during periods of conflict.[24]

The HIV/AIDS epidemic has also affected urban growth patterns in Africa. Life expectancy in Southern Africa has dropped from 62 years in 1990 to 49 years in 2005. Zambia's capital, Lusaka, grew only 0.7 percent annually from 1990 to 2000, and other Zambian cities such as Luanshya, Ndola, and Mufulira have declined. HIV/AIDS is not the only factor leading to this decline, but it certainly is a leading factor. Zambia's urban populations have an HIV/AIDS rate twice that of the rural population. Cities in Tanzania and Burundi reflect similar trends.[25]

---

19   UN-Habitat, *State of the World's Cities*, 99.

20   Michael J. White, Blessing U. Mberu, and Mark A. Collinson, "African Urbanization: Recent Trends and Implications," in *The New Global Frontier*, ed. Martine et al., 302.

21   UN, *World Urbanization*, 74, 75.

22   White, Mberu, and Collinson, "African Urbanization," 301.

23   UN-Habitat, *State of the World's Cities*, 17, 18.

24   Ibid., 18.

25   Ibid.

North America

From 1990 to 2000, cities in North America grew the fastest of all cities in the developed world.[26] In 1950 North America was 64 percent urbanized. In 2005 it was 81 percent urbanized and projected to be 87 percent urbanized in 2030.[27] The rate of urbanization in the United States is identical to North America for all three periods, and Canada's rate is similar.[28]

From 2001 to 2006, Canada had the highest growth rate in population (5.4 percent) among all G8 countries. Two-thirds of this growth came from international immigration. Nearly 90 percent of the entire population growth was located in Canada's 33 census metro areas, though there are signs that immigrants are beginning to choose smaller metros.[29] According to the 2006 census, four out of every five Canadians live in an urban area. In fact, 13.9 million of 31.6 million Canadians in 2006 lived in the country's three largest metros: Montréal, Vancouver, and the Greater Golden Horseshoe (Toronto and surrounding environs).[30]

International immigrants now account for one in every five Canadians. In 2006 Asians, including the Middle East, were the largest percentage of immigrants at 58.3 percent. Immigrants from other regions of the world included Europe (16.1 percent), Central and South America and the Caribbean (10.8 percent), and Africa (10.6 percent). Nearly 70 percent of these immigrants settled in just three metros: Toronto, Montréal, and Vancouver.[31]

The US has urbanized rapidly, and the nature of that urbanization is changing. First, metropolitan areas, even regions, are taking the place of cities. Second, edge cities, urban cores in the outer rings of metropolitan areas, are exhibiting substantial growth. Third, the Sun Belt represents

---

26 UN-Habitat, *State of the World's Cities*, 14.

27 Ibid., 80, 81.

28 Ibid.

29 Statistics Canada, *Portrait of the Canadian Population in 2006, 2006 Census* (Ottawa: Minister of Industry, 2007), 22 [on-line], accessed 9 December 2009; available from http://www12.statcan .ca, p8-eng.cfm; Internet; Statistics Canada, "2006 Census: Immigration in Canada: A Portrait of the Foreign-born Population, 2006 Census: Highlights" [article on-line]; accessed 9 December 2009; available from http://www12.statcan.ca/census-recensement/2006/as-sa/97–551/index-eng .cfm; Internet.

30 Ibid., 5.

31 Statistics Canada, "Immigration in Canada: A Portrait of the Foreign-born Population, 2006 Census: Immigrants in Metropolitan Areas" [article on-line]; accessed 9 December 2009; available from http://www12.statcan.ca/census-recensement/2006/as-sa/97–557/index-eng.cfm; Internet.

a historic population shift as industrial cities of the Northeast and North-central lose their dominance to cities in the South and West from Virginia to California.[32]

The 100 largest metro areas are home to 65 percent of the US population, though they represent only about 12 percent of the US land mass. Additionally, they produce 75 percent of the US gross domestic product (GDP). Seattle and Chicago are prime examples. Seattle represents 51 percent of the population of the state of Washington and 69 percent of its GDP. Chicago represents 67 percent of the population and 78 percent of the GDP of the state of Illinois.[33]

The recession that began in the latter part of 2007 has directly affected metros throughout the US. From 1990 to 2000 several metros grew at astounding rates. The Las Vegas and Naples metros grew 83.3 percent and 65.3 percent, respectively. The largest metros in the US with 5 million inhabitants or more averaged 10.8 percent growth, with Dallas-Fort Worth having the highest rate at 29.3 percent.[34] Since 2007 the migration picture has changed, and domestic migration within the US has slowed noticeably. Metros in Florida have been among the hardest hit with stark downturns, including Orlando, Tampa St. Petersburg, and Cape Coral Fort Myers.[35]

Indications are that international migration, especially from Mexico, has slowed significantly from 2007 to 2008.[36] From 1990 to 2006, the foreign-born population in the US increased an average of one million people annually, most of them settling in urban areas. Yet even if the immigration rate stabilizes or slows, the US population will become "minority white" about 2042. The preschool population will achieve this status in 2021.[37]

---

32 J. John Palen, *The Urban World*, 8th ed. (Boulder, CO: Paradigm, 2008), 90–113.

33 Bruce Katz, "The Great Recession: What Comes Next for America" (speech given at the Urban Age Conference, Istanbul, Turkey, 27 October 2009) [on-line]; accessed 9 December 2009; available from http://www.brookings.edu/speeches/2009/1027_istanbul_katz.aspx; Internet.

34 Marc J. Perry and Paul J. Mackun, "Population Change and Distribution: Census 2000 Brief," US Census Bureau (April 2001) [on-line]; accessed 9 December 2009; available from http://www.census.gov/prod/2001pubs/c2kbr01–2.pdf; Internet.

35 William H. Frey, "The Great American Migration Slowdown: Regional and Metropolitan Dimensions," The Brookings Institute (December 2009), 10, 14 [on-line]; accessed 9 December 2009; available from http://www.brookings.edu/~/media/Files/rc/reports/2009/1209_migration_frey/1209_migration_frey.pdf; Internet.

36 Ibid., 14.

37 William H. Frey, Alan Berube, Audrey Singer, and Jill H. Wilson, *Getting Current: Recent Demographic Trends in Metropolitan America* (Washington, DC: The Brookings Institute, 2009), 6

Two trends stand out. First, the Southeast has become the fastest-growing destination for immigrants in the last part of this decade. Cities such as Raleigh, Nashville, Atlanta, and Orlando saw strong increases in immigrant populations. Other locations with noteworthy increases were Knoxville and Little Rock. Second, immigrant populations in small metros of fewer than 500,000 inhabitants had the highest rate of growth (124 percent) from 1990 to 2007. During the same period, the immigrant population in larger cities grew 60 percent.[38]

Our world is urbanizing at warp speed, and global migration is a leading characteristic. Increase in passion, resources, and effort for urban missions is insufficient. We need to listen with fresh ears to what God says about the city and what He says about living in them and doing missions and ministry in them.

BIBLICAL INTERSECTIONS

Cities are frequently located at significant intersections that define a city's growth and serve as a life source for the flow of products, people, and power. Similarly, urban missions and ministry must be developed upon intersections of biblical teaching. Different teachings from the Word of God overlap and give us a comprehensive understanding of God's will. From the center of this intersection, we gain a full view of His vision and plan for cities and disciples of Jesus who live and work in them. Each text is necessary; neglect one, and we weaken our understanding of God's will. We become unbalanced, and our missional efforts miss His plan for the city.

While we cannot address every text that relates to cities, we will consider three significant teachings of Jesus, and at their intersection begin to develop an urban vision with which to engage cities with the gospel. The Great Commission (Matt 28:18–20), the Lord's Prayer (Matt 22:37–40), and the Great Commandment (Matt 6:9–13) speak powerfully to urban missions and ministry.

[on-line]; accessed 9 December 2009; available from http://www.brookings.edu/~/media/Files/rc/reports/2009/03_metro_demographic_trends/03_metro_demographic_trends.pdf; Internet.

38 Ibid., 10.

The Great Commission

Jesus never started an evangelism program, yet His disciple-making results were extraordinary. Fortunately, He did more than give a few clues as to how we can effectively evangelize our cities. Matthew 28:18–20 has become a primary text for the church's call to evangelism and missions: "Then Jesus came near and said to them, 'All authority has been given to me in heaven and on earth. Go, therefore, and make disciples of all nations, baptizing them in the name of the Father and of the Son and of the Holy Spirit, teaching them to observe everything I have commanded you. And remember, I am with you always, to the end of the age.'" Therefore, it is imperative we take a careful look at what Jesus commissions His church to do.

The epicenter of the Great Commission, and urban missions for that matter, is the command to make disciples of all nations. In fact, it is the primary command in all the phrases that make up the Great Commission. Going, baptizing, and teaching, while vital, are secondary to the command to make disciples. A Great Commission Resurgence in the world's cities will require more going, more giving, and more praying, but to what end should we increase our efforts? Jesus defines the Great Commission in quality (make disciples) and scope (of all nations).

Today, a primary reason we need a Great Commission Resurgence in which churches become more missional is that we have drifted away from the mission. We continue to preach and teach about the Great Commission, while using our resources primarily to increase our church attendance and maintain our level of comfort.

A missional drift has been felt even in our cities. Homelessness, violence, poverty, addictions, hunger, unemployment, and an innumerable list of needs face the city church. Driven by compassion and mercy to meet these needs, the church finds it easy to drift away from its *primary* mission. Job training, after-school ministries for at-risk children, and AIDS testing are noble ministries that can become the functional mission of the urban church—at the expense of the Great Commission. Roger Greenway reminds us of the centrality of making disciples as it relates to holistic ministry when he says,

> But at the same time the holistic perspective on urban mission recognizes that nothing is more crucial for social change in the city than the conversion of persons, families, and groups to

evangelical Christianity. There is both theological and empirical evidence to substantiate this position.[39]

What is a disciple? When we realign our ministries to be more missional, we must not become satisfied with increased missional activity. Jesus gives simple instructions that are sufficient to impact the entire world and the most complex cities: make disciples of all nations. These instructions also serve as our goal. Certainly, we should increase our going, our serving, our teaching, and all manner of means to make disciples. Nonetheless, these activities are not the aim, just as adding a few more people to our churches will fail to complete the Great Commission.

For now, avoid thinking in terms of a church member. Instead, think about one of the prominent themes of the Gospel of Matthew: being a *disciple* of Jesus. The first of five discourses in the Gospel is Jesus' teaching that we call the Sermon on the Mount (Matt 5–7). Both its content and location are important because in it Jesus teaches who disciples are and how they are to live. From this sermon, we trace to the very end of the Gospel Jesus' instructions and model for making disciples that live their lives according to His teaching. The Gospel concludes by coming full circle with a commission for the disciples Jesus made to do what He had done with them—make disciples that multiply and live according to His teachings.

Thus, New Testament scholar D. A. Carson plainly describes disciples as "those who hear, understand, and obey Jesus' teaching."[40] Disciples are ordinary Christians living continually in relationship with Jesus, seeking to imitate and obey Him in every area of life. Making this kind of disciple must be a goal of a Great Commission Resurgence.

How do we make disciples? Our Great Commission problem goes beyond the need for increased mobilization and financial resources. Increasing the number of church members (attendance) has often been the aim of our efforts without consciousness that a gulf too frequently exists between the life of a disciple and that of a church member. The fact is, there should be no difference in the life of a disciple of Jesus and that of a church member.

---

39   Roger S. Greenway, "The Urban-Mission Movement in the New Testament" in *Cities: Missions' New Frontier*, ed. Roger S. Greenway and Timothy M. Monsma, 2nd ed. (Grand Rapids: Baker, 2000), 43.

40   D. A. Carson, *Matthew*, in vol. 8 of *The Expositor's Bible Commentary*, ed. Frank E. Gaebelein (Grand Rapids: Zondervan, 1984), 596.

Our evangelism and discipleship methods have played a leading role in making church members who do not always look much like disciples of Jesus. Bill Hybels laments this situation when he comments on the study of his own church, Willow Creek, and several other churches that revealed a gap between the life styles of the church members and that of fully devoted followers of Christ: "When I first heard these results, the pain of knowing was almost unbearable. Upon reflection, I realized that the pain of not knowing could be catastrophic."[41]

We need to return to the simple teachings of Jesus about the Great Commission. Our cities do not need evangelism efforts that result in people who claim to be Christians and passively attend church, while living, thinking, and talking like the world. In *Breaking the Missional Code*, Ed Stetzer and David Putman conclude that our evangelistic methods need to change. Again, for a Great Commission Resurgence in our cities, that change must be a deliberate effort to make multiplying disciples of Jesus Christ. Stetzer and Putman say it this way: "Those who break the [missional] code are committed to making and multiplying disciples. Many pastors have learned the hard way that you can attract a crowd and still not have a church. You can build a church and not make disciples."[42] We must get this one right in our cities.

What characterizes urban disciple making according to Jesus is ordinary Christians who intentionally imitate Him in the city. Paul was an urban missionary who modeled his disciple making after Jesus. He describes this process with these few words, "Be imitators of me, as I am of Christ" (1 Cor 11:1). We have depended on programs, classes, events, and Bible study curriculum to make disciples. Jesus' approach was to proclaim broadly the good news, invest His life in His disciples, saturate them with the Word of God, expect them to obey it, keep them connected with Himself and each other, and send them out among nondisciples to make new disciples. How can we improve on what He did?

I have been involved in church-starting ministries for nearly twenty years, so it might seem odd that I have not discussed church starting in the context of the Great Commission. The reason is that we need to let the Great Commission speak to us. We need to hear again clearly the

---

41   Greg L. Hawkins and Cally Parkinson, *Reveal: Where Are You?* (Barrington, IL: Willow Creek Resources, 2007), Foreword.

42   Ed Stetzer and David Putman, *Breaking the Missional Code: Your Church Can Become a Missionary in Your Community* (Nashville: B&H, 2006), 75, 104.

commission to make disciples of Jesus. Too often our energy and focus have been on congregating people and enlarging these congregations with diminished attention on making disciples of all nations. If we will focus on making disciples that imitate Jesus and obey His teachings, the congregating results will be healthier and will multiply more rapidly. Yes, we need to start churches, but we need to do so by making vibrant, devoted disciples of Jesus Christ.

The Lord's Prayer

The second teaching in our intersection comes from Jesus' sermon we call the Sermon on the Mount (Matt 5–7). He had been preaching and teaching the good news of the kingdom and healing the sick in the region of Galilee. This region had upwards of three million inhabitants living in 204 cities and villages.[43] Large crowds from Galilee, the Decapolis, Jerusalem, Judea, and from beyond the Jordon were following Him. He preached and taught as well as healed many who suffered from disease, illness, demon possession, and seizures (likely describing some mental illnesses as well). In addition to the message He proclaimed, His ministry of miracles gave evidence that the kingdom had arrived, though not fully. His ministry was in proximity to the urban milieu of the day. Most of His audience would have heard and seen Him with urban ears and eyes.

Historian Rodney Stark describes these cities well: "Greco-Roman cities were small, extremely crowded, filthy beyond imagination, disorderly, filled with strangers, and afflicted with frequent catastrophes—fires, plagues, conquests, and earthquakes."[44] Water was limited, and public baths were not available for the general public. Sanitation was minimal. Stench and incense were inescapable. Open ditches in the streets served the sewage needs of most urbanites. Insects abounded.

People lived in cramped quarters. More people per acre lived in Antioch than currently live in Calcutta. Nearly everyone lived with the effects of parasites, disease, and illness. Mortality rates were so high that only the steady stream of migrants kept cities from declining in size. This urban migration brought a wide range of ethnic groups to the city where most

---

43   Carson, *Matthew*, 121

44   Rodney Stark, *Cities of God: The Real Story of How Christianity Became an Urban Movement and Conquered Rome* (New York: HarperOne, 2006), 26.

lived in ethnic enclaves. Religious pluralism abounded. Crime, especially at night, was a dark force coursing through the streets. Fires, political conquests, and natural disasters further defined urban life. Living in the city was difficult.[45]

City life is in Jesus' view when He teaches His disciples on the mount, instructing them about how to live each day. Part of this instruction focuses on the prayer commonly called the Lord's Prayer (Matt 6:9–13). It serves as a model and teaches us the perspective we should have when we pray. It helps us align our prayers with biblical truths. Urbanites of Jesus' day would have heard this prayer in very practical terms as it addresses issues they faced daily. Here, we will look at just two of the urban applications.

"Our Father." First century urbanites worshiped hundreds, even thousands, of gods. These were not personal, intimate gods. The beginning words of this prayer, "Our Father," required a reorientation for people living in the press of cities whose inhabitants exalted thousands of capricious, impersonal gods. To pray to one God, the Creator of the universe and the Savior of their souls, with such intimate words gave city dwellers dignity and reminded them they were part of a family. This teaching on prayer reveals they were more than a mass of people; each had a personal, exclusive relationship with the Father.

"Our Father" unleashes a revolution in the kingdom against class and ethnic distinction. The poor and wealthy have the same Father. The slave and the master are siblings. All members of the family are privileged. The redeemed prostitute and the liberated Pharisee have equal moral status. While life in the city is defined by social status, power, and possessions, life in the kingdom is defined by a relationship with the Father. One's status in the city, high or low, is of no importance in the kingdom. In Christ all disciples have a common heritage that supersedes DNA, skin color, culture, language, accent, tribe, and nationality. We are one family in Christ.

The kingdom present and future. Jesus teaches His disciples to pray: "Your kingdom come, Your will be done, on earth as it is in heaven" (Matt 6:10). We need to linger over this phrase and drink in the richness of urban application. This part of the prayer seems simple enough, but what does it mean for the city? The answer to that question provides an essential element of our biblical intersection.

The kingdom is God's kingly reign over all of the earth, over all the peoples, and over all the cities. When Jesus declares we must repent because

---

45   Ibid., 26–32.

the kingdom of God is at hand, He is saying we must submit to God's authority. We must yield and enter His kingdom. The latter part of Matthew 6:10 confirms it: "Your will be done, on earth as it is in heaven." Jesus instructs His disciples to pray there would be complete submission and obedience to the Father's will on earth as it is in heaven. George Ladd explains, "This prayer is a petition for God to reign, to manifest His kingly sovereignty and power, to put to flight every enemy of righteousness and of His divine rule, that God alone may be King over all the world."[46]

The kingdom is both present and future.[47] The Scriptures speak of the kingdom being present with the coming of Christ and His resurrection. Paul teaches in 1 Corinthians 15:20–28 that there are three temporal events that are part of Christ's establishing the kingdom: the resurrection of Christ at the end of His earthly ministry; the resurrection when Christ returns at His *parousia*; and the time when Christ abolishes all His enemies and gives the kingdom to the Father. The writer of Hebrews declares in Hebrews 9:26 that the cross is a marker in world history and indicates a new era has dawned.[48] In the letter to the disciples in Colossae, the apostle Paul tells the disciples they have already entered the kingdom when he writes, "He has rescued us from the domain of darkness and transferred us into the kingdom of the Son He loves, in whom we have redemption, the forgiveness of sins" (Col 1:13–14).

Urban disciples should pray for the kingdom to come and for God's will to be done in every domain of their cities and among every people group. They should display the kingdom by living according to kingdom ethics (e.g., Matt 5–7) as members of their families and tribes and as citizens of their cities and nations. Creating heaven on earth is, though, far from what this text teaches, except as the disciples reflect kingdom values in the way they live and in their roles in society. The mission of the church is not to

---

46 George Eldon Ladd, *The Gospel of the Kingdom: Practical Expositions on the Kingdom of God* (Grand Rapids: Eerdmans, 1959), 21.

47 "Kingdom of God" and "kingdom of heaven" are interchangeable, and Matthew uses both without distinction (Matt 19:23, 24). Kingdom of God, kingdom of heaven, salvation, eternal life, salvation, the age to come, and the end are related and all speak to the fulfillment of God's redemptive plan. See, Ladd, *Gospel of the Kingdom*, 32, 33. The expression "this age" refers to the present period when Satan has dominion and sin and unrighteousness are prevalent (Matt 12:32, 13:39, 40, 49; 2 Cor 4:4; Gal 1:4; Eph 1:21, 2:1–2; Titus 2:12).

48 Other texts teach that disciples of Jesus no longer live under the dominion of this age (Matt 12:28; Luke 10:9,17; John 8:12, 12:46; Acts 26:18; Rom 6:14, 8:4–17, 12:2, 14:17; Gal 4:8, 24; Eph 5:8; 1 Thess 5:4, 5; 1 Pet 2:9; 1 John 1:5, 6, 2:8–11).

transform the city. Yet, as the power of the gospel transforms disciples, they actively display and exert kingdom values in their cities and beyond. David Hesselgrave explains this perspective:

> Though God is always building his kingdom, he is in this age building his church as an expression of that kingdom. Nowhere in Scripture are we specifically called upon to obey "kingdom mission" in the way we are called upon to obey the Great Commission. "Kingdom mission" was and remains uniquely the mission of Christ, though we are to witness to it in very practical ways. "Great Commission mission" is uniquely ours and requires us to make disciples by preaching, baptizing, and teaching the people of the earth. Christ will *bring* his kingdom and so he teaches believers to pray that God's kingdom will come *on earth as it is now in heaven*. Christ is *building* his church so he commands believers to witness and work for its completion, now and in this age. God's kingdom will come because his "is the kingdom of power and the glory forever" (Matthew 6:13). His church will be built because God will be glorified "in the church and in Christ Jesus throughout all generations, forever and ever" (Eph. 3:21).[49]

The Great Commandment

The third teaching that makes up our biblical intersection is the Great Commandment. It is only possible to make disciples that obey all that Jesus commanded if we fully embrace the Great Commandment. We will focus on the Lukan account found in Luke 10:25–37, where an expert in the law poses a question to Jesus about eternal life: "Teacher, what shall I do to inherit eternal life?" (Luke 10:25). This question begins a discussion with Jesus that provides profound insight for life and ministry in cities.

First, eternal life, that is entrance into the kingdom, centers on our relationship to God. Jesus confirms here that the means of salvation in the Old Testament and the New Testament are identical. He asks the lawyer to answer his own question according the Scriptures, and the lawyer quotes two Old Testament texts (Deut 6:5; Lev 19:18). The first part of

---

49   David J. Hesselgrave, *Paradigms in Conflict: 10 Key Questions in Christian Missions Today* (Grand Rapids: Kregel, 2005), 347, 348, emphasis original.

the answer, "You shall love the Lord your God with all your heart and with all your soul and with all your strength and with all your mind" (Luke 10:27a; Deut 6:5), is the most fundamental element of what it means to be a disciple of Jesus. Our love for God should be all-consuming. This expert in religious law would have known much about God, but Jesus leads him to see that knowledge of God and religious devotion are insufficient. God expects intimate, passionate love that saturates the emotions, consciousness, motivation, and intelligence.[50]

Second, Jesus reveals that love for God is inseparably linked to a horizontal response of loving "your neighbor as yourself" (Luke 10:27b and Lev 19:18). The lawyer would have understood this command to mean loving another Jew. Out of this cultural context, he halfheartedly asks Jesus to tell him who his neighbor is, and he could have hardly expected Jesus' response. The Good Samaritan parable is more than a teaching on doing an act of kindness. The parable of the Good Samaritan and the Great Commandment form one unified teaching.[51] Through them, Jesus describes in graphic detail what it means to be His disciple and how He expects us to live, even in cities with many hurting people all around us.

Notice how Jesus describes the man who was robbed: "A man was going down from Jerusalem to Jericho, and he fell among robbers, who stripped him and beat him and departed, leaving him half dead" (Luke 10:30). Jesus does not reveal the man's ethnicity, social status, or religious affiliation. They do not matter.

The contrast between the Samaritan and the two Jewish characters, the priest and the Levite, was a sour illustration for the lawyer. Jews despised Samaritans, and Jesus made the Samaritan the "hero" of the story. Jesus says the Samaritan is the one who had compassion for his neighbor, and who is living like one who will receive eternal life in the kingdom.

In the end, Jesus asks the lawyer, "Which of these three do you think proved to be a neighbor to the man who fell among the robbers?" (Luke 10:36). The subtle shift in the question is hugely important for urban life. Jesus teaches that being the right kind of neighbor is the focus of the second part of the Great Commandment. He pokes the self-righteous heart of this expert in the law by telling him he should be neighborly like the Samaritan. Defining your neighbor has no place or value in the kingdom.

---

50   Robert H. Stein, *Luke*, New American Commentary 24 (Nashville: Broadman, 1992), 316.
51   Ibid.

We easily miss the sharpness of this teaching if we rip the parable from its context. The message is greater than simply teaching us to do good toward a neighbor in need. Acts of kindness and service fulfill the Great Commandment when they extend from and display an intense love of God. The commands to love God and love our neighbors are inseparably joined, but they are not equal. The first is just that, the first.

Out of this love relationship with God flows a generous, Christ-like love of any and every neighbor, especially those in need. The Samaritan personally involved himself in the injured man's life. Without rubber gloves, he cleaned and bandaged his wounds. He placed him on his animal and went to an inn where he spent the night with the man, continuing to care for him. Before leaving, he told the innkeeper he would return and pay any remaining expenses. With each additional detail Jesus drew a stark contrast between the religious travelers that passed by and the generous love the Samaritan showed his neighbor.

We herald Baptist missionary William Carey as the father of modern missions, yet we fail to emphasize adequately he was an urban missionary, spending much of his ministry in cities like Calcutta, Mudnabatty, Kidderpore, and Serampore. He fearlessly and plainly proclaimed the gospel. He also loved his neighbor. He opposed slavery, *ghat* murders (the practice of leaving aged and ill people on the banks of the Ganges River to die), infanticide, abortion, and the *sati* (the Hindu practice of a widow sacrificing herself on her deceased husband's funeral pyre). He boycotted West Indian sugar produced by slaves and rescued people from the banks of the Ganges. He pleaded with widows and crowds at funeral pyres to preserve life and dignity. He called upon the government to intervene and prevent inhumane practices, resulting in government policy changes that restricted infanticide and banned the *sati*.[52]

Right priorities are essential in urban ministry. Neighbors in need are countless. Sometimes loving our neighbor requires our involvement to the level that we seek change in cultural practices and governmental policies. Always, though, we must preach the gospel. Carey's social reform efforts serve as a good model for urban ministry today. Timothy George notes, "Carey never permitted his involvement in movements for social reform to substitute for, or take precedence over, the clear proclamation of

---

52 Timothy George, *Faithful Witness: The Life and Mission of William Carey* (Birmingham, AL: New Hope, 1991), 149–52.

salvation through faith in Jesus Christ alone."[53] This clarity guided Carey throughout his fruitful, urban ministry.

We cannot leave this teaching without looking at the implications for time and possessions. In *The Mission and Expansion of Christianity in the First Three Centuries*, Adolf Harnack's detailed investigation of the early church reveals ten areas where disciples gave their time and possessions to love their neighbors:

1. Alms in general, and their connection with the cultus [i.e., the Christian religion] and officials of the church.
2. The support of teachers and officials.
3. The support of widows and orphans.
4. The support of the sick, the infirm, and the disabled.
5. The care of prisoners and people languishing in the mines.
6. The care of poor people needing burial, and of the dead in general.
7. The care of slaves.
8. The care of those visited by great calamities.
9. The churches furnishing work, and insisting upon work.
10. The care of brethren on a journey (hospitality), and of churches in poverty or any peril.[54]

This list reflects both corporate and individual acts of service, sacrifice, and love. So remarkable was this way of living that Roman Emperor Julian complained in 362 in a letter to the high priest of Galatia that the pagans needed to match the virtue of Christians. By this request, Julian attempted to launch an effort that would minimize the growth and influence of the Christian movement. In a letter to another priest, he noted that the "Galileans" supported not only their own poor, but also the poor who were not Christians.[55] Julian's complaints are especially important to us, as early Christianity was an urban movement. Cities throughout the empire felt the impact of Jesus' disciples.

---

53   Ibid., 152.

54   Adolf Von Harnack, *The Mission and Expansion of Christianity in the First Three Centuries*, 2nd rev. ed., trans. and ed. James Moffatt (New York: G. P. Putnam's Sons, 1908), 1:153.

55   Rodney Stark, *The Rise of Christianity: How the Obscure, Marginal Jesus Movement Became the Dominant Religious Force in the Western World in a Few Centuries* (New York: HarperOne, 1997), 83, 84. See Harnack's various quotes of Julian, especially where Julian attributes the growth of Christianity to its adherents' philanthropy toward strangers and their burying the dead: Harnack, *Mission and Expansion*, 162, 165.

Jesus' teaching on the Great Commandment and the parable of the Good Samaritan create a new culture in which the use and value of time and possessions change. The parable shows us that we must hold them more loosely than our self-indulging culture teaches us. We must live constantly in the perspective that God will bring us into the lives of hurting people where He desires that we act neighborly to them. Being neighborly will be messy and inconvenient. It will be intimate as God desires that we love our neighbors rather than in most cases passing them off to a church committee or Christian organization. Being neighborly will require a level of generosity, especially toward non-Christians, that we seldom see in our churches today. Being neighborly is the life of a disciple.

From the center of this intersection, these three teachings give us vision and perspective sufficient to engage any city in the world. They form an intersection of urban theology, urban life, urban ministry, and urban missions. To complete the foundation of our intersection, though, we need to look further at one part of the Great Commission. Jesus' command to make disciples of "all nations" has considerable bearing on the priority given to reaching cities and the way we seek to fulfill the Great Commission.

PANTA TA ETHNĒ AND THE CITY

Why should cities be a Great Commission priority? Many answers are possible. Certainly, the enormous numbers of people should draw our attention. The apostle Paul's strategy was to go to the major urban centers of his day. He was an urban missionary and Acts contains the history of early urban missions. Cites are the centers of culture, commerce, communication, construction, and people. It is possible to touch and be touched by more types of people and elements of society in the city than in villages and rural territories.[56]

---

56 Many cities today are global cities, influencing other cities and the people living in them. The 2008 Global Cities Index looks at 60 cities and ranks their global influence according to various categories. Saskia Sassen notes that 19,000 foreign firms are operating in Turkey, and more than half of them are located in Istanbul, one of the 60 cities with significant global influence. Saskia Sassen, "Global Flows of Urban Change" (speech given at the Urban Age Conference, Istanbul, Turkey, 27 October 2009) [on-line], accessed 10 December 2009; available from http://www.urban-age.net/conferences/istanbul/media/materials/presentations/05_SASSEN.pdf; Internet.

In recent years, a *people-group* approach has superseded almost all other priorities in missions.[57] The concept of unreached people groups burst onto the missiological stage in 1974 with Ralph Winter's disturbing address at the Lausanne Congress on World Evangelization about "people blindness." Since that time, missions according to people groups has become a global norm. This approach has also given an answer to the question, "Why should cities be a Great Commission priority?"

People-group thinking has become so widespread it is common to hear pastors talk about UPGs (unreached people groups) and UUPGs (unengaged, unreached people groups) as easily as they talk about how many people attended their services the previous week. Missions leaders encourage churches to adopt a people group. Web sites such as www.joshuaproject .net and www.peoplegroups.org (maintained by the IMB and NAMB) make available to anyone with Internet access the latest information on people groups including their status of evangelization. It might seem that our understanding of people groups is settled and sufficient. Reality, however, is not so clear, especially in cities.

Panta ta Ethnē *and the Bible*

People-group thinking comes from Matthew 28:19a, "Go therefore and make disciples of all nations." Today, it is commonly known that the phrase "all nations" is the translation of *panta ta ethnē*. John Piper has helped us with an extensive study of Old and New Testament texts that speak of nations, ethnicity, language, tribes, and clans. He concludes that "one would have to go against the flow of the evidence to interpret the phrase *panta ta ethnē* as 'all Gentile individuals' (or 'all countries'). Rather, the focus of the command is the discipling of all the people groups of the world."[58]

---

57 A *people group* is defined as "a significantly large grouping of individuals who perceive themselves to have a common affinity for one another because of their shared language, religion, ethnicity, residence, occupation, class or caste, situation, etc., or combination of these." For evangelistic purposes, it is "the largest group within which the gospel can spread as a church planting movement without encountering barriers of understanding or acceptance." An unreached people group is "a people group within which there is no indigenous community of believing Christians able to evangelize this people group." See Ralph Winter and Bruce Koch, "Finishing the Task: The Unreached Peoples Challenge," *International Journal of Frontier Missions* 16, no. 2 (1999): 69.

58 John Piper, *Let the Nations Be Glad: The Supremacy of God in Missions*, 2nd ed. (Grand Rapids: Baker, 2003), 186–87. See Piper's detailed comments in Chapter 5, "The Supremacy of God among 'All the Nations.'"

Other texts also speak to this matter. Revelation 5:9–10 reveals worshipers from every tribe (*phulē*), tongue (*glōssa*), people (*laos*), and nation (*ethnos*) will praise God. With these words we must include the promise in Genesis 12:3 that God would bless all the families or clans (*mishpehōt*) through Abraham.

Panta ta ethnē in Matthew 28:19 can certainly apply to "the largest group within which the gospel can spread as a church planting movement without encountering barriers of understanding or acceptance." It must also apply to a group as small as a clan.[59] While much emphasis is given to *ta ethnē*, we should remember the importance of *panta*. The Great Commission calls us to make disciples of the wide array of human groupings, including every clan, tribe, people, nation, and language.[60]

Urbanizing Panta ta Ethnē

People-group strategies have been driving many missions organizations for the last three decades. Terms and phrases such as "countdown," "final frontier," "finishing the task," and "closure" reflect the urgency and passion that have come to be part of the people-group approach. It is regrettable that for most of the last 35 years, cities have played a lesser role in the strategies to reach unreached people groups. "I'm distressed," says Harvie Conn, "that so little attention goes to the cities and the urban character of so many peoples. Tribal, animistic groupings get a lot more attention."[61] Others have detected this anti-urban bias. Wilbert Shenk, agreeing with Conn, states even more pointedly, "By making people groups the strategic key it seems to me to seriously distort the actual situation. This approach biases our thinking and action toward rural, primal peoples, whereas the dominant phenomenon of this generation is

---

59 Ibid., 191.

60 David J. Hesselgrave, "Measured by the Master's Piece, How Well Are We Doing?" *International Journal o f Frontier Missions* 13, no. 2 (1996): 72.

61 James W. Reapsome, "Definitions and Identities: Samples from the Ongoing Discussion," in *Reaching the Unreached: The Old-New Challenge,* ed. Harvie M. Conn (Phillipsburg, NJ: Presbyterian & Reformed, 1984), 72. Reapsome reported in this chapter his findings from a survey of prominent missions leaders. See also Frank M. Severn, "Some Thoughts on the Meaning of 'All Nations,'" *Evangelical Missions Quarterly* 33, no. 4 (1997): 415.

urbanization worldwide. While not all of the major language-ethnic groups are urbanized, urbanization has touched nearly all of them."[62]

The people groups of the world, however, have a pro-urban bias. Migration has filled cities with individuals from nearly every people group. In 2000, Shanghai, a city of 16.4 million residents, had 5.5 million migrants as part of its population. Sixty percent of the explosive growth in Dhaka, Bangladesh, is from migration.[63] From 1961 to 2001, the number of Indian-born migrants in the United Kingdom increased from 166,000 to 470,000.[64] From 1960 to 2005 the number of international migrants in Asia doubled from 28 million to 56 million.[65] Residents of Los Angeles speak 232 different languages. An ethnographer working with NAMB in New York City has identified 500 people groups. Houston has upwards of 362 people groups using 220 languages. From 1990 to 2004 the number of foreign-born residents in Louisville, Kentucky, increased 388 percent.[66] One area of Louisville is home to foreign-born residents from more than 60 countries.

The connection between immigrants and their people or place of origin is well documented.[67] To say that by reaching one person in the city it is possible to reach an entire village or tribe thousands of miles away is more than missionary fantasy. In Africa it is quite common for migrants living in a city to return to their home village more than once a year. Some 5.8 million Bangladeshis work abroad. Most of them work in cities in the Middle East and the US and send 70 percent of their income home. After a few years of service, most of them return home. In China the economic slowdown is resulting in a number of factories reducing their labor force. Migrants

---

62   Reapsome, "Definitions and Identities," 69.

63   UN-Habitat, *State of the World's Cities* (New York: United Nations, 2008), 24.

64   Daniel Naujoks, "Emigration, Immigration, and Diaspora Relations in India" (Washington, DC: Migration Policy Institute, October 2009) [on-line]; accessed October 15, 2009; available from http://www.migrationinformation.org/Profiles/display.cfm?id=745; Internet.

65   United Nations Economic and Social Commission for Asia and the Pacific, *Key Trends and Challenges on International Migration and Development in Asia and the Pacific* (United Nations Expert Group Meeting on Intl. Migration and Development in Asia and the Pacific, Bangkok, Thailand, 20–21 September, 2008) [on-line]; accessed 1 December 2009; available from http://www.un.org/esa/population/meetings/EGM_Ittmig_Asia/BGpaper_ESCAP.pdf; Internet.

66   Randy Capps et al., *A Profile of the Foreign-Born in the Louisville Metropolitan Area* (Washington, DC: The Urban Institute), 6 [on-line]; accessed 16 November 2009; available from http://www.urban.org/411391_Foreign-Born_Louisville.pdf; Internet.

67   Peggy Levitt, *Transnational Migrants: When "Home" Means More Than One Country* (Washington, DC: Migration Policy Institute, October 2004) [on-line]; accessed 15 October 2009; available from http://www.migrationinformation.org/display.cfm?ID=261; Internet.

working in urban factories are returning home to their villages, and in some cases they are returning as devoted followers of Jesus Christ.[68]

When migrants live in ethnic enclaves, a classic people-group approach is effective. In this case, the waffle illustration applies well. The idea is that each cavity of the waffle represents a different people group. If the gospel is syrup (just for the sake of this illustration), we need to pour it intentionally into each cavity. The challenge with people groups and cities is that ethno-linguistic groups can be more like an omelet than a waffle. Issues such as first, second, and third generation migrants redefine classic ethno-linguistic perspectives. Orville Boyd Jenkins, whose definition of people groups appears on the IMB's Web site, states, "This process of detribalization involves what is called secularization, both religious and ethnic. . . . New ethnic groups are developing constantly—the cities are a major cooking pot for new ethnicity."[69] The point is not to abandon a people-group approach. The challenge is to discover how people relate to one another, and cities increase the diversity and complexity of relationships exponentially as compared to homogeneous people groups.

Recently, I communicated with a missionary working in an Asian city who has given much thought to the application of people groups in an urban context. His comments on ethno-linguistic peoples groups in the city are insightful:

> While I understand and support focus on ethnicity to finish the task, I think when considering the urban challenge it is much more important to see the pockets of lostness in the cities. People are much more isolated and disconnected from their natural support lines and while more open to hearing are in many cases harder to engage. Time is much more demanding in the city, and those who work to reach urban dwellers have to be available when they are available, even into early morning. Many of the strong national believers come from more rural contexts, and they face

---

68 Manohar Sharma and Hassan Zaman, *Who Migrates Overseas and Is It Worth Their While? An Assessment of Household Survey Data from Bangladesh* (Washington, DC: World Bank, August 2009), 2 [on-line]; accessed 12 December 2009; available from http://www-wds.worldbank.org/WPS5018.pdf; Internet; Harley C. Schreck, "African Urban People Groups," *Urban Mission* 4 (1987): 47.

69 Orville Boyd Jenkins, "Ethnicity in the Cities" [on-line]; accessed 31 October 2009; available from http://orvillejenkins.com/ethnicity/cities.html; Internet. It is common for second-generation migrants to detribalize even further than their parents. Their children, the third generation, frequently retribalize, along the lines of their grandparents.

similar challenges of crossing culture to reach those in the city. In some ways, segmenting according to socio-economic strata is a more efficient way to segment and develop strategy. [70]

The same is true for people groups in North American cities. Chris Clayman, a missionary working in New York City, recently wrote me his thoughts on this matter when responding to a question about the number of people groups in New York. You will see they complement the comments of the missionary quoted above:

> This is a complicated question [the number of groups in NYC]. Number of people groups represented in NYC based on ethnolinguistic definitions in their home countries? Thousands and thousands, but sometimes there might just be a small amount of people representing a certain people group, so they reshape their ethnic identity to identify with a majority group. Migration reshapes people group boundaries. Even in their home countries this takes place with urbanization, and many immigrants to NYC came from urban areas that are not considered "their ethnic homeland." So, we have many immigrants here that have been through, or are going through, two or more urban filtering processes in regards to their ethnic identity. Many of these start having a much broader sense of their people group identity as a result.[71]

Can "urban" be a people group? Jenkins thinks it can, explaining, "Urban relational groups exhibit complex, but identifiable patterns common to human identity. This allows, or even requires, a concept of 'people group' in which 'urban' is a primary characteristic of some people."[72] Cities do not negate a people group approach. In fact, when we let the Scriptures define what a people group is, we see that urban areas should be among our highest missional priorities. People groups from around the world, even from some of the remotest regions of the world, are present in cities.

Furthermore, some people groups, including those forming daily, are found only in cities. Unprecedented growth, the presence of unreached people groups from around world, and the formation of new people

70 E-mail message to author, 23 November 2009. Author's name withheld for security purposes.
71 Chris Clayman, e-mail message to author, 23 November 2009.
72 Jenkins, "Ethnicity in the Cities."

groups validate the priority of urban missions. The apostle Paul was an urban missionary who understood clearly the mission to make disciples of all peoples. His example indicates the role cities should play in fulfilling the Great Commission. Paul's understanding of the Great Commission led him to the cities and the gospel spread to the ends of the earth.

CONCLUSION

The staggering numbers of people moving to and being born in cities is like a human tsunami. Its force will not be stopped, and it will change entire nations. For a denomination known for its rural heritage, the task will be formidable, but the future is bright. In addition to the disciples who were born in the city, some of us are becoming first-generation urban migrants, and we love our new home. Pray that many more join us. Also, pray that God would call out from the millions living in cities a tsunami of multiplying disciples.

We Need a Global Resurgence of the Great Commission in Cities

Imagine what might be possible if we selected 200 of the most missionally strategic urban areas of the world and established a global urban missions unit to coordinate a network(s) of disciple-making and church-starting partners who would engage them. We could select these cities according to three criteria: their global influence, the size and number of unreached people groups,[73] and the ratio of Christians to the total population.

Recognizing that cities are connected to one another and to the hinterlands surrounding them, it would be important that Southern Baptist stakeholders such as the IMB, the NAMB, state conventions, seminaries, universities, associations, and churches collaborate as needed regardless of whether a given city is located in the US or in South America. Likewise, it would be beneficial to collaborate with other missions organizations that share our values, vision, and goals.

---

73 As of November 2009, the IMB had identified 924 urban people segments located in 700+ cities. Of the UN's 50 largest cities, 39 cities are represented in the IMB's database. This work reflects significant improvement in the effort to understand and engage cities. It also demonstrates that much work remains to be done. Scott Peterson, email message to author, 25 November 2009.

We Must Do the Work of Making Disciples of All Peoples in the City

The "what" of urban missions and ministry is remarkably simple. The context in which we do the work is complex, and we must not allow the complexity of the environment to cloud the mission of urban missionaries and urban churches. We are commissioned to make multiplying disciples of Jesus who pray for His kingdom to come and His will to be done while simultaneously loving and obeying God with all that they are and loving their neighbors sacrificially.

We should be discontent until there are disciples of Jesus from every clan, tribe, people, nation, and language who form multiplying churches in our cities. Imagine what might be possible if every church set aside 10 percent of its undesignated gifts next year and devoted them to making multiplying disciples among unreached peoples in urban areas around the world.

We Must Love Our Neighbors Because of Who We Are in Christ

In the city we love our neighbor, every neighbor, because that is who we are. Love is not a strategy. It is not a method of evangelism. We do it individually. We do it with our households. We do it as a church. Sometimes, we organize and plan carefully how to love. On the other hand, we are ever ready to love spontaneously. We love our neighbors without public notice, though when necessary we draw public attention in order to change harmful and oppressive cultural practices and governmental policies.

Loving our neighbor should never become our purpose in life. The truth is, we love our neighbor out of an overflow of our love relationship with God. Some of our greatest spiritual growth will come as God leads us to love a neighbor through personal sacrifice. Imagine what could happen if your church had a capital funds campaign, but instead of buying brick and mortar, you used the money to care for people in Zambia dying from AIDS and to help the 1.1 million AIDS orphans in that country.

We Must Prepare Disciples to Be Urban Leaders

The next generation of Christian leaders must be urban leaders. We need to take the finest of Bible college and seminary classroom instruction and couple it with urban apprenticeships. We train plumbers and pilots by giving them both formal training through curriculum and supervised experience in the field. They must complete both. The dynamics and complexity of urban ministry necessitate that these kinds of apprenticeships be an integral part of Christian leadership development.

Not only do we need to prepare church and missions leaders for urban contexts, but we also need to develop ordinary urban disciples who are leaders in government, business, education, healthcare, the sciences, and the arts. Cities desperately need disciples of Jesus in every domain of society who live according to His teachings. The church can never become an enclave in the city. On the contrary, the church (and its seminaries and universities) needs to equip leaders to imitate Christ at home, in their neighborhoods, and in their roles in society.

Imagine what might happen if the IMB, the NAMB, seminaries, and churches partnered together to equip each church's university students to be part of an urban church-starting team when they graduate. Think of the architects, teachers, CPAs, managers, artists, linguists, coaches, nurses, journalists, cinematographers, scientists, engineers, etc., we could scatter to the cities of the world. They could work in the urban marketplace and make disciples as part of a team starting new churches.

We Need to Engage Cities with an Urbanized People Group Perspective

What is God doing in the world? One of His most prominent activities can be seen in the global urban migration. The world is moving to the city. We need to align our missional efforts with Him and make disciples of every people group, including those in the cities. Some urban people groups resemble homogenous groups in rural areas. A number of them do not. We need to urbanize our understanding of people groups, noting especially that relationships in the city are different than relationships in the village. The "*ethne*" understanding of ethno-linguistic people groups can take on a different meaning in the city than is common in smaller, more homogenous communities.

Imagine what could happen if partnerships formed between churches, universities, seminaries, and missions organizations to study our cities. Such partnerships would go a long way toward removing our urban blindness and helping us find and better understand the peoples of the city. Such partnerships would go a long way toward a Great Commission Resurgence.

GREAT COMMISSION MULTIPLICATION
CHURCH PLANTING AND
COMMUNITY MINISTRY

J. D. Greear

A Great Commission Resurgence will happen only when we return to the strategy God has established for the propagation of His gospel. That strategy is the planting of healthy, local churches in strategic cities in the world. This is what we see in the book of Acts. Following Jesus' issuing of the Great Commission in Acts 1:8, the Holy Spirit planted the congregation of Acts 2:42–47. As the church was being simply "the church" (i.e., fellowshipping, worshipping, preaching the Word, experiencing answers to prayer, and being radically generous with one another), a "fear came over everyone, and many wonders and signs were being performed through the apostles" (v. 43) and "every day the Lord added to them those who were being saved" (v. 47).

This first church was a blessing not only to its members, but also to its city. The overwhelming majority of miracles recorded in the church happened outside the walls of the church, on the streets of the city and in the marketplaces. Wherever the apostolic community went, there was joy in the city because of the extraordinary things done for the poor and needy by early Christians (see, for example, Acts 8:7; 9:36–39; 19:11–12; more on this below).

God's strategy for a Great Commission Resurgence is this: planting in every city vibrant, healthy local churches that are committed to blessing their communities. When our major cities are saturated with local, Acts 2:42–47-style churches, we will see God add to our number daily. Like the first church, these churches must be committed to blessing the city and doing "their miracles" in the streets.

THE CONTROVERSY?

The role that community ministry should play in establishing churches is a much-debated question among evangelical theologians and church planters, with opinions ranging from community restoration being the goal of church planting to community ministry being a dangerous distraction for churches. In this chapter, I will argue that the preaching of the message is the primary task of the local church (and, by preaching, I mean both that which happens from the pulpit and, more importantly, what church members do from "house to house" and on the streets of the community).

I also will argue that preaching the gospel effectively in unchurched and dechurched cities today is best done when accompanied by a robust, radically generous community ministry. Thus, I will urge new churches to make blessing the city through the meeting of its physical needs part of its core strategy, even though they should see proclaiming the gospel to their city as their primary task.

COMMUNITY MINISTRY AND THE GREAT COMMISSION: FOUR VIEWS

First, let's consider a variety of opinions on this matter. When asked if evangelical churches should view community ministry as part of their commission to preach the gospel, evangelicals commonly respond in one of four ways.

"Churches Should Do Community Ministry Because in So Doing, They Are Extending the Kingdom of God on Earth"

This group believes that Jesus left us behind to build His kingdom on earth. Scripture, they note, presents God's work in salvation progressing in four major movements: creation, fall, redemption, and restoration. The purpose of the cross was not merely to forgive the soul of the sinner and whisk him off to heaven, but to redeem the physical creation from the curse and restore it to glory. Jesus' resurrection inaugurated the restoration, and believers must now take the power of the resurrection and apply it to all dimensions of the cosmos.

Jesus' resurrection was merely the "first fruit" of the new creation, and our personal redemption merely the first application of the resurrection. The whole creation "has been groaning together with labor pains until now" (Rom 8:22), waiting, like our own physical bodies, for the "redemption" of the body.[1] The kingdom Jesus preached was not simply about a home in heaven for forgiven souls, but about a coming, restorative kingdom to be experienced on earth. The point of the gospel, to use N. T. Wright's phrase, was "life after life after death."[2]

Thus, we are not simply to be evangelizing the people on the earth, as if the church were an "ark" that we are to fill up before God destroys the worthless world with fire, but we are actually restoring the earth to its glorified state. They point out that the final chapter of Revelation describes not a group of Christians being evacuated from earth into heaven, but rather a glorified city of God being placed on the earth (Rev 21:1–2). Just as Jesus' miracles brought the new creation to earth, so we are to take the power of this resurrection to all spheres of the world.

What about 2 Peter 3:11, one might ask, which seems to say that the present earth will only be "burned up"?[3] Doesn't that make any focus on the physical creation useless? They point out that what Peter actually says is that the world will be "purified" through fire and that the heavens and earth will "pass away." When the earth is purified by fire, the dross of

---

1 See, for example, N.T. Wright, *Surprised by Hope* (New York: HarperCollins, 2008), 189–205.

2 Ibid., 189.

3 Albert Wolters comments, "A passage that is sometimes adduced against this view (i.e., that the physical creation is being renewed and will continue into eternity) is 2 Peter 3:10, but in fact this passage lends support to it. In the RSV it reads, 'But the day of the Lord will come like a thief, and then the heavens will pass away with a loud noise, and the elements will be dissolved with fire, and the earth and the works that are upon it will burned up.' However, all but one of the oldest and most reliable Greek manuscripts do not have the final words 'will be burned up' but instead have 'will be found,' which makes quite a difference. [This is the Greek text accepted by the more recent translation, such as the NEB and NIV, which read, somewhat obscurely, "will be laid bare."] The text therefore teaches that in spite of the passing away of the heavens and the dissolving of the elements, 'the earth and the works that are upon it' will survive. And as for the passing away and the dissolving, this certainly does not refer to annihilation or complete destruction. A few verses earlier Peter had written that the world 'was destroyed' in former times (v. 6), referring to the catastrophic destruction wreaked by the Flood, and he is drawing a parallel between the judgment and the one to come. The day of the Lord will bring the fires of judgment and a cataclysmic convulsion of all creation, but what emerges from the crucible will be 'a new heaven and a new earth, the home of righteousness' (v. 13), and it is presumably there that 'the earth and the works that are upon it will be found,' now purified from the filth and perversion of sin." Albert M. Wolters, *Creation Regained: Biblical Basics for a Reformational Worldview* (Grand Rapids: Eerdmans, 1985): 47–48, bracketed information mine.

corruption and sin will be burned away, but the gold of God's kingdom will remain. Just as one day my physical body will "pass away" and my redeemed spirit will be clothed with its new body, so the dead outer body of the earth will dissolve, and only the kingdom (the Spirit-powered new creation that we have been building on earth) will remain. When Jesus comes again, He will simply finish what we have started. In that new, final glorified city that God brings down to the new, purified earth, "the glory and honor of the nations [i.e., earthly culture and beauty] will be brought in" (Rev 21:24, 26).

For this group, then, "community restoration" is the ultimate point of the church's work on earth. Just as the cross was the means to the resurrection, so the preaching of the gospel is the means to community restoration. Restoration is the end game and, ultimately, the more important work.

"Social Ministry Is Not the Domain of the Church; the Church Should Be Concerned Only with Preaching the Gospel"

By contrast, these Christians believe that our role is not to build the Kingdom, but to preach the gospel of the kingdom. Jesus, they say, builds the kingdom Himself. The power behind the new creation is as one-sided as that behind the first creation and the bodily resurrection of Jesus. Though Revelation does indeed end with a glorified city on earth, they point out that that city descends from heaven, not rises up from the earth. God Himself plants the eternal garden. In other words, we do not build the kingdom so Jesus can return to it. Jesus builds it and brings it down to us. He, not us, makes all things new.

The role of believers now on earth is to preach the message of the gospel—that Jesus has suffered once for all for sinners and has been declared to be the Son of God in power (Heb 10:12, Rom 1:4). Preaching is the one, primary work of the church. Other good pursuits (like social justice and community ministry) should not take the church away from that one task. Preaching the gospel is the greatest act of community service the church can do, and to get deeply involved in community ministry in a way that distracts our attention from preaching the message is unkind to people whose lives depend on hearing that message. The church has not been given, primarily, the ministry of restoration, but of reconciliation (2 Cor 5:16–21).

They argue that when Jesus was asked by the apostles in Acts 1:6 what they were to do after His resurrection (**"Lord, at this time are You restoring the kingdom to Israel?"**), He did not respond by saying, "Restoring the kingdom is your job. Now get on it." Rather, He said, "You will receive power . . . and you will be My witnesses" (Acts 1:6–8). The apostles could not restore the kingdom, since Jesus was preparing to ascend and there could be no kingdom without the King! The primary objective of the apostles was to be witnesses to the kingdom.

Furthermore, they point out that the book of Acts does not show the church doing much, if any, community restoration. The early believers did not run soup kitchens; they preached. When the apostles were presented with a legitimate social need (the widows were feeling neglected), they responded that others would have to see to this concern because they should not be distracted from preaching (Acts 6:1–5).[4]

They point out that even Jesus Himself did not meet every physical need. When He sent out the 72 (Luke 10:1 ESV, NIV), He did not send them to every place there was hunger, but only to places where He Himself planned to go and bring the message. And when the miracles were getting in the way of the message, He quit performing them.

For example, when the crowd in John 6 became fixated on the bread and fish that Jesus multiplied, Jesus refused to repeat the miracle and preached instead to the people about Himself as the bread of life (John 6:26–27). He turned down the chance to end world hunger, opting instead for the primacy of preaching. In Luke 12:13–14, when asked to solve the property dispute of a brother who had been cheated out of his property, He refused to intervene, saying that this was not His business, and opted to preach instead about the sin of greed.

---

4   D. Martyn Lloyd-Jones comments on the apostles' response to the problem of the hungry widows: "This is surely a most interesting and important statement, a crucial one. What was the church to do? Here is a problem . . . it was a social problem, perhaps partly a political problem, but certainly a very acute and urgent social problem. Surely the business of the Christian Church, and the leaders particularly, is to deal with this crying need? Why go on preaching when people are starving and in need and are suffering? That was the great temptation that came to the Church immediately; but the apostles under the leading and the guidance of the Holy Spirit, and the teaching they had already received, and the commission they had from their Master, saw the danger and said, 'It is not reason that we should leave the Word of God, and serve tables. . . . We are here to preach this Word, this is the first thing. We will give ourselves continually to prayer and the ministry of the Word.'" *Preaching and Preachers* (Grand Rapids: Zondervan, 1971), 23.

Individual Christians (or groups of Christians, as in charitable foundations, philanthropy groups, parachurch ministries, etc.), this group says,
should engage in community ministry, but not the local church body itself.
The focus of the organized church should be only on preaching.

These Christians see themselves like an EMT in an emergency. If
there were an earthquake that left many people dying, it would not be
prudent for a trained EMT to start cleaning up the debris. The most
loving thing an EMT could do is perform emergency procedures that he
trained to do and that save lives. In the same way, churches should not
get distracted from preaching the gospel by cleaning up the world's mess,
since preaching the gospel is the most needed thing and the one thing
that only they can do.[5]

"Churches Should Do Community Ministry Simply Because It Is Part of Loving Their Neighbor"

Other Christians believe that while our primary role as believers is to
preach the gospel and not physically to build the kingdom on earth,
churches should still actively be involved meeting the needs of their
neighbors. Giving bread to the hungry and clothes to the naked are
necessary acts of love that anyone who cares about his neighbors will
do—churches most of all! They note that, as James 2 says, we cannot
love our neighbors and see them physically impoverished and not meet
their needs. Churches cannot say they love their neighbors when they are
content to leave them in squalor with only a weekly message that they
proclaim, "Be warmed, and filled!"

As love is the most significant change the gospel makes in our hearts,
and loving people means feeding them when they are hungry, churches

---

5 See, for example, "Who Does Scripture Say Is to Care for the Poor?" *Capitol Hill Baptist
Church Monthly Messenger*, 58, no. 12 (December 2006): 7–8. The elders at Capitol Hill note here
that while some occasional social ministries are acceptable for a congregation, none is required: "It can
be harmful if the local church became diluted with other things that distract her from her primary
purpose. Yet, while the primary purpose of the church is the preaching of the gospel, she may pursue
that in ways which include caring for the physical needs of non-Christians. Such ministries to those
outside of the church are not Biblically required to be ministries of any congregation, but may be
employed to the end . . . of promoting the gospel in the community . . . [here quoting Ken Jones] 'If
the church never offers a single hot meal but preaches the gospel, then she is true to her calling . . .
the church is not called to economically empower anybody, but it is called to deliver the message of
reconciliation.'"

should do community ministry as an act of love. This community ministry, however, is not really part of the Great Commission. It is simply what people who love their neighbors do. Loving and serving our neighbors is not done in an attempt to convert our neighbors, but simply because we cannot bear to see them suffer when we can make a difference. I heard one person say it this way: "We don't serve to convert, we serve because we are converted."

"Community Ministry Should Accompany the Preaching of the Gospel as a 'Sign' of Its Message"

This final position (which I believe to be the correct one) combines aspects of each of the previous three. From position #1, I believe it is true that the purpose of Christ's work was not simply forgiveness but restoration. But, from position #2, I believe it is also true Jesus never commissions the church to build the kingdom on earth. He alone can do that. From #3, I believe that loving our neighbor means meeting their needs, but I also believe that this is one of the most effective apologetics for the gospel in a post-Christian society.

Thus, churches should engage in community ministry as a "sign" of the gospel—while not neglecting to make the preaching of the Word their primary task. Community ministry is more than just an act of kindness; community ministry/restoration serves the purposes of the Great Commission. We are not "restoring the kingdom," but we are restoring parts of the city as a sign of the coming kingdom. We give, to use Lesslie Newbigin's terminology, "signs amid the rubble."[6]

"Signs" always accompanied the message of Jesus. His miracles were not merely random acts of kindness or magic tricks to prove His power. He did not prove He was the Son of God by levitating or catching bullets in His teeth. While those things may have proven that He had power, His miracles had a grander purpose.

His miracles served a message, that He was the King who was coming to restore the earth. King Jesus healed blindness (Mark 8:22–25). He stopped

---

6 Lesslie Newbigin gave a lecture by this title, recorded in the book *Signs amid the Rubble: The Purposes of God in Human History*, ed. Geoffrey Wainwright (Grand Rapids: Eerdmans, 2003). The church is to be a "sign, instrument, and foretaste" of the coming Kingdom of God (103).

storms (Mark 4:35–41). He fed the hungry (Matt 14:13–18). Repeatedly the Gospels present Jesus as proclaiming the Word *and* doing signs (Luke 9:11; Matt 9:35; Luke 9:1-2). His miracles showed that His mission was to reverse the curse caused by sin. As Tim Keller has noted, "The point of his miracles is never to show the naked fact of his power. The point of his miracles is always to show the redemptive purpose of his power."[7] Keller notes that we often think of Jesus' miracles as a suspension of the natural order, but they were quite the opposite. They were a return to the natural order.[8] Miracles demonstrated, in a physical, tangible way the invisible message of the gospel. Jesus' miracles showed His audience what the kingdom He was preaching was like—a kingdom of justice and equality and without blindness or sickness or darkness or death.

Signs also characterized the apostles' ministry. Healing the sick, delivering from demons, radical generosity, living in harmony with those of other races and socioeconomic classes, and even raising the dead—these were all part of the apostolic ministry. They were "signs" of the kingdom that they proclaimed.

In the same way, community ministry "signifies" what the kingdom of God is really like to our communities. Our main responsibility in the present age is indeed to witness to the King through speaking His message (Acts 1:8), but we should also be giving signs of the kingdom through acts of physical and social healing, showing that the kingdom is one of justice, progress, equity, health, and sacrificial love—just as Jesus and the apostles did.

All physical signs, however, whether done by Jesus or by us, are only temporary (contra position #1). They are not the actual building of the kingdom. The blind eyes that Jesus healed went blind again (think about it: all blind men Jesus healed are dead now, which means their eyes have descended again into decay!). The people Jesus fed got hungry again. The dead people Jesus raised died again (has anyone seen Lazarus lately?). The simple fact is that Jesus left without fully establishing the kingdom, and when He left, all of His physical miracles were slowly undone.[9] Jesus gave only temporary pictures of what the kingdom was like. He "sketched out

---

7   Tim Keller, "Doing Justice," accessed at http://www.theresurgence.com/r_r_2006_session_eight_audio_keller.

8   Tim Keller, *The Reason for God* (New York: Dutton, 2008), 95–96.

9   Some theologians assert that had Israel accepted Jesus as the Messiah He would have inaugurated the kingdom, in which case the healings He gave would have become permanent and the actual institution of the kingdom. Even so, Jesus is not here now, and ultimate, permanent healing awaits His return.

in pencil what He would one day paint over with indelible ink" and gave "signs amid the rubble."

In the same way, our works of physical "restoration" in our city are only temporary signs of the future, permanent restoration. The bodies we feed will become hungry again. The neighborhoods we rebuild might likely descend back into ghettos. We are not building the kingdom for Jesus; we are giving signs of that kingdom that He will one day build while calling people through proclamation to be reconciled to King Jesus.[10]

Attempting to build the kingdom will ultimately be a futile and frustrating activity for Christians—God alone builds His kingdom, and, as said earlier, there can be no kingdom without the King. Giving signs of the gospel, however, is an important part of preaching the gospel in every age, and especially in ours. Community "healing" is more than simply being obedient to the command to love our neighbor; it is a sign of the kingdom that Jesus inaugurated. The signs make our message intelligible to those who are alienated from the gospel. In an increasingly secularized society, showing the peacefulness, generosity, and beauty of the gospel enhances the gospel's persuasiveness.

EXAMPLES OF "SIGNS" AS A CENTRAL PART OF THE APOSTOLIC MESSAGE AND CHURCH PLANTING STRATEGY

Our primary task is to be Christ's witnesses to the ends of the earth (Acts 1:8). Like the early church, we are to call all people everywhere to turn from sin to God (Acts 17:30). At the same time, we see that "signs" were an important part of apostolic ministry.

---

10 To those who think we are restoring our cities and ushering in the kingdom, perhaps historical reflection would be helpful. Some of the Christians who came to America in the seventeenth century to build a new country believed they were establishing the foundations of God's kingdom, a government which ultimately would help usher in the return of Jesus. Many American Christians today still suffer from the vestiges of those roots, believing America to be "God's country" and their government a "Christian government." The irony is that many of those who today advocate "renewal of cities" and "building of the kingdom" are greatly critical of the "Constantinianism" of the "Christian right." However, they themselves appear to be working according to the same ideology and toward the same ends. When we teach our church members to "build the kingdom" in their government, how will they not come to see their rule as synonymous with God's kingdom?

For example, in the midst of Peter's two great sermons in Acts 2 and Acts 4, he performs a sign (4:16) of the gospel that amazes the community (3:10) by making the lame man walk. Paul also made "community ministry" a central part of his evangelism strategy in Acts 16. As Paul plants the church in Acts 16, he brings three Philippians to Christ. He brings each to Christ in a different way. First, Lydia, a God-fearing woman from Asia, comes to Christ through one of Paul's Bible studies (16:9–15). Second, a servant girl comes to Christ through Paul's economic and spiritual deliverance (16:16–19).[11] Finally, the Philippian jailor, an employee of the cynical Roman ruling class, comes to Christ after watching Paul and Silas's radical generosity (first to the servant girl and then to himself) and their unfailing joy in the midst of great suffering (16:19–31).

What is significant in this account is that apparently neither the servant girl nor the Philippian jailor came to Christ through Paul's Bible studies or his sermons, though we must assume that they had heard the gospel (Rom 10:14). The servant girl was persuaded as she experienced liberation from her oppression through the ministry of a Christian. The Philippian jailor was persuaded as he saw the love and power of Paul's life. The same will be true for the oppressed and the cynical in our cities.

Sometimes the apostolic signs were miraculous, as with the signs Philip performed in Samaria that caused the people of Samaria to rejoice (Acts 8:7). Sometimes they were simply demonstrations of love and peace to the community, as with Tabitha who generously made garments for her community (Acts 9:36, 39) or Paul's kindness toward the Philippian jailor (Acts 16:25–31).

The Local Church Is Itself a Sign of the Gospel

The local church itself was, though, the greatest kingdom sign of the gospel in Acts. Acts 2:40–47 describes a community characterized by unity (Acts 2:5, 44), generosity (2:44–45), and answered prayer (Acts 2:43). As a result, there was a sense of awe in the community, they had favor with "all" the people of Jerusalem (Acts 2:46–47), and people were saved and added daily to their number.

---

11 The text never says, directly, that she came to Christ. The context, however, gives some support to that assumption. Her conversion (though important to her) is not essential to the point I am making here, which more concerns methodology than results.

A gospel-centered church is a community of unity and love the world cannot explain. Jesus said that the world would know that He was the Messiah by the love of His disciples for one another (John 13:35). The church should be a mystery of communal unity where people who have historically been alienated from one another enjoy a close brotherhood around the cross. This is why Paul placed such emphasis on the unity of Jew and Gentile in the epistles. Paul said that the unity of Jew and Gentile in the church was a sign of the "new man" established in the cross (Eph 2:15), and it was through "the church" that the manifold wisdom of God is made known to the rulers of the world (Eph 3:10). As Francis Schaeffer said, the church is the final apologetic of the gospel.[12]

The church in Philippi is, again, a great example. Jewish men, like Paul before his conversion, were notorious for praying each morning, "God, I thank you I am not a woman, a slave, or a Gentile." Yet, Paul's first three converts in Philippi were a Jewish woman, a slave, and a Gentile. In no other community on earth would a Jewish woman, a slave girl, and a Gentile jailor call each other "family." This was a great, and compelling, display of the power of the gospel in the ancient world.

The Example of the Early Church

Rodney Stark has noted that the reason the church grew so quickly in the first few centuries was because they so pursuasively *signified* the gospel in their community. In his excellent book, *The Rise of Christianity*, Stark explains that the early church grew rapidly in Greco-Roman cities because it was unique in at least three areas.[13]

First, when disease swept through the Greco-Roman world, Christians did not flee the cities as others did, but stayed to minister to the dying. They reasoned that because Jesus was a healer who had risen from the dead, they as His followers should stay to help bring healing to the sick. They would not fear death since they served death's Conqueror. This demonstrated the gospel to their community.

Second, Christians were forgiving even under persecution. Christians, like many other minorities in the Roman Empire, faced fierce persecution. However, unlike other minorities, Christians did not form vigilante groups

---

12 See Francis Schaeffer, *The Great Evangelical Disaster* (Wheaton: Crossway, 1984), 164-65.

13 See Rodney Stark, *The Rise of Christianity* (San Francisco: Harper Collins, 1997), 161–67.

to fight back or seek justice. They forgave their persecutors. Their reasoning was that Jesus' greatest victory had come in persecution; therefore, they could endure and wait for victory to come through their persecution. Again, this demonstrated the gospel they proclaimed.

Third, Christian churches were one of the few places modeling peace among the multiethnic groups living together in the city. Ethnic tension ran high in the new Greco-Roman urban centers because, for one of the first times in history, communities of different origin were thrust together. In churches, however, the varying ethnicities got along and treated each other respectfully. They understood that Christ was the Lord of all humanity, and, for that reason, all races were essentially one in Him.

Each of these behaviors was a direct response to, and demonstration of, the gospel. This radical approach to life made Christians unique in the Greco-Roman world, and the result, says Stark, was their rapid growth. Emperor Julian, one of early church's fiercest opponents, explained in a letter why he believed he could not keep the church from growing. Julian famously said in disgust, "The godless Galileans feed not only their poor but ours as well!"[14]

IMPLICATIONS FOR LOCAL CHURCHES

What, then, should our local churches do—especially in an interest in refocusing on the work of the Great Commission? How might Southern Baptists use these insights to experience a Great Commission Resurgence?

We Must Look for Ways to Give Signs of the Gospel to Our Community

Just as Jesus and the apostles gave signs of the kingdom they were announcing, local churches must also be devoted to performing signs of that kingdom in their communities. They must accompany and substantiate their preaching with signs that put the message of the gospel on display. They should seek to heal the sick, feed the hungry, and clothe the poor, sometimes by natural means and sometimes supernatural.

---

14 Stephen Neill, *A History of Christian Missions* (Middlesex, England: Penguin, 1964), 42.

Those of us who are pastors must realize that the primary work God wants to do is in the community, not in our churches. The overwhelming majority of miracles recorded in Acts happen outside the church. Talk to most pastors about the "miracles" they have seen in their church, though, and they point to a powerful sermon or a capital campaign! The primary miracles the Holy Spirit wants to do are in the community through the hands of God's people.

Ephesians 4:11–13 says that God has appointed pastors "for the training of the saints in the work of ministry." The primary "ministry" does not happen at the hands of pastors, but through the saints. I often tell my congregation that when I became a pastor, I "left" the ministry. The people in my congregation, unlike me, spend the majority of their week working side by side with unbelievers in the community. God wants to use them to do "miracles" in the community. I tell them that the majority of God's expressions of His miraculous power await them outside the walls of the church.

Many churches today are seeking to do this. Pastor-at-Large of Fellowship Bible Church in Little Rock, Arkansas, Robert Lewis says in his book *The Church of Irresistible Influence* that churches should be so ingratiated into the community through their good works that the community cannot imagine functioning apart from the church.[15] Erwin McManus, pastor of the Mosaic Church of Los Angeles says, "We want our community to say, 'We may not believe what those crazy people at Mosaic believe, but thank God they're here, because if not, we'd have to raise our taxes!'"[16] Tim Keller, pastor of the Redeemer Church in New York City, started a ministry called "Hope for New York" that seeks to help New York City residents do everything from finding jobs to overcoming addictions.[17]

Our church has seen some of its most effective outreach happen through community ministry. In 2004, I was preaching through the first half of the book of Acts to our congregation at the Summit Church. The Sunday I preached on Acts 8, I read 8:6–8, "The crowds paid attention with one mind to what Philip said, as they heard and saw the signs he was performing. . . . So there was great joy in that city," and I asked our church if there was "great joy" in the city as a result of our message and the miracles we were doing in the city. Then I read Acts 9:36–39 that talks about an

---

15 Robert Lewis, *The Church of Irresistible Influence* (Grand Rapids: Zondervan, 2001).

16 Erwin McManus, quoted at the 2007 Evangelism Conference, Baptist State Convention of North Carolina, Greensboro, North Carolina, 12 February 2007.

17 See http://hfny.org/about-us/our-history/.

early church disciple named Tabitha who "was always doing good works and acts of charity." Verse 39 says that when she died the community of widows gathered at her bedside and wept at their loss of her. I asked our church, "If the Summit Church 'died,' do we think our community would weep that we were gone?"

We believed the answer to both those questions was "no." The extent of our organized community ministry at that point had been mail-outs, billboards, annual fall festivals, and token gifts to local charities. If anything, the community may have been excited that we had "died," as they would have regained access to a currently tax-exempt piece of property, and they would have had one less mail-out to throw away at Easter!

We repented as a church and asked that God help us become a blessing to our city—to make us the kind of place about which the unbelievers of our city might also say, "We may not believe what they believe . . . but thank God they're here, because, if not, we'd have to raise our taxes!" We asked God to show us ways we could demonstrate the peace and love of the kingdom.

The first project God brought to us was a needy public elementary school in downtown Durham. The school was the worst ranked school in Durham County and was on track to be shut down within two years. We approached the principal and asked her if we could do our annual "fall festival" on their property, for their people, free of charge. We told her that we did not expect to preach, hand out Bibles, or do anything to promote the church. We told her we just wanted to love and serve and bless them. It took some persuading, but she finally consented.

That led to several facility renovation projects that we undertook for the school, and throughout the next year many of our people got involved tutoring many of the school's children. People in our church have adopted classrooms and teachers, housed refugees, and met physical needs of families in the school. One soon-to-be-married couple in our church asked that any wedding gifts for them go instead to a family in the school whose house had been destroyed in a fire.

At the end of that first year, the principal asked us if we would pray for her kids during the end of the year exams because their scores would be the primary criteria by which the school would be evaluated. We did, and we have every year since then. In the fourth year of our involvement, the school (which previously had the lowest scores of any school in the county) had the highest percentage of kids to pass the end of year exams. In a report chronicling our involvement with the school, the principal credited the church's efforts with helping to improve the school's academic performance.[18]

This past year the principal came to our church and presented me with an award, saying, "You have made a difference in our school. You have been a picture of the love of God to us." At a teachers' banquet we put on recently, one of the teachers at the school stood up and said to us, "I have always known you Christians believed you should love your neighbor. . . . I've never known what it looked like until now."

For seven years now, we have done our best to love, serve, and demonstrate the gospel to the people of Eastway Elementary School. Our kindness to the people of this school is only a dim shadow of Jesus' great kindness of us, but it has helped people in that school to understand the gospel better. Our kindness to that school is not simply an act of love, but an adornment of the gospel. It has made tangible the "invisible" kingdom we preach.

As inheritors of the apostolic commission, we do acts of kindness that are neither random nor senseless. We do not have time for that. Our actions are to signify the gospel of the King. Our works do not restore the kingdom, but they testify to it. We "sketch out in pencil what Jesus will one day paint over in indelible ink" so they can see the gospel and believe it.

We Must Discipline Our Ministries to Keep the Message Central

I hope I have demonstrated that the primary task of the church is the preaching of the gospel. Like the apostles, we have a single agenda—being His witnesses—and we must therefore go everywhere preaching. That is because the gospel is an announcement about what Jesus has done on our behalf to save us, not instructions about what we are to go and do for Him. The gospel is not spelled "D-O" or "D-O-N-T," but "D-O-N-E." As it has been said, the gospel is not good advice; it is good news.

No act of compassion or love, no matter how beautiful, should supersede the preaching of the gospel in our ministries. To say "preach the gospel; if necessary, use words" is like saying, "Tell me your phone number; if necessary, use digits." The gospel is an announcement of words about

---

18 "Church Efforts Earn Family Status at Elementary School," *Biblical Recorder*, 12 September 2009, 7.

what Jesus has done for us, not about what we can do for others. Preaching that announcement must remain primary.

Racial reconciliation, radical generosity toward the poor, and holy living are all vital fruits of conversion, but they are the effects of the gospel and not the gospel itself. Local churches should discipline their ministries so that community ministry enhances, and never distracts from, the preeminence of the message.

The apostles knew when they should walk away from table waiting to focus on the Word (Acts 6:1–5). Jesus did not stop with feeding the hungry but went on to preach about Himself as the bread of life (John 6:26–27). Jesus also refused to get overly embroiled in every social justice issue so that He could preach against the idolatry of the human heart (Luke 12:13–14). These examples show us that we must be disciplined enough not to allow the signs of the gospel to take either our or our community's attention away from the gospel. And if they have, we must turn away, in Jesus' name and for love of our neighbor, from the community ministry and get back to preaching!

Any time our message becomes more about what we should go and do for others than about what God has done for us, we preach heresy. Any time the focus of our churches is on what we are doing for the community rather than on what God has done for all of us in Christ, we exemplify heresy. What we are doing may be good and worthy, but if it receives greater emphasis than the actual gospel message, it has become heresy. As Arthur Pink said years ago, "Error is truth out of proportion."[19]

We Must Lead Churches That Are Themselves Clear Signs of the Kingdom

Local churches should be such miracles of diversity, love, and generosity that their communities stand in awe. The church is to be like a window into another world. In many ways, it is like a star. The light we see from most stars was generated thousands of years before our eyes actually see it. The light we are seeing in the present results from action that took place in another time. The local church is the light of God in the present that points to action at another time—the light of the church points the world backward to Jesus' activity in the cross and forward to the restoration He

---

19 Arthur W. Pink, *An Exposition of Hebrews* (Grand Rapids: Baker, 2003), 601.

will bring. The local church shows the radical generosity of Jesus' cross and the radical victory of His coming kingdom.

Churches characterized by racial diversity—as well as age, cultural, and socio-economic diversity—will be a compelling display of the gospel, especially in our globalized age. People are more aware than ever of the ethnic strife in our world. Like the early church, local churches can be a demonstration of the one "new man" that God created in Christ.

In 2007 I had a chance to have breakfast with a small group of pastors that included Pastor Bill Hybels. Hybels's Willow Creek Community Church served as a pattern for megachurches in the 1990s. Hybels shared that one of the mistakes he made in growing Willow Creek was adhering to the homogeneity principle. The homogeneity principle has been understood to teach that churches can grow fastest if they "target" a specific type of person and go after only them. Hybels said that the principle worked at Willow Creek—their church grew, rapidly, to 20,000 people—but said that if he could do it over again, he would not pursue the homogeneity principle and instead write diversity into the fabric of Willow Creek.

I asked him if he would do so even if he knew it meant Willow would grow only half as large. Without hesitation he said, "Yes." I asked, "How could you, who have been so outspoken about the need for evangelism in the church, espouse anything that would result in reaching fewer people?" His response, I believe, was profound: the corporate witness of the body of Christ, he said, a witness magnified by cultural diversity, will have a larger evangelistic impact on our world than will a numbers surge at any one congregation.

Church Planting Should Be Our Primary Missions Strategy

Finally, we must dedicate ourselves to planting other churches, both in our city and in other cities around the world. As Tim Keller notes, the entire strategy of Paul in the book of Acts can be summed up as "finding the most strategic cities in the world and planting churches."[20]

As I noted above, it is not coincidental that the Holy Spirit's first act following Jesus' issue of the Great Commission in Acts 1:8 was to plant

---

20 Tim Keller makes this observation in his *Church Planting Manual*, used by the Redeemer Church Planting Center in New York City. This manual contains many helpful insights about urban church planting in North America, and is available online from http://www.redeemer2.com/rcpc/rcpc/.

the congregation of Acts 2:42–47. As shown earlier, it was in the presence of a Spirit-filled church that "fear came over everyone, and many wonders and signs were being performed through the apostles" (v. 43), and "every day the Lord added to them those who were being saved" (v. 47). God's strategy for fulfilling the commission of Acts 1:8 was the planting of Acts 2:42–47-style churches in every city of the world.

The presence of a local church is the greatest catalyst for evangelism— and thus, for a Great Commission Resurgence—on our planet. Churches are uniquely equipped to demonstrate the multifaceted beauty of the gospel to their communities. Local churches can preach the gospel from their pulpits, equip their members to preach the message "from house to house," and can adorn that gospel by teaching people to live out the peace, purity, and generosity of the gospel in the community. Local churches can organize their members to minister healing signs of the gospel to the neediest parts of the community. The *koinonia* and love within the local church is the most compelling sign of the kingdom in this age. As Ephesians 3:10 says, it is through the local church that God's "multi-faceted wisdom" would be made known to the rulers of the world.

Community ministries, street evangelism, evangelistic crusades, social justice, racial reconciliation, prayer initiatives, Promise Keeper rallies, and other such activities are worthy ministries, but they are most effective when done side by side with a church planting strategy (or, in conjunction with and in service to the ministries of existing local churches). Local churches are the hub of New Testament work.

The churches we plant must be committed to bold, clear proclamation of the message, radical demonstration of the gospel's power and generosity in the community, and miraculous diversity in congregations unified around the gospel. In such a way, Jesus intends to fulfill the Great Commission through His church. The local church is, to quote Hybels again, the hope of the world.[21] Planting churches that are committed to blessing their cities is the Southern Baptist's hope of a Great Commission Resurgence.

---

21   Bill Hybels, *Courageous Leadership* (Grand Rapids: Zondervan, 2002), 70.

SECTION 5
THE WAY FORWARD

AXIOMS FOR A GREAT COMMISSION RESURGENCE[1]

Daniel L. Akin

INTRODUCTION

Following His resurrection, Jesus spent time with His disciples for 40 days preparing them for their assignment once He had ascended. He led them out to Mount Olivet where He would return to the Father. However, just prior to His ascension, the disciples wanted to have a theological conversation concerning matters of eschatology. Specifically they wanted to know, "Lord, at this time are You restoring the kingdom to Israel?" (Acts 1:6).

Jesus did not rebuke them for asking what is certainly an interesting question. His response did indicate, however, that it was not the most important question. His response reveals that the better question is this: "What should we do until You do come again and establish Your kingdom?" To that question, He provides a definitive answer in the Acts version of the Great Commission found in verse 8: "Be my witnesses." In essence, Jesus was saying to His followers, "Do not get distracted over issues that are secondary and nonessential. Stay focused on the main thing. Make sure your priorities line up with the Father's. Be my witnesses and advance the gospel until I return."

Like the disciples, Southern Baptists today run the risk of being distracted from the main thing. Many of the issues we are emphasizing and debating are interesting things, but they are not the most important things. They do not line up well with the priorities we find revealed in

---

1 This chapter is a revised and expaned version of the author's original sermon, preached in Binkley Chapel, Southeastern Baptist Theological Seminary, April 16 2009 (audio available from http://apps.sebts.edu/chmessages/resource_2452/04–16–09_Dr_Daniel_L_Akin.mp3).

Holy Scripture. The result: we are fractured and factionalizing. We are confused, having lost our spiritual compass. We have reached, many of us believe, what Alvin Reid describes as "a tipping point." We have tragically devolved into "a giant movement now in decline," experiencing far too much ineffectiveness in gospel ministry and the fulfillment of the Great Commission.

How do we change this situation and experience a much needed course correction? How do we, by God's grace and for His glory, get in sync with the Savior's heart, a heart that cried, "For the Son of Man has come to seek and to save the lost" (Luke 19:10)?

I share, humbly and with no illusion that I have all the answers, twelve axioms (or values) that I believe can move us in the right direction. People are talking about many of these principles all across the Southern Baptist Convention, and they get excited and energized when that happens. The Great Commission has been defined for us in Matthew 28:18–20. These principles or axioms describe what the implementation of a Great Commission Resurgence for Southern Baptist might look like.

It is not too bold to say that both frustration and anticipation are building among our people, and the time is right to put the former behind us and to pursue the latter with a laser beam focus directed by what so many believe God is leading us to embrace. It is hard to imagine the evil one leading us to intensify our involvement with what the blogging demon Wormwood calls that "cursed Commission!" I do think all the demons of hell would do all that they can to distract us from it.

What must happen to make us ready for and get us moving in a God-sent Great Commission Resurgence? My agenda is purposefully positive and forward-looking. I share what I pray will be an encouragement to all of us.

AXIOM #1: WE MUST COMMIT OURSELVES TO THE TOTAL AND ABSOLUTE LORDSHIP OF JESUS CHRIST IN EVERY AREA OF OUR LIVES (COL 3:16–17, 23–24)

Jesus Christ must be our passion and priority. We must aspire to both know Him and love Him more fully. We must long to see Him "come to have first place in everything" (Col 1:18). To miss this is to miss everything and never to get out of the starting blocks. Southern Baptists need to become more than ever "a Jesus-intoxicated people," returning to our first love (Rev 2:4–5). A Christ-centered life must, and it will, inform our theology and inspire our missional service.

We must love Him, worship Him, adore Him, exalt Him, share Him, and exemplify Him. Within the family of Southern Baptists, we have often been described as "people of the Book." This is a good thing, and it must never be lost. However, if we are indeed a people of the book, then we need to be in love with the Person to whom the book points us: Jesus! When the world thinks of us, they should think first, "Those are the folks in love with Jesus. They are the people obsessed with Jesus. There is a people that talk and act and serve and love like Jesus. Southern Baptists are Jesus people!"

We need the ministry of the Holy Spirit to lead us to a new and fresh intimacy and communion with Jesus. This must be first and foremost. Any other agenda is to get the first and most important thing wrong.

AXIOM #2: WE MUST BE GOSPEL-CENTERED IN ALL OUR ENDEAVORS FOR THE GLORY OF GOD (ROM 1:16)

The Lordship of Jesus Christ and His gospel is what it is all about. It is why we exist as the people of God. Being "gospel-centered" means that we are "grace-centered." It means loving the people Jesus loves and reaching out to those rejected and even scorned by the Pharisees of our day. We must expose, confess, and repent of the legalism of our day embedded in our traditions to which we are often blind. A gospel-centered agenda can make this happen.

Being gospel-centered means that we proclaim the victory that Christ won over death, hell, the grave, and sin by His substitutionary atonement and glorious resurrection. We must be gospel-centered for our justification, our sanctification, and our glorification. We must be gospel-centered from beginning to end.

Pursuing in all things the "glory of God" means that we will be theocentric and not anthropocentric in our worship and work. The supremacy of God in Christ through the Spirit in all things must be the engine that drives us. A radically gospel-centered life will ensure that the bloody cross of a crucified King is the offense to nonbelievers—not our styles, traditions, legalisms, moralisms, preferences, and sourpuss attitudes!

A radically gospel-centered life will promote a grace-filled salvation from beginning to end, putting on display the beauty of the gospel in all of life's aspects. It will remind us that we do not obey in order to be accepted; we obey because we *are* accepted by God in Christ! Once more an attractive and contagious joy in Jesus will draw people to the Savior whose glory radiates through transformed lives made new in Christ (2 Cor 5:17).

Too many of our pulpits have jettisoned the proclamation of the gospel. Too many of our people have lost the meaning and therefore the wonder of the gospel. We must get it right once again if we are to experience a Great Commission Resurgence. No gospel, no Great Commission Resurgence. It really is that simple.

AXIOM #3: WE MUST TAKE OUR STAND ON THE FIRM FOUNDATION OF THE INERRANT AND INFALLIBLE WORD OF GOD, AFFIRMING ITS SUFFICIENCY IN ALL MATTERS (MATT 5:17–18; JOHN 10:35; 17:17; 2 TIM 3:16–17; 2 PET 1:20–21)

Southern Baptists won the "battle for the Bible" that began in 1979. Wonderful men of God like Jimmy Draper, Paige Patterson, Paul Pressler, Adrian Rogers, and Jerry Vines put their ministries on the line because they saw what the poison of liberalism was doing to our Convention and its institutions. These men are heroes of the faith, and what they did must be honored and never forgotten.

However, and hear me well, the "war for the Bible" is not over, and it will never end until Jesus returns. Launched by Satan in the garden of Eden, "has God said?" will continue to be the question that assaults us, and we must be on guard and ready to answer those who question Scripture's veracity and accuracy. Already, as Greg Beale warns in the book *The Erosion of Inerrancy*, evangelicals are backing away from or redefining into insignificance the idea of inerrancy.[2] A younger generation of Southern Baptists will eventually face this challenge, and you must not squander away precious theological ground that is essential to a Great Commission Resurgence.

Russ Bush was absolutely correct when I heard him say in a seminary classroom in the early 1980s, "the question of biblical inspiration is ultimately a question of Christological identity." Why? Because Jesus believed the Holy Scriptures to be the completely true and trustworthy Word of God! Even Rudolf Bultmann said this—he just believed Jesus got it wrong!

---

2   G. K. Beale, *The Erosion of Inerrancy in Evangelicalism* (Wheaton: Crossway, 2008).

Hear me, and hear me well. To deny inerrancy is to say that Jesus was wrong and that you are smarter than He was. That is both heresy and blasphemy. It is spiritually suicidal!

Are you questioning inerrancy? Then repent! Do you deny inerrancy? Then go join another denomination. We will love you and pray for you, but we do not want you infecting our people with a spiritual disease that is always fatal to the Church of the Lord Jesus. Inerrancy and the sufficiency of the Bible in all matters of faith and practice are not up for debate in the Southern Baptist Convention. It alone will give us the necessary weapons to take on and take down what *Newsweek* calls "a newly muscular secularism."[3]

AXIOM #4: WE MUST DEVOTE OURSELVES TO A RADICAL PURSUIT OF THE GREAT COMMISSION IN THE CONTEXT OF OBEYING THE GREAT COMMANDMENTS (MATT 28:16–20; 22:37–40)

A devoted follower of Jesus Christ gets excited about (1) reaching the nations for Christ, (2) reaching our nation, the United States of America, for Christ, and (3) doing so in a manner that is biblically-theologically sound and driven. Why? Because all three are in the DNA of the Great Commission. However, a real Great Commission Resurgence will not only possess Great Commission DNA; it will also be alive with Great Commandment DNA too.

The ultimate motivation for the Great Commission is love of God and a passion to be on mission with Him. After all, the Great Commission is His mission! But flowing out of love for God also will be a genuine love for people, something too many of us have lost somewhere along the way. The results have devastated our witness. If we do not love them, we have no right to expect them to listen. If we do not serve them, we have no reason to expect them to trust us.

Much could be said here, but I will narrow my focus to one area of particular concern. A Great Commission Resurgence is not the same thing as a moral reformation, and it is certainly not a revival of political activism. Now, do not misunderstand. It is our Christian duty to be good citizens, vote our convictions, and promote good and godly policies. The end of slavery, the right of all Americans to vote, and Civil Rights legislation

---

3 Jon Meacham, "The End of Christian America," *Newsweek*, 13 April 2009. Available online from http://www.newsweek.com/id/192583.

quickly and easily come to mind. However, our commission is to promote the gospel and not crawl in bed with the government, political parties, and politicians. As John MacArthur so well says, "True Christianity is more concerned with saving souls than it is with gaining votes. . . . Rather than concentrating on political issues and debates, believers should be *consumed* with their responsibility as Christ's ambassadors."[4]

Governmental legislation will not stop the moral plunge of our nation and the world, but the gospel will! Our hope is not in Republicans or Democrats, Congress or Capitol Hill. Our hope, the world's hope, is in Calvary's hill and a crucified and risen Savior named King Jesus. Love for God and love for our neighbor demand that we not get sidetracked by political machinations. Neither Jesus nor His disciples exhausted their time trying to change the government. They spent their time trying to change people's hearts. We must do no less. Do not forget, it is Jesus who said, "My kingdom is not of this world" (John 18:36).

If we love Jesus as we should, we will love sinners as we ought and pursue them as He did. We will not condemn them; that is the business of God. We will love them, serve them, and tell them of a Savior who cares for their soul. The silence of our gospel witness may be an evidence of the coldness and hardness of our hearts. The Great Commission and the Great Commandments—they always go hand in hand.

AXIOM #5: WE MUST AFFIRM THE 2000 *BAPTIST FAITH AND MESSAGE* AS A HEALTHY AND SUFFICIENT GUIDE FOR BUILDING A THEOLOGICAL CONSENSUS FOR PARTNERSHIP IN THE GOSPEL, REFUSING TO BE SIDETRACKED BY THEOLOGICAL AGENDAS THAT DISTRACT US FROM OUR LORD'S COMMISSION (1 TIM 6:3-4)

What do we as Southern Baptists agree on doctrinally and theologically? The answer, praise God, is a lot. For example:

- We affirm the inerrancy, infallibility, authority, and sufficiency of the Bible.

---

4 John MacArthur, *Right Thinking in a World Gone Wrong* (Eugene, OR: Harvest House, 2009), 122, emphasis added.

- We affirm the Triune God who is omnipotent, omniscient, and omnipresent.
- We affirm God as Creator and reject naturalistic evolution as nonsense.
- We affirm both the dignity and depravity of man.
- We affirm the full deity, perfect humanity, and sinlessness of Jesus the Son of God.
- We affirm the penal substitutionary nature of the atonement as foundational for understanding the cross work of our Savior.
- We affirm the gospel as the exclusive and only means whereby any person is reconciled to God.
- We affirm the biblical nature of a regenerate church witnessed in believer's baptism by immersion.
- We affirm salvation by grace alone through faith alone in Christ alone for the glory of God alone.
- We affirm the reception of the Holy Spirit at the moment of regeneration/conversion and the blessing of spiritual gifts for the building up of the body of Christ.
- We affirm the literal, visible, and historical return of Jesus Christ to this earth when He will manifest fully His kingdom.
- We affirm the reality of an eternal heaven and an eternal hell with Jesus as the only difference.
- We affirm a "sanctity of life" ethic from conception to natural death.
- We affirm the sanctity of heterosexual marriage, the goodness of sex in marriage, and the gift of children—lots of them.
- We affirm the complementary nature of male/female relationships, rejoicing in the divine ordering of them for the home and the church.
- And the list could go on.

Now, there are also some things about which we do not agree doctrinally and theologically. For example:

- the exact nature of human depravity and transmission of the sin nature;
- the precise constitution of the human person;
- the issue of whether or not Christ could have sinned (We all agree He did not!);

- the *ordo salutis* ("order of salvation");
- the number of elders and the precise nature of congregational governance;
- the continuance of certain spiritual gifts and their nature;
- whether baptism requires only a right member (born again), right meaning (believer's), and right mode (immersion), or whether it also requires the right administrator (however that is defined);
- the time of the rapture (pre-, mid-, or post-trib; partial rapture or pre-wrath rapture);
- the nature of the millennium (pre-, amill-, or post-);
- and, saving the best for last in our current context, we are not in full agreement about Calvinism and how many points one should affirm or redefine and affirm.

Now, what are we to make of all this? Can we—and if so, how can we—move ahead and work together? No one has been more helpful in helping us think rightly and wisely in this area than Al Mohler, president of The Southern Baptist Theological Seminary. His paradigm of "theological triage" gets to the heart of how we can think well theologically. In *A Theology for the Church*, he addresses the subject, and here is how he puts it:

> One essential task of the pastor is to feed the congregation and to assist Christians to think theologically in order to demonstrate discernment and authentic discipleship. . . .
>
> The pastor's concentration is a necessary theological discipline. Thus, the pastor must develop the ability to isolate what is most important in terms of theological gravity from that which is less important. I call this the process of *theological triage*. . . .
>
> The pastor must learn to discern different levels of theological importance. First-order doctrines are those that are fundamental and essential to the Christian faith. The pastor's theological instincts should seize upon any compromise on doctrines such as the full deity and humanity of Christ, the doctrine of the Trinity, the doctrine of atonement, and essentials such as justification by faith alone. Where such doctrines are compromised, the Christian faith falls. . . .
>
> Second-order doctrines are those that are essential to church life and necessary for the ordering of the local church but that, in themselves, do not define the gospel. That is to say, one may

detect an error in a doctrine at this level and still acknowledge that the person in error remains a believing Christian. . . . At the same time these differences can become so acute that it is difficult to function together in the local congregation over such an expansive theological difference.

Third-order doctrines are those that may be the ground for fruitful theological discussion and debate but that do not threaten the fellowship of the local congregation or the denomination. Christians who agree on an entire range of theological issues and doctrines may disagree over matters related to the timing and sequence of events related to Christ's return. Yet such ecclesiastical debates, while understood to be deeply important because of their biblical nature and connection to the gospel, do not constitute a ground for separation among believing Christians.

Without a proper sense of priority and discernment, the congregation [and denomination] is left to consider every theological issue to be a matter of potential conflict or, at the other extreme, to see no doctrines as worth defending if conflict is in any way possible.[5]

Brothers and sisters, some things are worth fighting over, and some things are not. Some things are worth dividing over, and some things are not. At the *Building Bridges Conference*, I put it like this, and I have not changed my mind:

Our agreement on the BFM (2000) is an asset, not a weakness. It is a plus and not a minus. If I were to pen my own confession, it would not look exactly like the BFM (2000). But then I do not want nor do I need people exactly like me in order to work together for the proclamation of the gospel of Jesus Christ and the building of His church.

Our confession is a solid foundation for a sound theology that avoids the pitfalls and quicksand of a straightjacket theology. Do we want or need a theology that rules out of bounds open theism, universalism and inclusivism, faulty perspectives on the atonement, gender-role confusion, works salvation, apostasy of true believers, infant baptism and non-congregational ecclesiologies just to name a few? Yes, we do. These theological errors have never characterized

---

5   R. Albert Mohler Jr., "The Pastor as Theologian," in *A Theology for the Church*, ed. Daniel L. Akin (B&H Academic, 2007), 930–31, emphasis original.

who we are as Southern Baptists, and they have no place in our denomination today. Inerrancy is not up for debate. The deity of Jesus and His sinless life are not up for debate. The triune nature of God as Father, Son and Holy Spirit is not up for debate. The perfect atoning work of Christ as a penal substitute for sinners is not up for debate. Salvation by grace alone through faith alone in Christ alone is not up for debate. A regenerate church is not up for debate. Believers' baptism by immersion is not up for debate. The glorious historical and personal return of Jesus Christ is not up for debate. The reality of an eternal heaven and an eternal hell is not up for debate. There is nothing soft about this kind of theology, and we must avoid a soft theology at all cost. . . .

Because of our passionate commitments to the glory of God, the lordship of Christ, biblical authority, salvation by grace through faith, and the Great Commission, we should be able to work in wonderful harmony with each other.[6]

We have a sound theology. The 2000 *Baptist Faith and Message* is a solid confession for building theological consensus for Great Commission cooperation. The promise of the Conservative Resurgence was that eventually we would find common, biblical, theological ground that would be more than enough to get us focused on the Great Commission. I think we have it, and I, for one, am ready to move ahead, and I believe the vast majority of Southern Baptists are as well!

AXIOM #6: WE MUST DEDICATE OURSELVES TO A PASSIONATE PURSUIT OF THE GREAT COMMISSION OF THE LORD JESUS ACROSS OUR NATION AND TO ALL NATIONS, ANSWERING THE CALL TO GO, DISCIPLE, BAPTIZE, AND TEACH ALL THAT THE LORD COMMANDED (MATT 28:16–20; ACTS 1:8; ROM 1:5; 15:20)

Southern Baptists were born, in part, out of a racist context and have a racist heritage. That will forever be to our shame. By God's grace and the Spirit's conviction, we publically repented of this in 1995 on our one-hundred-fiftieth anniversary, but there is still much work to do. The Southern

---

6   Daniel L. Akin, "Answering the Call to a Great Commission Resurgence," in *Calvinism: A Southern Baptist Dialogue*, ed. E. Ray Clendenen and Brad J. Waggoner (Nashville: B&H Academic, 2008), 253–54.

Baptist Convention remains a mostly middle-class, mostly white network of mostly declining churches. If you doubt what I am saying, look around today, visit a State Convention, attend an annual Southern Baptist Convention meeting, or drop in on 99 percent of our churches on any given Sunday. We can integrate the military, athletics and the workplace, but we can't integrate the body of Christ! Shame on us!

Until we get right about race, I am convinced God will not visit us with revival. The call for a Great Commission Resurgence will not move heaven, and it will be scoffed at by the world for the sham that it is! "We will love you and welcome you if you look like us and act like us!" What kind of gospel madness is this?

Starting at home, we must pursue a vision for our churches that looks like heaven. Yes, we must go around the world to reach Asians and Europeans, Africans and South Americans. But we must also go across the street, down the road, and into every corner of our local mission field where God in grace has brought the nations here.

This will demand little boys sitting down and men of God standing up. Reaching, for example, Muslim men, will require Christian men! This will demand a radical reorienting of lifestyles, priorities, commitments, and perspectives. Business as usual as a denomination and as individuals will not be an option if a real Great Commission Resurgence is to take place. We must take seriously each essential component of the Great Commission: Go . . . disciple . . . baptize . . . and teach them to obey all that Christ has commanded.

This means planting authentically Bible/Baptist churches and filling them with authentic followers of Jesus, irrespective of nationality, race, economic or social status. Genuine discipleship is not negotiable. We must train them and equip them to reproduce and then move on to those fields yet to hear the name of Jesus, inviting them to join us in the glorious assignment our Lord has given to all of His disciples.

AXIOM #7: WE MUST COVENANT TO BUILD GOSPEL-SATURATED HOMES THAT SEE CHILDREN AS A GIFT FROM GOD AND AS OUR FIRST AND PRIMARY MISSION FIELD (DEUT 6:1–9; PSS 127, 128; EPH 6:4)

The sirens of modernity have seduced Southern Baptists in a very important place. We have been seduced in how we do family and how many we should have in the home.

We have been seduced with respect to the gift of children. "Children are a burden, not a blessing. Less is best, or at least less is better. Result: have less children!"

We have been seduced with respect to the importance of motherhood. "It is an inferior calling. It can be delegated, at least in part, to another."

We have been seduced with respect to the role of dad. "He is a bumbling idiot. He is not necessary, maybe not even needed."

We have been seduced with respect to what a good home is and does. Let me clarify what a good home looks like. It loves Jesus. It honors God. It teaches the Bible. It casts a vision for spiritual greatness. It has fun! It lets go so that our children may soar for the glory of God!

Will you pray for God to call your children and grandchildren into vocational ministry? To go to the nations far away and to the hard places as an international missionary? Will you get a Godward perspective for life, for marriage, for family?

AXIOM #8: WE MUST RECOGNIZE THE NEED TO RETHINK OUR CONVENTION STRUCTURE AND IDENTITY SO THAT WE MAXIMIZE OUR ENERGY AND RESOURCES FOR THE FULFILLING OF THE GREAT COMMISSION (1 COR 10:31)

Here we address what will probably be most controversial and generate the most debate, discussion, and even opposition. However, it is here that the most frustration is felt. Too much of the Southern Baptist Convention is aiming at a culture that went out of existence years ago. Using mid-twentieth-century methods and strategies, we cannot understand why they are not working in the twenty-first century.

In addition, we have become bloated and bureaucratic. It is easier to move some things through the Federal government than through the Southern Baptist Convention. Overlap and duplication in our associations, state, and national conventions is strangling us. If folks in the pew knew how much of their giving stayed in their state, they would revolt and call for a revolution! Praise God, I live in a state where our Convention leaders are trying to do something about this. Their tribe must increase. We waste too much time and too many resources, and many are fed up saying, "Enough is enough!" The rallying cry of the Conservative Resurgence was, "We will not give our monies to liberal institutions." Now the cry of the Great Commission Resurgence is, "We will not give our money to bloated bureaucracies."

LifeWay president Thom Rainer has challenged us to do simple church.[7] I want to challenge us to do simple Convention. Let's streamline our structure, clarify our identity, and maximize our resources. How? I put forth the following as food for thought in the days ahead. This list is by no means exhaustive. Ask:

- Is there not a way to have annual meetings on the national and state levels that are attractive, inspiring, and worth attending? I confess if I were not required to attend, I am not sure I would go to our yearly meetings either! So much of what we do is unnecessary and will never allow us to build momentum for the Great Commission.
- Is the name "Southern Baptist Convention" best for identifying who we are and want to be in the future?
- Do we need all the boards and agencies we currently have, or could there be some healthy and wise mergers?
- Do we have a healthy structure and mechanism for planting churches that will thrive and survive past a few years?
- Do we have a giving program that fairly and accurately reflects the gifts many Southern Baptist churches are making to the work of our denomination?
- Are we distracted by doing many good things but not giving our full attention to the best things?

Church planting in the United States, pioneer missions around the world, and theological education that starts in the seminaries but finds its way to the local church is a three-legged stool I believe most Southern Baptists would gladly occupy! Let others do what they can do. Let us focus on what only Christ has commissioned us to do. Prioritize and simplify.

Our mission will require aggressive and intentional cooperation in church planting. The churches we plant must be sound in their doctrine, contextual in their forms, and aggressive in their evangelistic and mission orientation. In order to make this work, we need renewed commitment from our churches, local associations, and state conventions. For local associations, this is an opportunity to demonstrate that we still need them and

---

7 Thom S. Rainer and Eric Geiger, *Simple Church* (Nashville: B&H, 2006).

that their existence matters. In days gone by, local associations provided local churches with mission resources and advice that other institutions, networks, and people now provide. For state conventions, this provides an opportunity to return to their roots and stem the tide of churches that are bypassing (and many more that will) state conventions because they refuse to give money to what they consider to be bloated and inefficient bureaucracies with red tape a mile long.

We need to kill and bury all sacred cows. We need to start talking publicly about what so many are whispering privately. Nothing less than a new vision and a new paradigm for effective and efficient cooperation will inspire a new generation to get on board and stay on board.

AXIOM #9: WE MUST SEE THE NECESSITY FOR PASTORS TO BE FAITHFUL BIBLE PREACHERS WHO TEACH US BOTH THE CONTENT OF THE SCRIPTURES AND THE THEOLOGY EMBEDDED IN THE SCRIPTURES (2 TIM 4:1–5)

Today I sense a real hunger in a younger generation for strong Bible teaching and Christian theology. That is a wonderfully positive sign. With the waning of a cultural Christianity that cannot survive the attacks of a sophisticated and growing secularism, only faithful teaching of the Bible will equip twenty-first-century believers to stand strong as defenders of the faith once for all delivered to the saints (Jude 3).

We need a new battalion of well-trained expositors who preach the whole Bible book by book, chapter by chapter, verse by verse, phrase by phrase and word by word. Those who expound the Bible faithfully, theologically, and practically will work the hardest, sweat the most, and wrestle with God and His Word with the greatest time investment and intensity.

Walt Kaiser is exactly right when he says, "One of the most depressing spectacles in the church today is her lack of power. . . . At the heart of this problem is an impotent pulpit."[8] I am absolutely convinced there is a genetic connection between an impotent pulpit and an indifference concerning the Great Commission. Too many of our people know neither the content of Scripture nor the doctrines of Scripture. The cross of Christ, His bloody atonement, and the lostness of humanity are often absent from

---

8 Walter C. Kaiser Jr., *Toward an Exegetical Theology* (Grand Rapids: Baker, 1981), 235–36.

preaching. Some pulpiteers simply want to be cute or edgy. If the Bible is used at all, it is usually as a proof-text out of context with no real connection to what the biblical author is saying.

Such men are guilty of ministerial malpractice on their congregation. Some topical preaching, narrative preaching, emerging preaching, and yes, even some types of doctrinal preaching, fundamentally suggest by their method and practice that the Holy Spirit should have packaged the Bible differently. This is spiritually ignorant at best and arrogant at worst.

What our churches need is "expository preaching that is text driven and honors the truth of Scripture as it was given by the Holy Spirit." Mark Dever well says, "The first mark of a healthy church is expository preaching. It is not only the first mark; it is far and away the most important of them all, because if you get this one right, all of the others should follow."[9] Mark is absolutely right in my judgment.

The faithful expositor will be humbled, even haunted, by the realization that when he stands to preach he stands to preach what has been given by the Holy Spirit of God. J. I. Packer, referring to the Westminster Directory (AD 1645), captures well what we are after: "The true idea of preaching is that the preacher should become a mouthpiece for his text, opening it up and applying it as a word from God to his hearers . . . in order that the text may speak . . . and be heard, making each point from his text in such a manner 'that [his audience] may discern [the voice of God].'"[10]

A faithful minister of the Word will bombard every text with questions that many preachers of the Holy Scripture never ask, questions that will inspire and equip a congregation to become competent systematic theologians.

1. What does this text say about the Bible (and the doctrine of Revelation)?
2. What does this text say about God (also Creation, angelology)?
3. What does this text say about humanity (and sin, our fallenness)?
4. What does this text say about Jesus Christ (His person and work)?
5. What does this text say about the Holy Spirit?
6. What does this text say about salvation?

---

9   Mark Dever, *Nine Marks of a Healthy Church* (Wheaton: Crossway, 2004), 39.
10   J. I. Packer, *God Has Spoken* (London: Hodder and Stoughton, 1979), 28.

7. What does this text say about the Church?
8. What does this text say about last things?

In particular, he will take note of what Jesus said in John 15:26, "When the Counselor comes, whom I will send to you from the Father—the Spirit of truth who proceeds from the Father—He will testify about me," and again John 16:14, where Jesus adds, "He [the Holy Spirit] will glorify Me." Call it what you will, preaching that does not exalt, magnify, and glorify the Lord Jesus is not Christian preaching. Preaching that does not present the gospel and call men and women to repent of sin and place their faith in the death and resurrection of Jesus Christ is not gospel preaching. We are not Jewish rabbis or scribes. Good and faithful exposition will be Christological in focus. It will carefully interpret each text in the greater context of the grand redemptive storyline of Scripture showing Jesus as the hero of the Bible.

Brothers, we are not journey guides, self-help gurus, positive thinkers, entertainers, comedians, or liberal or conservative commentators, parroting the wisdom of the world. We are gospel preachers, Jesus-intoxicated heralds! Any theology that does not compel you to plead with people to be reconciled with God is a theology not worth having. Any preaching that does not expect the living and powerful Word of God to produce results and usher in conversions is preaching that should be retired to the graveyard where it rightfully belongs.

Bad preaching will sap the life of a church. It will kill its spirit, dry up its fruit, and eventually empty it. It is preaching that will torpedo a Great Commission Resurgence.

AXIOM #10: WE MUST ENCOURAGE PASTORS TO SEE THEMSELVES AS THE HEAD OF A GOSPEL MISSIONS AGENCY WHO WILL LEAD THE WAY IN CALLING OUT THE CALLED FOR INTERNATIONAL ASSIGNMENTS BUT ALSO EQUIP AND TRAIN ALL THEIR PEOPLE TO SEE THEMSELVES AS MISSIONARIES FOR JESUS REGARDLESS OF WHERE THEY LIVE (EPH 4:11–16)

Missions is not a ministry of the church; it is at the heart of the church's identity and essence. The strategic and biblical importance of the local church in this regard must be recaptured. Our churches do not exist to serve the Southern Baptist Convention. The Southern Baptist Convention at all levels exists to serve the churches—end of discussion!

The local church is to be ground zero for the *missio dei*. Here is the "spiritual outpost" for the invasion of enemy territory as we reclaim lost ground for its rightful owner King Jesus. A new vision that I pray will grip the churches of the Southern Baptist Convention is, "every church a church-planting church!"

Pastors must be seized by a vision for the strategic importance of their calling as the head of a gospel mission agency called the local church. This will involve:

1. Being used by God to call out the called who have an overseas assignment given by our commander-in-chief, the Lord Jesus.
2. Partnering in strategic and vibrant church planting that assaults the major population centers of North America following closely the pattern of the apostle Paul. This alone will inspire and energize a younger generation because of the excitement entailed in a new work. Furthermore, and we must never forget, urban centers such as New York, Washington, Boston, Los Angeles, and Seattle are powerfully influential in national and international affairs, and almost completely bereft of evangelical influence.
3. Working to help revitalize existing local congregations so that we do not lose a meaningful past and squander massive assets built by our parents and grandparents.
4. Training all of our people to see themselves as God-called missionaries no matter what their vocation or location happens to be. God has gifted them, and we must equip them for their service of ministry and missionary service in their community, school, workplace, and places of recreation.

Religious practices and traditions are not the same as missionary and gospel living. We must help our people recognize the difference. No one has addressed this better than Tim Keller, who in The Missional Church [and if you don't like the word "missional" then think "missionary"] writes:

> The missional church avoids "tribal" language, stylized prayer language, unnecessary evangelical pious "jargon," and archaic language that seeks to set a "spiritual tone." The missional church avoids "we-them" language, disdainful jokes that mock people of different

politics and beliefs, and dismissive, disrespectful comments about those who differ with us. The missional church avoids sentimental, pompous, "inspirational" talk. Instead, we engage the culture with the gentle, self-deprecating, but joyful irony the gospel creates. Humility + joy = gospel irony and realism. The missional church avoids ever talking as if non-believing people are not present. If you speak and discourse as if your whole neighborhood is present (not just scattered Christians), eventually more and more of your neighborhood will find their way in or be invited. Unless all of the above is the outflow of a truly humble-bold gospel-changed heart, it is all just "marketing" and "spin."[11]

AXIOM #11: WE MUST PLEDGE OURSELVES TO A RENEWED COOPERATION THAT IS GOSPEL-CENTERED AND BUILT AROUND A BIBLICAL AND THEOLOGICAL CORE AND NOT METHODOLOGICAL CONSENSUS OR AGREEMENT (PHIL 2:1–5; 4:2–9)

There are essential and nonnegotiable components of biblical worship and work. There is no specific biblical style or method ordained by our God. Look all you like—it is not there!

What will unite Southern Baptists in the future will not be style, methodology, and preference. Any past hegemony of methods and programs is gone, and it is not coming back. How we do things will be expansive and diverse. The key will be that what we do is filtered through the purifying waters of Scripture so that we honor Jesus and glorify the Father in all that we do.

Different contexts will demand different strategies and methods. Cultivating the mind of a missionary, we will ask, "What is the best way to reach the people I live amongst with the gospel?" Waycross, Georgia, will look different than Las Vegas, Nevada. Montgomery, Alabama, will look different than Portland, Oregon. Boston will be different than Dallas. Memphis will have a different strategy than Miami. Various ethnic believers and social/cultural tribes will worship the same God, adore the same Jesus, believe the same Bible, and preach the same gospel. However, they may

---

11 Tim Keller, "The Missional Church," available online from http://www.redeemer2.com/resources/papers/missional/pdf.

meet in different kinds of structures, wear different kinds of clothes, sing different kinds of songs, and engage in different kinds of ministries.

The point is simply this: we must treat the United States missiologically and do so with the same seriousness that our international missionaries treat their people groups missiologically. As long as it is done for the glory of God, has biblical warrant, and theological integrity, I say, Praise the Lord! So, let's stop griping about organs, choirs and choir robes, guitars, drums, coats and ties, and get on with the real issue of the Great Commission.

If we seek to build a consensus around style or methods, we will continue to balkanize, fracture, and lose important ground. If we will build a consensus around Jesus and the gospel, we can—we will—cooperate for the advancement of God's kingdom, and He will bless us.

Theology should drive our cooperation, not tradition. The message of the gospel will unite us, not methods.

AXIOM #12: WE MUST ACCEPT OUR CONSTANT NEED TO HUMBLE OURSELVES AND REPENT OF PRIDE, ARROGANCE, JEALOUSY, HATRED, CONTENTIONS, LYING, SELFISH AMBITIONS, LAZINESS, COMPLACENCY, IDOLATRIES AND OTHER SINS OF THE FLESH, PLEADING WITH OUR LORD TO DO WHAT ONLY HE CAN DO IN US AND THROUGH US AND ALL FOR HIS GLORY (GAL 5:22–26; JAS 4:1–10)

Pride—young leaders saying, "I do not need the insights of godly, seasoned ministers." Or, we look at ourselves and say, "Look at what the Southern Baptist convention is and has done!" God does not need the Southern Baptist Convention. We think more of ourselves than we ought.

Arrogance—veteran pastors saying, "We know what is best because we have been there and done that. Younger brothers and sisters need to sit back and be quiet. When we need them, we will let them know."

Jealousy—the attitude that does not want God to bless others and leave me/us out.

Hatred—loathing others you should love.

Contentions—fighting over things that are not essential and acting as unchristian as the world.

Lying—purposefully misrepresenting others or not taking the time to accurately understand them.

Selfish ambition—wanting a place of leadership rather than earning it. A love for running a church or denomination more than a love for serving it.

Laziness—not doing the hard work of ministry because it is costly.

Complacency—being satisfied with the status quo and being in denial that we are in a crisis moment that could be fatal.

Idolatries—putting anything or anyone in the place of Jesus and His agenda for His church.

CONCLUSION

I am convinced we can be better than this. I also am convinced that we can do more together than we could ever do apart. That is why I am in this to the end whenever or however it may come.

However, we have to stop doing everything we do "for us!" In many ways, we have become a selfish people. We must once more start doing what we do for others, beginning with Jesus.

God is going to turn this world upside down. We can be a part of this if we are more passionate for His glory than for our conveniences and comfort. God is going to turn this world upside down, and we can be a part of it if we humble ourselves and focus on loving each other and working with each other to seek and save the lost. Older believers need to acknowledge, "We need the energy and fresh ideas of a younger generation." Younger believers need to realize, "We need the wisdom and experience of our parents and grandparents." We really do need each other.

Finally, we desperately need the heart of Jesus. We need the eyes of Jesus. If we can get to that, we will have what we need to move forward as a mighty Great Commission army going forth to do battle for the Captain of our Salvation and the Savior of Souls. If not, we will find ourselves on the sidelines playing silly and meaningless games while God's mighty army moves on without us.

Brothers and sisters, I have found the army with whom I want to fight. It's called the church. I have found the Commander-in-Chief I want to serve. His name is Jesus. I have found the enemy I want to destroy. It is Satan, sin, death, and hell. Will you join me? There is victory for the taking!

READY OR NOT, A NEW SBC IS COMING

PARTNERING WITH OUR SONS AND DAUGHTERS FOR A GREAT COMMISSION FUTURE

Ed Stetzer and Philip Nation

The SBC is struggling with generational transition, but that should not surprise us. Generational change is always fraught with challenges in our families, homes, and churches, so we should not be surprised to see the same in our denomination. It is normal.

The first day of school makes little boys and girls nervous. But most parents are terrified by the thought of letting them go. Multiple concerns race through the minds of parents who want the best for their children. Out of the apparent safe haven of home, children must confront the world for the first time. Are they ready? Will they succeed? Will they be hurt? Will they fail? How well did we prepare them? Questions continue to torment nervous parents.

Fast-forward to another vivid image—teaching your teenager to drive. Maybe you are not there yet. Good for you. If you have been there, you can relate. Even more terror grips your soul as you fear everything from wrecked cars, to insurance rates, to the personal safety of your teenager and other passengers. You have major legitimate concerns. How can I guarantee my child will be safe? How can I protect my personal property? Are they ready for such a responsibility? Here is something, in your darkest moment, you never consider. You never consider stopping them. Why? Well there are many reasons you do not seriously consider stopping them. On the top of the list is something to the effect of, "It will not do any good to try, I could not stop them even if I wanted to."

Parenting is filled with fears, challenges, and transitions. When the transition involves "letting go," your life as a parent feels like a movie. Time stands still at the kindergarten class, the driver's license bureau, the college dorm room, and the wedding altar. Your babies are coming of age. Children become "grown-ups" right before our eyes. Your relationship with them changes through every major passage. You learn something about yourself as well as them. Letting go is never easy, but there is no way to stop the process. Time makes change happen. We can't control time or change. We can only prepare for the inevitabilities of our future.

There may be a knot in the stomachs of current SBC leaders, but the reality is a new generation of leaders is coming of age. Our young SBC leaders are ready and able to get behind the wheel. So, what are our options?

OPTION #1: TRY TO STOP THEM

I guess if I wanted to stop my daughters from driving I could rent construction barriers and line them on the streets in my neighborhood. I could make it as complicated as possible to test their maturity and commitment to my values. None of this will work if my goal is to keep them from behind the wheel. Eventually they will drive with or without my support.

We can do the same things to our sons and daughters who are becoming the young leaders in the SBC. We can challenge their commitment level and test their loyalty. We can create roadblocks to fellowship and cooperation. We can make church planting as complicated as possible. We can do all kinds of things to make us feel better. We may feel it is to protect the faith or the Southern Baptist movement. But eventually they will lead with or without our permission.

The reality may be that we are not ready to pass the mantle of leadership. Embedded in the first option is an attitude that we can force young leaders to be loyal to the denomination. Be it right or wrong, young leaders do not possess the same sense of duty toward the denomination as past generations. But remember, they are going to drive—something. To try to stop them does more harm than good. Engaging them and learning together can make all the difference.

OPTION #2: ALIENATE THEM

Alienation occurs when the conversation moves from theological and methodological realms and degenerates to the personal realm. Don't get me wrong, theological and methodological discussions can be personal. But when the integrity, competency, intelligence, and motivation of next generation leaders are questioned, a whole new level of damage is done. Young leaders are actively pushed away.

The first step in organizational decline is that you lose your creative people, who decide to go on to more entrepreneurial settings. We have already lost many of these creative thinkers. In fact, some have actively pushed many of them out by teaching and preaching against them in many SBC conferences and conventions. The next step in decline is that the most competent begin to leave. They become convinced that the effort is not worth the hassle. As they perceive the current leaders defending systems with what they see as ineffectual means to the missional task of the church, they rightly feel like an outsider and walk away disaffected.

Many Purpose-Driven/contemporary church pastors believe we have already told a generation they are not really needed or wanted in today's SBC. Are we intent on communicating this same message to the next generation?

When then-LifeWay president Jimmy Draper was planning the first national "Young Leaders" meeting, he asked me for suggested speakers. I told him what we needed most was a nationally known pastor who had credibility with young pastors and who was also still clearly connected with the denomination. His voice went up with excitement: "Exactly! Who?" With sadness I replied, "That's my point."

Some deconstructionists among us scream "the sky is falling" concerning the young leaders and the SBC. I am not convinced. God uses prophetic voices to wake us up to reality. And the reality is that our track record since the Conservative Resurgence has not been stellar in embracing younger leaders, their ideas, or their methodologies. But new leaders are emerging every day.

On a positive note, I am glad to report that this is changing in today's SBC. I have seen the environment begin to shift over the last several years, and I believe that younger leaders are increasingly ready to respond. Their bent is more toward kingdom and cooperation than you might realize. The potential for a stronger Great Commission-driven SBC over the next twenty years may be better than you think. But we must be careful not to alienate the young leaders who love Christ and His gospel but practice ministry differently from previous generations.

OPTION #3: BE APATHETIC

In my years of denominational work I have met many pastors and church leaders who invest extra energy in the denomination. I respect that investment. I understand how exhausting it is to lead a single church, much less serve on an associational, state, or national committee for our convention. It is easy to say that you do not have the emotional energy to invest in one more activity, one more person. Deciding to invest in a young leader will require an amount of energy many are simply unwilling to give. Yet by doing so, you are investing in the fulfillment of the Great Commission through the SBC.

Our leaders have become apathetic toward helping young leaders for a myriad of reasons. It takes too much time, the generational divide, the methodological divide, and the difference in how to assign value to the convention are a few of the major reasons some leaders will simply not engage with younger leaders. But to invest nothing in our sons and daughters is not an option if we care about the future of the SBC.

OPTION #4: BE HESITANT

No question, the young leader issue is complex. I am not proposing a unilateral "be nice to a young guy" emphasis regardless of what he says, does, or believes. Both young leaders and experienced leaders have responsibilities in the matter. But as we engage and invite young leaders to lead in the SBC, intentionality is critical. Lack of consistency kills our influence and relationships.

Young leaders need to know where they belong in SBC life. A safe place for them is critical to our future. Do they need to be challenged? Yes, but in a way that will cause them to grow as individuals and help the churches they lead. When hesitancy is shown, the possibility of influence wanes quickly. Too many young leaders have been greeted with suspicion, welcomed with a hesitant handshake, and ignored for most of their ministry.

We must be particularly careful about the meetings we expect young leaders to attend. We smile, call, shake hands, and in some instances even pay for them to come to our conventions. Upon arrival, they hear a speaker rail against them as the reason the world is going to hell. Let us not expect to have things both ways.

OPTION #5: TAKE A DEEP BREATH, HAND THEM THE KEYS, MENTOR, AND PRAY

I like this option. Our sons and daughters soon become adults. If we are willing to commission them into the leadership positions God has designed for them, we will see a return on our kingdom investment. We must commit ourselves to building relationships of mutual respect in order to build receptivity for the leadership lessons that we need to give them.

At times, young leaders will drive you nuts and you will feel disrespected. Do not worry—they sometimes feel the same way about you. So remember this equation:

Respect = Receptivity
Receptivity = Influence
Influence = Leadership

The truth is, we can build walls or we can build bridges for our sons and daughters. What makes the most sense in light of our current reality? Being driven by the Great Commission and the need for billions of people to see and hear the gospel, each harvester is mission critical. In fact, we will see a harvester as a more important investment than the harvest. Let me say it another way: *An investment in a harvester is a true investment in the harvest.* The multiplication of harvesters is the key to our hopes for the harvest. If we are not thinking multiplication, then we are not thinking harvest. Jesus said it this way, "Therefore, pray to the Lord of the harvest to send out workers into His harvest" (Matt 9:38).

WHAT VALUES WILL DRIVE OUR RELATIONSHIPS WITH YOUNG LEADERS?

In his influential book, *The Present Future*, Reggie McNeal proposed six mindset shifts critical to the future of the local church. I believe one shift in particular is essential for the transition in leadership to our sons and daughters in the body of Christ. McNeal's proposed shift from planning for the future to preparing them for the future is vital. Planning involves prediction and assumes control. Preparing involves prayerful strategy and succession plans.

McNeal wrote, "God is making waves all around the North American church. Some churches are going to get to ride them. These are the churches prepared to get in on what God is up to."[1] In this matrix, the difference between planning and preparing is simple: relationships. Planning assumes a first-person execution of the work. Preparing assumes the rise of others to lead the work. The decision to value and prepare young leaders is critical for the future of our churches. But the preparation must be in the context of relationships

To my dismay, too often in denominational leadership, when a young leader is elevated, work behind the scenes is done to make sure that leader can be trusted. By trusted, I mean that those in power have control over his ascent, thinking, and methodology. For some, young leaders must be robots who think, talk, and dress just like us. They must speak our code language. Everything must be neatly scripted. We must reject the need for generational clones and choose new generation leaders.

Our sons and daughters seldom become carbon copies of us. It is a fact that frustrates some parents. When they do copy us, too often it is our bad traits they retain. They may embrace our values, but our sons and daughters tend to wander in their younger years. Though they will operate differently, we should welcome them into close community in order to prepare them as leaders.

New leadership is emerging in the SBC. We must prepare by investing in those who will lead. Often our relationships are formed by circumstance, fears, and feelings. Our relationships with our new leadership must be shaped by values, not feelings. Here are some critical values to consider. But this is a process being shaped by God Himself. We should join Him if we want to be part of the new thing He will do.

Preserve the Relationship

Young leaders need connectedness to those who went before them. In turn, spiritual parents need to release them. Ironic, is it not? We both need each other desperately, but are dysfunctional in the realities of our relationships.

Paul and Timothy are models for the need for an ongoing relationship between generations. A spiritual son relating to a spiritual father is a

---

1 Reggie McNeal, *The Present Future: Six Tough Questions for the Church* (San Francisco: Jossey-Bass, 2003), 92–93.

relationship worth keeping. Young leaders should not be forced to learn to navigate the complexities of life and ministry alone. When joined together, both young and seasoned leaders fulfill their personal callings while the influence of the gospel multiplies.

We all know that relationships, like gardens, require attention, time, and patience for long-term health. Unfortunately, those who have the potential to be a spiritual sponsor to a young leader can sabotage the opportunity through uninformed opinions. One pastor hears rumors about what a young pastor is doing at his church and lashes out at him in a local meeting. Consider the impact if instead the mentor remained in constant contact with the young leader to give guidance, reproof, and shelter from unwarranted attacks at said meetings. Younger leaders are worth the energy and investment long-term.

Shallow, short-term attempts to relate to young leaders will be counterproductive in the long haul. High-profile lunches and "bridge builder" meetings are only as good as the personal investment that comes out of the meeting.

Keep Listening to Their Heart

When is the last time you invested in a young leader to the level that you could hear his or her heartbeat? If you were close enough to hear their heartbeat your opinion might change. You might see who that leader is and why that leader does what he does in a new light. What would a relationship like that look like? How could you keep that kind of closeness to young leaders?

Not too long ago, I was a young leader. I now spend much of my time around young leaders. Without hesitation, I find them to have a great heart for God's kingdom expressed through His church. The future of the SBC and their future depend on people like you who care enough to listen to their heart.

Keep Communication Channels Open

I am amazed at the commitment young leaders have shown just to sit down and talk with me. It is humbling. They will travel for miles at great personal expense just to talk for an hour. Why? Young leaders are hungry to learn. They are hungry to learn from you, too. What are you doing to make yourself accessible to young leaders? How do they really know you would invest in them?

Become an Advocate

I was moved when Daniel Montgomery, founder and lead pastor of Sojourn Church in Louisville, Kentucky, shared about our relationship via video at the *Baptist21* meeting during the 2009 Southern Baptist Convention annual meeting. He confessed that he made many mistakes. And yes, I took some arrows for him, but I am glad I did. God has used him in powerful ways. I remember back when Sojourn was only two people. Now it is a great force for the gospel in urban Louisville. I have stood up for other young pastors. They have made mistakes and we have worked through them together. But I believe that the results of patience and exhortation are worth the arrows along the way.

Our convention would be different if older leaders stood with the younger leaders—encouraging, admonishing, and helping. After all, these are your children. We can walk with one another, not work against each other. We can fight for one another, not with one another.

Become a Strategic Intercessor

We naturally pray for our sons and daughters. Some of our prayer is based on concern for their future. They will make choices and face challenges that are beyond anything we have seen or known. One of the ways we prepare for the future is to pray for our leaders. How encouraging would it be for a young leader to know that a senior pastor of a local church was investing time praying for him or with him? We can be an agent of God's plan for change through those prayers.

View Young Leaders as Family

I think you are beginning to get the idea here. Emotional detachment from young leaders will demoralize them and put the SBC's future in jeopardy. To ignore or criticize people from a distance, however, is lazy and irresponsible. In fact, let me get a bit more prophetic . . . to ignore and criticize young leaders from a distance is dysfunctional and ungodly. It is unwise for the SBC and it is unbiblical.

The New Testament is clear that collectively we are the household of God. Treating our own children as many have treated the young leaders of our convention would be seen as dysfunctional at best.

What if the next church planter who called you was your own son? How would you handle the conversation? How well would you listen? He is somebody's son. The next generation of leaders is made up of our spiritual sons and daughters. We should treat them as the prize possession they are in Christ.

GET TO KNOW YOUR SONS AND DAUGHTERS— WHAT ARE THEY REALLY LIKE?

One thing is for sure: your sons and daughters are not like you. That statement is not meant as an insult but simply as an observation of reality. Were you like your mother and father? Did you value what they valued? Did you listen to their music? Did you watch their television shows? Did you wear the clothes that they wore? Did you even eat the same food they ate? If your answer is anything close to yes, it was not the case for very long.

If you were churched you experienced a "youth ministry" wave that was near movement proportions in the 1970s and 1980s. You were separated from your parents the minute you set foot on the church property. Why? Because you were different from them. Your church was committed to give you church the way you liked it. Oh, they had an agenda for you—to find and follow Jesus. But they cared enough to show you Christ in your language, through the lens of your world. Your youth minister stayed in trouble for everything—from the length of guys' hair, to loud music, to the girl you kissed during the church lock-in. It is critical, however, that the discussion eventually moves beyond generational differences and beyond youth culture, as there are greater realities.

Take for example the high school graduating class of 1977. They listened to the Bee Gees, The Eagles, and Stevie Wonder music via eight-track tapes (try Google images if you are clueless here). Their president (Jimmy Carter) claimed to be "born again" yet confessed (much to everyone's discomfort) that he had lusted after many women. Cable television was coming of age. The class of 1977 would see more in their teenage years than their parents (every generation does). The US population that year was 216 million, and the average cost of a house was $49,000.[2] In 1977 Elvis Presley died, *Star Wars* was a hit movie, and the miniseries *Roots* profoundly influenced America.

The big idea behind presenting this snapshot of 1977 is to illustrate *how much and how rapidly America changes*. In fact, more specifically, America changes because people change. Much has been written about these subjects. The class of '77's parents generally graduated in the 1950s. How different was America for them? The big idea can be illustrated over and over again.

Most of the class of '77 turned 50 years old in calendar year 2009. The majority of their children would have been born in the 1980s. Now, their children are between 20 and 30 years old. To fast forward this discussion we will not attempt to document their world, jammed with fast-paced, rapidly evolving technology. Their music, politics, and fashion information is easily accessible . . . via the Internet. The real question is, "How much has the mission field of America changed since 1977?" An even more relevant question is, "How much have the missionaries of America changed since 1977?"

George Barna called the children of the 80s the "Third Millennium Teens" in his 1999 research report.[3] He predicted they would represent the "changing of the generational guard." Since then they have been tagged "Millennials," those born from 1981 to 2000. Barna's prediction has come true. The Millennials are our sons and daughters. The generation born from 1965 to 1980 might be who we perceive is of immediate importance to the SBC (ages 31–45). They are important. But a historically unprecedented characteristic of both groups could inform our relationships. Barna connected the characteristic with both generations. He made a critical observation about Third Millennium Teens:

> One of the most important of these insights is that teenagers are quite comfortable with contradictions. While their parents tend to focus on reconciling competing points of view–e.g., assessing blame, identifying appropriate and inappropriate, choosing the better of the options–young people are more relaxed about the

---

2 "The Year 1977" [article on-line]; accessed 6 January 2010; available from http://www.thep eoplehistory.com/1977.html; Internet.

3 See George Barna, *Third Millennium Teens: A Report by George Barna* (Ventura, CA: Barna Research Group, 1999).

tensions that reside in the world. This comfort level is partially a function of their thinking style (i.e., mosaic rather than linear) and partly a reflection of their comfort with diversity and inclusivity.[4]

A key to understanding other people is to listen to them. Young leaders have reasons for the decisions they make and the ways they act. God is speaking to them, too. At times they struggle to know and do the will of God . . . just like you. So understand them first as you engage them in relationship.

Our younger leaders see the world differently. They have learned to live with the contradictions inherent to the current culture. Their world of politics, entertainment, church, and family is filled with inconsistencies. The issues move beyond moral and spiritual contradictions. They see the world through different lenses because they were raised in a different world. The argument is not that they see the world better, just differently than the previous generation.

Critical to knowing the younger generation is to understand that generational differences are not always theological differences. But many older leaders have sabotaged relationships with younger leaders by interpreting the differences as such, and many younger leaders have done the same by misunderstanding those older. Certain theological differences do exist and we should explore them. My fear, however, is that without healthy relationships, leaders from the previous generation will not have the credibility to engage the discussion with young leaders. Our sons and daughters need our mentoring and support as they navigate their world.

God prepared you to do ministry in your generation. Your context for ministry still exists. Meaningful roles and assignments will be here until God is finished with you on earth. The way you have "done" ministry has likely evolved, too. Why? Because the world has changed.

Do a quick journaling exercise. On a piece of paper, write down your ministry years in ten-year increments and give a 2–3 sentence answer to the questions below for each increment (you may even want to consider five-year increments). Then compare your increments.

- What was the world like?
- What was I doing in ministry?

---

4 Ibid., 61.

- How was I doing it?
- What were the important ministry tasks to me?
- What changes did I make since the previous period?

Few of you are doing ministry exactly the way you did ministry in the 1980s. And don't forget that few of you were concerned with what previous generations thought about the way you did ministry in the 1980s. We are holding our sons and daughters to a standard to which we did not adhere. You are a missionary *in* your generation. Your sons and daughters will do ministry in a different generation. Should they think like you in order to reach people like them? Could you have thought like your father and mother and remained effective in your ministry contexts?

So, how do we proceed? First, we need to acknowledge that God is working in many different ways. God is raising an army of new missionaries to carry the gospel to the next generation. The only reason that we should ask them to be like you is if God calls them to reach people exactly like you. Mostly, that will not be the case. Instead, we should celebrate the difference found in them that will allow God to work through them to reach the lost indigenous cultures of America and the world.

It is high time for us to stand with our sons and daughters! God is shaping new missionaries with new passions to engage their generation with the Gospel of Jesus Christ. They bring different strengths to the table. These strengths are not better than yours but they are different. What do you need to know to help understand them? What are younger leaders like? The suggestions below are by no means exhaustive, but they will give you an overview of younger leaders in the SBC.

Socially Conscious

Frank (not his real name) grew up in a wealthy family in the old South. After earning undergraduate and graduate degrees and working for a number of years he began a pattern of major drug and alcohol abuse. Frank also began living an openly homosexual lifestyle. Through relationship failure and lost jobs, Frank continued to dig deeper into the world of drugs. Frank, despite his educational degrees, found himself on the streets as a homeless man who had nothing. He was in deep depression and in search of the next drug he could get his hands on.

Through some believers pouring their lives into Frank, sharing the gospel with him, and exposing him to Christian community, Frank surrendered his life to Christ. Frank is now working, off the streets, and living in a transitional home in a downtown Southern city. He is involved in the church and is working through sin issues. Frank is looking forward to being at a place to be able to help others who have been where he was.

Frank's story came through the ministry of Midtown Fellowship in Columbia, South Carolina. The church of twenty-somethings is four years old. Midtown engages thousands of people through social ministries to the homeless, sick, orphaned, and poor. Pastor/Planter Dustin Willis, 29, said, "Too many times we see needs and are maybe even moved to tears, but do nothing. That is us being sentimental. The truth is we are called to do something about it. That is compassion." Hundreds of next generation churches throughout America have similar stories to that of Midtown.

Young leaders have engaged the needs of their community in new and deeper ways. They have a fresh sense of optimism about God's desire to change the lives of people on the margins. At LifeWay Research, we completed a survey of 1,002 Protestant pastors asking about their political ideologies and engagement with aspects of social justice in their ministries. It was our intent to compare their views and their reported actions. We also asked if they were evangelical, mainline, or Pentecostal (allowing them to select more than one option).

When the sample of 1,002 Protestant pastors is filtered by evangelicals (592 self-identified evangelicals), one question shows a statistical significance between age segments, and it deals with community service. Younger pastors speak of their churches being involved in community service at a higher level than their older counterparts. Higher than all other age groups, 35 percent of young pastors say that over 34 percent of their adult attendees are involved in ministries or projects that serve people in their community. On the other end of the spectrum, the 18 percent of young pastors who say 1–10 percent of their adults do so is significantly lower than 55–69 and 70+ age pastors.[5]

In simple terms, young pastors see a more active engagement in social ministries in their churches than older pastors. The obvious explanation is that younger pastors lead the people of their congregations to do so. But

---

5 Originally cited in a research paper by Ed Stetzer for the American Society for Church Growth, "The Gospel, The Kingdom, and Evangelism . . ." as "forthcoming from LifeWay Research," September 14, 2008.

there seems to be a fear over a return to the Social Gospel which causes conversations and relationships to break down between generations of leaders. The reactions that come have been swift and strong—rejecting this social justice as the Social Gospel in new clothes. For others, it has challenged presuppositions about how Christians might be engaged in issues that Jesus and the writers of Scripture spoke about often.

Young leaders are deeply passionate about sharing the gospel. Churches that miss out on opportunities to help them express that desire through ministries of mercy will soon miss younger leaders. Young leaders read passages from the Bible and see the concern for social justice displayed by the early church, such as the example of serving the widows in Acts 6. They believe that, by serving those less fortunate and advocating for causes outside of the reach of standard church programming, evangelism and changed lives will result. Younger leaders see this in such scriptures as this one: "So the preaching about God flourished, the number of the disciples in Jerusalem multiplied greatly, and a large group of priests became obedient to the faith" (Acts 6:7).

Young leaders see an imperative for serving those who are in need by coming around them and caring for them for the sake of and with the gospel. They embrace a faith that is deeply generous in its expression and care for others. Younger leaders are passionate about issues of social justice because they have an integrated view of justice and evangelism. Rather than replace disciple-making, as occurred during the Social Gospel era, the young leaders of the SBC are engaging in both the verbal witness and the living work inherent to redemption.

Relationally Wired

How did Paul do his apostolic work? Obviously not with training manuals, DVDs, or books. Yes, the Spirit inspired him to write letters to pastors and churches that would be included in Scripture. But, on the whole, even the Spirit-inspired letters were a part of ongoing conversations with people to whom Paul related.

Paul worked through relationships. Notice in one example, Paul's core value:

> But as for us, brothers, after we were forced to leave you for a short time (in person, not in heart), we greatly desired and made

every effort to return and see you face to face. So we wanted to come to you—even I, Paul, time and again—but Satan hindered us. For who is our hope, or joy, or crown of boasting in the presence of our Lord Jesus at His coming? Is it not you? For you are our glory and joy! (1 Thess 2:17–20)

Paul was the ultimate coach because he was thrilled by the "wins" experienced by those he helped. Paul valued people.

Hopefully, all leaders in the church place a high value on relationships. This is certainly the case for younger leaders. Relationships are what keep them coming back to anything. You seldom speak to young leaders that place a high value on institutionally sponsored training and resources. They may take advantage of these offerings but they can find events and financial support through many avenues. Southern Baptists are just one of many opportunities for such resources. But the perceived value of the denomination for young leaders is the relationships. As our hope is to keep them engaged, a high value must be placed on personal relationships in the SBC structure.

One way to ensure such efficiencies is to keep learning connected to relationships. Learning is another characteristic of young leaders. They are constantly seeking opportunities. Often times we embarrass ourselves when we try to create our own denominational version of an event like Catalyst. We just can't complete, nor should we. It would be a waste of our valuable time and resources trying. Events like Catalyst (an event that was first organized by John Maxwell and Andy Stanley among others in 1999) are designed to gather leaders across the spectrum of the church in America once a year. But our denominational learning events should seek to connect leaders in long-term relationships in the field. Some conferences (like Catalyst) are striving to do this, but we have a ready-made system to do it in our denominational structure.

As leaders, we should be able to understand and help young leaders to engage their communities. By using events, older leaders (and the denomination) can establish cohorts or clusters to meet for peer coaching and follow-up from the training events (whether denominational or parachurch like Catalyst). Focusing on relationships will allow us to leverage our resources and complement the premier events for greater kingdom impact in our communities.

Centralized denominational personnel can become communication and relationship experts. Coaching is another great value centralized denominational personnel can bring to the field. Properly trained centralized personnel can coach and use technology (video conferencing) to gather small groups of leaders and never leave the office. Again, think of the efficiency as well as the effectiveness the new way of thinking would produce by thinking like the relationally wired generation of young leaders.

To change the culture, the conversation needs to change. A consistent theme throughout this chapter has been forming more and deeper friendships with young leaders. Informal relationships, since biblical times, have been the best delivery system for Kingdom influence. But this generation may be more influenced by relationships than previous ones.

Methodologically Diverse

As previously stated, younger leaders have learned to live in a world of contradictions. All the contradictions do not necessarily have to be resolved. Because of their world of diversity, they are driven toward relating to people who are lost. Many are comfortable in the space of lost people. A high level of energy is invested in making their Sunday morning environments comfortable and relevant to people far from God.

You may have a heart for the lost as well. Your vision is similar but may have some different emphases. You may first cite this passage, "But how can they call on Him in whom they have not believed? And how can they believe without hearing about Him? And how can they hear without a preacher? And how can they preach unless they are sent? As it is written: How welcome are the feet of those who announce the gospel of good things" (Rom 10:14–15). *The "information" of the gospel is critical for those who need to know Him.*

But your sons and daughters might have a different starting point for evangelism. They may cite, "Then Jesus went to all the towns and villages, teaching in their synagogues, preaching the good news of the kingdom, and healing every disease and every sickness" (Matt 9:35). *The demonstration of the gospel may be a more likely starting point for a young leader.* One is not right and the other wrong—we need both. Hearing is needed in both cases. Compassion is also needed in both cases. The sides reconcile when we trust our sons and daughters instead of deeming one method as better than the other.

Style of worship is another methodological controversy with young leaders in our day, as it has been in every generation of the church. How many of our churches are battling through worship tensions at this moment? Successfully understanding the tensions over worship styles can provide a template for us to address other differences with young leaders. Ignoring the differences is not an option if we hope to come to a sincere understanding of this new generation of leaders. Here are four ideas to better the understanding between generations.

Truth is crucial. Jesus prayed that His church would be one (John 17:21–22). He also prayed that we would be sanctified by the truth of God's Word (John 17:17). The church often assumes that "music" equals "worship." But the truth is that worship occurs in the whole of life. We are always worshiping. Our affections are always oriented somewhere or to someone.

Discussions between older and younger generations must be based on truth rather than preferences. When we hold personal style preferences loosely, greater unity in the body of Christ and the advancement of God's mission will result. The truth God seeks is His glory among the nations. Worship is about Him and for Him. Yet we have reduced the issue to debating if we will have two hymns and three choruses or three hymns and two choruses this Sunday. Jesus told the woman at the well, "God is spirit, and those who worship Him must worship in spirit and truth" (John 4:24). Healthy dialogue about worship begins with truth.

In getting to know the younger generation of leaders in the SBC, begin with the issues of truth. Having been raised in a culture that has surrendered the ideal of truth, they are ready to learn how to understand the truth and its origins.

Preferences are personal. Preferences exist because we have a passion to do a certain thing in a certain way. Whether dealing with a pedestrian issue such as clothing style or a heavenly issue such as worship, people are passionate about their preferences. The same is true for both the "contemporary praise" and "traditional" tribes. Neither appears willing to give up ground. One group perceives themselves to be pushing forward toward the next generation (relevance). Another group is trying to pull back to a once-honored method (reverence). One group thinks a more casual style will suit the current generation and appeal more to the lost. Meanwhile, the other group thinks it is worldly compromise and an affront to a holy God. Both groups have, at times, made the mistake of elevating preferences to the level of principles. Both groups should embrace the mission of God and the good of the community as what ultimately drives worship consensus.

Relevance and reverence are complementary. Relevance for relevance's sake never helped anybody. A smart church will be biblically-driven and culturally discerning. Playing a shocking song at the front of your Easter service may get headlines and upset religious people, but that's about all it does. Neither is the traditionalist placement of reverence on external styles a solution. Reverence is a quality of the heart, not necessarily an outward expression.

The best of our leaders (both older and younger) see the two ideals of relevance and reverence as working together rather than pulling apart from one another. As my colleague Mike Harland, director of LifeWay Worship, has said, "You will never achieve spiritual goals with musical means." We see music as important in Scripture, but never a particular form or function as necessary for discipleship.

Humility wins! When I was young in the ministry, I was charged with ministry to both youth and seniors (go figure). One day I was invited to lead worship at a nursing home, so I took my guitar. I'll never forget this 92 year-old woman, Miss Langley, who put her hand on my arm and said "Don't worry about the guitar, young man, we're just gonna sing and you can sing with us." I was bringing a relevance they didn't need, and I had to be mature enough to see the hindrance I was about to become.

Imagine what would happen if worship warriors actually took on the attitude of Jesus (cf. Phil 2:5–6) and did not regard their agendas as something to be grasped. What would it look like if all of us took on the servanthood posture of seeking to approach worship consensus? What if we actually tried to outdo one another in showing honor (cf. Rom 12:10)? Humility works and is a "win" for every generation. To know the younger generation, offer to learn from them and offer yourself for them to learn from you.

Healthy relationships will seek dynamic understanding rather than sterile compromise. Rather than pandering to one generation or another, we should seek a way for all leaders to engage in mission and relationships together. If we merely seek methodological compromise, we will fight until the return of Christ about who has the better plan. Working for consensus regarding the convention's future will bring us together as leaders for the kingdom in one accord.

Theologically Conservative

Unlike most Southern Baptist pastors, I wasn't reared or redeemed in an SBC church. I was raised nominally Catholic and came to Christ in a denomination that drifted away from the gospel. Talk about "broadening the tent" theologically does not generally appeal to me. Been there, done that, seen the compromise that follows. If young leaders are not serious about theology, preaching, and cooperation, then this denomination is not the place for them.

As I wrote in *SBC Life* some years ago, doctrine matters to missions—and it matters when we seek to be "missional" as well.[6] I've learned that we constantly need to talk, think, and learn better theology. From my observations both from research and personal travel, I find that the vast majority of our SBC young leaders are theologically conservative. They care deeply about the gospel mission of the church and are willing to resource its global advancement.

Now, some young leaders consider themselves theologically conservative and methodologically liberal. I am not a big fan of the terminology, but their point is clear—they want to hold firmly to the Word of God and engage the culture in fresh new ways. That's not liberal (unless you want to call Jesus and the disciples liberals), that's just missiologically-driven.

Sometimes when young leaders use the wrong code language and their methods are foreign to us we assume something about their theology. That assumption is often unfair. If you ever wonder what young leaders believe, you can find out by checking their Web sites. By the way, most young leaders go to great lengths to explain their beliefs on their Web sites. But an even better way to find out what young leaders believe is to invest time with them. As you become better acquainted, talk about their theology (and yours). But do not forget to trust the young leaders first, as that is the key to having a solid relationship. If the new Baptist pastor down the street looks like you, dresses like you, and has VBS once a year, do you check his theology before you invite him to lunch? Give a young leader the same chance.

Baptist21 is a group of young leaders who, in their own words, are "seeking to be Baptist in the twenty-first century." They are a group of young leaders who are methodologically diverse yet theologically conservative. As they describe their purpose you can see that they represent a generational shift back to theological conservatism:

---

6 See Ed Stetzer, "Can We Do Missions Without Doing Doctrine?", *SBC Life*, February 2003 [article on-line]; accessed 14 January 2010; available from http://www.sbclife.org/articles/2003/02/sla4 .asp; Internet.

Baptist21 exists to contend for "the faith once for all delivered to the saints" (Jude 3).We embrace our past, believing this faith has been proclaimed in our Southern Baptist heritage. We work in the present, believing the Kingdom effectiveness of Southern Baptists will be in proportion to our fidelity to the Gospel. We cooperate for the future, believing the only hope for the people of the world is the Gospel of King Jesus.[7]

The B21 group is made up of our sons and daughters, in some cases literally. For example, B21 members Nathan and Jonathan Akin are sons of Danny Akin, President of Southeastern Baptist Theological Seminary. The 2000 *Baptist Faith and Message* is one of their doctrinal statements, but the list goes further, including the *Abstract of Principles* (1858), the *Chicago Statement on Biblical Inerrancy* (1978), and the *Danvers Statement on Biblical Manhood and Womanhood* (1987).

Young leaders in the SBC represent a clear shift back to a more conservative theology. Their mission field, filled with syncretism, demands such a shift. So far they seem up to the task. As you get to know them, you will be encouraged and even challenged by their clear commitment to conservative biblical theology.

Technologically Savvy

Technology changes at an incredible pace. Younger leaders have become so accustomed to the change it has become cliché to them. What amazes Boomers and other older generations does not gain the attention of the Millennials. Probably the best way to relate is to try not to act amazed. When we are amazed, we tell how old we really are!

The Pew Research Center will study the Millennial generation through a series of surveys in 2010. Preliminary reports have already provided some interesting shifts. If we are drawn to relationships, we need to understand their cultural changes. The study will be worthwhile as we think about the future of the SBC. The Pew Research Center provided early observations from the research thus far. Millennials are being described as ". . . the first generation in human history who regard behaviors like tweeting and texting, along with Web sites like Facebook, YouTube, Google, and

---

7   http://www.baptisttwentyone.com/?page_id=107; accessed 6 January 2010.

Wikipedia, not as astonishing innovations of the digital era, but as everyday parts of their social lives and their search for understanding."[8]

Many of us enjoy the advancements in technology and take advantage of Macs and smart phones. But we will never fully understand the world of the younger leaders because we can never be them. God is raising missionaries who will be able to comfortably navigate technology and leverage it for His purposes. What an incredible thought!

The above list only begins the journey to understanding young leaders. Young leaders are culturally engaged. Their environments and technology have cultivated a high level of creativity. Their generation is the least religiously engaged in the history of our country. They appreciate the arts. Some believe they are the most politically engaged generation in history. All this information is to show you that young leaders are fascinating and worth getting to know. Young leaders are being used by God and an incredible asset to His Great Commission.

WHAT'S NEXT?

We need go no further than the apostle Paul to learn what to do next. His advice can move us from our current realities to a movement that touches the world for the cause of Christ. Paul struggled with the young leader Mark, but multiplied himself through young men like Timothy and Titus. It will not always be easy but it will always be worthwhile. He gave ministry away to young leaders. He valued them as sons. He released them as co-laborers. He knew the future of the movement was beyond what he could physically protect and accomplish.

Here is how Paul embraces young leaders:

> "To Timothy, my true child in the faith . . ." (1 Tim 1:2)
>
> "To Titus, my true child in our common faith. Grace and peace from God the Father and Christ Jesus our Savior. The reason I left you in Crete was to set right what was left undone and, as I directed you, to appoint elders in every town . . ." (Titus 1:4–5)

---

8   Scott Keeter and Paul Taylor, *The Millennials*, Pew Research Center Publications, 11 December 2009 [report on-line]; accessed 5 January 2010; available from http://pewresearch.org/pubs/1437/millennials-profile; Internet.

"I thank God, whom I serve with a clear conscience as my forefathers did, when I constantly remember you in my prayers night and day." (2 Tim 1:3)

"Now you, man of God, run from these things; but pursue righteousness, godliness, faith, love, endurance, and gentleness. Fight the good fight for the faith; take hold of eternal life, to which you were called and have made a good confession before many witnesses." (1 Tim 6:11–12)

Here is how Paul taught Timothy to embrace spiritual fathers and mothers:

"Do not rebuke an older man, but exhort him as a father, younger men as brothers, older women as mothers, and with all propriety, the younger women as sisters." (1 Tim 5:1–2)

You can provide what no technology or trend can do. You can become a leader to the next leaders. You can become that person who cares enough to pray and invest in young leaders. You can help keep them accountable and encouraged as they take the keys and get behind the wheel of the new SBC.

I love the Southern Baptist Convention and pray that other young leaders can feel the same way. If we "invite" but do not "welcome" them, our overtures will go unheeded. Let us do what it takes to remain biblically conservative, but in the process still encourage different missional expressions. If we do, young leaders will find the SBC to be the kind of partnership we all know it can be.

One day our sons and daughters will possess everything that once belonged to us. They may sell it, give it away, abuse it, enjoy it, or make more out of it than what they received. As Southern Baptists we must embrace the reality that our spiritual sons and daughters will soon lead our churches and denomination. For now, it is the task of those who are mature in their faith and leadership abilities to prepare the next generation. The greatest legacy that you may leave behind is not a large ministry but the ability in another person to lead in the grandness of God's kingdom and His church.

CONVICTIONAL YET COOPERATIVE
THE MAKING OF A GREAT
COMMISSION PEOPLE

David S. Dockery

One cannot understand who Southern Baptists are apart from the distinctive idea of voluntary cooperation. It is in light of this historical reality that Southern Baptists, with God's help and guidance, will be able to work together in carrying forth the task of making disciples of the nations through the cooperative and collaborative efforts of Great Commission partners.

The official Web site of the Southern Baptist Convention (SBC) contends that "since its inception in 1845, the Southern Baptist Convention has always had one mission—the Great Commission (Matt. 28:19–20)."[1] In 1919, two years after the establishment of the Executive Committee, Convention leaders proposed the Seventy-five Million Campaign, a five-year campaign to support the various mission agencies and ministries of the SBC. From these efforts, the Cooperative Program, under the leadership of M. E. Dodd, was adopted at the 1925 convention in Memphis.

The Cooperative Program is a cooperative partnership whereby churches across the Southern Baptist Convention combine financial gifts, given to and through state conventions, which are then passed on to support the work of national convention entities and agencies. These financial gifts are employed to send and support missionaries, equip pastors and church leaders, enable educational institutions, and address benevolent, social, ethical, and moral concerns. The Cooperative Program is the glue that pulls together more than 44,000 Southern Baptist congregations for the purpose of advancing the gospel around the world. With a global

---

1 The direct link can be found online at http://www.cpmissions.net/2003/what%20is%20cp.asp.

population exceeding 6.8 billion and a commission to take the gospel to every nation (Matt. 28:18–20), Southern Baptists must enhance our spirit of cooperation and expand our collaborative efforts if we are going to fulfill Christ's command. We must work, pray, give, and go—and do so together in the spirit of Christian unity.[2]

CHURCHES AND COOPERATION

Understanding the distinctive nature of Baptist polity will be essential for developing Great Commission partners to work together toward a Great Commission Resurgence. Baptist churches may choose to form associations or conventions. Southern Baptist churches have organized both state conventions and a national body. These churches actually do not join associations or conventions so much as they choose voluntarily to cooperate through these institutions.

There have been few times in the history of Southern Baptist life when the commitment to cooperation needed to be more highly prized than today. Morris Chapman has observed that, "without cooperation, without trusting each other, our Convention shall cease to have the dynamic mission enterprise that reaches to the far corners of the earth."[3] Southern Baptists now find themselves at a critical juncture in terms of both cooperation and conviction. In order to move forward with cooperative conviction and with convictional cooperation toward a Great Commission Resurgence, we need to recognize how we arrived at this moment and what we need to do to move forward together.

DEVELOPMENT OF CONFESSIONAL AND COOPERATIVE COMMITMENTS

At the 1925 annual convention in Memphis, the messengers not only received the report to approve the Cooperative Program, but they also approved the recommendation to adopt the *Baptist Faith and Message* as

---

2   Portions of this material have been adapted from David S. Dockery, *Southern Baptist Consensus and Renewal* (Nashville: B&H Academic, 2008).

3   Morris H. Chapman, "Axioms of a Cooperating Southern Baptist," in *Southern Baptist Identity* (Wheaton: Crossway, 2009), 160.

the confessional statement for the SBC. While it had been the case since the founding of the SBC eight decades earlier in 1845, the convention now, in a formal way, declared that both conviction and cooperation mattered.

While no doctrinal statement was adopted when the Southern Baptist Convention was organized, one should not assume that early Southern Baptists were not a confessional people. The leaders of the young Southern Baptist movement emphasized that their differences with northern Baptists were about missions and mission strategy, not doctrines. Early Southern Baptists were both missional and doctrinal, cooperative and convictional.

As I noted above, the Southern Baptist Convention, in 1925, for the first time adopted a complete confession of faith. The confessional statement was needed to address mounting concerns about evolution and to clarify Southern Baptist doctrinal commitments in the midst of the Modernist–Fundamentalist controversy that raged across the country in the early decades of the twentieth century.

The 1925 *Baptist Faith and Message* was largely a restatement of the 1833 *New Hampshire Confession* with minor revisions. The Southern Baptist Convention in 1925, however, chose to move beyond the realm of classic doctrinal affirmations not only by addressing the evolution question, but also by making declarations regarding the importance of stewardship, cooperation, education, evangelism, missions, and social ministries.

The Southern Baptist Convention, by adopting the 1925 statement, placed themselves in the great tradition of Nicea, Chalcedon, the Reformers, and the Pietists on the doctrines of God, Christ, and salvation, while maintaining and articulating significant Baptist distinctives such as regenerate church membership, the priesthood of believers, congregational church government, believer's baptism, and the Lord's Supper.

The reports in the state Baptist papers at that time reveal that the adoption of the *Baptist Faith and Message* was seen as the major story coming out of the 1925 convention. Though the Convention also approved the twelve-page report from the Committee on Future Programs to develop a general outline of plans for the next forward movement of Southern Baptists (which came to be known as the Cooperative Program), it was only barely noticed because of the importance given to the *Baptist Faith and Message*.[4] This marvelous plan outlined in that twelve-page report has been

---

4   See Albert McClellan, *The Executive Committee of the Southern Baptist Convention* (Nashville: Broadman, 1985), 453–70; Chad Owen Brand and David E. Hankins, *One Sacred Effort: The Cooperative Program of Southern Baptists* (Nashville: B&H, 2006).

used of God to advance the collaborative work of Southern Baptists in this country and around the world since 1925.

From the time of the 1925 convention to the "Million More in '54" campaign (in 1954), the SBC was characterized by the growth of denominational organization and efficiency. Since 1925, the Cooperative Program has probably been the key entity to hold together an expanding and diverse denomination for more than 80 years. The SBC entered the second half of the twentieth century as an efficiently run and largely unified organization, but the denomination's consensus and identity during those years tended to be shaped by adherence to a unified programmatic model, an assumed orthodoxy more so than an intentionally formed theological orthodoxy. We might say that an emphasis on cooperation took priority over matters of doctrinal conviction.

Many believed that from 1954 to 1979 the SBC was on the road to becoming yet another "mainline Protestant denomination"—by this time the largest Protestant denomination in the country, having surpassed the United Methodists. In 1963, Herschel H. Hobbs, in his role as SBC president and chair of the *Baptist Faith and Message* Committee, led the convention to reaffirm the SBC's commitment to Scripture, as well as other historical Baptist tenets.[5] The conflict that has characterized the SBC for the past thirty years is well known, but it was actually a conflict in the making since those challenging days in the early 1960s.

Most people have interpreted the past three decades as a battle between "conservatives" and "moderates." While such a statement is generally true, it is probably too broad and somewhat superficial. In the late 1980s, many started recognizing at least four groups: Fundamentalists, Evangelicals, Moderates, and Liberals. The reality is that there were several subgroups among each of these. Now, most all of the moderate and liberal groups have disconnected from that national convention, though many have remained involved with state conventions.

Those who have remained involved with the various conservative groups within the SBC are quite diverse. They included a loose knit coalition of several groups—all of whom wanted some kind of course correction to bring about a more faithful Baptist orthodoxy. All of these groups were needed to bring about the theological course correction/conservative resurgence in the SBC. They all wanted a recovery of the gospel while emphasizing the full truthfulness of Scripture.

---

5   See Jesse C. Fletcher, *The Southern Baptist Convention: A Sesquicentennial History* (Nashville: B&H, 1994); also Robert A. Baker, *The Southern Baptist Convention and Its People, 1607–1972* (Nashville: Broadman, 1974).

Now that the doctrinal course correction is complete, there is a need to reestablish the importance of cooperation in order for Southern Baptists to point toward a hopeful future. Today Southern Baptists need to begin to build a new theologically and historically informed consensus that will help us understand our past, our identity, and our beliefs so that we can move forward to carry the gospel around the world and disciple the nations in the twenty-first century.

We need a new generation that will be both convictional and cooperative. Sometimes when the emphasis is placed primarily on matters of conviction, people can appear to be cantankerous. On the other hand, when the emphasis is placed solely on cooperation, people tend to compromise. Neither of these is a good option. It is time for us to take a fresh look at the need to balance conviction with cooperation and cooperation with conviction, with a new gospel-centered consensus. In doing so, we can develop a renewed appreciation for developing a theologically, historically, and biblically informed identity of what it means to be a Southern Baptist.

Such a renewed identity is needed since the once clear programmatic and cultural identity of Southern Baptists has now all but disappeared. In order to move toward a new convictional cooperation and a spirit of cooperative conviction, we need simultaneously to focus on a biblically informed commitment to unity and truth.

A CALL FOR UNITY

The Gospel of John gives us a picture of Jesus' heart for the kind of unity that our Savior desired for His disciples. Just before He was arrested, Jesus prayed for authentic spiritual unity for His followers (John 17:21). John 17 is our Lord's own prayer, the greatest prayer recorded in Holy Scripture, where we see Jesus Christ pouring out His heart to the Father for His followers on the night before He died for us. This prayer is not only for Jesus' immediate followers, but also for the church through the ages, which means this prayer has application for Southern Baptists in the twenty-first century. Romans 8:34 and Hebrews 7:25 remind us that Jesus still prays for His own today from His exalted position at the right hand of God. His prayers for believers today reflect the words of John 17, which is a prayer for unity and a prayer for truth—bringing about a holy uniqueness and a unique holiness for His followers.

In verses 20–26 of John 17, we read that Jesus prayed that His followers would experience a spiritual unity that exemplifies the oneness of the Father and the Son. Southern Baptists in the twenty-first century are different and diverse—young, old, educated, uneducated, Southerners, non-Southerners, red, yellow, black, brown, and white. But in spite of our many differences, we must recognize that we belong to the same Lord and thus to each other. Yet, far too often Southern Baptists have been characterized by controversy, infighting, fragmentation, selfishness, competition, and disunity. What unity that we have experienced has too often come from our cultural homogeneity. If we believe the Bible as we proclaim we do, and if we take seriously the words of John 17, then we must think afresh about a biblical understanding of unity and cooperation.

The Nicene Creed, an important confession from the early years of Christianity, describes the church as "one, holy, universal, and apostolic."[6] It is universal in that it crosses all geographical, social, racial, and ethnic lines. The church is one because it is founded on the person and work of Jesus Christ and the common salvation we share in Him (John 17:2–5).

One of the things that impresses the world and authenticates the message of the gospel and the efforts of our missionaries is the way Christians love each other, they way they live and serve together in harmony. It is the witness that our Lord wants and expects from us in the world so that the world may believe that the Father has sent the Son (John 17:21). The lost world cannot see God, but they can see Christians. Let us pray that we will represent Christ to them in a faithful and winsome way.

If the world sees constant fighting, bickering, and discord, they likely will misunderstand and reject the gospel message. If the world sees Christ's followers exemplifying love and unity, they will be open to believe the good news that "God loved the world in this way: He gave His One and Only Son, so that everyone who believes in Him will not perish but have eternal life" (John 3:16).[7]

A TIME FOR CONVICTION

Southern Baptists over the past thirty years have been embroiled in controversies focusing on the truthfulness of the Bible and the uniqueness of the

---

6 http://www.creeds.net/ancient/nicene.htm.

7 See Richard D. Phillips, Philip G. Ryken, and Mark E. Dever, *The Church: One, Holy, Catholic, and Apostolic* (Phillipsburg, NJ: P & R, 2004); Francis Schaeffer, *The Church Before the Watching World* (Downers Grove, IL: InterVarsity Press, 1971).

gospel. Such controversies cause us to ask if indeed there are times when it is necessary to separate over such first-order issues or, to phrase it differently, are there times when it is best not to cooperate? The answer to such questions is extremely difficult, especially in light of the prayer for unity in John 17, and requires much prayer and wisdom.

Christ calls His followers to exemplify both love *and* truth. Certainly, we are to promote Christian unity at every opportunity. True believers belong to the same Father and are called to the same service. Believers trust the same Savior and have received the same gift of grace, and thus share a common salvation. Yet ultimately, true unity is based on biblical truth. Any other kind of unity is earthly, worldly, temporal, and thus falls short of the John 17 ideal.

A unity that exists without truth is mushy, misguided, and meaningless. Yet, truth without a concern for love and unity is hardly consistent with scriptural truth. Jesus' prayer was not only for spiritual unity but also for sanctified truth. Jesus prayed that the Father would sanctify His followers in truth, for His Word is truth (John 17:17). So, as affirmed in the Nicene Creed, the church is not only one and universal, but it is also characterized as holy and apostolic.

True holiness is based on truth taught by the apostles and made known to us in Holy Scripture (see John 14:6; 16:3; 17:17). Just as it saddens the Father and the Son and harms the witness of the church when we fail to love one another and demonstrate biblical unity, so likewise, the witness of the church is harmed when we look to the world to be our guide on matters of belief and practice rather than to the truthfulness of God's Word.

AN APPEAL FOR LOVE AND TRUTH

Faithful Christ-followers are called to be separate from and to be distinct from the world (John 17:15, 16: Eph 4:17–32; Col 3:5; 1 Pet 2:11; 1 John 2:15–17). Having been redeemed and regenerated by the Lord, believers are to be different in their lifestyles and beliefs from the unbelieving world. Holiness is the calling for all believers. How do we know when our calling to truth and holiness is not only a call to be different from the world, but from other professing believers? Is there ever such a time?

This question has been the subject of much debate. As early as the time of Tertullian (c. 155–220) and the Montanists (c. 170), and especially the debate surrounding Augustine (354–430) and the Donatists, these disputes existed. In American Christianity, the Fundamentalist-Modernist controversy in the early twentieth century brought about splits in major denominations, and parallel splits between conservatives and liberals took place in a number of churches in the United States and Canada. Fundamentalists separated from those who espoused any form of liberalism, evolutionary thought, or modernism, as well as those who participated in card playing, theater attendance, or alcohol use. Fundamentalists soon became unable to distinguish between less important concerns such as card playing and ultimate concerns regarding the liberal denials of cardinal doctrines such as the deity of Christ or the uniqueness of the gospel. Such separatism soon became characteristic of fundamentalism as a test of true faith.

Fundamentalists in the middle of the twentieth century even refused to cooperate with Billy Graham and other evangelicals. Such misguided secondary separation practices coupled with withdrawal from social and cultural concerns caused Carl F. H. Henry to pen his important work, *The Uneasy Conscience of American Fundamentalism.*[8] Certainly, the Bible teaches that heresy is not to be tolerated. Yet, Henry's words of sixty years ago seem like a fresh warning to Southern Baptists of our day. He contended that the church's witness to the world is stronger when Christ's followers are united (John 17:11, 21, 23; Eph 4:1–6) and that separation often leads to additional and unnecessary fragmentation—thus diminishing opportunities for reform and renewal.

We are called to live in tension, engaging the world without becoming characterized by it, emphasizing both truth and love, holiness and unity. As Southern Baptists move out of our cultural isolation and move forward from the years of controversy, it is more important than ever to balance truth and love, holiness and unity. We must make every effort to love one another while seeking to live pure and holy lives pleasing to our Lord. As we think about the importance of both cooperation and conviction for a Great Commission Resurgence, let us turn to the apostle Paul to find guidance to help us move forward together in unity as we seek to exemplify love and truth while cooperating in the work of the Great Commission.

---

8 Carl F. H. Henry, *The Uneasy Conscience of American Fundamentalism* (Grand Rapids: Eerdmans, 1947).

MOVING FORWARD TOGETHER

As we move into the second decade of the twenty-first century, there is a need to reestablish the identity of Southern Baptists toward a helpful and hopeful future.[9] We must recognize that the theological controversy of the past three decades was primarily a call for conviction without equal attention given to cooperation. There have been various responses and calls from time to time from some Baptists appealing for cooperation. Unfortunately, while there is merit in conviction and much to be said for cooperation, we need a new model that calls for both. One without the other will not provide the visionary roadmap needed for the future of the SBC.

In calling for a spirit of cooperation at this time, we need not spend our time longing for the past when our denominational identity was almost inseparable from the cultural similarities around us. The SBC world in which many of us were nurtured—Bible drills, GAs, RAs, Training Union, WMU, Brotherhood . . . not to mention uniform Sunday school lessons, the Baptist hymnal, and similar worship patterns—no longer exists in most Southern Baptist churches across the country. For almost five decades in the second half of the twentieth century, Southern Baptists followed the same organizational patterns, the same programs, and the same Sunday school lessons.

Those practices were to Southern Baptists what the Latin Mass was to Roman Catholics. They provided all within the SBC a sense of continuity and security. This programmatic uniformity all hung together around a ubiquitous commitment to missions and evangelism, best expressed in giving through the Cooperative Program and special offerings for Lottie Moon for international missions and Annie Armstrong for work in North America. It was ingenious. Among all of these things, a renewed priority on the Cooperative Program and the special missions offerings will be a right step toward a new spirit of cooperation for our day.

Throughout most of the twentieth century, being a Southern Baptist had a cultural and programmatic identity to it unlike anything else. This kind of intactness provided Southern Baptists with a denominational stability unmatched by any other denomination in the country. Martin Marty was not exaggerating when he said that Southern Baptists were the Roman Catholic Church of the South because its identity was so intact,

---

9 See David S. Dockery, ed., *Southern Baptist Identity: An Evangelical Denomination Faces the Future* (Wheaton: Crossway, 2009).

its influence so pervasive, providing an umbrella over the entire culture in almost every dimension of life.[10] Southern Baptists were a very practical people with heart religion, carried out in rather uniform pragmatic and programmatic expressions. But for a variety of reasons, this intactness has been challenged by growing fragmentation.

Even without the controversy of the past thirty years, the intactness had started to unravel due to a variety of factors. These included the growth of multiple Bible translations, the impact of parachurch groups, the expanding diversity of music, varied worship patterns, and the unexpected reality that church models and heroes for many Southern Baptists, especially for younger pastors and leaders, now come from outside the SBC. Today, in many ways, Southern Baptists seem to be a gathering of loosely connected, if not balkanized, groups. What is now needed, in light of the complex challenges in Southern Baptist life today, is a fresh look at the teaching of the apostle Paul. In Ephesians 4 we find not only an appeal to biblical unity, which Southern Baptists need to hear, but also the necessary virtues and guidelines that can help bring about this kind of authentic unity, which will be foundational for convictional cooperation in our shared work.

When we turn to Ephesians 4, we are struck by Paul's repetition of the word "one," which occurs seven times. Further observation reveals that the seven "ones" are grounded in the three members of the Holy Trinity ("one Spirit," 4:4; "One Lord," 4:5; and "one God and Father of all," 4:6). Believers who have been reconciled to Christ (Eph 2) have new standards and expectations. Paul urged his readers, "walk worthy of the calling you have received" (Eph 4:1). Ephesians 4:2 presents five virtues that characterize and exemplify life worthy of the Christian calling. "Humility" points to our ultimate dependence on God and is an absolute necessity to unity, because pride often stands behind discord. We need humility before God, but also in our relationships with others, thinking of others as more important than ourselves (Phil 2:1–4).

"Gentleness" suggests strength under control. Gentleness should not be associated with weakness; rather, it is a work of divine grace that produces patience, quiet restraint, and submission to God. The third virtue is "patience." Patient people demonstrate long-suffering in dealing with insulting and aggravating people, seeking to follow the example of how God in Christ has acted toward us (Rom 2:4).

---

10   Martin E. Marty, "Concerns about Membership Decline in the Southern Baptist Convention," available from http://divinity.uchicago.edu/martycenter/publications/sightings/archive_1999/sightings-051099.shtml.

The next quality, "accepting one another," emphasizes forbearance, which expresses a mutual tolerance without which no group of people can live together in peace. "Love" is the final quality that embraces the previous four. Paul grounded the virtues of Christian unity "in love." If Southern Baptists are to demonstrate unity before a watching world, love—as the embracing and crowning virtue of all virtues—must characterize God's people. Jesus said that love is the mark of His followers (John 13:34–35). Southern Baptists will have a genuine spirit of cooperation only when these Christian virtues characterize our lives individually and corporately.[11]

Believers are to make it their business to pursue unity in the body of Christ. We are not to take a wait-and-see attitude, but we are to be eager to do what we can "to keep the unity of the Spirit with the peace that binds us" (Eph 4:3). God's Spirit energizes the church to exemplify unity to an observing world. When believers cultivate and practice the virtues described in Ephesians 4:2–3, they display and preserve the unity of the Spirit. God is the author of the peace, and stirring up dissension among His people is detestable to Him (see Prov 6:16–19).

From his admonition to unity, Paul moved to the basis of this unity. In Ephesians 4:4, "one body" refers to the church, the body of Christ (Eph 1:23; 2:16). This "one body" is comprised of diverse people (1 Cor 12:13; Gal 3:28). Cohesion of the "body" comes from the Holy Spirit who indwells, seals, and energizes it (Eph 1:13; 4:30). As there is one body with many members, so there is one Spirit whose gifts and operations are many (Eph 4:7–12).

Paul continues by claiming that "one hope," "one faith," and "one baptism" exist because there is only one Lord. The "one hope" of our calling is the hope of sharing Christ's glory. The "one hope" is the calling for all believers; the believing community has no favored members for whom better things are reserved.

The "one faith" refers to the sum and substance of the church's belief. No Christian cooperation is possible unless believers share a common conviction about "the faith that was delivered to the saints once for all" (Jude 3). The "one faith" of Ephesians 4:5 also points to the common experience of faith in Christ and the same access to Him shared by all believers.

"One baptism" pictures the outward expression of believers exercising faith in the one Lord. Baptism is the visible sign in water by which persons who believe the gospel and repent of their sins publicly acknowledge Jesus as Lord and identify themselves with the body of Christ (Rom 6:3–4; Gal 3:27).

---

11   See Timothy George and John D. Woodbridge, *The Mark of Jesus* (Chicago: Moody, 2005).

The final emphasis of Ephesians 4:1–6 concerning the new humanity is that all believers belong to the "one God and Father of all, who is above all and through all and in all." A call to unity is one that Southern Baptists need to hear and exemplify in order with integrity to proclaim the one Christian faith, to share one hope, to experience one baptism, and to participate in one body. The infighting and discord that have often been part of our history remind us of how far we have fallen short of God's expectations. The larger context of Ephesians 4 indicates that true Christian unity is expressed through variety (Eph 4:7–12), bringing about maturity (Eph 4:13–16) and purity (Eph 4:17–32) in the body of Christ.

As we move forward, we will need convictional boundaries grounded in truthfulness of Scripture while at the same time we will need to build bridges of cooperation. We cannot ignore necessary boundary markers. Yet, we need to recognize the ultimate danger to the gospel lies not in our variety or in the nuances of our differences, but in the rising tides of liberalism, neo-paganism, and postmodernism that threaten to swamp our Baptist identity in cultural accommodation.

A call for a Great Commission Resurgence must be supported by a confessional and convictional faith and a collaborative and compassionate sense of cooperation. We offer thanks that the recovery of a convictional confessionalism has kept Southern Baptists from going the way of so many mainline denominations who have become untethered from Scripture and have lost their way. Yet the need of the hour also includes the need to regain a spirit of collaborative cooperation.

Many wonder if Southern Baptists can once again find a way to cooperate. After all, we are so different. No longer can a programmatic pragmatism or a cultural homogeneity alone be the foundation for our cooperation. The call to cooperate in the twenty-first century differs greatly from the 1925 world of M. E. Dodd, but we need to reclaim the spirit of M. E. Dodd for our day. While a recommitment to the work of the Cooperative Program is essential, it is not an end in itself and is just a first step toward reenvisioning a future for Southern Baptists.

Southern Baptists in the twenty-first century have dark and light skin, we are young and old, our churches are small and large, and we worship in rural communities and in sprawling metropolitan areas. We are educated and uneducated, well-known and anonymous, rich and poor, social media magnets and Luddites, theologians and practitioners, and while we remain predominantly Southerners, SBC congregations are now found across this land in the West, East, and North as well. One of the things, however, that will get the attention of others will be the way in which we love one another, celebrate our diversity, and serve together in harmony and heart-felt cooperation.

We thus call for churches and church leaders to renew their commitments to the Cooperative Program, the genius of which is that it allows us to do things together that we could not do alone, including facilitating the work of colleges, universities and seminaries, church planting and global missions efforts, and, of course, benevolent, social, and ethical ministries as well. We are thankful to God for each and every one of these effective and faithful partners in Great Commission work at all levels: associational, state, and national. Many of these partners employ wise stewardship of Cooperative Program dollars; we should offer them generous praise and bountiful support.

CONSENSUS AND RENEWAL: FROM HANDWRINGING TO HOPEFULNESS

Together we can begin to build a new and much-needed consensus around the gospel of the Lord Jesus Christ—a consensus present at the first Triennial Convention of Baptists in 1814, seen at the inaugural convention of Southern Baptists in 1845, and evident once again at the important gathering of Southern Baptists in 1925.

In calling for a Great Commission Resurgence, we need to take a step back not just to commit ourselves afresh to evangelism, church planting, and global missions, as significant as these priorities are. We need to commit ourselves foremost to the gospel, the good news found only in Jesus Christ, His atoning death, and resurrection. We trust God to bring renewal to our shared service, to our theological commitments and convictions, and to our cooperative and collaborative efforts. We must prepare and educate a new generation who will, in the spirit of William Carey, the "father of modern missions," plan, pray, give, and go.

Cooperating churches, associations, state convention entities, and national convention ministries must work together in a renewed partnership grounded in the gospel. We recognize that denominations, like the Southern Baptist Convention, are a God-honored means for carrying forth the work of Christ in the world. When any denomination becomes an end in itself, it will invariably end with itself, and history is replete with examples of such.

As we move further into the twenty-first century, we will need to ask hard questions about historical structures to see if they are continuing to be faithful and effective for the new challenges of our day. We must together pray for the wisdom of the Holy Spirit as we pursue answers to these questions. We believe that all Baptists can and must serve together in a new spirit of cooperative conviction and convictional cooperation.

One final observation seems important as we move toward a conclusion. A re-envisioned future for the Southern Baptist Convention might have the same or similar organizational structure on paper, but in reality and in practice our commitment to a convictional cooperation and a spirit of cooperative conviction might result in a developing structure that will be appropriate for our changing context. In addition to associations, state convention entities, and national convention entities will be the presence of various networks. For many people, networks will replace denominational structures altogether. That need not be the case if we respond in the right way to this change in the twenty-first century landscape. Networks can strengthen and augment established entities and structures in an auxiliary way.

There can be a bright future for Southern Baptists if we remain convictionally connected to Scripture, the gospel, and the best of our theological tradition. In doing so, Southern Baptists will need to move out of our insularity and explore ways to partner with affinity groups and networks that will help us understand better the changing global context around us.

Learning to work afresh in cooperative ways will be essential. We must see other Christ followers, in various Southern Baptists contexts, as co-laborers together in the gospel. We must look for commonalities rather than rivalries. With fresh eyes, a cooperative spirit, and genuine convictional grounding regarding doctrinal matters, the future of the SBC can be very bright. We will need conviction and cooperation, boundaries and bridges, and denominational structures that will be open to the fresh winds of God's Spirit.

All of these things will be important to move forward in a dynamic and constructive way in the years to come. Tension between all of these must be held together in balance without ignoring any or overemphasizing one to the neglect of the others. In doing so, we can move from a time of hand-wringing to a spirit of hopefulness.

A Great Commission Resurgence will require renewed efforts in building Great Commission partnerships with local churches, networks, associations, and other denominational entities. Let us join in praying that God, by His Holy Spirit, will bring renewal to Southern Baptist churches, ministries, entities, and institutions—and may He bring guidance and hope to our cooperative efforts as we seek together to take the good news of Jesus Christ to a lost and needy world.

CONCLUSION

Adam W. Greenway

As I write these words, my wife and I are just days away from the expected birth of our first child—a son! Contemplating my impending paternity over recent weeks has caused me to reflect more upon my own childhood and upbringing. I have a renewed appreciation for my mother and father and their positive influence in my life. Though certainly not perfect, my parents gave me an example that I hope to emulate for my own children. Yet I am cognizant that the world my son will grow up in is far removed from my hometown of Frostproof, Florida—a distance measurable not only in terms of mileage but also milieu. While I harbor great hopes for my son and soon-to-be namesake, I also know there will be many challenges along the way as my wife and I endeavor to train him up in "the way he should go" (Prov 22:6). Looking backward gives me greater confidence and determination as I move forward into this new phase of life.

My thoughts concerning the state of the Southern Baptist Convention vis-à-vis the call for a Great Commission Resurgence in many ways mirror my mental musings about fatherhood—I cannot help but reflect over my life's course as a Southern Baptist as I also envision what the future holds for our Convention. At the outset, I must confess that Southern Baptists have indelibly impacted my life. My first educational experience outside the home was an SBC church's pre-kindergarten program. I came to a saving knowledge of Christ as an eight-year-old through the witness of a Southern Baptist couple passionate about children's ministry. That same local Southern Baptist congregation in my hometown baptized me, discipled me, affirmed my calling, licensed me, and ordained me.

I am a graduate of a Southern Baptist university (Samford),[1] and proud alumnus of two of our six SBC seminaries (Southwestern and Southern). I have served as pastor and interim pastor of Southern Baptist churches, and am currently privileged to serve as a professor and administrator at the SBC's "mother seminary." I would be neither *who*, nor *what*, nor *where* I am were it not for Southern Baptists. My pondering over the past can easily segue into praise, with a heart that eagerly cries out, "Thank you, Lord," and, "Thank you, Southern Baptists."

Gazing forward, however, I am both excited and concerned as I consider the SBC's future as a Great Commission instrument in our Redeemer's hands.[2] The Conservative Resurgence in the Convention was indeed a *necessary* condition[3] for a Great Commission Resurgence, for without a clear and unequivocal reaffirmation of the inspiration, inerrancy, and infallibility of the Bible as the Word of God, there can be no true gospel to proclaim. Indeed, it must be our conviction that because God *has* spoken we *must* speak (Acts 4:20; cf. 5:41–42). As one who "came of age" after the Conservative Resurgence was largely over, I remain eternally grateful for what our Lord did through grassroots Southern Baptists to return our denomination to "the faith of the fathers."

Yet such is not a *sufficient* condition,[4] for the embracing of correct biblical theology does not guarantee automatic evangelistic fervency and

---

1 Technically, the Southern Baptist Convention does not own or operate any colleges or universities, as that responsibility historically was within the purview of the SBC-affiliated state conventions, while the national Convention concerned itself solely with graduate theological education. Most of these colleges and universities were members of the Association of Southern Baptist Colleges and Schools (now International Association of Baptist Colleges and Universities), hence the moniker "Southern Baptist university." The Conservative Resurgence contributed to an altering of this structure, with many Baptist colleges and universities altering or severing their state convention relationships, starting graduate-level schools of divinity or theology, or both, like my undergraduate *alma mater*. The six SBC seminaries responded to this trend by launching baccalaureate programs to provide a conservative alternative to the predominantly center-left state Baptist schools.

2 Phraseology used here adapted from Paul David Tripp, *Instruments in the Redeemer's Hands* (Phillipsburg, NJ: P&R, 2002).

3 In logic, a *necessary* condition for some state of affairs X is a condition that must be satisfied in order for X to obtain. To illustrate, a *necessary* condition for a student to receive a final grade of "A" in my Personal Evangelism course is to submit seven (7) personal evangelism reports. Students who fail to submit their seven witnessing reports will not receive an "A" in my class. Put another way, a student who receives an "A" in my course is one who *at least* submitted his or her seven personal evangelism reports. For further discussion on *necessary* conditions, see Norman L. Geisler and Ronald M. Brooks, *Come, Let Us Reason: An Introduction to Logical Thinking* (Grand Rapids: Baker, 1990), 171.

4 In logic, a *sufficient* condition for some state of affairs X is a condition, that, if satisfied, guarantees that X obtains. To illustrate, a *sufficient* condition for a student to receive a final grade of

fruitfulness. As several of this volume's contributors have reminded us, we have a long way to go as a denomination in terms of bringing the gospel to *all peoples* and *all nations*. Perhaps a true Great Commission Resurgence would begin if each of us decided actually to share the good news of Jesus Christ with *some person* in *our nation*. Maybe we should pray, slightly modifying that revival plea of old, "Lord, give us a Great Commission Resurgence, and let it begin in me."

Integrity, however, should demand from us the honest admission that our hearts do not break and our eyes do not weep over the lostness that surrounds us in our own states, much less our subdivisions. Despite our needed public reaffirmations of doctrinal orthodoxy, the overwhelming abandonment of that most central responsibility of our faith—to personally engage individuals who are not yet believers in Jesus Christ, sharing with them that He is the only Savior and Lord—produces the practical result of contradicting the very faith we claim to embrace. As one state Baptist paper editor recently opined:

> As evangelicals, Baptists seem to have become practical universalists because we talk about evangelism and witness and salvation and baptisms all the time but we leave few footprints in the sand behind that talk. . . . "Practical universalism" simply says that no matter what we say about our conviction of the need to introduce Christ to friends and neighbors so they might be saved, the fact that we don't do it says we believe all will be saved–or we don't care.[5]

To put the question more pointedly, is there really any functional difference between the mosque, Kingdom Hall, or Mormon temple—all places where the biblical gospel of grace cannot be found—and the Southern

---

"A" in my Personal Evangelism course is to earn an "A" on each individual assignment in the class. In other words, a student who receives an "A" grade on each class assignment will receive an "A" for the course. Submitting seven (7) personal evangelism reports, while a *necessary* condition, is not a *sufficient* condition, as it is possible for students to submit all their witnessing reports but not receive final grades of "A" (they might have failed the midterm examination, for example). Likewise, earning an "A" on each individual assignment, while a *sufficient* condition, is not a *necessary* condition, as it is possible to receive a final grade of "A" without having received an "A" grade on some particular assignment (given that all assignments are not weighted equally percentagewise toward the final grade). For further discussion on *sufficient* conditions, see Geisler and Brooks, *Come, Let Us Reason*, 171–73.

5 Norman Jameson, "Are Southern Baptists Evangelicals?" *Biblical Recorder*, 29 December 2009 [editorial on-line]; accessed 9 January 2010; available from http://www.biblicalrecorder.com/post/2009/12/29/Are-Southern-Baptists-evangelicals.aspx; Internet.

Baptist congregation that baptizes zero individuals because its members, though they know "the truth" (cf. John 14:6), never actually share it? I trust the answer is painfully self-evident, despite the fact that the number of SBC churches falling into such a noxious category seemingly increases with every Annual Church Profile, now upwards of one in four.[6]

Part of the SBC's problem at hand, however, lies not merely in the *lack* of evangelizing (abysmal of a reality as that may be), but also in *how* our evangelism has been conducted. This charge should come as no surprise to the thoughtful observer of Southern Baptist life. Consider for a moment one last batch of statistics. In a provocatively disconcerting article entitled "Southern Baptists: An Unregenerate Denomination," Jim Elliff wrote in 2005:

> Although the Southern Baptists claim 16,287,494 members, on average only 6,024,289 people (guests and non-member children included), a number equal to only 37% of the membership number, show up for their church's primary worship meeting (usually Sunday morning). . . . If your church is anything like normal, and is not brand new, your statistics are probably similar. In other words, if you have 200 in attendance on Sunday morning, you likely have 500–600 or even more on your roll. Many churches have an even worse record.
>
> Discerning who among us is regenerate is not an exact science, but a closer look at these numbers will at least alert us to the fact that *most* Southern Baptists must certainly be dead spiritually. That is so, unless, of course, you claim that there is no difference between a believer and a non-believer.

---

6   In 2007, for example, the Annual Church Profile reported a total of 44,696 Southern Baptist churches. 8,217 churches reported "Zero Total Baptisms." An additional 3,943 churches reported "Null/Blank Total Baptisms," which when totaled equals 12,160 SBC churches reporting "Null or Zero" baptisms in 2007, or 27 percent. Information gathered from the 2007 Annual Church Profile Summary [report on-line]; accessed 9 January 2010; available from http://www.lifeway.com/lwc/files/lwcF_LifeWay_Research_2007_ACP_Summary_Charts_Part_1.pdf; Internet.

In fairness, however, there are certainly those Southern Baptist congregations who faithfully proclaim the gospel but, because of remote geography, small surrounding population, or other extenuating circumstance, might see no conversions in a single year's time and thus record zero baptisms. Given the sheer number of SBC churches in this statistical category, however, it seems likely that many are chronic repeat offenders rather than isolated cases (worth undertaking would be a research project to determine how many years each of these "Null or Zero" churches have been so classified).

In the average church you can cut the 37% Sunday morning attendance by about two-thirds or more when counting those interested in a Sunday evening service, or other gatherings held in addition to the principal meeting of the church. In 1996, the last time the SBC kept these statistics, the number of Sunday evening attenders was equal to only 12.3% of the membership (in churches that had an evening meeting). One might ask what makes us claim that the rest are Christians, if they involve themselves with God's people only on such a minimal, surface level? How are they any different from the people who attend the liberal church down the street—the "church" where the gospel is not even preached?

And remember that the numbers of those attending include many non-member children and guests, often making up a third of the congregation's main meeting attendance. When all factors are considered, these figures suggest that nearly 90% of Southern Baptist church members appear to be little different from the "cultural Christians" who populate other mainline denominations.

To make matters worse, we tell a lot more people that they are true Christians (because they prayed a prayer sincerely) than we can convince to be baptized. Our largest pizza supper may bring in a hundred new "converts," but we will likely get only a few of those on the roll. *After that*, the percentages that I have been mentioning kick in. In other words, if you compare all we *say* have become Christians through our evangelistic efforts, to those who actually *show signs* of being regenerate, we should be red-faced.[7]

Red-faced indeed! Not only has no appreciable increase in baptisms occurred in the SBC, but one must also wonder about the true spiritual condition of the legions of those who have gone under the water. God have mercy on us! We desperately need a true Great Commission Resurgence!

Yet as tempting as it may be to abandon all optimism concerning our future, I remain hopeful—first and foremost because of my firm and unwavering belief in the absolute sovereignty of God in all things. In the last epistle he wrote this side of heaven, Paul reminded Timothy that

---

7 Jim Elliff, "Southern Baptists: An Unregenerate Denomination" [article on-line]; accessed 17 March 2010; available from http://www.ccwtoday.org/article_view.asp?article_id=150; Internet, emphasis original. Used by permission of the author.

"even if we are faithless, He remains faithful, for He cannot deny Himself" (2 Tim 2:13). No matter how discouraging our situation, our Lord "will not abandon His people" (Ps 94:14). Despite what statistics and data might lead some to conclude, the biblical gospel remains "God's power for salvation to everyone who believes" (Rom 1:16). Our problem really is not "the message"—to quote that oft-repeated cliché. The Conservative Resurgence tackled that issue head-on in SBC life, and while we must remain ever vigilant—as the "battle for the Bible" never truly ends—we should regularly give thanks to God that the major battles that needed to take place did occur and with a positive outcome.[8] The Conservative Resurgence was indeed a "God-moment," despite the real and perceived frailties and failings of those human beings involved in it. I, for one, gladly and publicly acknowledge the debt of gratitude I owe, and I am confident that all my fellow contributors share that sentiment.

But as grateful as we all should be for the past, we can easily be seduced into thinking that we *only* need to look backward and all our current problems will be solved. It may be tempting to think everything will get better if we can just "recapture the magic" of some halcyon days of yore. The reality, however, is that we dwell neither in sixteenth-century Geneva—for which the occasional student of mine seemingly pines, nor in 1950s America—those supposed Southern Baptist "good ole days" too often treasured for sentimental reasons over and against statistical realities. (Most of us probably either never heard or largely forgot that we baptized less than half of

---

8 For example, one of those "major battles that needed to take place" focused on the Southern Baptist Convention's flagship seminary (my *alma mater* and current employer). Founded in 1859, just fourteen years after the Convention itself, The Southern Baptist Theological Seminary had been established on a strong foundation of biblical orthodoxy best expressed by the seminary's *Abstract of Principles*, the oldest confession of faith produced by Southern Baptists. For most of the twentieth century, however, the seminary had largely forsaken this "sure foundation" and instead embraced the "sand pile" of higher criticism, neo-orthodoxy, and apostasy. Anyone tempted to argue that a "course correction" was unnecessary needs only to read Susan M. Shaw and Tisa Lewis, "Once There was a Camelot: Women Doctoral Graduates of The Southern Baptist Theological Seminary, 1982–1992, Talk about Seminary, the Fundamentalist Takeover, and Their Lives Since SBTS," *Review & Expositor* 95 (1998): 397–424 (available online from http://www.rande.org/SHAW.doc), to have all such doubts erased.

Though indeed tumultuous at times, the Conservative Resurgence succeeded in bringing about a new administration, an almost complete faculty turnover, a return to confessional fidelity, record enrollments, and not insignificantly, the founding of the first graduate school of an SBC seminary dedicated to Great Commission studies—the Billy Graham School of Missions and Evangelism. For the definitive history of these events see Gregory A. Wills, *Southern Baptist Theological Seminary, 1859–2009* (New York: Oxford University Press, 2009).

our "Million More in '54" goal anyway.) Attempts to ignore or minimize the challenge of evangelizing a twenty-first century populace much closer in terms of worldview and culture to the first century AD rather than the twentieth are tragically misguided. Bob Dylan was right, "The times they are a-changing." Likewise, our methodologies—to quote the rest of that afore-mentioned cliché—must indeed be constantly changing to meet the task.

That point leads me to the second reason underlying my hope, namely the encouraging signs of what I observe God doing in our midst. As a seminary professor, I have the distinct personal privilege of being directly involved in the training process God is using to call and deploy the next generation of equippers—pastors, missionaries, evangelists, support staff members, and even lay leaders. From my interactions with students, both inside and outside the classroom, I see God raising up and sending out a generation of leaders genuinely seeking to be "biblical," "theological," and "missional" in all they do.

I am also blessed to have opportunities to serve as interim pastor and preach regularly, allowing me both to maintain direct connection with the local church and to fulfill my own calling as a minister of the gospel. With greater frequency I am finding believers not content with the "status quo" and who genuinely want God to work in and through their own lives and their local congregations. Lest one think I am naïve, let me quickly affirm—as long as seminary classrooms and church buildings are populated with people, there will be knuckleheads and kooks, critics and complainers aplenty! Even our Lord was not immune from such earthly vanities (cf. John 6:61).

This reality points to a larger one—that true faithfulness in the Christian life always entails a cost to the believer. Nothing worth having in the Christian life ever comes without a "price to be paid," so to speak. That cost can often be measured in terms of comfort, criticism, and change. The Great Commission Resurgence is no exception, and believers must be willing to personally "count the cost" (Luke 14:28) of unashamed and unreserved obedience to our Lord's imperative.

In a sense, dear reader, you have already paid a small "cost." You (or somebody) bought this book, so there has been a financial "cost" paid. You have digested and reflected on the contents within (or you are reading this conclusion to determine whether or not you will), so there has been a time "cost" paid. In reality, of course, these "costs" are quite insignificant. The *money question* (no pun intended) for all of us remains: "What cost are we *not* willing to pay to see a true Great Commission Resurgence occur in our lives, our churches, and our denomination?" Answering that question must take precedence over any debate about percentages, programming, and personalities, for the latter cannot be rightly adjudicated until the former is settled. *How* we respond will not only dictate the future of the Southern Baptist Convention, but will most likely also determine who will and will not stick around to experience it.

I do not claim to have *the* answer, but I think I can eliminate some possibilities fairly easily. For starters, an unacceptable option would be to do nothing, or closely related, to choose simply to maintain our present situation. That type of response immediately brings to mind the famous quip, "The definition of insanity is doing the same thing over and over and expecting a different result."[9] If all were well in the Southern Baptist Zion, perhaps such alternatives might be acceptable. Our evangelistic malady has been convincingly documented throughout this book, however, and remains the *raison d'être* behind the call for a Great Commission Resurgence. An answer of this sort would only guarantee a terminal diagnosis for the SBC.

Repudiating the Conservative Resurgence is not the answer either. While some discordant voices may clamor for a return to a pre-1979 SBC, spinning yarns about a paradise lost due to power lust and political labeling, one can probably safely say that had such a turnaround not occurred, the even more precipitous rates of decline that have characterized mainline Protestantism would also be true of the Southern Baptist Convention. In the same vein, our annual meetings would likely be given over to endless division and needless debates over subjects the Scriptures declare to be settled matters. Persons enticed by such prospects should seriously consider making the Cooperative Baptist Fellowship a home for their hearts.

In closing, the present discussion concerning the Great Commission Resurgence has hopefully helped to awaken us from our evangelistic slumber and move us away from trusting in our own advertising slogans like "America's largest Protestant denomination" and toward candid admission that the SBC has a problem—the necessary first step. Let us acknowledge that this problem is not someone else's fault, for ultimately the Southern Baptist Convention is not some "bloated bureaucracy," but rather the SBC is you, and it is me. Let us acknowledge that God has given us a window of opportunity to make things right. Instead of looking simply to assign blame, may we accept personal responsibility, knowing that Great Commission obedience calls me to "go, therefore, and make disciples" (Matt 28:19–20). May we do so, not only for our own sake, but also for the sake of those who have yet to hear and believe the gospel (Rom 10:9–15).

---

9   Variously attributed to Albert Einstein and Benjamin Franklin, among others.

NAME INDEX

SUBJECT INDEX

Subject Index

SCRIPTURE INDEX

Scripture Index

428